Are Muslims Distinctive?

ARE MUSLIMS DISTINCTIVE? A LOOK AT THE EVIDENCE

M. Steven Fish

OXFORD
UNIVERSITY PRESS

Oxford University Press, Inc., publishes works that further
Oxford University's objective of excellence
in research, scholarship, and education.

Oxford New York
Auckland Cape Town Dar es Salaam Hong Kong Karachi
Kuala Lumpur Madrid Melbourne Mexico City Nairobi
New Delhi Shanghai Taipei Toronto

With offices in
Argentina Austria Brazil Chile Czech Republic France Greece
Guatemala Hungary Italy Japan Poland Portugal Singapore
South Korea Switzerland Thailand Turkey Ukraine Vietnam

Published by Oxford University Press, Inc.
198 Madison Avenue, New York, NY 10016

www.oup.com

Oxford is a registered trademark of Oxford University Press

Library of Congress Cataloging-in-Publication Data
A CIP record is available from the Library of Congress

ISBN 978-0-19-976920-9 (cloth)
ISBN 978-0-19-976921-6 (pbk.)

Printed in the United States of America
on acid-free paper

For my wife,
Olga,
and the lights of our lives,
Nate and Max

Contents

Acknowledgments

This book could not have been written without the help and support of many friends and colleagues. I am deeply indebted to Sener Akturk, Kathleen Collins, Amaney Jamal, Francesca Jensenius, Mujeeb Khan, Danielle Lussier, and Valerie Sperling, all of whom read the manuscript in its entirety and offered a wealth of comments. I owe a special debt to Danielle Lussier. She joins me as coauthor of chapters 2 and 3, reflecting the extent to which she became a real partner on the project as it progressed. I also benefited from Francesca Jensenius's skillful assistance. Katherine Michel furnished invaluable help as well. Her knack for gathering and coding data and her research prowess were particularly important to the production of chapter 5.

Many students whom I have taught as undergraduates at the University of California-Berkeley contributed to narrowing my ignorance of Islam over the past decade. They include Mohammad Isaqzadeh, Farah Mahesri, Fatima Mojaddedi, Kiana Sharifi, Sanaz Tofighrad, and Hannah Zarkar.

My students and colleagues at the Airlangga University of Surabaya, Indonesia, where I was stationed as a Fulbright Fellow in 2007, also contributed a great deal to that cause. I owe a special debt of gratitude to Airlangga Pribadi, my friend and colleague who did so much to help me gain access to political and religious leaders throughout Indonesia. For help with forging contacts and for tutoring me on substantive matters while I lived in Indonesia, I am also indebted to more people than I can possibly acknowledge here. Those who graciously extended their assistance and expertise include Andy Alfatih, Bima Arya Sugiarto, Budiman Sudjatmiko, Dedi Prihambudi, Dimas Oky Nugroho, M. Faishal Aminudin, Hanafi Rais, Herdi Sahrasad, Kemas Iskandar, Kris Nugroho, Roby Abror, Sukardi Rinakit, and Yudi Latif. Pritta Hapsari managed, with skill and good humor, the heroic and thankless task of teaching me Indonesian. Cornelia Paliama of Fulbright Indonesia and Esti Durahsanti of the U.S. consular office in Surabaya helped in myriad ways to make my stay in Indonesia enjoyable and productive.

My parents, Michael Fish and Cherrie Robinson, and my sister, Diana Fish, remain pillars of support and love on which I rely.

My greatest debt is to my wife, Olga, and our stunning little achievements, Nathaniel and Maximillian. Olga is my best friend and closest confidante as well as my love, and Nate and Max make everything complete. No man could hope to be part of a better team, and I dedicate this book to the three of them.

How to Read the Tables in this Book

Some of the statistical techniques used in this book are complex, and a short introductory note obviously cannot replace coursework in probability theory, econometrics, and applied statistics. But a few simple guidelines may help the reader with little or no experience with statistical hypothesis testing better to comprehend the material presented in this book.

WHAT IS STATISTICAL SIGNIFICANCE?

Statistical significance in all of the models presented in this book is indicated by the number of stars following a coefficient. The greater the number of stars after a coefficient, the greater is our confidence in the results. One star indicates 95 percent certainty that the result observed did not happen by chance, two stars indicate 99 percent certainty, and three stars indicate 99.9 percent certainty. For the models in which countries are the units of analysis our sample sizes are quite small and I also indicate a lower level of statistical significance with the dagger symbol (†). For coefficients with a dagger symbol, we are 90 percent confident that the variable in question is indeed having an impact on the outcome of interest. In other words, we are 90 percent confident that the result observed did not happen by chance; there is a 10 percent chance that the relationship is the result of random error.

WHAT DO THESE COEFFICIENTS MEAN?

Four different types of statistical models are use in this book: ordinary least squares (OLS) regression, negative binomial regression, hierarchical linear models (HLM), and hierarchical generalized linear models (HGLM). Each type of model relies on a specific set of statistical assumptions. The meaning of the coefficients in the tables depends on the type of statistical model being employed.

Ordinary least squares (OLS) regression is the simplest regression form. The first table using OLS is table 4.3, which is reproduced below. The circled number, –0.017, is the regression coefficient. Regression coefficients are determined by an equation that represents a linear combination of the outcome variable and the predictor variables. The regression coefficients change across the different model specifications (model 1, model 2, model 3, and so on) because different combinations of variables are present in the various models. When we include multiple variables in the same equation, we are "controlling" for their possible effects on the dependent variable. In this way, the coefficient helps us to understand the relationship between a single predictor variable and our outcome of interest while holding other possible influences constant. In some cases the coefficients might vary also because of the number of cases being analyzed varies (for example, between the 150 cases present in models 1 and 2 and the 119 cases present in model 3). Regression coefficients in OLS models represent the amount the dependent variable (also called the outcome variable) changes when the corresponding independent variable (also called the predictor) changes by one unit. Since our independent variable of interest is percent Muslim, we focus on the coefficients following percent Muslim in the table. The dependent variable in this table is the Corruption Perceptions Index (CPI). The coefficient –0.017 tells us that, on average, as the percentage of Muslims in a country increases by 1 percent, the score on the CPI decreases by 0.017.

Negative binomial regression models are used to estimate models where the dependent variable is counted and many cases have very low scores on the dependent variable. The first set of negative binomial regression models is found in table 4.9, which is reproduced below. The coefficient –0.015 is the negative binomial regression coefficient for the variable percent Muslim in the first model. In negative binomial models, the regression coefficients can be interpreted as the rate of change between the independent variable and the log of expected counts of the dependent variable. Since log odds do not lend themselves to direct and clear interpretation, in the case of negative binomial coefficients we mostly are just looking for information about the statistical significance of a variable and its direction—does it have a positive or negative effect on the dependent variable and is the relationship statistically significant? The coefficient circled in table 4.9 tells us that percent Muslim is statistically significant and has a negative effect on homicide. The number shows that societies with proportionally larger populations of Muslims have lower murder rates.

Hierarchical linear models (HLM) and *hierarchical generalized linear models (HGLM)* are both first introduced in chapter 2. In both of these forms of models, there are two levels of analysis: the individual level and the country level. Throughout the book, we are interested in two predictor variables: (1) self-identification as a Muslim at the individual level (that is, whether or not an individual is a Muslim), and (2) the proportion of Muslims in the population at the country level. The coefficients of HLM models are generally similar to those of OLS models with one important exception: The variables are "centered" around the group means for individual-level variables and the grand means for country-level variables, which basically means that the overall mean for the variable is subtracted from each

How to Read Tables: Regressions of Corruption Perceptions on Hypothesized Predictors

Table 4.3 Regressions of Corruption Perceptions on Hypothesized Predictors

	Model 1	Model 2	Model 3	Model 4	Model 5	Model 6
(Intercept)	4.533*** (0.231)	1.968*** (0.487)	0.644 (0.832)	1.080 (0.707)	1.546** (0.533)	0.840 (0.644)
Percent Muslim	−0.017*** (0.004)	−0.003 (0.002)	0.004 (0.003)	−0.002 (0.003)	0.003 (0.002)	0.005⁺ (0.003)
Income per capita		0.207*** (0.019)	0.185*** (0.024)	0.200*** (0.023)	0.186*** (0.021)	0.193*** (0.023)
Life expectancy		0.007 (0.009)	0.005 (0.012)	0.013 (0.013)	0.006 (0.009)	0.000 (0.010)
Ethnic diversity			−0.306 (0.500)		−0.328 (0.355)	
Postcommunist country			−0.278 (0.198)	−0.403⁺ (0.223)	−0.307⁺ (0.181)	
Fuels dependence			−0.002 (0.003)		−0.005* (0.003)	−0.004 (0.003)
Former British colony			0.287 (0.242)		0.159 (0.201)	
Unitarism of state structure			0.114 (0.072)	0.148* (0.073)		0.089 (0.070)
Level of democracy			0.240** (0.087)		0.171* (0.066)	0.244** (0.092)
N	150	150	119	119	150	119
Adjusted R^2	.071	.810	.826	.812	.831	.825

Note: OLS models with robust standard errors in parentheses.

⁺significant at $p < .10$; *$p < .05$; **$p < .01$; ***$p < .001$.

How to Read Tables: Regressions of Murder Rates on Hypothesized Predictors

Table 4.9 Regressions of Murder Rates on Hypothesized Predictors

	Model 1	Model 2	Model 3	Model 4	Model 5
(Intercept)	2.095*** (0.139)	1.942* (0.789)	-0.764 (0.747)	-0.778 (0.689)	1.766⁺ (0.923)
Percent Muslim	-0.015*** (0.003)	-0.018*** (0.003)	-0.013*** (0.003)	-0.012*** (0.002)	-0.018*** (0.003)
Income per capita		-0.077*** (0.016)	-0.057*** (0.013)	-0.063*** (0.014)	-0.077*** (0.014)
Life expectancy		0.012 (0.013)	0.025* (0.011)	0.021* (0.009)	0.013 (0.016)
Ethnic diversity			0.202 (0.432)		0.211 (0.535)
Income inequality			0.044*** (0.011)	0.044*** (0.011)	
Level of democracy			-0.069 (0.084)		-0.003 (0.083)
N	151	151	132	132	150
AIC	849.300	814.274	720.404	717.611	814.977
BIC	873.438	862.550	801.122	775.267	887.232
log L	-416.650	-391.137	-332.202	-338.805	-383.488

Note: Negative binomial models with robust standard errors in parentheses.

⁺significant at $p < .10$; *$p < .05$; **$p < .01$; ***$p < .001$.

observation.* Variables are centered in this way to ensure numerical stability in estimating hierarchical models. Because of centering, the HLM coefficients are not as easy to interpret with a quick glance as OLS coefficients are. We need to remember to consider how the variables have been transformed in analyses using HLM.

HGLM models are used for hierarchical data in which the outcome variable is categorical, such as a "yes" or "no" question, or a question in which there is an ordered set of responses, such as "strongly agree," "agree," "disagree," and "strongly disagree." Like the negative binomial regression models, the coefficients in HGLM models defy direct interpretation. They generally constitute the rate of change in the log odds of the dependent variable as the predictor variable changes by one unit. As with the negative binomial models, the only information that can be readily gleaned from HGLM coefficients is statistical significance and the direction of an effect. Because it is not easy to ascertain the effect of independent variables from HGLM coefficients, after presenting the HGLM models we also calculate and present several predicted probabilities for models. Log odds are difficult to interpret and they are noncontinuous, which further confounds direct interpretation since the rate of change might be greater or smaller at different levels of the independent variables. Many scholars believe that the most direct approach for interpreting models for categorical dependent variables is to examine the predicted probabilities of the event occurring for different values of the independent variables. That is what we do. We provide predicted probabilities of particular outcomes for Muslims and non-Muslims who are otherwise similar with regard to the remaining independent variables in the models.

WHAT ARE THE NUMBERS AT THE BOTTOM OF THE TABLES?

At the bottom of all of the tables in this book, I provide some measures of model fit. Scholars evaluate these statistics to try to determine the usefulness or appropriateness of the models. Each of the four types of models presented in this book requires different statistics to evaluate goodness of fit. All of these measures are the subjects of vigorous debate; specialists differ in their opinions about the best way to evaluate different model specifications.

For the OLS models, the measure I use is the adjusted R^2. The adjusted R^2 tells us the fraction of the sample variance of the dependent variable that is explained by the predictor variables in the model, adjusted to take into account the number of predictor variables in the model. This statistic is included to give us a sense of how much variance is explained across different model specifications. If we look back at table 4.3, we see that in model 1, 7 percent of the variance in the Corruption Perceptions Index is explained by the percent Muslim variable, while in model 2, which includes three independent variables, 81 percent of the variance is explained.

For the negative binomial models, I present the Akaike's information criterion (AIC) and the Bayesian information criterion (BIC), which are two popular and very similar measures for comparing maximum likelihood models. The measures capture the tradeoff between bias and variance in a model, since they reward goodness of fit and penalize including more variables than are needed. The AIC or BIC cannot be interpreted alone but are used to compare across different model specifications. The model with the lowest AIC or BIC is the best.

The debates about the merits of goodness-of-fit statistics for HLM and HGLM are even less settled than for the other models used. In the book, we provide sophisticated consumers of HLM with the raw variance components with which they can calculate their own tests of model fit. Variance components are the random effects that are not accounted for by the model at each level of analysis. For HLM models, we provide the variance components for individual-level random effects (σ^2) and the country-level random effects (τ). For HGLM models, we provide the variance components for the country-level random effects (τ). Alone, these numbers are not particularly meaningful, but they can be used to calculate various statistics or tests that can be compared across the models.

*When a predictor is centered around the group mean, the overall mean for the group (e.g., "Muslims") is subtracted from the predictor value for each observation in the data set. When a predictor is centered around the grand mean, the overall mean for all of the predictors in the data set is subtracted from the predictor value for each observation in the data set. For more on centering, see Stephen W. Raudenbush and Anthony S. Bryk, *Hierarchical Linear Models: Applications and Data Analysis Methods* (Thousand Oaks, CA: Sage, 2002), pp. 31–35.

Are Muslims Distinctive?

1 Introduction

Are Muslims distinctive? How, if at all, do they differ from non-Muslims? Are they more (or less) religious than non-Muslims? Do they feel differently than non-Muslims about matters such as divorce, sex, and abortion? Are they more (or less) prone to violence? Is the status of women worse (or better) in Muslim communities than in others?

Such questions spur spirited discussion among people the world over, in Muslim and non-Muslim lands alike. They are raised in glittering skyscrapers and government office buildings in Jakarta, London, Delhi, Washington, and Moscow. They come up in kitchen-table conversation in village huts in East Java, council tenancies in Bradford, lean-tos in Bihar, trailer parks in Michigan, and miners' cabins in Novokuznetsk. Yet we still lack even provisional answers to these questions.

This book provides no definitive answers and addresses only a portion of the large issues. But it does take on a substantial chunk of the big questions and it examines them using hard evidence. Unbiased by prejudice and unconstrained by political correctness, this book treats the assumptions about Muslims that rattle around public debate as hypotheses, rather than as unassailable truths or as unconscionable falsehoods. The book aims to shift the grounds of the debate from hot and wispy rhetoric to fact-finding and hypothesis testing.

WHY WE KNOW SO LITTLE AND WHY WHAT LITTLE WE KNOW IS UNSATISFACTORY

Why We Know So Little

Given the great scope and intensity of global public interest in Islam, it may seem surprising that a book such as this one was not written years ago. Why do our bookshelves not groan under the weight of such volumes?

One reason might have to do with the division of labor among scholars. Few specialists on religion, including theologians, historians, and philosophers, are in the business of testing hypotheses. They may know a great deal about Islam or other confessions. Some even specialize in multiple religions and are adept at comparing faiths.[1] But such people do not normally treat their own insights, and those of their colleagues, as hypotheses. For the most part, they aim to deepen our understanding of belief systems, not to uncover empirical facts about the adherents of this or that religion. And just as most specialists on religion do not test hypotheses, few scholars who do test hypotheses study religion. Social scientists who work on discovering empirical regularities gravitate toward subjects such as international trade, voting patterns in the U.S. Congress, or public opinion in France—that is, matters on which we enjoy an abundance of good data. The data we must rely on to study the links between a given religious tradition and this or that social condition or practice are not as fine-grained or abundant, making study of such matters less attractive to empirically minded scholars. Furthermore, few social scientists who test hypotheses have a strong intellectual interest in religion.

A second reason for the shortage of books such as this one is that generalizing about the adherents of a given religion leads the investigator into politically perilous terrain—a place most of us would prefer to avoid. The investigator invites charges of ethnocentrism and insensitivity just by posing the questions. The same is true for generalizing about members of one or the other sex or about people of a given nationality. But religion may be the most politically touchy topic of all. Since September 11, 2001, when terrorists acting in the name of Islam hijacked commercial airliners and slaughtered nearly 3,000 people in the United States, making generalizations about Muslims has become particularly explosive. The U.S. invasion and occupation of Iraq, the widespread perception among Muslims of Western indifference to mass violence against Muslims in the former Yugoslavia and in Chechnya, the escalation of conflict in Israel and the Palestinian Territories, and what some observers regard as an erosion of civil protections for Muslims in the West have only heightened sensitivities.[2]

In public consciousness in the West, as well as in non-Muslim regions of Asia and Africa, there is widespread unease about Islam.[3] Many people assume, for example, that Islamists regard committing violent acts as the route to personal and political salvation. After all, the headlines seem to overflow with evidence. And that evidence may heighten a feeling of superiority about one's own religion—be it Christianity, Judaism, Hinduism, or some other creed. On the other side, many Muslims feel under siege. They perceive an unjustified growth of Islamophobia in the world. They regard non-Muslims as willfully ignorant of Islam and reflexively hostile to Muslims. Most Muslims, like adherents of other faiths, regard their faith as true and as superior to others. As Mohammed Arkoun states, "Islam is still imagined as inferior (to Jewish and Christian traditions), unchanging, and militant by the West; and superior, dynamic, and peace loving by Muslims."[4] It is little wonder that social scientists who specialize in dispassionate analysis of social facts do not find wading into these waters enticing.

Why What We Know Is Inadequate

We do have some books that speak to some of the big questions addressed in this volume. But few qualify as social science or begin to answer our questions. Most works suffer from one (or both) of two shortcomings. First, they rely on evidence that is ill-suited to making broad generalizations. Second, they lack objectivity; their authors knew what they wanted to "find" before they found it. Let us briefly consider each of these problems.

The first problem is that the evidence authors rely on is insufficient for making generalizations. A great deal of public discussion about Muslims and Islam takes place in an arena where rhetorical prowess substitutes for evidence. The discussion that takes place among pundits and commentators on the airwaves, on op-ed pages, and in blogs has this character. One argument might sound more convincing than the other, but the author or speaker relies on glibness rather than facts. For example, one commentator says that women are treated shabbily in Muslim societies and presents his or her argument forcefully. Another commentator, perhaps with equal or greater flair, argues that women in Muslim communities are not oppressed, and that any perception of bad treatment is due to the observer's bias. Yet both rely on rhetorical muscle rather than hard facts.

Some scholarly writing does provide real evidence, but usually that evidence is insufficient to support broad generalizations. Often authors produce valuable information about a single country or community, and then make generalizations that cover a much larger realm. For example, in an engaging study, Lara Deeb delves into the lives of women in Shi'i Muslim communities in Lebanon. These women, as Deeb shows, are sophisticated. They defy stereotypes of the oppressed, voiceless female. Their association with Islamism, moreover, does not make them radical extremists. Although they are associates of Hezbollah, an Islamist organization, they are not advocates of reckless violence. But rather than stop there, Deeb states that her study "aims to dislodge" what she calls the common assumption "that Islam and modernity are incompatible."[5]

Deeb's claims about her case are compelling. But her general claim about Islam may outstrip her evidence, which is about a particular community in Lebanon. Her story shows that Islam and modernity are not always and everywhere incompatible. It demonstrates that Islam and modernity can go together. But does it "dislodge" the notion "that Islam and modernity are incompatible"? Some readers may be convinced that it does. But others may question that the findings drawn from a case study of a particular community in Lebanon, even if based on impressive investigation, can dislodge doubts about the compatibility of Islam and modernity.

An author may focus on individuals rather than countries or communities. For example, Amir Taheri argues that Islam is incompatible with democracy. For evidence, Taheri relies on statements from the likes of Ayatollah Ruhollah Khomeini, the leader of Iran's Islamic revolution, who called democracy "a form of prostitution," and Sayyid Qutb, the influential Egyptian Islamist who equated self-rule with forsaking God's authority.[6]

But again, the evidence cannot support the weight of the conclusions. Taheri shows that some Muslim leaders are hostile to democracy. But that is all he shows. Any conclusions that reach further than that are reaching too far. A handful of prominent Muslim leaders—or even many Muslim leaders—voicing antipathy for democracy does not demonstrate that Islam is incompatible with democracy.

In short, the first major problem found in works that address the big questions about Muslims is that they present insufficient evidence. Authors use anecdotal data based on a small part of the world, or a handful of people, to draw inferences that are more expansive than the evidence can bear.

The second common problem is lack of objectivity. No study can be entirely objective. Every author is blinkered and enlightened by his or her own habits of thinking. Our personal backgrounds, experiences, and inclinations color our worldviews. Yet the writer can strive to set aside his or her preconceptions, even while accepting that such a goal cannot be fully realized. So too can he or she let the findings lead where they will, without subordinating them to an overarching agenda.

Writings that rate high on objectivity are uncommon in scholarship on Islam and society. In most works, one finds little in the authors' conclusions that is not in their original assumptions. Many authors use evidence selectively to bolster preestablished arguments; they do not follow the evidence wherever it leads them. In the works of John Esposito, for example, one knows that Islam will be portrayed as a peaceful, enlightened faith.[7] The same is true for the works of Karen Armstrong, Bruce Lawrence, and many other authors.[8] To such scholars, misunderstanding on the part of non-Muslims is to blame for any negative impressions that non-Muslims might have of Islam and its adherents. Ever resistant to prejudice and intent upon overcoming ethnocentrism, these writers assume that Muslims cannot be, say, more prone to violence, inequality, or authoritarianism than non-Muslims are—at least not without just cause. Such thinking is common in the academy.

In the works of some other writers, one finds a similar lack of commitment to open-ended investigation, but the assumptions and conclusions cut the other way. In the writings of Daniel Pipes, for example, contemporary Islam is invariably portrayed as problematic and potentially menacing.[9] The same is true of Samuel Huntington's writings.[10] In the United States and Europe, these views figure prominently among conservative politicians and commentators. Such thinking sometimes manifests as a superiority complex. It assumes that Islam lags behind Christianity and Judaism and that Muslims are hostile to what Westerners consider progress.

The authors just cited are not minor figures. They are among the most influential scholars currently writing on the big questions on Islam and society. Nor are they intellectual lightweights; they are experts of great erudition. Yet their conclusions are invariably indistinguishable from their prior assumptions. It would be inconceivable for Pipes or Huntington to find that Islam is a peaceful faith whose adherents incline to democracy. It would be unthinkable for Esposito or Armstrong to find otherwise.

These authors' works lack not only objectivity. They are also deficient in evidence. In a recent volume, Esposito and a coauthor do adduce some numbers in what the authors claim is a broad-gauged, global look at Muslim opinion.[11] Huntington similarly offers what he calls evidence, including some descriptive statistics.[12] Yet these works present only the evidence that confirms the author's preestablished position. Each work uses data selectively. None uses rigorous methods to test hypotheses— or for that matter even treats the main assertions as hypotheses in need of testing. These works are polemics, not investigations. They present opinions, not findings. They leave us in a world of dueling, untested assumptions.

GOALS AND GENERAL APPROACH OF THIS BOOK

We need systematic, open-ended scientific investigation. Selective use of evidence in service of preestablished conclusions does not advance our understanding of the crucial issues at hand. We also need research that uses evidence drawn from the whole world or at least a broad sample of countries. Case studies of this or that country or community or individual are relatively abundant in studies of religion and society. They have contributed greatly to our stock of knowledge. Case studies are good at drawing out and illustrating causal links, since the author can train attention on processes and actors and assess precisely how and why things turned out the way they did. But case studies are less good at establishing whether a meaningful correlation exists at all, at least outside a circumscribed universe of specific contexts. For this purpose, a quantitative approach that draws on a large number of observations may be useful. It may furnish a strong basis for answering the "whether" questions. Once we know whether there is reason to suspect that a causal link exists, case studies can help us understand why the link exists and how it came into being. But for establishing whether there is any relationship in the first place, quantitative methods may be indispensable. In order reliably to assess, for example, whether there is a robust correlation between the proportion of the population that adheres to Islam and the status of women, statistical analysis of quantitative data has a great deal to offer.

We still do not have even provisional answers to many of the "whether" questions. We still do not know whether Muslims are more or less prone to violence than non-Muslims, whether socioeconomic inequalities are higher or lower in predominantly Muslim societies than others, or whether Muslims are more or less religious than non-Muslims. Despite intense public interest in such questions, they have been debated largely in an evidentiary vacuum. This situation leaves us in the dark about the basic facts on some of the most vital issues of our time.

In addition to bringing systematic hypothesis testing to bear on the "whether" questions, we also need to strive for objectivity. Research that is motivated by a political passion—say, by a desire to dispel stereotypes or to warn readers against this or that threat—has its place. Some valuable works have been inspired by such concerns. But such studies are already rife in the literature on contemporary Islam. Genuine investigations—meaning studies that authors undertook without having decided the answers in advance—are in much shorter supply.

Aim of the Study

This book aims to remove discussion of whether Muslims differ from non-Muslims from the arena of polemics, accusations, and apologetics and place it in the realm of social-scientific investigation. Of course the polemics, accusations, and apologetics will continue, but I seek to provide some hard evidence that is relevant to the debates.

My central purpose is to shed some light on the "whether" questions; my primary aim is descriptive rather than explanatory. I seek to assess whether Muslims are more religious than non-Muslims, whether Muslims are exceptionally likely to favor the fusion of religious and political authority, and so on. I am concerned only secondarily with the "why" questions. Thus, if I find evidence that Muslims are more (or less) religious than non-Muslims, I examine why. Still, my answers to the "why" questions are provisional and speculative. I do not engage in the in-depth investigation needed to nail down complete answers. I instead provide a menu of possible answers to the "why" questions, size up the items on that menu, and offer my best assessment. I cover a good deal of territory on the "whether" questions, taking on a separate big issue in each chapter. This approach does not leave space to delve deeply into the operation of causal mechanisms and dynamics. I hope that some of the countless scholars whose knowledge of Islam and its country- or community-specific incarnations is superior to my own will take up questions of causation in their own work.

The book aims to reveal general tendencies. It does violence to nuance and context. In order to get a look at the forest, it overlooks many trees. Among the book's shortcomings is its lack of focus on the enormous diversity that exists among Muslims. Indeed, some people would argue that there is no "Muslim world"—or, for that matter, "Christian world" or "Hindu world" either. This is a reasonable point, and in strictly political terms it is accurate. A united front of Muslims or Muslim countries is certainly nowhere to be found in the world.[13] In sociological terms, however, little is gained by simply assuming the nonexistence of commonalities among members of a faith group, asserting that all religions are endlessly complex and heterogeneous, reciting the bromide that this or that group is "not monolithic," and abandoning any effort to discern general tendencies. Social science is at least in part about discovering the presence—or absence—of regularities. I will attempt to unearth regularities rather than to deepen our appreciation of variety and complexity.

Method, Data, and Presentation

Statistical methods are used extensively in this book. There is no way to uncover whether corruption is more (or less) pervasive among Muslims than non-Muslims or whether Muslims are or more (or less) prone to political violence than non-Muslims without digging into some numbers.

Now, before the reader panics and returns this book to the shelf, I ask that he or she consider the following: All the findings are presented in the prose in a manner that enables the reader to skip the tables of numbers. People who know nothing about statistics but who want to access the information that statistical analysis reveals will find this book useful. The reader who is more interested in the findings than in how I arrived at them and who prefers words to numbers can skip the technical discussions. The introductions and conclusions to the chapters and numerous places within the chapters summarize the findings.

The mode of presentation in each chapter is straightforward. For each question, I formulate rival hypotheses about how Muslims and non-Muslims might differ. For example, in the second portion of chapter 4, I ask whether Muslims are more (or less) prone to violent crime. I consider some ideas about why one might expect Muslims to be more (or less) inclined to criminal violence. I choose an indicator for the dependent (or "outcome") variable, which here is criminal violence. The indicator I use for criminal violence is national homicide rates, measured as the number of people murdered each year per 100,000 inhabitants.

Here, like everywhere else in the book, I am concerned with how Muslims and non-Muslims differ from one another. So here as elsewhere, I present the averages for Muslim and non-Muslim countries. I run the numbers and find that the average murder rate in predominantly Muslim countries is 2.4 and in non-Muslim countries it is 7.5. Since Islam and Christianity are by far the world's largest faiths, and since

Christians comprise the referent group that is (implicitly or explicitly) used by many people in thinking about Muslims, I then provide a table with the raw numbers for the largest predominantly Muslim countries and the largest predominantly Christian countries, along with an average for each of the two groups.

I then present the results of statistical analyses. The first model is a simple bivariate regression. It represents the correlation between the proportion of the country that is made up of Muslims and the scores on the outcome variable. In subsequent models, I add controls for variables other than the proportion of the population that is Muslim that might be correlated with the outcome variable. Thus, when looking at the determinants of murder rates, I add controls for socioeconomic development, ethnic diversity, socioeconomic inequality, and level of democracy. Writings on violent crime hold that these factors might influence murder rates, so we must control for them.

Our aim is to see whether Muslims differ from non-Muslims and, if so, by how much. All the variables besides the variable for Muslims are included only as controls. The goal is to see whether Muslims and non-Muslims differ when we include the controls. In the case of murder rates, there is indeed evidence of a difference between Muslims and non-Muslims. The proportion of a country's population that adheres to Islam matters when the control variables are included. In statistical jargon, the variable for Muslims is robust to the inclusion of the controls and is a statistically significant predictor of murder rates. Any way you slice it, more Muslims spells less murder.

If the data analysis suggests that Muslims are distinctive, I consider why and how. That is, once we know whether Muslims differ from non-Muslims, we consider in greater depth why they might differ. In the case of murder, this matter leads us to the criminological literature and consideration of how life in Muslim communities might curb the risk of homicide. Yet, here as elsewhere in the book, my discussion of why Muslims are (or are not) distinctive is cursory; I have no pretensions of providing definitive statements on causation.

For some of the questions this book addresses, countries are the units of analysis. These analyses are cross-national, meaning that they assess variation across countries at a given point in time. Data on individuals are generally superior to data on countries, but unfortunately individual-level data are sometimes unavailable. For example, the information we have for homicide rates for most of the world is available by country. We do not know the religious identity of everyone who committed murder, but we do have numbers on the rate of homicide in (most) countries and the proportion of each country that is made up of Muslims. So we must assume that the higher the proportion of Muslims in a country, the higher the probability that the person who committed the murder was a Muslim. Methodologists call this kind of work "ecological inference," and they tend to consider it terribly inadequate. Some economists and political scientists have abandoned cross-national analysis altogether, since they view the results it produces as crude and unreliable.

I agree that it would be better to have higher quality data and admit that my results produce only rough estimates that leave us seeing through a glass darkly. But we must use what we have and do the best we can. Specialists in American politics and society enjoy good numbers for everything imaginable, but our data for Bahrain, Bolivia, and Bulgaria, not to mention Mali, Moldova, and Mozambique, are not as abundant. Furthermore, many things, such as ethnic identities, political party affiliations, and regions of residence, which can readily be used in single-country studies, often are not comparable across countries. Eventually, we may have better data on all or most countries of the world than are now available. But until the dawn of that golden age, we must stick with the blunter, lumpier information we have, while suppressing our covetousness of our colleagues who generate their data in the psychologist's experimental laboratory or in the less controlled, but still data-rich, arena of American society.

When individual-level data are available, I use them. Chapter 2, which focuses on religiosity and attitudes toward religion and politics, and chapter 3, which examines social capital and people's views on social issues, are based on individual-level data drawn from the World Values Survey (WVS). Parts of chapters 6 and 7 also draw on and analyze these data.

Even the individual-level data are highly imperfect. I intend not to defend the quality of either the individual-level or the country-level data. I aim instead to do the best we can with what is available to us, with an eye toward establishing a baseline for further discussion and eventually developing improved indicators. What is more, my main goal throughout the book is to assess whether Muslims and non-Muslims differ from each other, not to determine precisely the degree of difference, which our data do not allow us to do.

WHAT SOCIAL SCIENCE CAN OFFER

Statistical analyses open possibilities for advancing our understanding of how Muslims and non-Muslims differ from one another. Contrary to popular belief, it is actually harder to lie with statistics than without them. Still, it is true that one can use statistics to concoct especially impressive and "scientific"-looking deceptions.

Why Social Science Does Not Always Contribute to Better Understanding

Indeed, in works that rely on scientific methods, be they quantitative or qualitative, we sometimes encounter essentially the same problem found in more publicistic works. That problem might be dubbed "motivated results," meaning "findings" that are tailored to the author's desired outcome.

Empirically minded scholars sometimes use the data that make their case and ignore the data that do not. Furthermore, after selecting and analyzing the data, scholars sometimes present only the results that suit their favored arguments. In quantitative analysis this approach involves showing the results only of the statistical models that "work"—meaning that support the author's pet argument. In qualitative analysis such an approach involves constructing narratives that exclude information that contradicts the author's preestablished argument. In addition to using data selectively and failing to present contrary findings, scholars may engage in operations that make the outcome of the analysis congenial to the author's theory. One prominent scholar who possesses sophisticated statistical skills alerts graduate students that they will frequently encounter the following approach as they immerse themselves in the literature:"First, you analyze the data. If that doesn't work, you massage the data. If even that doesn't work, you pound the data into submission." Social scientists who rely on qualitative evidence, by using verbal (instead of mathematical) sleight-of-hand, may do essentially the same thing.

Why do we engage in such dubious practices? We scholars develop pet theories, and the temptation to defend them is strong. For example, if I make a name for myself early in my career by showing that electoral rules are more important than economic conditions for determining outcomes in elections, I become associated with that argument. I subsequently have a stake in defending it and ignoring or suppressing contrary evidence. Or my political convictions might motivate me. If I have a strong normative commitment to state support for the poor, but in the course of analyzing the data I find no stable correlation between state spending on social welfare and changes in poverty rates, I might be tempted to discount the finding. I might disregard good data and seek alternative sources of data and indicators for my variables until I find numbers that are more amenable to making my argument. I might also carry out the analysis in every possible way until I hit upon a model that supports my viewpoint. I might be loath to admit that in most of the statistical models I constructed the evidence actually failed to support my argument.

Herein lies an important reason why policy makers, analysts outside academia, and the attentive public so often ignore academic social science. Jargon and statistics often get the blame. But intelligent people are capable of learning a few new terms and glancing over columns of numbers, at least provided the authors define their terms and explain in the prose what the numbers mean. But many people suspect that scholars tailor their findings to their theories, rather than the reverse. That suspicion is often justified. Scholars do sometimes offer motivated results—findings that are tailored to the author's sought-after outcome.

How Social Science Can Contribute to Better Understanding

This will not do. If we social scientists want to speak to audiences outside our insular communities, and if we wish to improve the intellectual life of our own communities, we must invariably fit our conclusions to our findings and not the reverse.

We have some laudable examples. One is found in the collaborative project on anti-Americanism in world politics headed by Peter Katzenstein and Robert Keohane, two leading scholars of international relations. Katzenstein and Keohane, scholars of a liberal orientation, clearly set out to find that American arrogance in world affairs was fueling anti-Americanism, and that the growth of anti-Americanism damaged American interests. But to their surprise, the authors found—and frankly reported—that anti-Americanism, while real and growing, had not inflicted great harm on U.S. interests.[14] Here we have an example of real investigation. There is much in the findings that was not in the original assumptions. But not all studies are so stern in their pursuit of the truth. Subordinating our own hopes and expectations to the facts as we find them is not universal practice.

Some simple steps can help us take care that our conclusions fit the evidence rather than the other way around. Making a sincere effort to use a wide variety of good data and indicators for our variables is, of course, one important step. Selecting data or indicators with an eye to producing "clean," unequivocal findings or findings that fit the author's pet theory is not the path to unearthing the truth. Where they are available, multiple sources of data for each indicator and multiple indicators for each variable should be used to provide a check on the findings. For some phenomena, there exist multiple sources of data, and using more than one source is possible as well as desirable. Thus, in chapter 4, where I try to assess whether Muslims are more or less corruption-prone than non-Muslims, I tap both of the two good sources of data that provide national ratings on corruption. In some instances, a variable can be measured in a variety of ways, meaning that there exist multiple possible indicators for the same phenomenon. For example, there are many ways to indicate inequality between the genders. The female-to-male earned income ratio is one indicator; the representation of women in high office is another; and the female-to-male literacy ratio is yet another. We may profit from using all of them. Thus, in chapter 6, which assesses whether Muslims differ from non-Muslims in terms of inequality between the genders, all of these indicators and still others are used as well. Using multiple indicators provides a check on the findings. We must resist not only tailoring the findings to pet theories but also striving to produce "clean" findings that allow for unequivocal conclusions. If all the evidence cuts in the same direction, we may have more confidence in our findings. If not, we must qualify the conclusions or refrain from making generalizations at all.

For some variables, however, we are stuck with few indicators and sparse data. For example, while indicators for gender-based inequality (as well as sources of data for most indicators) are plentiful, information on class inequality is much scarcer. Measuring class inequality is harder than measuring gender-based inequality. There is but one widely accepted indicator for class inequalities, the Gini score, and our data even for it are spotty. Creating Gini scores requires complicated household surveys that have never been conducted in some countries. We have multiple sources of data, but most sources are dated and none provides information for all of the world's countries. Thus, in chapter 6, when investigating how Muslims and non-Muslims differ in terms of class inequality, I am limited to a single indicator (Gini scores) and one main source of data that provides the most complete and up-to-date numbers.

For some variables data are even harder to come by. For example, although large-scale political conflict and terrorism are the subjects of enormous public interest, high-quality data on them are scarce. I therefore had to create the databases, one on episodes of mass political violence and one on terrorist incidents. As a starting point, I relied on lists of events that were scrupulously compiled by another scholar, as will be discussed in chapter 5.

Now, when we create our own data, the opportunities for mischief are rife. We must be grimly frank on this point. The scholar may shift the criteria for inclusion of cases or alter coding rules in a manner that influences what analysis of the data shows. This kind of thing happens all the time in social science, though it is seldom discussed in polite company and never admitted in print. I make my best effort to engage in no such shenanigans. Working with a talented research assistant, I completed work on the databases entirely in advance of using them to investigate the substantive questions at hand. I did not double back and make any changes in the dataset after viewing the findings that use of the data yielded. Such a "naïve" approach is essential to sound scholarship.

A firm commitment to an accurate presentation of findings is also crucial. Scholars who use statistics know well that one can alter the results by including or excluding this or that variable; findings may depend on how one specifies the equation. One may mask the statistical and substantive significance of a variable whose effects one seeks to minimize by including other variables in the equation that are correlated with it. One way to hold ourselves accountable to is to show multiple specifications of statistical models with a variety of combinations of predictors. Another trick we must shun is making a variable appear statistically significant by omitting crucial control variables. The problem of "omitted variable bias" can never be overcome fully. But we can make a theoretically informed effort to include the variables that might be of greatest importance.

Of course, no amount of methodological self-consciousness—or for that matter, statistical wizardry—can substitute for a plain commitment on the part of the author not to engage in the crimes of commission or omission to begin with. As in all works that rely on statistics, I report only a tiny fraction of the results obtained over long hours of crunching the numbers. But the results presented here represent the empirical facts that emerged from crunching the numbers. The results I report are those that best fit the evidence. Everything I report here is faithful to the facts as I found them.

The statistics in this book have been subjected to neither the delights of massage nor the agonies of being pounded into submission. There is no place for such practices in scholarly inquiry. Members of the policy community and the attentive public must depend on scholars to tell the truth, the whole truth, and nothing but that truth—at least to the best of their ability. If scholars do otherwise, their findings may be used as ammunition by this or that advocacy group or partisan cause; but they will not be and should not be taken seriously by anyone else.

SCOPE AND LIMITATIONS OF THE STUDY

What the Book Does Not Do

As mentioned above, this book focuses primarily on description and employing statistical methods to test propositions on Muslims in social and political life. Such a modest agenda admittedly limits the scope and perhaps appeal of the volume. But the absence of overriding explanatory aims also has advantages. As John Gerring notes, "We need good descriptive work. We would also like to know why things happened and what things are going to happen, but few studies manage to adequately fulfill all three goals at once. Arguably, description is more sure, more nuanced, and more impressive generally when not confounded by the expectation to predict or explain." Gerring adds, "Intuitively, I have greater faith in a descriptive analysis where description is the *summum bonum*. Such accounts are less likely to be skewed by the analyst's search for a knockout causal or predictive theory." As an example of the need for descriptive work in social science and the drawbacks of "long-standing preferences for causal or predictive work," Gerring cites the problem of American exceptionalism. He points out that "while an enormous literature addresses the question of why America is exceptional, relatively few studies address (in a rigorous and empirical way, that is) the antecedent question: Is America exceptional, and if so, in what ways?"[15]

Gerring is right. Few studies have addressed whether America is exceptional (compared to, say, other advanced industrialized countries), and our understanding of America (and perhaps other countries as well) would be enhanced by studies that assessed, in a rigorous fashion, the "whether" question on American exceptionalism. The current volume resembles those few studies that have addressed this question, though I seek to assess whether the adherents of a particular religion, rather than the inhabitants of a particular country, are exceptional, and if so, in what ways.

Even in the realm of description the book's coverage is incomplete. The book takes up questions that have already been widely debated, including whether Muslims are especially prone to political violence or resistant to democratic governance, as well as topics that have not yet been investigated extensively, such as whether Muslims are more (or less) religious and more (or less) inclined to socioeconomic inequality. But this volume, while attempting to cover a good deal of territory, by no means addresses all of the big questions. For example, one question that has sparked great interest is whether Muslims are particularly resistant to technical innovation. Milton Viorst holds that the conventional interpretation of the Qur'an that guides the conduct of most Muslims in the contemporary world "serves to suppress individual creativity and innovation. It has transformed a culture whose brilliance once bedazzled the world into a social backwater."[16] Similarly, Akbar Ahmed has objected to the absence of Muslim intellectual giants such as Ibn Khaldun from the syllabi of courses in contemporary Islamic schools. According to Ahmed, Ibn Khaldun is considered too "scientific" and therefore excluded, much to the detriment of the development of critical thinking among contemporary Muslims.[17] This is a weighty issue. Still, I do not take it up. Addressing it effectively would require global data on how Muslims' attitudes toward innovation differ from those of non-Muslims, and on how school curricula in Muslim communities differ from those elsewhere. We have some anecdotal data and we find discussion of the matter among scholars and even politicians. But we still lack the data needed to subject the question to the kind of testing I rely on in this volume.

Not only are some of the big questions put aside here, but even the questions that are addressed are not answered fully. The data and the methods I bring to bear have advantages for generalizing about broad populations, but they are not sufficiently comprehensive or sophisticated to provide anything more than provisional insights. The evidence presented here is intended to be suggestive, not definitive.

The findings, moreover, are time-bound. This book offers only a snapshot of conditions in the late twentieth and early twenty-first century. Much of what I find may not hold for previous decades—not to speak of previous centuries. I do not track change over time or assess how the findings might hold up in the future. I trust that interest in present conditions is sufficient to render this book of some value to readers today.

Nor do I focus on accounting for diversity within the Muslim world. I sometimes mention differences between this and that predominantly Muslim country, and such differences are captured (often dramatically) in the tables that present raw data on the largest predominantly Muslim countries. But my primary concern is to compare Muslims with non-Muslims, not to compare Muslims with other Muslims. I assume that readers are aware that Muslims are not monolithic and that there is as much diversity among them as there is within any group of people that encompasses nearly one-quarter of humanity.

A Word on Classification of People

Who gets counted as Muslim, or as an adherent of another faith, depends on self-identification. Sources of data on the religious composition of societies, including those I use, rely on self-identification. We have nothing else to go upon, since no one besides people themselves can possibly decide who counts as a Muslim, or for that matter a Hindu or a Jew or a Christian or a Zoroastrian. Of course a Muslim is not a Muslim any more than a Christian is a Christian or a Buddhist is a Buddhist; there is vast variation across and within societies in terms of how people understand their own confession and enact it in their lives. To many Christians in the southern and midwestern parts of America where I grew up, membership in the faith means not only accepting Jesus Christ as one's personal savior but also attending mammoth churches in which the cross is projected on vast video screens alongside an American flag (which often looms larger than the cross). Patriotic themes often rival the Gospel for prominence and are treated as integral parts of the faith. By contrast, among many Orthodox friends I made during years of residence in Russia, being Christian means getting baptized and wearing the crucifix, each of which is considered important for warding off evil spirits.

Syncretism is obvious in both cases. The American example mixes nationalism and Christianity, and the Russian one blends traditional pagan beliefs and Christianity. Such syncretism, as well as the more general tendency to tremendous variety in beliefs among adherents, is found among Muslims as well as Christians. Yet, people the world over still generally identify themselves as adherents of a certain religion (or of no religion), and their self-identification is what we must accept in defining their confessional identities.

A Word on Classification of Countries

When relying on individual-level data or percentage Muslim (or Christian), classifying whole countries according to their predominant faith tradition is unnecessary. The analyses in this book for the most part rely on individual-level data and on data on the percentage of the country made up of members of a religion. In some places, however, including in some tables that provide descriptive data, I will have reason to classify whole countries by religious tradition. A word is therefore in order about how countries are classified. In order to qualify as a "Muslim country" or a "Christian country," one of those religious traditions must clearly predominate. There are about a dozen countries in the world with Muslim or Christian populations in the 35–50 percent range, some of which have large populations of the other religion as well. They cannot readily be classified as either "Muslim countries" or "Christian countries." For example, according to the main source I use for data on religious composition, the Association of Religion Data Archives (ARDA), Burkina Faso is about 48 percent Muslim and 20 percent Christian.[18] The highest estimate of Burkina Faso's Muslim population available in other sources is 50 percent. Nigeria is, according the ARDA, 44 percent Muslim and 46 percent Christian; the *CIA World Factbook* states that it is 50 percent Muslim and 40 percent Christian. The Muslim population of Ethiopia ranges, depending on the source, from 30 to 50 percent, with the Christian population also covering such a range. Kazakhstan is about 50 percent Muslim according to the ARDA and 47 percent Muslim according to several other sources. Thus, Burkina Faso, Nigeria, Ethiopia, and Kazakhstan have large Muslim populations; in Burkina Faso and Kazakhstan, Muslims clearly constitute a religious plurality. But in all of these cases religious demography is deeply mixed and it is difficult to say that Muslims really predominate.

Tanzania presents another ambiguous case. According to the ARDA, Tanzania is 53 percent Christian and 37 percent Muslim. Some other sources list the Christian population as low as 30 percent and consider up to 35 percent of Tanzanians adherents of "indigenous beliefs" or local religions. Tanzania has a large Christian population, but it is not large enough for us to categorize it as a "Christian country." It differs from neighboring Kenya, which by all accounts is at least three-quarters Christian.

In labeling countries by religious affiliation, I adopt the following criterion: To qualify as a "Muslim country," a country must be at least 55 percent Muslim according to the ARDA as well as a preponderance of other available sources. The same rule holds for designation as a "Christian country"; the ARDA plus other sources must consider the Christian population to be at least 55 percent of the total. In addition to the countries mentioned above, the marginal cases that have large but not predominant Muslim or Christian populations are Côte d'Ivoire (which sources list as between one-quarter and three-fifths Muslim), Eritrea (about half Muslim and half Christian), Guinea-Bissau (40–45 percent Muslim), South Korea (one-quarter to 45 percent Christian), and Sierra Leone (45–60 percent Muslim). In these countries, like in Burkina Faso, Ethiopia, Kazakhstan, Nigeria, and Tanzania, it is difficult to say that a single tradition predominates. I therefore do not classify these countries as either "Muslim" or "Christian." Using the criteria I do, 44 of the countries of the world under examination in this volume are classified as predominantly Muslim and 128 countries as not predominantly Muslim.

Using the terms "Muslim country" or "Christian country" for any country might bother some readers. Some might point out that the presence of substantial religious minorities in this or that country renders classification problematic. Others might object to labeling any society according to its predominant religion. I cannot fully placate such concerns. At least using the terms only for countries in which a clear majority adheres to the faith in question lowers the risk that the differences we find in the data between Muslim countries and non-Muslim countries are accounted for by non-Muslims in Muslim countries or by Muslims in non-Muslim countries.

Let us begin our study by aiming squarely at a question about the value and practice of faith among its adherents. Namely, are Muslims especially religious?

2 Personal Religiosity and Religion in Politics

Are Muslims more religious than non-Muslims? To some people, Muslims seem to be especially religious. Says Ernest Gellner, "In the social sciences, one of the commonest theses is the secularisation thesis, which runs as follows. Under conditions prevailing in industrial-scientific society, the hold of religion over society and its people diminishes. By and large this is true, but it is not completely true, for there is one major exception, Islam." According to Gellner, "In the last hundred years, the hold of Islam over Muslims has not diminished but has rather increased. It is the one striking counter-example to the secularisation thesis."[1] Some Muslims share this view. The charge of "godlessness" that conservative Muslim establishments in places such as Saudi Arabia level at the United States is not a reference to the fact that most Americans are not Muslims. It is rather an accusation that they are not serious about their Christianity (or Judaism). Islam is sometimes seen, by its very nature, as calling its followers to a greater level of devotion than other faiths demand of their adherents. According to Yilmaz Ensaroğlu, a Turkish Muslim activist and human rights advocate, "Islam is not like the other religions, it's a 24-hour lifestyle. Devout Muslims pray five times a day."[2] Adherents.com, a major online database on world religions, estimates the world's Christian population to be 2.1 billion and its Muslim population to be 1.5 billion but notes, "Many Muslims (and some non-Muslim observers) claim that there are more practicing Muslims than practicing Christians in the world."[3] The emphasis here is on *practicing*. The implication is that Muslims are generally more Muslim than Christians are Christian.

Are Muslims exceptionally religious and resistant to secularism? We do not have a large scholarly literature on the subject, in part, because defining religiosity is so difficult and data are in short supply.[4] Our views to date have been based mostly on hearsay or impressionistic evidence.

But we do have cross-national data that can help sharpen our understanding. The World Values Survey (WVS) furnishes an especially valuable source. Data from the WVS have not yet been used as effectively as they might be to strengthen our grasp of what is and is not distinctive about opinion and values among Muslims around the world. In this chapter and the next, we tap these data extensively. The WVS has queried people from about half of the world's countries on hundreds of matters, including religiosity, over several decades, though many questions have been added only recently and data are scarce for some survey items. We use data from the most recent waves of surveys, which were conducted during 1999–2004 (the fourth wave) and 2005–2008 (the fifth wave).[5]

The WVS does not give us perfect information. The data are inferior to those generated by some studies conducted in single countries, such as the American National Election Studies (ANES), which produces numbers on voting and public opinion in the United States. The data-gathering process is decentralized, occasionally leading to differences in the quality of sampling and interviewing across countries.[6] Furthermore, like in all surveys, responses to questions posed in the WVS may be affected by the timing of the poll. People's recent political, social, and economic experiences may affect their responses to questions. The data that surveys produce therefore cannot fully reflect deep underlying values and psychological orientations. We must bear in mind, moreover, that even fundamental beliefs may change over time.[7] Surveys give us only blurry snapshots. They do not provide a full-length movie or even perfect pictures. In surveys that cover multiple countries, we also encounter the thorny problem of context and meaning. Even assuming good translation of questions, when a Chinese is asked about the value of democracy, does she understand the premise of the question the same way that a Swede does?

Still, we use the surveys anyway. The reason is simple. The WVS provides the best data we have. We cannot hope fully to surmount problems such as differences in how people in diverse national contexts understand certain concepts. Such is the nature of comparative social science—which helps explain why, as one leading political scientist has lamented, "comparative politics is scandalously data-poor."[8]

Yet the nature of the comparative enterprise is to grasp large truths about the whole world (or at least large parts of it) with nothing like the data resources that, say, specialists on elections in the United States enjoy. So we will be living in scandal for the foreseeable future. The question is not whether the data that the WVS produces are perfect. The issue is rather whether they provide useful information and are better than nothing. The answer to that question is yes.

What, then, do the surveys tell us about religiosity among Muslims and non-Muslims? The first major section of the chapter deals with personal religiosity. It focuses on individuals' religious beliefs and practice. The second major section examines popular attitudes toward religion and politics. It aims to assess how closely people think religious and political authority should be aligned. The third section discusses the findings of the first two sections, placing them in a broader framework. Before proceeding to these matters, however, a word is in order about the survey data and the religious composition of the survey's respondents.

In order to test our hypotheses on the largest possible sample, we have combined cases from the two most recent waves of the WVS. They include fifty countries that were surveyed in 2005–2008 as part of the fifth wave of the survey[9] and thirty-three cases from the fourth wave, which was carried out in 1999–2004. We only included older cases to add countries for which fifth-wave data were not yet available at the time of this writing. A list of the countries in which the surveys were conducted appears in appendix 2.A. This sample of eighty-three countries includes 114,440 individuals.[10] Respondents in the WVS are asked if they belong to a religious denomination, and if so, which one.[11] We used the information from these questions to place respondents in groups that correspond with dominant faith traditions and spiritual practices: Muslim, Protestant, Catholic, Orthodox Christian, other Christian, Jewish, Hindu, Buddhist, Sikh, and pagan/spiritist.[12] We also created an "other" category for traditions with a relatively small number of adherents. People who did not list a religious tradition were categorized as "nondenominationalist."

Unfortunately, there is no distinction in the data from the 2005–2008 surveys between individuals who answered that they had no religious denomination and those who were not asked or did not answer the question. In this case, we used information from another survey question to try to arrive at a more precise categorization. In the 2005–2008 question ordering, after respondents were asked about religious denomination they were asked if they considered themselves religious. If responses for an individual were missing from both of these questions, we assumed that the questions were not asked. These respondents were not included in the analysis. All other individuals who did not list a denomination but provided a response when asked if they were religious are treated as nondenominationalists. Table 2.1 provides a breakdown of the respondents in our sample according to religious denomination.

As table 2.1 shows, individuals identifying with a religious tradition other than Christianity or Islam constitute only 8.8 percent of the sample. Together, Muslims and Christians constitute 74.2 percent of the sample, while those listing no religious

Table 2.1 Religious Denomination as Self-Reported in the World Values Survey

Denomination	Number of Respondents	Percentage of Total
Christians[a]	57,870	50.6
Muslims	26,971	23.6
Buddhists	3,416	3.0
Hindus	2,251	2.0
Pagans/spiritists	1,690	1.5
Jews	1,267	1.1
Other[b]	1,405	1.2
No Denomination	19,570	17.1

[a]Comprised of Catholics, Protestants, Orthodox Christians, and other Christians.
[b]Includes Sikhs.

adherence comprise 17.1 percent. Obviously, Christians and, to a lesser extent, Muslims are overrepresented in the survey. This is due in large part to the fact that the vast majority of the world's people who identify neither as Muslims nor as Christians live in China and India. These countries are included in our data, but their inhabitants are not represented in the survey in proportion to their share of the world's population, which would have required including tens of thousands of respondents for each country. The data, such as they are, have their limitations, but have the advantage of being especially useful for comparing Muslims and Christians on a global scale.

Across the countries included in our sample, the percentage of respondents describing themselves as Muslim ranges from 0 to 99.4. There are no Muslims among the respondents in Argentina, Brazil, Chile, Croatia, Czech Republic, Greece, Hungary, Iceland, Ireland, Italy, Japan, Lithuania, Malta, Peru, Portugal, Slovakia, and Venezuela. The upper bound of the empirical range of 99.4 is in Morocco. Similarly, the percentage of respondents who claim a Christian denomination ranges from 0 to 99.3. There are only two countries in the World Values Survey with no Christian respondents—Pakistan and Turkey. In Romania, 99.3 percent of respondents identify as Christian. The percentage of respondents claiming no religious denomination also varies considerably across country cases. All respondents in Egypt, Israel, Jordan, and Morocco listed a religious denomination, while 88.9 percent of respondents in China did not.

Countries containing large Muslim populations have significantly smaller percentages of individuals who did not identify with a religious denomination. The one exception is Pakistan, in which 29.2 percent of respondents did not list a religious denomination.[13] Large percentages of individuals without religious denominations are located in Western Europe, the postcommunist region, Australia, Canada, and the United States. A considerable number of individuals in the "nondenomina-tional" category would be considered by many analysts and scholars as nominal Christians; they inhabit countries with a predominantly Christian religious history and probably have parents or grandparents who adhered to Christianity. For example, 49 percent of respondents in the United Kingdom and 41 percent of respondents in Latvia did not name a religious denomination. These individuals did not choose to identify themselves as Christian and, as such, are not considered Christian in our analysis, even though analysts using alternate measures of religious identification might count them as Christians.

PERSONAL RELIGIOSITY

Let us now turn to analyzing the data from the WVS. The most telling questions are those that shed the most light on people's level of religiosity. Defining religiosity precisely is impossible. Still, while admitting that we see only dimly, we may examine data that illuminate aspects of personal religious devotion. The WVS asks respondents numerous questions on religion. Some touch on religion but do not directly elicit information about personal religiosity.[14] Other questions do a good job of targeting an aspect of personal religiosity but do not yield plentiful data. In some such cases the questions are recent additions to the WVS, and surveys that include the questions have to date been carried out in only a handful of countries.[15]

But several questions are right on target for assessing personal religiosity and have yielded abundant data. Three questions are especially useful. The first asks how important God is in the respondent's life.[16] The second asks the respondent whether he or she is a religious person.[17] The third asks how often the respondent attends religious services.[18] Responses to these questions give us a good look at the place of religion in people's lives.

The WVS does not score the answers to the questions in identical fashion. For the first question, respondents are asked to assess the importance of God in their lives on a 1–10 scale, with 1 signifying "not at all important" and 10 "very important." We look at average scores on this scale as the measure of religiosity. For the second question, the respondent can answer in one of three ways: "a religious person," "not a religious person," or "a convinced atheist." Here the percentage of people who answered "a religious person" is our indicator of religiosity. For the third question, respondents are offered multiple categories that reflect a continuum of frequency of attendance at religious services (more than once a week, once a week, once a month, and so on). The total percentage of respondents who said that they attend services "more than once a week" or "once a week" is our indicator of religiosity.

We begin with a look at the average scores on each of the survey questions for Muslims and non-Muslims. We then proceed to the statistical analyses on the data for each of the questions.

Are Muslims More Religious? A Preliminary Look at the Data

Using respondents' replies to the question of how important God is in their lives as the measure of religiosity, it appears that Muslims are unusually religious and are moderately more religious than Christians. Table 2.2 presents the numbers. Notably, however, the average for Christians is also very high—over 8 points on a 10-point scale.

The numbers on the second survey question, which asks each respondent whether he or she considers himself or herself a "religious person," are presented in table 2.3. Examining all three response categories provides useful information about our sample and about interpreting measures of religiosity. There is considerable heterogeneity in the non-Muslim category. The category is primarily Christian but also includes individuals belonging to other religious traditions as well as people who did not select a religious denomination. If we look at the separate responses for Christians and those not selecting a denomination, a clearer picture emerges. Christians are only slightly (about 1 percentage point) less likely to consider themselves "religious persons" than are Muslims. About one-third of nondenominationalists call themselves religious, while about half say they are "not religious." Among Muslims and Christians, about 15 percent of adherents of each confession say they are not religious. Finally, a miniscule percentage of both Muslims and Christians consider themselves "convinced atheists."

The data for the third question, which asks people how often they attend religious services, are presented in table 2.4. Before discussing the numbers, however, a word about the source of data is in order. In the fifth wave of the WVS, conducted between 2005 and 2008, the question about attendance at weekly services was not posed in a uniform manner across countries. In some predominantly Muslim countries, such as Malaysia, respondents were asked how often they *prayed*, while in others, such as Indonesia, they were asked how frequently they *attend religious services*. This

Table 2.2 How Important Is God in Your Life? (1 = least importance, 10 = greatest importance)

Muslims	All Non-Muslims[a]	Christians	No Denomination
9.5 ($N = 26,689$)	7.3 ($N = 85,703$)	8.1 ($N = 57,142$)	4.5 ($N = 18,707$)

[a]Includes all individuals who adhere to a religious denomination other than Islam as well as individuals who did not state adherence to a religious tradition.

Table 2.3 Do You Consider Yourself a Religious Person?

	Muslims (%)	All Non-Muslims (%)	Christians (%)	No Denomination (%)
A religious person	85.1	69.2	84.0	29.5
Not a religious person	14.5	25.2	15.0	51.8
A convinced atheist	0.5	5.5	1.1	18.7
N	25,258	82,815	55,893	18,760

Note: This question was not asked in Israel and Singapore.

Table 2.4 Attend Religious Services at Least Once per Week

Muslims (%)	All Non-Muslims[a] (%)	Christians (%)
42.7 ($N = 24,195$)	28.1 ($N = 70,110$)	36.9 ($N = 46,978$)

Note: This question was not asked in Israel.

[a] Includes all individuals who adhere to a religious denomination other than Islam as well as individuals who did not state adherence to a religious tradition.

inconsistency in question wording is problematic. It represents a glitch in the survey, and renders comparison across cases impossible on this question. Fortunately, however, in the fourth wave of the WVS survey, conducted between 1999 and 2004, the question appears to have been asked uniformly across country cases. We therefore rely on data from the fourth wave for the question on attendance at religious services.[19]

In contrast to the two other indicators of religiosity, which are strictly attitudinal, frequency of attendance at religious services is a behavioral indicator. It measures an actual commitment to an act, rather than a person's self-assessment of an attitude. The meaning of the data on this matter are roughly comparable across Muslims and Christians, since Muslims consider weekly attendance at Friday noon prayers and sermons at mosque an important practice of their faith, much as Christians consider weekly attendance at Sunday morning worship services a centerpiece of theirs. One cannot say that Friday prayer services mean exactly the same thing to a Muslim as Sunday church services mean to a Christian, but it is not unreasonable to suppose that there is some rough equivalence, particularly since the question wording is general enough also to include Muslims attending mosque for daily prayers on days other than Friday as well.

When we examine attendance at religious services as a measure of religiosity, we see that, on average, a higher percentage of Muslims than Christians attend religious services at least once a week. Table 2.4 shows the numbers.

Table 2.5 Attend Religious Services at Least Once per Week (Christian subgroups)

Catholics (%)	Protestants (%)	Orthodox (%)
41.9 ($N = 25,248$)	43.8 ($N = 12,441$)	13.1 ($N = 9,127$)

Upon closer inspection, however, we find that the difference between Muslims and Christians is due to variation across subgroups of Christians. Table 2.5 presents the data. Almost 42 percent of Catholics and 44 percent of Protestants attend religious services at least once a week, while only 13 percent of Orthodox Christians do. Thus, both the Catholic and the Protestant averages are virtually identical to the Muslim average of about 43 percent. There is far greater variation within Christianity than between Christians and Muslims. Low levels of church attendance among Orthodox Christians, most of who live in postcommunist Eastern Europe and the countries of the former USSR, accounts for the entire difference in religious observance between Muslims and Christians.

Statistical Analysis

We now extend the analyses by controlling for other variables that may affect religiosity. The averages presented above provide a helpful starting point, but they are not adequate. We must also include the proper controls. Doing so requires that we conduct statistical analysis.

We therefore control for the variables that are commonly considered as potentially influencing religiosity. In survey research, gender, age, and educational attainment are often regarded as individual-level determinants of religiosity, and we control for these variables. Gender is a binary variable (female–male). We measure age in years. Educational attainment we treat as an ordinal variable measured 0–1, in which 0 = incomplete elementary education or less; 0.20 = complete elementary; 0.40 = incomplete secondary or incomplete vocational/technical secondary; 0.60 = complete secondary or complete vocational/technical secondary; 0.80 = incomplete higher education; and 1 = complete higher education.

Gender, age, and education are all individual-level characteristics. Another individual-level variable that theorists posit as an important component of modernization and the subsequent effect it has on various outcomes is income. Like education, income is a measure of individual-level socioeconomic status, which some scholars hypothesize weakens attachment to religion. The WVS includes a question about income but does not measure income in currency terms that can be readily compared across cases. Rather, the survey in each country provides respondents with a range of ten income brackets based in local currency and asks them to which category their family belongs.[20] As a result, the income variable only measures relative income deciles within countries and is of little use in comparing income levels across cases.[21]

In order to consider potential country-level effects, we also tested several controls for socioeconomic development. Socioeconomic development plays an important role in modernization and secularization theories that posit a decline in commitment to religious values. Modernization is a broad concept that describes the major social changes that occur when an economy moves from an agrarian to an industrial basis. This transformation is accompanied by urbanization, an expansion of education, and reliance on wage-based household economies. These shifts may have a profound effect on traditional social institutions, including religious practice. The secularization thesis, as formulated by social theorists such as Karl Marx, Max Weber, and Émile Durkheim, posits that as societies move toward higher levels of modernization, secular values and institutions grow in importance while religious values and the authority of religious institutions wane.

There are many ways of measuring socioeconomic development. Income per capita, urbanization, occupational structure, life expectancy, infant mortality, maternal mortality, fertility, and literacy are among the most widely used indicators. When selecting indicators for hierarchical linear models (HLM) and hierarchical generalized linear models (HGLM), however, we need to be parsimonious. Here and elsewhere in this book where we use HLM and HGLM, we will rely mainly upon two indicators: the log of the gross domestic product (GDP, or income) per capita in U.S. dollars, adjusted for purchasing power parity (PPP), in the year 1998, and average age.[22] Income per capita is the most commonly used indicator in social science. It does a reasonably good job of capturing the "economic" part of "socioeconomic" development. Average age better captures the "socio" part of "socioeconomic" development. Higher average age is the product of longer life expectancy and lower fertility rate, each of which indicates a more advanced level of development.[23] Countries with older populations are more developed; those with younger populations, less.[24] Using these indicators together provides a good way to control for development.

At the level of countries, in some analyses it also makes sense to control for the openness of political regime (which we will also refer to as the level of democracy). We use a five-year average of scores from the Freedom House survey (1994–1998).[25] We also control for the proportion of a country's population made up of Muslims and the proportion of the population made up of Christians.

Ideally we should control for both individual-level factors (e.g., the gender, age, and educational attainment of respondents) and country-level factors (e.g., the level of socioeconomic development and democratic attainment as well as the religious composition in the country in which the respondents live). We are able to do so by using hierarchical linear modeling (HLM) and hierarchical generalized linear modeling (HGLM). Given the nature of the data we have and the questions we are asking, HLM and HGLM are the best and most sophisticated methods available. HLM and HGLM, which are forms of multilevel modeling, allow us to consider that there are two levels of potential variation that may affect any individual's religiosity. At the individual level, characteristics such as gender, age, and education may explain why some people are more religious than others. Yet, the individuals in our sample come from eighty-three countries, and it is likely that country-level characteristics, such as a country's socioeconomic conditions or its religious composition, might also influence religiosity. In a traditional regression analysis, we would have to limit our investigation to one level. If we examined variation between countries, we would be throwing away potentially useful information about differences between individuals in the same country. Yet if we looked exclusively at variation between individuals, we would be ignoring the potentially powerful impact of country-level differences. By analyzing these questions in a hierarchical context, we can consider both sources of possible variation.[26] Additionally, since HLM and HGLM first analyze trends within each country and then look across countries, the technique prevents the imbalance of each country's sample size from influencing the overall results. While we cannot change which countries are sampled in the WVS and the overabundance of Christians compared to other denominations, HLM and HGLM make it possible to compare individual-level and country-level effects with standard errors that are adjusted to the appropriate level.

Now, to return to the substantive matter at hand: Do the broad similarities in religiosity that we find between Muslims and Christians still hold when we control for other factors that may affect religiosity?

When conducting HLM on a continuous dependent variable, we begin by assessing the differences between how much variance is due to differences between countries and how much is due to differences between the traits of individuals. First, we conducted an analysis of variance of the importance-of-God scale. This analysis allowed us to calculate how much of the variance in response to the question is between countries and how much is between individual-level characteristics. We find that 40 percent of the variance is between countries and 60 percent is between individual-level characteristics.

Table 2.6 presents the results of the HLM analyses that treat the importance-of-God scale as the indicator of religiosity and the dependent variable. Because the importance-of-God scale is measured continuously, the coefficients in table 2.6 can be interpreted similarly to the coefficients in an ordinary least squares (OLS) regression. That is, they tell us the change in the importance-of-God scale when the independent variables increase by one unit.

Models 1–3 test individual-level variables that may influence one's religiosity, as measured by the importance-of-God scale. As models 1 and 2 demonstrate,

Table 2.6 HLM Analysis of the Importance of God in Life (1 = least importance, 10 = greatest importance)

Predictors	Model 1	Model 2	Model 3	Model 4
Intercept	7.55*** (.21)	7.55*** (.21)	7.55*** (.21)	7.55*** (.00)
Individual-level[a]				
Female			0.51*** (.04)	0.51*** (.04)
Age			0.01*** (.00)	0.01*** (.00)
Education level			−0.37*** (.07)	−0.37*** (.07)
Muslim	1.43*** (.17)		2.81*** (.21)	2.89*** (.22)
Christian		1.66*** (.17)	1.97*** (.15)	1.99*** (.15)
Country-level[b]				
GDP per capita (log)				−0.01 (.00)
Average age				−0.00 (.00)
Average Importance of God				1.00*** (.00)
Proportion Muslim				0.00 (.01)
Proportion Christian				0.01 (.01)
Variance Components[c]				
σ^2	5.28	4.69	4.33	4.32
τ	$u_0 = 3.53$	$u_0 = 3.53$	$u_0 = 3.53$	$u_0 =$ fixed to 0
	$u_M = 1.67$	$u_C = 2.30$	$u_F = 0.13$	$u_F = 0.13$
			$u_A = 0.00$	$u_A = 0.00$
			$u_E = 0.38$	$u_E = 0.38$
			$u_M = 3.21$	$u_M = 3.40$
			$u_C = 1.80$	$u_C = 1.83$

Note: For details about the equations used in these and other HLM and HGLM models throughout the chapter, see appendix 2.B. Entries are restricted maximum likelihood coefficients with robust standard errors, calculated on HLM 6.06.

$N = 111{,}350$ individuals in 83 countries.

[a]All individual-level variables are centered at the group mean; all individual-level error terms were treated as random coefficients and were statistically significant at $p < .001$.

[b]All country-level variables are centered at the grand mean. In model 4 the intercept error term was constrained to zero following a deviance test, which determined that the intercept error term was not statistically significant from zero.

[c]The variance components for a null model including only the random Level-2 intercept are: $\sigma^2 = 5.38$; $\tau = 3.53$.

*$p < .05$; **$p < .01$; ***$p < .001$.

self-identification as a Muslim or Christian has a statistically significant and positive effect. This result is to be expected given the nature of the question; we would expect people who identify themselves as Muslims or Christians to be more religious than average, given that nondenominationalists figure prominently among respondents who identified themselves as neither Muslim nor Christian. Model 3 includes three individual-level socioeconomic predictors of religiosity: age, gender, and education level, together with the Muslim and Christian dummy variables. In the analysis, all of the variables are highly statistically significant. Being a female and being older correspond positively with religiosity, while being more highly educated corresponds negatively. Even when we control for these characteristics, self-identification as a Muslim or Christian is statistically significant and positive.[27]

Model 4 introduces five country-level predictors: national income measured as GDP per capita for 1998, the average age of the country's population, a country's average score on the importance-of-God scale, the proportion of Muslims in a country, and the proportion of Christians in a country.[28] If we average the scores on the importance-of-God scale for all individuals in a country, we can develop a measure of the overall level of religiosity in that country. In our sample, the scores for country-level religiosity vary from a low of 3.58 in China to a high of 10 in Pakistan. The average across all the country cases is 7.54. In contrast to what we would expect from the standard tenets of modernization theory, which include the notion that wealthier societies tend to be less religious, neither of our socioeconomic controls—national income or average age—is statistically significant. Rather, countries' overall levels of religiosity play a more important role and have a greater effect on individuals' assessments of the importance of God in their lives than do their countries' levels of socioeconomic development. The difference in a person's predicted score on the importance-of-God scale if he or she lives in a country that has an average religiosity level one point above or below the average (7.54) is a full point. Interestingly, neither the proportion of Muslims nor the proportion of Christians in a country is a statistically significant predictor. Therefore, while self-identification as a Christian or a Muslim is a strong predictor of individual-level religiosity, the proportion of Christians or Muslims in one's society does not appear to play a role.[29]

Thus, people in wealthier countries tend to rate God's importance in their lives as about the same as people in poorer countries; there is no visible difference in the importance-of-God scores based on national income. Furthermore, the proportion of one's fellow religionists who live in a country has no effect—not even a modest one—on the intensity of religiosity. Individuals, whether Muslims or Christians, are not more likely to regard God as more important if they live in societies that are proportionally higher in Muslims or in Christians. Yet the religiosity of one's environment does appear to influence one's own personal intensity of religiosity, and the

Table 2.7 HGLM Analysis of the Question "Are You a Religious Person?"
(1 = yes, 0 = not religious or "convinced atheist")

Predictors	Model 1	Model 2	Model 3	Model 4
Intercept	1.19*** (.12)	1.28*** (.13)	1.34*** (.14)	1.22*** (.03)
Individual-level[a]				
Female			0.52*** (.03)	0.51*** (.03)
Age			0.01*** (.00)	0.01*** (.00)
Education level			−0.29*** (.08)	−0.28*** (.08)
Muslim	1.03*** (.16)		2.30*** (.16)	2.22*** (.16)
Christian		1.60*** (.16)	1.97*** (.13)	1.97*** (.13)
Country-level[b]				
GDP per capita (log)				−0.11 (.07)
Average age				0.00 (.01)
Proportion religious persons				6.21*** (.27)
Proportion Muslim				−0.19 (.19)
Proportion Christian				−0.44** (.19)
Variance Components[c] (τ)	$u_0 = 1.24$ $u_M = 0.96$	$u_0 = 1.37$ $u_C = 1.84$	$u_0 = 1.51$ $u_F = 0.06$ $u_A = 0.00$ $u_E = 0.40$ $u_M = 1.36$ $u_C = 1.31$	$u_0 = 0.07$ $u_F = 0.06$ $u_A = 0.00$ $u_E = 0.40$ $u_M = 1.35$ $u_C = 1.22$

Note: Entries are restricted maximum likelihood coefficients with robust standard errors for the unit-specific model, calculated on HLM 6.06.

$N = 107,073$ individuals in 81 countries

[a]All individual-level variables are centered at the group mean; all individual-level error terms were treated as random coefficients and were statistically significant at $p < .001$.

[b]All country-level variables are centered at the grand mean.

[c]The variance component for a null model including only the random Level-2 intercept is $\tau = 1.21$.

*$p < .05$; **$p < .01$; ***$p < .001$.

effect is substantial. Living in an environment with people who are more religious makes one more religious; living in an environment with people who are less religious makes one less religious.

While self-identification as a Muslim or as a Christian has a positive effect on one's score on the importance-of-God scale, the size of the effect of being a Muslim is greater. For example, if we take two men of the same age and educational status living in the same country, the Muslim man is predicted to have a score on the importance-of-God scale that is 0.9 points higher than that of the Christian man. A woman is predicted to have a score that is 0.5 points higher than a man of the same confession, whether she is Muslim or Christian.

We may now examine the results of analyses that treat people's responses to the question of whether or not they consider themselves "a religious person" as our indicator of religiosity. Those results are presented in table 2.7.

The models presented in table 2.7 are HGLM models for a binary outcome. The models are estimated using a logit link function, and therefore the coefficients in table 2.7 can be thought of as logit coefficients. Logit coefficients are interpreted as the rate of change in the "log odds" of our dependent variable as the predictor variable changes by one unit.[30] While logit coefficients can provide clues about statistical significance and whether an independent variable has a positive or negative effect on the outcome of interest, log odds provide little directly interpretable information about the magnitude of these effects. In order to examine the substantive effect of different independent variables, it is useful to calculate predicted probabilities for some hypothetical values for actual people, which we will do here.[31]

The results of the individual-level models evaluating whether one considers himself/herself a religious person are broadly similar to the results we obtain when using the importance-of-God scale as the indicator of religiosity. At the individual level, being a female and being older are each positively associated with identifying as a religious person. Higher levels of education are negatively associated with religiosity. Self-identification as a Christian or Muslim is also positively correlated with identification as a religious person. If we consider a Muslim man and a Christian man of average age and education level, according to model 3 the Muslim man would have a predicted probability of .86 of describing himself as a religious person, while the Christian man would have a predicted probability of .82. Hypothetical Muslim and Christian women of the same average age and education status would have predicted probabilities of describing themselves as "religious" of .92 and .89, respectively. Thus, we see that while Muslims are a bit more likely to consider themselves "religious" than are Christians, the differences are modest. Similarly, while being a female is positively associated with religiosity, the differences between women and men are not substantial. These patterns largely mirror those that we observed in table 2.6.

The country-level variables also show similar patterns when we use the "are you a religious person" question to assess religiosity. First, in both tables 2.6 and 2.7, the two variables measuring country-level socioeconomic status—national income and average age—are not statistically significant. Second, a country's average religiosity level is statistically significant and positive. In the models presented in table 2.6 we saw that as a country's average score on the importance-of-God scale increased, an individual's score on the scale also increased. A similar trend is present in table 2.7; as the proportion of individuals in a country that consider themselves "religious" increases, the likelihood of identifying as "a religious person" also increases. Third, the proportion of Muslims in a country is not statistically significant. The one variable that shows different results in the models presented in tables 2.6 and 2.7 is the proportion of Christians in a country. While this variable is not statistically significant in analyzing the importance-of-God scale, the models in table 2.7 show that the proportion of a country that is Christian is statistically significant and negative when we use the question of whether the respondent considers himself/herself as a "religious person." As the proportion of Christians in a country increases, the likelihood that an individual will consider himself/herself "a religious person" actually decreases.

How do these country-level variables affect the predicted probability of considering oneself "a religious person"? Let us consider three men—one Muslim, one Christian, and one who does not identify as the adherent of any religious denomination—of average age and education. If we place these three men in the same country, and that country has average levels of income, average age, and proportion of religious persons, the predicted probability that they would consider themselves "religious" is .84 for the Muslim man, .81 for the Christian man, and .37 for the man who claims no religious denomination. While the Muslim man has the highest predicted probability for identifying as a religious person, this probability is only slightly higher than that predicted for the Christian man.

Yet, as model 4 in table 2.7 suggests, the proportion of a country's population that considers itself religious also plays a significant role in explaining individual-level religiosity. While the average proportion of people who call themselves religious across all countries is 72 percent, the empirical range spans from a low of 22 percent in China to a high of 98 percent in Mali. If we consider two hypothetical Muslim men of average age and education, one living in Mali, where 98 percent of people say they are religious, and the other living in Saudi Arabia, where 70 percent say they are religious, we find that the predicted probability that the Malian Muslim will consider himself religious is .97, while the predicted probability that the Saudi Arabian Muslim will consider himself religious is .83. The analogous probabilities for Christian men would be 96 percent in Mali and 80 percent in Saudi Arabia. The higher level of overall national religiosity in Mali contributes to a similar level of predicted individual-level religiosity among Muslims and Christians. The Christians

Table 2.8 HGLM Analysis of Attendance at Religious Services at Least Once a Week (1 = attends at least once per week, 0 = attends less regularly/never attends)

Predictors	Model 1	Model 2	Model 3	Model 4
Intercept	−1.06*** (.17)	−1.23*** (.19)	−1.32*** (.20)	−1.36*** (.05)
Individual-level [a]				
Female			0.16 (.12)	0.15 (.12)
Age			0.02*** (.00)	0.02*** (.00)
Education level			−0.03 (.08)	0.01 (.08)
Muslim	0.43* (.16)		2.00*** (.22)	1.95*** (.22)
Christian		1.51*** (.19)	1.89*** (.20)	1.87*** (.19)
Country-level [b]				
GDP per capita (log)				0.14 (.14)
Average age				−0.02 (.01)
Proportion attending services weekly				6.26*** (.21)
Proportion Muslim				0.47 (.30)
Proportion Christian				0.55 (.33)
Level of democracy				−0.01 (.04)
Variance Components [c] (τ)	$u_0 = 1.89$ $u_M = 0.84$	$u_0 = 2.38$ $u_C = 2.21$	$u_0 = 2.56$ $u_F = 0.93$ $u_A = 0.00$ $u_E = 0.33$ $u_M = 2.00$ $u_C = 2.26$	$u_0 = 0.12$ $u_F = 0.93$ $u_A = 0.00$ $u_E = 0.34$ $u_M = 2.04$ $u_C = 2.05$

Note: Entries are restricted maximum likelihood coefficients with robust standard errors for the unit-specific model, calculated on HLM 6.06.

$N = 90,627$ individuals in 65 countries.

[a] All individual-level variables are centered at the group mean; all individual-level error terms were treated as random coefficients and were statistically significant at $p < .001$.

[b] All country-level variables are centered at the grand mean.

[c] The variance component for a null model including only the random Level-2 intercept is $\tau = 1.88$.

*$p < .05$; **$p < .01$; ***$p < .001$.

in Mali have a substantially higher predicted probability of considering themselves religious than do the Muslims in Saudi Arabia. Thus, as when we measured religiosity using the importance-of-God scale, when we use the question on whether respondents consider themselves to be "a religious person" living in a more religious environment may be conducive to higher levels of personal religiosity. The influence of the overall religiosity of one's environment, moreover, is stronger than the effect of either the concentration of adherents to either Christianity or Islam in that environment or whether one is Muslim versus Christian.

Let us turn to treating attendance at religious services as the measure of religiosity. The results of statistical analyses that treat this indicator as the outcome variable are presented in table 2.8, which is also a binary outcome model using HGLM.[32]

In analyzing attendance at religious services in a multiple regression context, we see that the differences between Muslims and Christians are minimal. The models in table 2.8 demonstrate that being a Muslim or a Christian has a statistically significant and positive effect on the likelihood of attending religious services at least once a week, even when individual- and country-level socioeconomic characteristics are taken into consideration. As model 3 shows, the only other individual-level socioeconomic characteristic that has a statistically significant effect is age. As one's age increases, the likelihood of attendance also increases.

When we include the country-level controls, we find that, in contrast with our analyses that used the other two survey questions to assess religiosity, gender is not a statistically significant predictor of attendance at religious services. Upon closer inspection, however, we see that gender corresponds with attendance at religious services in distinct ways across denominations. Specifically, among Muslims, men are more likely to attend religious services than women are, while among Christians the reverse is true. In our sample, 56 percent of Muslim men attend religious services weekly compared to 29 percent of Muslim women. Thirty-three percent of Christian men attend religious services weekly compared to 40 percent of Christian women.

As we saw when analyzing the importance-of-God scale in table 2.6, the proportion of Muslims or Christians in a country does not have a statistically significant effect on the likelihood of an individual attending religious services at least once a

Table 2.9 Predicted Probabilities of Attending Religious Services at Least Once a Week

	Model 1	Model 2	Model 3	Model 4
Muslim	.33	—	.31	.30
Christian	—	.38	.29	.28

Table 2.10 HGLM Analysis of Weekly Attendance at Religious Services for Muslim and Christian Subgroups (1 = attends at least once per week, 0 = attends less regularly/never attends)

Predictors	Muslim Sample (N = 23,686)		Christian Sample (N = 45,873)	
	Model 1	Model 2	Model 1	Model 2
Intercept	−0.54*** (.22)	−.58*** (.12)	−0.70*** (.18)	−0.68*** (.07)
Individual-level [a]				
Female	−1.08*** (.22)	−1.06*** (.22)	0.51*** (.04)	0.51*** (.04)
Age	0.02*** (.00)	0.02*** (.00)	0.02*** (.00)	0.02*** (.00)
Education level	−0.32 (.18)	−0.16 (.18)	0.15 (.08)	0.17* (.08)
Country-level [b]				
GDP per capita (log)		0.21 (.18)		0.36 (.18)
Average age		−0.04** (.02)		0.00 (.02)
Proportion attending services weekly		4.90*** (.39)		6.16*** (.31)

Proportion Muslim	−0.69** (.20)	−1.57*** (.29)
Proportion Christian		
Level of democracy	0.06 (.04)	0.02 (.06)
Variance Components[c] (τ)	$u_0 = 1.70$	$u_0 = 2.07$
	$u_F = 1.32$	$u_F = 0.07$
	$u_A = 0.00$	$u_A = 0.00$
	$u_E = 0.75$	$u_E = 0.21$
	$u_0 = 0.16$	$u_0 = 0.25$
	$u_F = 1.32$	$u_F = 0.07$
	$u_A = 0.00$	$u_A = 0.00$
	$u_E = 0.59$	$u_E = 0.23$

Note: Entries are restricted maximum likelihood coefficients with robust standard errors for the unit-specific model, calculated on HLM 6.06.

$N = 63$ countries.

[a] All individual-level variables are centered at the group mean; all individual-level error terms were treated as random coefficients and were statistically significant at $p < .001$.

[b] All country-level variables are centered at the grand mean.

[c] The variance component for a null model including only the random Level-2 intercept is $\tau = 1.44$ for Muslims and $\tau = 1.92$ for Christians.

$^*p < .05$; $^{**}p < .01$; $^{***}p < .001$.

week. National wealth, average age, and level of democracy do not appear to have an influence on attendance at religious services either. We also see another trend that we observed when we used the other two indicators for religiosity, which is that societal religiosity influences individual religiosity. Here, higher national levels of attendance at services increase the likelihood that an individual will attend services, irrespective of his or her confession. Living in a society in which an individual's fellow residents go to mosque/church/temple appears to make it more likely that he or she will do so as well.

Since logit coefficients, which are presented in the analyses here, are difficult to interpret in a straightforward way, it is again useful to consider predicted probabilities. Table 2.9 presents the predicted probabilities of attending religious services at least once a week for a hypothetical Muslim man and a hypothetical Christian man, both of average age and education level, living in a hypothetical country with average levels of income, level of democracy, and proportions of Muslims and Christians. Each column shows the probability under a set of controls, and those controls correspond to the models shown in table 2.8.

As table 2.9 shows, the predicted probabilities of attending religious services at least once a week for Muslim and Christian men who share similar socioeconomic characteristics are virtually identical. When we control for individual-level socioeconomic characteristics alone (model 3), a Muslim man has a predicted probability of .31 of attending religious services at least once a week—that is he has a 31 percent chance of attending. A Christian man has a 29 percent chance of attending. That difference in percentages holds when we control for country-level characteristics. According to model 4, a Muslim man has a 30 percent chance of attending religious services once per week, while a Christian man has a 28 percent chance.

Since the likelihood of female attendance at religious services varies according to one's religious denomination, it is useful to analyze the Muslim and Christian subgroups separately. Table 2.10 considers the predictors of weekly attendance at religious services for Muslims alone and for Christians alone.

When we analyze the Muslim and Christian populations separately, rather than in a pooled sample that includes individuals belonging to other religious traditions and nondenominationalists, we see several differences. First, being a female has a statistically significant and positive effect on attendance at religious services for Christians, yet has a negative and statistically significant effect for Muslims. Age is statistically significant and positive for both groups, which is consistent with the models of the overall sample presented above. Older people, among both Muslims and Christians, are more likely to attend services. Education is not statistically significant for Muslims, but is for Christians once we control for country-level predictors.

Looking at country-level characteristics, we see that national income and level of democracy are not statistically significant. Average age is statistically significant and

Table 2.11 Predicted Probabilities of Attending Religious Services at Least Once a Week According to Models in Table 2.10

	Muslim Sample		*Christian Sample*	
	Model 1	*Model 2*	*Model 1*	*Model 2*
Man	.51	.50	.26	.26
Woman	.26	.26	.37	.37

negative for Muslims, but is not statistically significant for Christians. Living in a country with higher rates of attendance at religious services increases the likelihood of attendance for both individual Muslims and individual Christians. In contrast to the models presented above that analyze the full sample, when we look separately at the Muslim and Christian subgroups we see that the proportion of Muslims and Christians in a society has a statistically significant and negative effect on the likelihood of attending religious services at least once per week. In other words, living in a country with a large proportion of Muslims decreases the likelihood that a Muslim will attend religious services at least once per week; and living in a country with a large proportion of Christians decreases the likelihood that a Christian will attend religious services at least once per week. This differs from the analyses of our other indicators of religiosity, in which the proportion of Muslims and Christians in the country was not statistically significant (except for the proportion of Christians in model 4 of table 2.7).

Table 2.11 shows the predicted probabilities of attending religious services at least once a week using the models for the separate Muslim and Christian samples. The numbers are for hypothetical Muslim and Christian men and women with average age and education, living in a country with average levels of income, democracy, and proportions of Muslims and Christians in the population. The predicted probabilities for model 1 consider only individual-level socioeconomic characteristics; country-level predictors are included in model 2. The addition of country-level variables produces only a slight change in predicted probabilities for individuals of average age and education. While the differences in predicted probabilities between Muslim and Christian attendance rates in table 2.9 are very small, the differences in predicted probabilities generated when looking separately at Muslims and Christians are substantial. This is because of the opposite way that gender predicts attendance at religious services among Muslims and Christians.

When we analyze the full sample, the low attendance rates of Muslim women compared to Muslim men reduce the overall likelihood of a Muslim attending religious services weekly. As a result, as table 2.9 shows, a Muslim man is only 2 percentage points more likely to attend religious services at least once a week than is a Christian man, once individual and country-level characteristics are considered (model 4). In contrast, when we look separately at the Muslim and Christian samples (table 2.11), the predicted probability of attending religious services at least once a week for a Muslim man with average socioeconomic characteristics is considerably higher—51 percent compared to 31 percent when we look only at individual characteristics, and 50 percent compared to 26 percent when country-level characteristics are considered. Meanwhile, the predicted probabilities for the Christian man are essentially the same when we compare the models generated by analyzing Christians and Muslims together versus Christians separately. Although Christian women are more likely to attend religious services at least once a week than are Christian men, the differences in attendance based on gender are less dramatic among Christians than among Muslims. According to model 4 of table 2.9, a Christian man has a 28 percent chance of attending religious services at least once a week; while according to model 2 of table 2.11, he has a 26 percent chance. Thus, when both individual- and country-level socioeconomic characteristics are considered, according to table 2.11, a Muslim man is 24 percentage points more likely to attend religious services at least once a week than is a Christian man living in the same country with the same age and education level.

The differences between Muslim women and Christian women are also considerable. According to model 2 in table 2.11, a Muslim woman is 11 percentage points less likely to attend religious services weekly than is a Christian woman. There is a bigger difference, however, in the predicted probability of attendance between Muslim men and Muslim women. Muslim women are 24 percentage points less likely to attend religious services weekly than are Muslim men. The difference between Christian men and women is less extreme. According to model 2 in table 2.11, Christian women are 11 percentage points more likely to attend religious services than are Christian men.

Here we must consider the possible effect of confession-specific factors and how the concept of "religious services" is understood. In some Muslim communities, women are not expected to attend mosque and their absence is not considered a sign of laxness in matters of faith. In some communities, men's regular attendance at Friday prayers is viewed as fulfilling religious obligation for an entire family. One could argue that in Christian communities, something resembling the opposite norm has evolved, with women often "representing" the family at church and, by their presence, making their husbands' less frequent attendance socially acceptable. Certainly we may not consider a Muslim woman's absence from the mosque a sign of lack of piety. Muslim group prayer involves ritual prostrations and rubbing shoulders with those in close proximity. That aspect of prayer, combined with concern that women's presence might distract men, means that women who do attend mosque typically pray behind an enclosed section of the mosque, which is not visible to men. In some places such a separate section does not exist in mosques, and in such locations women are often discouraged or even banned from attending mosque and are encouraged to pray at home instead. These conditions suggest that Muslim women should not be seen as less observant than their Christian counterparts because they do not attend religious services as frequently.

Yet we also must be open to variation in how the concept of "religious services" is conveyed in the survey and understood by respondents. It is useful to look more specifically at how this item is translated in some of the large Muslim countries where the WVS was conducted. For example, in Morocco and Turkey, the question specifically asks about mosque attendance. In Nigeria and Singapore, where the survey was conducted in English, the term "religious services" was employed. In Indonesia, the question was translated to as "practice religious traditions." In some contexts, women might answer the question based on their engagement in locally accepted forms of religious practice that are not limited to mosque attendance. For example, in Indonesia women regularly gather for collective religious prayer and study outside of the mosque. Regular participation in these organized prayers is viewed as appropriate and acceptable religious practice and Indonesian women respondents likely had these prayer groups, and not mosque attendance specifically, in mind when they answered the survey question. Indeed, in Indonesia, rates of men's and women's attendance according to the survey are virtually identical, as they also are in Egypt and Pakistan. They are also almost the same among Muslim men and women in Tanzania, which is not a predominantly Muslim country but which has a large Muslim population and many Muslim respondents in the survey. The data show that the notion that Muslim women are universally discouraged from engaging in organized religious practice is mistaken. Yet rates are lopsided (in favor of men) in Saudi Arabia, Jordan, Morocco, Turkey, and several other countries. Appendix 2.C provides a list of the numbers on attendance at services among Muslims, broken down by gender, in the countries in which one-quarter or more of the respondents are Muslims.

The results of the measure for attendance at religious services, and in particular the findings comparing Muslims and Christians, need to be evaluated in light of this confession-specific condition and the plurality of norms found across Muslim communities. If women were universally encouraged to attend mosque in Muslim settings, it is possible that we would find a significant difference between Muslims and Christians in terms of attendance at services, and that Muslims would exceed Christians on this measure.

Yet our findings on the disparity in church attendance among Christians also merit attention. As reported at the end of the previous subsection above, the overall Christian average is pulled down by Orthodox Christians, who attend services at rates that are dramatically lower than those of Protestants and Catholics. Most Orthodox Christians, in the world and in our sample, reside in countries in which Soviet-type socialist regimes infiltrated and destroyed church organizations, and physically demolished church buildings themselves, over the course of many decades prior to the 1990s. We cannot possibly know what the rate of attendance among Orthodox Christians would be in the absence of a legacy of Soviet state-sponsored atheism, any more than we can guess what attendance rates would be for Muslim women if they were welcomed into mosques in all settings. Here we can only mention the need for caution in interpreting the results, the necessity of considering confession-specific factors, and the advisability of taking all three of the indicators into account rather than relying solely on the attendance-at-services indicator alone (or either of the other indicators alone) to assess religiosity.

Pondering the Findings

It is difficult to offer a sweeping generalization that fits all of the findings reported above. In general, however, the evidence suggests that Muslims are not dramatically more religious than non-Muslims and are only slightly more religious—if even that—than Christians. Once we apply the proper controls and analyze the data using appropriate methods, we find little support for the notion that Muslims are extraordinarily religious. They rate the importance of God in their lives mildly more highly than Christians do, while the proportion of Muslims and Christians who call themselves "religious persons" is virtually identical. Rates of attendance at religious services are essentially the same among Muslims and Christians, though we find interesting, asymmetric gaps between the genders in participation in religious services between the adherents of the two religions.

What makes the correlation between Muslim faith and degree of religiosity mild is not necessarily a deficit of religiosity among Muslims. It may instead be the abiding religiosity that is found among non-Muslims. As we see in table 2.2, Muslim respondents rate the importance of God in their lives as (a very high) 9.5 on a 10-point scale. Yet Christians, at 8.1, are not far behind. As table 2.3 shows, about 85 percent of Muslims consider themselves religious—but so do 84 percent of Christians. About 43 percent of Muslims attend religious services once a week or more. But 37 percent of Christians do so as well, and when we remove Orthodox Christians from the mix and compare Muslims with Protestants and Catholics alone, the numbers on frequency of participation in services are identical for Muslims and Christians. People in many countries that are not predominately Muslim clearly are as religious as those that are. Even in many predominantly Christian societies that are widely seen as highly secular, such as Italy, Ukraine, and Canada, substantial majorities consider themselves religious. Attendance at religious services in the United States, Mexico, the Philippines, South Africa, Poland, Uganda, Peru, Portugal, Slovakia, and Ireland is as high as or higher than the average level for the twelve Muslim countries for which we have data, which are Indonesia, Pakistan, Bangladesh, Egypt, Turkey, Iran, Morocco, Saudi Arabia, Iraq, Jordan, Kyrgyzstan, and

Albania. The data, and our analysis of the data, support the soundness of As'ad AbuKhalil's warning against "the mistaken association between secularism and Christianity."[33]

Why might these findings be surprising? We often tend to underestimate the endurance of religiosity even among the wealthy and sophisticated. The expectations of classical modernization theory are supported insofar as, in some of our models, higher educational attainment at the individual level is associated with lower religiosity. According to modernization theory, growth in prosperity gives people goods in the worldly realm that dampen their longing for things of the spirit. The changes in communal life associated with urbanization reduce people's dependence upon traditional authorities, including clerics. The growth of intellectual sophistication that attends rising educational attainment may render the supernaturalism of religious belief less plausible, while the increase in mastery over one's environment that accompanies technological advancement makes supernatural aid less needed. But while higher development does apparently reduce religiosity, it does not even come close to extinguishing it. Over three-fifths of Russians and Ukrainians label themselves as religious people after three-quarters of a century of indoctrination by the most aggressive antireligious propaganda machine the world has ever known. The same is true of the prosperous and world-weary Canadians, Americans, Austrians, Belgians, Greeks, and Danes. God has survived all manner of industrialism, materialism, postmodernism, and postmaterialism. God is not vanquished by "isms." And it is not just "spirituality" that survives; it is religiosity.

Yet—and here is where the basis for misunderstanding arises—nonbelievers, few though they are, are disproportionately represented among intellectuals. The people who write serious works of social science, such as the one you are holding, very often tend toward agnosticism or atheism.[34] At the university where your author works and many other leading research universities, Karl Marx, Friedrich Nietzsche, and Michel Foucault hold more sway than do Jesus, Muhammad, or Moses (though the Buddha may rival Marx, Nietzsche, and Foucault in some quarters). Since we human beings tend to confuse our own beliefs with everyone else's, creators of scientific and humanistic knowledge may underestimate popular religiosity—except perhaps in moments of despair when we contemplate the hold that belief in the Divine continues to exert on voters, and the ability of politicians (whose own religiosity we of course assume to be insincere) to exploit that belief. Those who do the most to create our knowledge about ourselves are among the least likely to embrace the supernaturalism—that is, the belief in miracles— that inheres in most religious doctrines, including those of Islam and Christianity. No wonder we may be surprised by the persistence of religiosity in our own societies.

But the problem is not just that we are misled by our own intellectuals. Another reason we tend to underestimate religiosity in our own midst, and therefore to exaggerate it, relatively speaking, in other settings, is the natural human tendency to regard what is well known as unremarkable and what is unfamiliar as imposing.

I remember well the impression I had shortly after taking up residence in Surabaya, the capital of East Java and Indonesia's second-largest city. On my first morning there, as the day's first *azan* (call to prayer) rang out from a stupendous loudspeaker at a nearby mosque, I awoke and felt my somnolent oblivion replaced by awe. As I lay in bed, the feeling turned to enchantment as the first, mellifluous baritone to pierce the silence was joined in rapid but uncoordinated succession by voices from other mosques, building to a cacophonous din that filled every corner of the city and went on for about fifteen minutes. Then, suddenly, silence. This all happened at about 4:00 A.M., two hours before sunrise. I remember lying in that sweltering tropical night following the return of silence, wondering how many of my countrymen across the Pacific would tolerate, much less embrace, such a practice. And what if many did, but someone in the neighborhood did not? If a single neighbor did not appreciate the intrusive ritual, it would not last long. In Surabaya that ritual would recur at regular intervals four more times over the next eighteen hours. Most of the residents of the bustling metropolis would participate in it every time it took place. Here, to be sure, was genuine mass religiosity.

During my early weeks in Surabaya I asked my new friends: If you pray, do you go back to bed afterwards or stay up? Isn't it, well, a pain to rise at 4:00 A.M.? As a night owl who sometimes had not yet retired at the time of the first *azan*, I stood in awe especially of anyone who not only prayed but also actually rose for the day at such an hour. Among the majority who did pray, some said that they stayed up. Many more said they prayed and returned to bed.

All responded to my naïve inquiries with utter graciousness. Never did I encounter so much as the hint of a patronizing smirk. Yet my questions did come as a bit of a surprise to some people. Morning prayers—all prayers—were, after all, so normal.

As my time in Indonesia passed they became normal to me, too. In one sense my attitude toward the prayers never changed. I continue to regard them as I did then—stirring and sublime. And yet, as my residence in Indonesia turned from weeks to months, the prayers became less dazzling. On mornings when I made it to sleep before the first *azan*, I stopped even waking up regularly at the sound of the call. Despite its magnificence and mighty decibel level, the call no longer stirred me. It became a regular part of the night, much like car alarms in New York City.

As I left Surabaya after nearly a half-year of residence, I still regarded Indonesians as religious. The data from the WVS support that impression. But I was no longer overwhelmed by the people's religiosity. Their confession and rituals had become familiar to me. I had acquired a host of friends and acquaintances who were observant Muslims who led lives that were largely similar to my own.

The experience reminded me that a process of internalizing Christian practices and symbols had also occurred in my life. It had just happened before I was old enough to be conscious of it. Having grown up in small cities and towns in the American Midwest and South, I rarely notice a sea of cross-topped steeples along the roads I traverse and announcers calling out the name of Jesus on every tenth station I cross on the radio dial. Yet some friends and colleagues from predominantly non-Christian societies who have spent time in America have a different view. What I see as unobtrusive manifestations of everyday life, they regard as striking signs that American society is steeped in (Christian) religiosity. As I drove together through the San Francisco Bay Area with one Muslim associate from the Middle East, he exclaimed, indicating with a sweep of his hand a landscape covered with churches: "If this is godlessness, where can faith be found?!" And the churches he beheld are not mere architectural relics. Americans' attendance at religious services outstrips that of the people in my colleague's native Iran, as well as that of the people of Turkey and all five of the Arab countries for which we have data (Egypt, Morocco, Saudi Arabia, Iraq, and Jordan).

Summary

To sum up the findings on personal religiosity: There does appear to be a difference in religiosity between Muslims and non-Muslims; Muslims are more religious. But the difference is modest and ranges between diminutive and nonexistent, depending on which indicator for religiosity we use, when we compare Muslims specifically with Christians. The one instance in which we see a more dramatic difference is in mosque attendance among Muslim men. It is true that Muslim men are more likely to attend religious services than are Christian men. But Muslim women are less likely to attend than are Christian women. Probing into the potential implications of this gender difference is beyond the scope of this chapter. On the whole, the findings furnish only the faintest evidence that Muslims are more religious than non-Muslims for reasons that are intrinsic to their religion.

POPULAR ATTITUDES TOWARD RELIGION AND POLITICS

Even if Islam does not necessarily dispose its adherents to extraordinary religiosity, does it not still have a strongly—even uniquely—favorable stance on combining religious and political authority? Few generalizations about Islam are more widely accepted. Leading scholars of diverse methodological and intellectual orientations embrace some version of this idea. Mark Tessler finds that more religious Muslims are no less favorably inclined to democracy than are less religious Muslims.[35] Yet he nevertheless holds, "There is a strong historic connection between religion and politics in the Muslim world, reflecting Islam's character as a religion of laws pertaining to societal organization as well as individual morality."[36] According to Bernard Lewis, "In Islam . . . there is from the beginning an interpenetration, almost an identification, of cult and power, or religion and the state: Mohammed was not only a prophet, but a ruler. In this respect, Islam resembles Old Testament Judaism and looks quite different from Christianity."[37] Mohammad Amjad echoes this sentiment, "In Islam, politics and religion are intertwined. The Prophet Mohammad was both the head of state and the administrator of religious affairs."[38] Samuel Huntington, in what has become a famous quip, states, "God and Caesar, church and state, spiritual and temporal authority, have been a prevailing dualism in Western culture." In contrast, Huntington states, "In Islam God is Caesar."[39] Jamal al-Suwaidi further argues that Muslims expect their political leaders to be religious leaders as well. According to al-Suwaidi, "Muslims have continued to assume that only a 'religious leader' can provide good government for the Muslim community."[40] Lahouari Addi says that "Muslim societies are pregnant with a religious utopia from which they would like to draw political order." This utopia is no local phenomenon; it is found, according to Addi, "in all Muslim societies." It is, moreover, deeply rooted. Addi asserts, "The Islamic utopia is not an accident of circumstances; on the contrary, it belongs to the long term of history," since "the Islamic world held itself apart from the social debates that the Renaissance unleashed in Europe. Untouched by the dynamic of social criticism, it remained faithful to apologetic historiography."[41] Mounira Charrad states, "There is no differentiation in Islam between the secular and the sacred, between theology and the principles guiding life in society. The sacred and the civil are one and the same thing."[42]

Such ideas are frequently asserted. They may be right, but we do not know until we test them. Numerous writings assert generalizations based on fragments of soft evidence, but we lack works that pose the questions as hypotheses and subject them to rigorous test. Below, we treat these notions as hypotheses and test them.

Attitudes toward Clerical Influence in Politics

The WVS includes two questions that are worded in a way that pointedly elicit views on whether respondents think the clergy should have a role in politics. One asks whether "religious leaders should not influence how people vote in elections."[43] The other asks respondents if they agree that "religious leaders should not influence government."[44] These questions provide a window on people's attitudes toward the involvement of religious authorities in political matters.

Here we focus on the first of these two questions. Data for the first are plentiful, while the second question was not asked in many major countries, creating a shortage of data and less confidence in the findings. We did analyze the second question as well as the first, however, and arrived at results that are substantively similar to what we found, and present here, on the first question.[45]

Table 2.12 Agreement with Statement, "Religious Leaders Should Not Influence How People Vote" (percentage who "agree" or "strongly agree")

Muslims	All Non-Muslims[a]	Christians	No Denomination
65.7 (N = 20,231)	72.2 (N = 71,336)	71.0 (N = 49,347)	79.1 (N = 14,374)

Note: This question was not asked in China, Colombia, Egypt, France, Israel, Netherlands, Russia, Saudi Arabia, Singapore, Switzerland, and the United Kingdom.

[a]Includes all individuals who adhere to a religious denomination other than Islam as well as individuals who did not state adherence to a religious tradition.

The raw percentages show that a large majority of respondents across religious affiliations agree or strongly agree with the statement that religious leaders should not influence how people vote. Muslims partake of that consensus, with roughly two-thirds holding that religious leaders should not influence voters. In comparative terms, however, Muslims are less likely to agree with this statement than are non-Muslims, including Christians. Table 2.12 presents the group averages.

When we analyze this question in a multiple regression context, however, we see that the differences between Muslims and Christians are not actually substantial. Table 2.13 presents the results from HGLM models using an ordered logit link function. The coefficients in table 2.13 can be viewed as the log odds for a cumulative logit model. As with the binary response models presented earlier, ordered logit coefficients provide little directly interpretable information other than statistical significance and direction of the effect. As models 1 and 2 in table 2.13 show, self-identification as a Muslim or as a Christian is negatively associated with agreement with the statement. Both Muslims and Christians are less likely to agree that religious leaders should not influence vote choice. This effect is amplified when socioeconomic characteristics such as gender, age, and education are added. Although age is not statistically significant, being a female has a small negative effect on agreement with the statement, while education is positively associated. Model 4 adds the importance-of-God scale as a control variable for religiosity.[46] This variable is statistically significant and negative, and appears to wash out the independent effect of being a female. Once the religiosity control is added, the size of the coefficients for the Muslim and Christian dummy variables are reduced. This result tells us that while self-identification as a Muslim or Christian has an independent effect on one's attitude toward the fusion of religious and political power, the size of the effect is lower once we consider individual religiosity. This finding holds when we consider country-level predictors as well, which are introduced in models 5 and 6.

Since odds ratios are difficult to interpret directly, it is useful to look at predicted probabilities for some hypothetical cases. Let us consider three men of average age, education, and level of religiosity who live in the same country, also with average

Table 2.13 HGLM Analysis of Statement, "Religious Leaders Should Not Influence How People Vote"[63T]

Predictors	Model 1	Model 2	Model 3	Model 4	Model 5	Model 6
Intercept	−0.76*** (.06)	−0.76*** (.06)	−0.77*** (.06)	−0.77*** (.06)	−0.77*** (.06)	−0.77*** (.05)
Individual-level[a]						
Female			−0.05** (.02)	−0.02 (.02)	−0.05** (.02)	−0.02 (.02)
Age			0.00 (.00)	0.00 (.00)	0.00 (.00)	0.00 (.00)
Education level			0.33*** (.05)	0.32*** (.05)	0.34*** (.05)	0.33*** (.05)
Muslim	−0.23** (.08)		−0.41*** (.07)	−0.28*** (.07)	−0.38*** (.08)	−0.26*** (.07)
Christian		−0.24*** (.06)	−0.33*** (.05)	−0.23*** (.04)	−0.35*** (.05)	−0.24*** (.04)
Importance of God			−0.06*** (.01)	−0.06*** (.01)		−0.06*** (.01)
Country-level[b]						
GDP per capita (log)					0.03 (.13)	−0.08 (.13)
Level of democracy					0.10** (.04)	0.09* (.04)
Average Importance of God						−0.14*** (.03)
Proportion Muslim					−0.09 (.07)	0.43* (.20)
Proportion Christian					−0.18 (.16)	0.27 (.18)
Thresholds	$\delta_1 = 1.73$ $\delta_2 = 2.65$ $\delta_3 = 4.31$	$\delta_1 = 1.74$ $\delta_2 = 2.66$ $\delta_3 = 4.32$	$\delta_1 = 1.75$ $\delta_2 = 2.68$ $\delta_3 = 4.35$	$\delta_1 = 1.75$ $\delta_2 = 2.68$ $\delta_3 = 4.35$	$\delta_1 = 1.75$ $\delta_2 = 2.67$ $\delta_3 = 4.34$	$\delta_1 = 1.75$ $\delta_2 = 2.68$ $\delta_3 = 4.35$

Variance Components[c] (τ)					
$u_0 = 0.22$	$u_0 = 0.22$	$u_0 = 0.22$	$u_0 = 0.23$	$u_0 = 0.19$	$u_0 = 0.14$
$u_M = 0.20$	$u_C = 0.21$	$u_F = 0.01$	u_F = fixed to 0	u_F = fixed to 0	u_F = fixed to 0
		$u_A = 0.00$	u_A = fixed to 0	u_A = fixed to 0	u_A = fixed to 0
		$u_E = 0.12$	$u_E = 0.38$	$u_E = 0.14$	$u_E = 0.14$
		$u_M = 0.18$	$u_M = 0.38$	$u_M = 0.19$	$u_M = 0.15$
		$u_C = 0.13$	$u_C = 0.38$	$u_C = 0.13$	$u_C = 0.10$
			u_I = fixed to 0		u_I = fixed to 0

Note: Dependent variable includes five response categories, "strongly agree," "agree," "neither agree or disagree," "disagree," and "strongly disagree." In the HGLM analysis, "strongly agree" is "1" and "strongly disagree" is "5." Entries are restricted maximum likelihood coefficients with robust standard errors for the unit-specific model, calculated on HLM 6.06.

$N = 89,415$ in 72 countries.

[a] All individual-level variables are centered at the group mean; with the exception of the error terms listed in Models 4–6, all individual-level error terms were treated as random coefficients and were statistically significant at $p < .001$. Error terms were fixed to zero in order to aid model convergence.

[b] All country-level variables are centered at the grand mean.

[c] The variance component for a null model including only the random Level-2 intercept is $\tau = 0.22$.

$*p < .05; **p < .01; ***p < .001$.

Table 2.14 Predicted Probabilities of "Agreeing" or "Strongly Agreeing" that "Religious Leaders Should Not Influence How People Vote" (model 4 from table 2.13)

Gender	Muslim	Christian	No Denomination
Male	.69	.72	.78
Female	.69	.71	.77

levels of GDP per capita, democracy, religiosity, and Muslim and Christian populations. According to model 4, the predicted probability of agreeing or strongly agreeing with the statement is 69 percent for the Muslim man, 72 percent for the Christian man, and 78 percent for the nondenominational man. The predicted probabilities for the woman under these conditions are essentially the same.

These individual-level effects remain relatively stable when country-level variables are added in models 5 and 6. GDP per capita and the proportion of the population that is Christian are not statistically significant. Not surprisingly, as model 6 shows, the average level of religiosity in a country is negatively associated with agreement with the statement that religious leaders should not influence how people vote. Higher levels of democracy, measured here by a five-year average in Freedom House scores, are positively associated with support for the separation of religious and political authority. Interestingly, and perhaps counterintuitively, when we control for average level of religiosity, living in a country with an above-average proportion of Muslims in the population is positively associated with agreement with preventing religious leaders from influencing voters. While self-identification as a Muslim means that one is less likely to agree that religious leaders should not influence how people vote, living in a country with a larger Muslim population increases the likelihood of agreement when controlling for all other factors, yet the effect is slight.

What is the impact of the magnitude of the Muslim population on Muslims' likelihood of advocating keeping religious leaders away from voters? A hypothetical Muslim man living in a country in which Muslims make up 70 percent of the population is predicted to favor keeping religious leaders away from voters at a probability of 74 percent. The same hypothetical Muslim man living in a country in which the proportion of Muslims is just 5 percent has a 68 percent predicted probability of holding such an opinion. Thus, the difference caused by living in a country with more Muslims is small.[47]

Attitudes toward the Influence of Religion on Political Leaders

We can obtain another angle on popular orientations toward the nexus between religion and politics by investigating what people expect from their political leaders in terms of religious commitment. The WVS includes two questions that get at the

Table 2.15 Mean Scores for Religious Groups on Attitudes toward the Influence of Religion on Political Leaders

Survey item	Muslims	All Non-Muslims[a]	Christians	No Denomination
Percentage who "agree strongly" or "agree" that "it would be better for this country if more people with strong religious beliefs held public office"	56.6 (N = 20,067)	37.0 (N = 70,387)	43.2 (N = 48,767)	15.0 (N = 14,085)
Percentage who "agree strongly" or "agree" that "politicians who do not believe in God are unfit for public office"	69.1 (N = 20,694)	32.0 (N = 70,925)	35.5 (N = 49,017)	15.9 (N = 14,297)

[a]Includes all individuals who adhere to a religious denomination other than Islam as well as individuals who did not state adherence to a religious tradition.

Table 2.16 HGLM Analysis of Statement, "It Would Be Better if More People with Strong Religious Beliefs Held Public Office"[64T]

Predictors	Model 1	Model 2	Model 3	Model 4	Model 5
Intercept	−2.08*** (.12)	−2.11*** (.13)	−2.15*** (.13)	−2.19*** (.09)	−2.29*** (.08)
Individual-level[a]					
Female			0.18*** (.02)	0.18*** (.02)	0.06** (.02)
Age			0.01*** (.00)	0.01*** (.00)	0.00*** (.00)
Education level			−0.58*** (.06)	−0.58*** (.06)	−0.51*** (.05)
Muslim	0.53*** (.12)		1.01*** (.12)	1.02*** (.12)	0.49*** (.09)
Christian		0.68*** (.09)	0.87*** (.07)	0.89*** (.07)	0.43*** (.04)
Importance of God					0.21*** (.01)
Country-level[b]					
GDP per capita (log)				−0.75** (.24)	−0.59** (.22)
Average age				−0.06* (.02)	−0.01 (.02)
Level of democracy				0.01 (.02)	−0.05 (.07)
Proportion Muslim				0.63 (.44)	−0.85** (.27)
Proportion Christian				0.55 (.41)	−0.62** (.23)
Average Importance of God					0.50*** (.05)

Thresholds				
$\delta_1 = 1.56$	$\delta_1 = 1.57$	$\delta_1 = 1.60$	$\delta_1 = 1.60$	$\delta_1 = 1.64$
$\delta_2 = 2.75$	$\delta_2 = 2.78$	$\delta_2 = 2.84$	$\delta_2 = 2.84$	$\delta_2 = 2.95$
$\delta_3 = 4.42$	$\delta_3 = 4.52$	$\delta_3 = 4.61$	$\delta_3 = 4.61$	$\delta_3 = 4.84$
Variance Components[c] (τ)				
$u_0 = 1.00$	$u_0 = 1.04$	$u_0 = 1.08$	$u_0 = 0.52$	$u_0 = 0.42$
$u_M = 0.69$	$u_C = 0.57$	$u_F = 0.02$	$u_F = 0.02$	$u_F = 0.02$
		$u_A = 0.00$	$u_A = 0.00$	$u_A = 0.00$
		$u_E = 0.24$	$u_E = 0.24$	$u_E = 0.20$
		$u_M = 0.60$	$u_M = 0.59$	$u_M = 0.20$
		$u_C = 0.30$	$u_C = 0.30$	$u_C = 0.08$
				$u_I = 0.01$

Note: Dependent variable includes five response categories, "strongly agree," "agree," "neither agree or disagree," "disagree," and "strongly disagree." In the HGLM analysis, "strongly agree" is "1" and "strongly disagree" is "5." Entries are restricted maximum likelihood coefficients for an ordered logit model using robust standard errors for the unit-specific model, calculated on HLM 6.06.

$N = 88,368$ in 72 countries.

[a]All individual-level variables are centered at the group mean.

[b]All country-level variables are centered at the grand mean.

[c]The variance component for a null model including only the random Level-2 intercept is $\tau = 1.43$.

*$p < .05$; **$p < .01$; ***$p < .001$.

matter nicely. The first asks whether it would be good if "more people with strong religious beliefs held public office."[48] The second asks whether "politicians who do not believe in God are unfit for public office."[49] In the two questions examined in the previous subsection of the chapter above, positive values represented greater secularism. In the two questions under examination here, positive values mean less secularism (to be precise, greater expectation of religiosity among one's political leaders). We take the percentage of people who "agree strongly" or "agree" as the measure of the belief that politicians should be religious.

As the descriptive statistics in table 2.15 show, the percentage of Muslims agreeing with each statement is considerably higher than the percentage of non-Muslims. When we separate out Christians from other non-Muslim groups, the percentage of Muslims agreeing still stands out as particularly high. A majority of Muslims agree or strongly agree that it would be better if more people with religious beliefs held public office, while the analogous percentage of Christians is about 43 percent. Almost twice as many Muslims as Christians hold that politicians who do not believe in God are unfit for public office.

Do these differences persist once we control for socioeconomic factors? We begin by analyzing the results for the question on whether it would be better for people with strong religious beliefs to hold public office. Analyses of this question in hierarchical level models that introduce individual- and country-level controls are presented in table 2.16.

Models 1 and 2 in table 2.16 show that self-identification as a Muslim or a Christian has a statistically significant and positive impact on the belief that it would be better if more people with strong religious beliefs held public office. This

Table 2.17 Predicted Probabilities of "Agreeing" or "Strongly Agreeing" that "It Would Be Better if More People with Strong Religious Beliefs Held Public Office"

	Model 1	Model 2	Model 3	Model 4	Model 5
Muslim man	.48	—	.43	.41	.41
Muslim woman			.47	.46	.43
Christian man	—	.44	.39	.38	.40
Christian woman			.44	.43	.44
Man, No Denomination	—	—	.21	.20	.24
Woman, No Denomination			.24	.24	.25

Note: Predicted probabilities are for individuals of average age and education, living in a country with average levels of income, age, democracy, and proportions of Muslims and Christians.

relationship holds once we include individual-level controls for age, gender, and education level in model 3.

Model 3 also shows that older age and being a female correspond positively with agreement with the statement, while increasing levels of education decrease the likelihood of agreement. When country-level variables are introduced in model 4, it is evident that as national income increases, likelihood of agreement decreases. A country's average age is also statistically significant and negative; as the average age of a country increases, the likelihood of agreement decreases. These are the only two variables that are statistically significant in model 4. A country's level of democracy, the percentage of Muslims in a country, and the percentage of Christians in the country do not have a statistically significant effect on agreement with the statement.

Model 5 introduces the importance-of-God scale as a measure of religiosity. We control for both individual responses to the question about the importance of God and the overall country-level average in responses to the question. Once we control for both individual- and country-level religiosity, our results change considerably. First, both individual religiosity and the average religiosity of a country are statistically significant and positive. As one's own religiosity increases, so does the likelihood that one will agree with the statement. Living in a country with a high level of average religiosity also increases the likelihood of agreeing with the statement, independent of one's own degree of religiosity or religious denomination. Second, the size of the coefficients for the female, Muslim, and Christian variables decrease considerably. Third, while the percentage of Muslims and the percentage of Christians in a country are not statistically significant in model 4, they are both statistically significant and negative in model 5. Thus, once we control for religiosity, living in countries with larger Muslim populations or larger Christian populations actually reduces the likelihood of agreement with the statement that it would be better if more people with religious beliefs held public office.

In order to understand the differences between these models more clearly, we calculated several predicted probabilities for hypothetical individuals of average age and education living in a country with average income, level of democracy, and proportions of Muslims and Christians. These predicted probabilities are listed in table 2.17. The probabilities correspond to the model numbers from table 2.16.

The predicted probabilities for models 1 and 2, which contained only the single variable for self-identification as a Muslim or Christian, are higher than the predicted probabilities for the models that include socioeconomic controls. Thus, once we control for factors other than people's religious adherence, the importance of the latter as a predictor of their opinions declines, albeit only mildly. According to model 4, on average a Muslim has a predicted probability of agreeing with the statement that is .03 higher than the predicted probability for a Christian. This is true for both men and women, although women have a higher predicted probability of agreement.

Muslims and Christians are actually quite close in their assessments of the value of having highly religious people in high office. The big difference is between Muslims and Christians together, on the one hand, and nondenominationalists, on the other. In model 4, the probability that a Muslim man will endorse having more strongly religious people in public office is 41 percent; the probability that a Christian man will hold that view is 38 percent; and the probability that a man who does not have a religious affiliation will hold that opinion is 20 percent. The analogous probabilities for a woman are 46, 43, and 24 percent, respectively.

The differences between Muslims and Christians decrease even further once we control for religiosity. Model 5 considers individuals with an average score on the importance-of-God scale for Muslims and Christians (8.56). With religiosity held at this level, we see that the differences in predicted probabilities for Muslims and Christians decrease. The difference in predicted probabilities between these groups and nondenominationalists decreases as well.

What happens to predicted probabilities when we vary the size of the Christian and Muslim populations in model 5? If we consider a hypothetical Muslim man and a hypothetical Christian man, both of average age, education level, and religiosity, living in the same country with a population that is 90 percent Muslim and 5 percent Christian, the Muslim man has a predicted probability of 35 percent of agreeing or strongly agreeing with the statement, while the Christian man has a predicted probability of 34 percent of agreeing. If the same two individuals were to live in a country that is 90 percent Christian and 5 percent Muslim, the predicted probability of agreement is 39 percent for the Muslim man and 38 percent for the Christian man. In this example, we see that the environment in which an individual lives—whether a country with a predominantly Christian or predominantly Muslim population—has an influence on attitudes that is independent of religious denomination. Muslims and Christians living in a predominantly Christian country are more likely to agree with the statement that it would be better if more people with strong religious beliefs held public office than are Muslims and Christians living in a predominantly Muslim country, yet the difference is not substantial.

Let us now turn to statistical analysis of responses to the question of whether politicians who do not believe in God are unfit for public office. Our previous question assessed whether people would like to see greater religiosity in their political leaders. The question we now examine measures people's forbearance of atheism in political leaders. The questions obviously resemble one another, but they provide distinct angles on popular attitudes toward the influence of religion on political leaders.

In table 2.15, we saw that Muslims were far more likely than Christians to agree with the statement that politicians who do not believe in God are unfit for public office. When we analyze this question as a hierarchical level model that allows us to control for both individual- and country-level socioeconomic factors, we see that

Muslims are more likely to agree with this statement than are Christians (models 3–5). Yet both Muslims and Christians are more likely than people who are neither Muslim nor Christian to regard atheists as unfit for office. As models 1 and 2 in table 2.18 show, self-identification as a Muslim or Christian increases the likelihood of agreeing with the statement, and this likelihood increases further when age, gender, and education level are introduced in model 3. Older individuals are more likely to agree with the statement, and women are more likely to agree than men. Higher levels of education decrease the likelihood of rejecting nonbelievers in public office.

When we introduce country-level variables in models 4 and 5, we see that as national wealth increases, an individual is less likely to agree that those who do not believe in God are unfit for public office. According to model 4, the percentage of Muslims in a country is positively associated with agreement with the statement; as the number of Muslims in a country increases, so does the likelihood of agreeing with the statement. The percentage of Christians in a country is not statistically significant.

In model 5 we introduce the importance-of-God scale as a control for religiosity, both at the individual level and at the country level. When we control for religiosity, the results change considerably. The size of the effect of being a woman, Christian, or Muslim is reduced. The results of country-level variables change as well. The size of the effect of national wealth decreases. Once we control for religiosity, the percentage of Muslims in a society falls out of statistical significance. Meanwhile, the percentage of Christians in a society becomes statistically significant and negative. Thus, once we consider the level of religiosity in a country as well as the percentage of Christians and Muslims, a higher number of Christians in the society decreases the likelihood of agreeing with the statement.

Table 2.19 includes the predicted probabilities for hypothetical Muslims, Christians, and nondenominationalists based on the models presented in table 2.18. The predicted probabilities are for individuals of average age and education, living in a country with average GDP per capita, age, level of democracy, and percentages of Muslims and Christians. Model 5 considers individuals with an average score on the importance-of-God scale for Muslims and Christians (8.56).

The predicted probabilities help us better to understand three important aspects of public opinion on atheists in office. First, the predicted probability of a Muslim or a Christian agreeing with the statement that politicians who do not believe in God are unfit for public office is less than 50 percent in all of the models. Once we control for individual- and country-level socioeconomic factors, both Muslims and Christians of average age living in a country with an average level of economic development are more likely to reject excluding atheists from office than to favor excluding them.

Second, if we compare the predicted probabilities in the different models moving from left to right, we see that the predicted probability of a Muslim agreeing with

Table 2.18 HGLM Analysis of Statement, "Politicians Who Do Not Believe in God Are Unfit for Public Office"[65T]

Predictors	Model 1	Model 2	Model 3	Model 4	Model 5
Intercept	−1.88*** (.16)	−1.90*** (.16)	−1.94*** (.17)	−1.96*** (.11)	−2.03*** (.09)
Individual-level[a]					
Female			0.14*** (.02)	0.14*** (.02)	0.04* (.02)
Age			0.01*** (.00)	0.01*** (.00)	0.01*** (.00)
Education level			−0.58*** (.07)	−0.58*** (.07)	−0.51*** (.07)
Muslim	0.59*** (.13)		1.06*** (.14)	1.06*** (.14)	0.52*** (.10)
Christian		0.50*** (.08)	0.66*** (.06)	0.75*** (.06)	0.31*** (.04)
Importance of God					0.19*** (.01)
Country-level[b]					
GDP per capita (log)				−0.70** (.26)	−0.53** (.21)
Average age				−0.04 (.02)	−0.00 (.02)
Level of democracy				−0.01 (.08)	−0.01 (.06)
Proportion Muslim				1.17** (.40)	−0.25 (.28)
Proportion Christian				0.13 (.38)	−1.20*** (.22)
Average Importance of God					0.44*** (.05)

Thresholds				
$\delta_1 = 1.27$	$\delta_1 = 1.27$	$\delta_1 = 1.30$	$\delta_1 = 1.30$	$\delta_1 = 1.32$
$\delta_2 = 2.25$	$\delta_2 = 2.26$	$\delta_2 = 2.30$	$\delta_2 = 2.30$	$\delta_2 = 2.37$
$\delta_3 = 3.94$	$\delta_3 = 3.99$	$\delta_3 = 4.08$	$\delta_3 = 4.07$	$\delta_3 = 4.24$

Variance Components[c] (τ)				
$u_0 = 1.44$	$u_0 = 1.48$	$u_0 = 1.53$	$u_0 = 0.63$	$u_0 = 0.36$
		$u_F = 0.01$	$u_F = 0.01$	$u_F = 0.01$
		$u_A = 0.00$	$u_A = 0.00$	$u_A = 0.00$
		$u_E = 0.31$	$u_E = 0.31$	$u_E = 0.26$
$u_M = 0.60$		$u_M = 0.74$	$u_M = 0.72$	$u_M = 0.30$
	$u_C = 0.40$	$u_C = 0.19$	$u_C = $ fixed to 0	$u_C = $ fixed to 0
				$u_I = 0.01$

Note: Dependent variable includes five response categories, "strongly agree," "agree," "neither agree or disagree," "disagree," and "strongly disagree." In the HGLM analysis, "strongly agree" is "1" and "strongly disagree" is "5." Entries are restricted maximum likelihood coefficients with robust standard errors for the unit-specific model, calculated on HLM 6.06.

$N = 89{,}477$ in 72 countries.

[a] All individual-level variables are centered at the group mean.

[b] All country-level variables are centered at the grand mean; with the exception of the error terms for the Christian variable in models 4 and 5, all individual-level error terms were treated as random coefficients and were statistically significant at $p < .001$.

[c] The variance component for a null model including only the random Level-2 intercept is $\tau = 1.43$.

$*p < .05; **p < .01; ***p < .001$.

Table 2.19 Predicted Probabilities of "Agreeing" or "Strongly Agreeing" that "Politicians Who Do Not Believe in God Are Unfit for Public Office"

	Model 1	Model 2	Model 3	Model 4	Model 5
Muslim man	.47	—	.45	.43	.43
Muslim woman			.48	.46	.44
Christian man	—	.40	.35	.36	.38
Christian woman			.38	.39	.39
Man, No Denomination	—	—	.22	.21	.31
Woman, No Denomination			.24	.23	.32

Note: Predicted probabilities are for individuals of average age and education, living in a country with average levels of income, age, democracy, and proportions of Muslims and Christians.

the statement that atheists are unfit for office decreases as we add socioeconomic controls. The difference in the predicted probability generated by model 1 and model 4 for the hypothetical Muslim man is .04. This difference is not particularly large, but it does suggest that the overall lower level of economic development in predominantly Muslim countries contributes to the large number of Muslims we see in table 2.15 agreeing with the statement that politicians who do not believe in God are unfit for public office.

Third, the differences between Muslims and Christians in predicted probability of agreement with the statement persist even when we control for socioeconomic characteristics. The differences in predicted probabilities for a Muslim man and a Christian man and for a Muslim woman and a Christian woman in model 4 are .07. The differences between Muslims and Christians and nondenominationalists are even greater. Nondenominationalist men and women are more than 20 percentage points less likely to agree with the statement than are Muslim men and women. The differences in these predicted probabilities decrease, however, when we consider personal religiosity. Model 5 compares predicted probabilities among Muslims, Christians, and nondenominationalists of the same level of religiosity. The differences between men and women decrease, as do the differences between the three denominational groups. Nondenominationalists who are as religious as the average Muslim or Christian are more likely to agree with the statement. In contrast to model 4, the predicted probability for the nondenominationalist man in model 5 is only 12 percentage points lower than that for the Muslim man, and only 7 percentage points lower than the probability for the Christian man. While self-identification as a Muslim does appear to influence attitudes about the religious credentials of political leaders independent of socioeconomic factors, when we consider personal religiosity the differences between Muslims, Christians, and nondenominationalists are smaller.

In sum, once we control for socioeconomic characteristics, Muslims are still more likely than Christians to express support for religiosity among political leaders, although the differences are not as extreme as one would expect when looking at the percentages in table 2.15. Moreover, personal religiosity and the level of religiosity in a country influence attitudes, independent of identification with a religious denomination. In both of our indicators on the influence of religion on political leaders, when we control for religiosity, the differences between Muslims and Christians decrease substantially.

Pondering the Findings

We find a substantial difference in the Muslim–Christian gap between the two questions we tapped to measure attitudes toward the influence of religion on political leaders. Muslims are only slightly more inclined than Christians to hold that it would be good "if more people with strong religious beliefs held public office." Thus, there appears to be little difference between Muslims and Christians on the importance of the *strength* of political leaders' religiosity. But Muslims are substantially more likely than Christians to reject outright atheism; they are notably more likely to hold that people "who do not believe in God are unfit for public office."

In fact, in the Muslim world, religious but non-Muslim leaders are not uncommon. Examples include George Habash, the founder of the Popular Front for the Liberation of Palestine; Léopold Senghor, the father of postcolonial Senegal and the country's president from 1960 to 1980; Amir Sjarifuddin, leader of the Indonesian Left during the struggles against Japanese occupation and Dutch colonialism and a prime minister of the new republic; and Boutros Boutros-Ghali, former foreign minister of Egypt and secretary-general of the United Nations. Each of these figures was a Christian in an overwhelmingly Muslim country. Sjarifuddin was a convert from Islam to Christianity. While none were Muslims, all—including Habash and Sjarifuddin, both of whom embraced Marxism—at least formally maintained identities as adherents to a faith. Their faith did not have to be pronounced; it did not even have to be Muslim. It was enough that they did not renounce belief in God.

These men were not only prominent political leaders; they were also (with the possible exception of Boutros-Ghali, whose association with the detested regime of Hosni Mubarak taints him) popular icons. Indeed, as we plumb the Muslim world for political heroes, pious people do not predominate. Most political giants have, of course, been at least nominal Muslims. But in most cases "nominal" would indeed be an appropriate adjective.

If Jamal al-Suwaidi is correct in his assertion that "Muslims have continued to assume that only a 'religious leader' can provide good government for the Muslim community," most of the Muslim world's political heroes should be clerics or at least devout religionists.[50] If Huntington is right to say that "in Islam God is Caesar," Muslims should expect their temporal leaders to have a demonstrably close relationship with God.[51]

But precious few political idols in Muslim societies fit that description. A Who's Who from the past century would likely begin with Egypt's Gamal Abdel Nasser, Turkey's Mustafa Kemal Atatürk, the Palestinian Territories' Yasser Arafat, Pakistan's Mohammed Ali Jinnah, Zulfikar Ali Bhutto, and Benazir Bhutto, Indonesia's Sukarno and Megawati Sukarnoputri, and Iran's Reza Khan and Mohammad Mosaddeq. Of course, assessing precisely the popularity of such leaders is difficult, since many of them came to power by force and were not elected democratically. Still, it would not be an exaggeration to say that each of these leaders is or was held in high esteem by a substantial segment of opinion among Muslim mass publics, including and especially in each leader's own country. None of these leaders was or is known for personal piety. Sukarno's sexual profligacy is legendary among Indonesians. Pakistanis know that Zulfikar Ali Bhutto had a weakness for distilled spirits. Turks know that Atatürk had a weakness for both women and distilled spirits. Iranians see Mosaddeq as the portrait of a Westernized liberal; the same may be said of Pakistanis' view of Jinnah. Nasser conjured Ramses more readily than Muslim-era heroes and often appeared to place his Arab nationalism above his Muslim faith.

To be sure, some political heroes are known for at least a degree of piety, and some have used politicized Islam to their own advantage. Malaysia's long-time prime minister, Mahathir bin Mohamad, Saudi Arabia's King Faisal bin Abdul Aziz, Bangladesh's founding father and first prime minister, Mujibur Rahman, and Libya's long-time dictator, Muammar al-Gaddafi, are examples. Still, to call any of these men "religious leaders" would be a stretch. They were, like all of the other figures listed above, lionized by their people for the same reason that political leaders are lionized outside the Muslim world: because they were viewed as promoters of national unity and glory, as modernizers, or both. There are exceptions. Iran's Ruhollah Khomeini, who commanded a large following and remains an object of popular veneration, was a cleric as well as a devout Muslim. But most popular political heroes in the Muslim world enjoy their status by virtue of their success (or at least ambitions) as wielders of the sword, crafters of nations, or expanders of the purse, not devotees of the faith. In this respect, they resemble political idols outside the Muslim world.

Thus, we find an interesting mix of evidence. Muslims are less accepting than non-Muslims of out-and-out atheism in their political leaders. On the other hand, they are not substantially more insistent that their political leaders be clerics or even especially observant of their religion. We can offer no definitive account for this particular pattern of opinion. We hope only that our empirical findings and accompanying ruminations provide a starting point for other scholars who are better qualified to explain an interesting and potentially consequential configuration of attitudes.

Summary

This section of the chapter has examined popular attitudes toward religion and politics using several different survey questions. We have investigated attitudes toward the influence of religious leaders on voters as well as attitudes toward the influence of religion on political leaders. We did not find that Muslims are especially prone to embrace clerical influence on voters. Muslims are part of the global consensus in favor of restricting the influence of professional religious leaders on citizens' behavior at the polls. The finding calls into question the widely held notion that Muslims are strongly disposed to regard the fusion of religious and political authority as legitimate.

On the importance of having political leaders who are religious, the evidence is mixed. Muslims are especially likely to consider atheists unfit for high office. But they are not disproportionately inclined to insist that their political leaders hold strong religious beliefs or be especially devout.

DISCUSSION OF THE FINDINGS

On balance, the empirical evidence suggests that Islam does not incline its adherents to extraordinary religiosity or enthusiasm for the fusion of religious and political authority. Muslims rate the importance of God in their lives more highly than non-Muslims as a whole, but the difference is not dramatic, and the gap between Muslims and Christians in particular is diminutive. In terms of actual behavior, which was assessed by examining attendance at religious services, there is no meaningful gap between Muslims as a whole and Christians as a whole, though there is a difference between Muslims and Christians in terms of the gender balance in attendance at services. Furthermore, Muslims appear to share in a global consensus in favor of dividing political and religious power. We do not find evidence that Muslims are particularly well disposed to the idea of religious leaders influencing people's political behavior, although they are unusual in the breadth of their opposition to atheism in public officeholders.

We did find, however, that the average level of religiosity of one's environment does matter. Individuals living in more religious communities, regardless of their individual-level religious identification, are more likely to agree that politicians who do not believe in God are unfit for public office and that it would be better if more people with strong religious beliefs held public office. They are also more likely to disagree with the statement that religious leaders should not influence how people vote. For scholars who seek to understand the impact of religion on a given outcome, these findings suggest the advisability of distinguishing between individual-level religiosity and the religiosity of one's immediate context.

That Muslims are neither extraordinarily religious nor inclined to favor mixing religion and politics may come as a surprise. Observers may overestimate the extent of fusion of religious and political authority in Muslim thought and practice. Writers often note Muhammad's dual role as ruler and Prophet, and contrast it with Jesus's renunciation of political power. Many observers also note the absence of a Muslim version of the Catholic Church; Islam has no centralized organization that continuously did battle with principalities and states down through the centuries. We tend to assume that the absence of the conditions that separated religious and temporal authority in the West necessarily produced nonseparation of religious and temporal authority outside Christendom. The quote from Huntington cited above reflects such an outlook.

But is it not possible that forces besides an otherworldly founder and a centralized religious organization could also do the job of separating religious and political power? The conditions that may have done so in Muslim lands include the imperatives of territorial administration and taxation, the centrality of coercive (as opposed to spiritual) power in binding together the principalities of the regions in which Islam predominated, the ethno-linguistic differentiation of elites including Turkish possession of military power and Arab and Persian preeminence in culture, the primacy of scholars (the *ulama*, also transliterated as *ulema*) rather than politicians as custodians of religious authority, and the generally inconclusive nature of the struggle for domination among social groups that characterizes most of human history in most places.

The distinction between the *amir* (also transliterated as *emir*), which means "commander," "prince," or "general," who controlled military power, and the *ulama*, the scholars who held religious authority, was evident from the earliest centuries of Islam. According to Marshall Hodgson, "However much the ulama cooperated with the amirs, it is clear that the distinction between the tradition of Muslim idealism and that of Muslim political responsibility, already adumbrated at the time of the Prophet, articulated under the Marwanids [a dynasty that existed 990–1085], and confirmed under the Abbasids [a dynasty that stretched from 750 to 1258], was now taken for granted and was reflected in a polarizing of Muslim institutions between those of the Shari'ah and those of the amir."[52] Competition between the holders of religious and political power is a recurring theme in Hodgson's panoramic and profound history of Islam.[53]

As Hodgson suggests, the distinction between temporal and religious power that was firmly established by the Middle Period (the time of medieval Islam, roughly 1000–1500) was "already adumbrated at the time of the Prophet." It has roots in the foundation of Islam itself. With the passing of the Prophet, it is therefore unsurprising that responsibility for what Hodgson calls "Muslim ideals" and "Muslim political authority" would not rest in a single place, and that Muslims would not necessarily expect it to do so.

As Jonathan Berkey shows, the notion that temporal and sacred power must be fused did not predominate even in theory. According to Berkey, "In Sunni Islam, there is no necessary connection between political and religious authority: prophethood as a legislative project came to an end with Muhammad, and what religious authority remained devolved upon the ulama as expressed through consensus." Berkey states that in Shi'i Islam, religious authority is indeed closely joined to political authority, with both vested in the Imam, or supreme leader. Yet, in practice, the Imam's political authority has often been "completely chimerical." During much of the middle and modern periods, "the cultural and social power of which the *shari'a* is a reflection carried with it no guaranteed access to the actual mechanisms of rule, and so politics in the later centuries would consist of constant negotiation between the Turkish military rulers and the native Muslim elites." Berkey notes that a central feature of the Middle Period was "a creative tension—sometimes symbiotic, sometimes competitive—between religious and political authority." He holds that "religion and politics were closely intertwined, but religious and political authority were never identical: in general the religious establishment was not an arm of the state, nor was the political power subservient to the religious scholars."[54]

Some writers hold that religion and politics are not normally fused even in Shi'i thought. Fazlur Rahman affirms that the *ulama* played a crucial role in Iran's 1979 revolution but doubts that the revolution showed "that in Shi'i Islam the state has little or no legitimacy in the absence of the imam—a thesis that has lately gained wide currency among Western scholars." According to Rahman, Iranian religious scholars in principle accepted the legitimacy of the state separate from the Imam. When they turned against their nonclerical rulers over the past century-and-a-half, it was because they saw those rulers as "collaborating with a foreign power at the expense of their country." Rahman contrasts Iran with Egypt and India, where "the rulers were perceived as having been overpowered by the foreign powers rather than as collaborating."[55]

What emerged over the centuries of Islam's appearance, through the high culture of the Middle Period and into modern times, has been a competition for sway over the masses between the scholars who hold religious authority and the rulers who control administrative and coercive power. This dynamic is not dissimilar to what one finds in Christendom. The absence in Islam of a universal Church and a formal priesthood does not make the distinction between religious and temporal authorities, and the struggle between those authorities for allegiance, any less real. In Muslim lands, the great temporal powers often have sought the support of the *ulama* for moral and ideological legitimation, much the way that the temporal powers of Christendom have sought the backing of the Church (or whatever churches command widespread allegiance in the society in question). Similarly, the *ulama*, much like religious leaders in Christendom, have sought favor and accommodation with the holders of administrative and coercive power in order to gain security and financial support. But the *ulama* have no more been the unchallenged custodians of political authority in Muslim lands than bishops have been in Christendom. Nor have the holders of political authority typically wielded more religious authority in the Muslim world than they have Christian dominions.

In most times and places over the centuries, ordinary Muslims, like ordinary Christians, have not looked mainly to their rulers for religious inspiration and guidance. Nor have they viewed their rulers as spiritual role models or expected them to act as such. In Muslim realms, as Hodgson notes, the governed have expected their rulers to guard the peace and furnish just administration that does not trample on the weak.[56] In this respect, there is nothing exceptional about Muslims. This reality helps explain how the likes of Nasser, Sukarno, Arafat, Jinnah, and Mahathir could become political heroes of the first rank in the Muslim world, even as puritanical religious leaders such as Sayyid Qutb of the Muslim Brotherhood in Egypt and Maulana Maududi of the *Jama'at Islami* in Pakistan bitterly denounced their lack of personal piety. Their people did not expect them to embody Muslim piety any more than Americans expected Franklin Roosevelt, John Kennedy, or Ronald Reagan to personify Christian piety—which is to say, people could hope for such a thing, but few really expected it.

There have been exceptions. As Berkey notes, in Shi'i Islam the Imam has often been regarded as a rightful keeper of political as well as religious authority, and he is expected to uphold high standards of personal devotion. This dynamic is evident in Iraq since the demise of Saddam Hussein, where some Shia look for political guidance to Grand Ayatollah Ali Husaini al-Sistani and to Muqtada al-Sadr, a son of another Grand Ayatollah, Mohammad Mohammad Sadeq al-Sadr. So too does the Grand Ayatollah and leader of the Iranian revolution of 1979, Ruhollah Khomeini, enjoy political prestige, in Iran and among the Shia in other countries. Bernard Haykel, writing of the Zaydi sect of Shi'i Islam in Yemen, notes, "Unlike Sunnis, Zaydis have continuously insisted upon having a just ruler who must fulfill rigorous qualifications and duties."[57]

Still, even in Iran, the one major Shia-majority country whose rulers in recent times have also been Shia, the people have not always had the benefit of devout rulers, and the absence of clerical status and overt piety in leaders such as Reza Khan and Mosaddeq has not prevented them from enjoying popular veneration. Nor in present-day Iran has the clerical authority of the current Supreme Leader, Ali Hoseyni Khamenei, and the former president, Akbar Hashemi Rafsanjani, or the ostentatious religiosity of the current president, Mahmoud Ahmadinejad, shielded these figures from becoming objects of mass popular disaffection.

Even in Shi'i communities, how many people really regard God as Caesar? Huntington's quip is droll, but is it true? Even among the many Muslims who believe that God should rule their own personal lives, how many identify their political leaders as God's delegates? How many Iranians really think that God rules through

President Ahmadinejad—or even Ayatollah Khamenei? Has the experience of the centuries really failed to teach most Iranians—or for that matter most people everywhere—that God is indeed God but normally does not choose to play Caesar, and that politicians fall short of the righteousness required to claim status as God's regent on Earth? How many people, Muslims or non-Muslims, really believe in theocracy? Even among leading Shi'i clerics, voices that dispute the fusion of religious and political authority are not difficult to find. Iraq's al-Sistani, who as of this writing is regarded by Shia worldwide as their highest religious authority, has shunned the Khomeini model and remained firmly outside and above the political fray in post-Saddam Iraq. Hussein-Ali Montazeri, the Grand Ayatollah who until his death in 2009 was widely regarded as the leading religious scholar in Iran, held that the amalgamation of political and sacred authority threatened to corrupt both religion and the state. Although originally picked as Khomeini's successor, Montazeri fell out with Khomeini shortly before the latter leader's death in 1989 and thereafter was politically marginalized.

Iran's clerical regime is only one of several political orders in the Muslim world that portray themselves as the embodiment of religious values. As Ibrahim Karawan has argued, there are three distinct types of regimes that pretend to represent "Islam in power." In addition to the "populist clerical regime" of Iran, Karawan names the "conservative dynastic regime" of Saudi Arabia and the "authoritarian military regimes" of Pakistan in the 1980s and Sudan.[58] Yet, writing at the beginning of the 1990s, Karawan noted that the authoritarian military regimes had already "lost, rather quickly, most of the popular support generated by the promise of Islamization." Karawan said that the verdict was still out on the ability of Iran's clerical regime and Saudi Arabia's conservative dynastic regime to "provide alternative models of governance worthy of emulation by other Muslim communities."[59] Almost two decades after Karawan penned his article, we can safely say that there is precious little commotion among the world's Muslim masses to adopt the Saudi dynastic model. Nor has the Iranian clerical paradigm even begun to live up to its promise of honest government by men who fear God. Both the Saudi and the Iranian regimes suffer from an acute shortage of prestige even among those they rule.[60]

To be sure, strains that idealize the unification of spiritual and temporal authority are found in some Muslim thought and have been present through the centuries. They are embedded in what is sometimes called the "traditional reformist movement" of modern Sunni thinkers such as Muhammad 'Abduh and M. Rashd Rida as well as in Shi'i thought.[61] At the very least, however, what Hodgson calls the "tension between the social ideals of Islam and political actualities" has tended, even in Shi'i lands, to play out in a manner that favors political actualities over social ideals.[62] Precisely the same may be said, of course, of Christendom and the realms of the other great world religions.

The immense complexity of the history of one-and-a-half millennia of relations between political and religious authority cannot be adequately explored here. But it is noteworthy that the empirical findings presented in this chapter, which suggest the presence of a legitimate separation between religious and political authority in the minds of contemporary Muslims, are largely consistent with long experience as described by leading historians of Islam.

3 Social Capital and Tolerance

Do Muslim and non-Muslim communities differ in their stocks of social capital? Do Muslims socialize with others more (or less) frequently than non-Muslims do? Are they more (or less) likely to participate in organizational life? The first section of this chapter examines these matters. It focuses specifically on how frequently people socialize with their fellows from various walks of life (which we will refer to as sociability) and people's rate of membership in formal organizations.

The second part of the chapter investigates socially relevant attitudes and opinions. It concentrates especially on tolerance. First, it examines tolerance of controversial behaviors. Are the opinions of Muslims distinctively conservative (or liberal) on the acceptability of controversial acts? Investigation then turns to tolerance of dishonest behaviors. Are Muslims particularly stern (or clement) in their opinion on the justifiability of dishonest deeds?

SOCIAL CAPITAL

Perhaps the best-known definition of social capital is what Robert Putnam offers in his celebrated analysis of associational life in the United States. Putnam defines social capital as "connections among individuals—social networks and the norms of reciprocity and trustworthiness that arise from them."[1] The notion that connections between individuals and social networks confer important benefits for society long predates Putnam. Social theorists such as Karl Marx and Émile Durkheim emphasized the importance of group interactions and group-led initiatives.[2]

Why examine social capital? At its core, social capital is about nonmonetary forms of interaction that generate resources that can be used for exercising power and influence. As a resource, social capital is often assigned a positive valence. Putnam, following Alexis de Tocqueville and others, holds that social capital shapes the vibrancy of society, the prospects for robust democracy, and even the health of individuals. Putnam and others who write in the tradition of Tocqueville generally regard higher levels of interpersonal interaction and membership in organizations as propitious.[3]

Yet, like any generator of resources, social capital may be abused as well as used. There may be reasons to hypothesize that high levels of social capital can foster outcomes that our general social norms would view as negative, such as gang violence, organized crime, and terrorism. Indeed, some scholars are skeptical about the implications of dense associational life for civil peace, self-rule, and other goods.[4] Whichever view one takes of the possible effects of associational life, there is broad agreement that it is a matter of interest and importance.

Why examine social capital specifically in a book the compares adherents of one particular faith with people who are not adherents of that faith? Despite the paucity of writings on the matter, there are good logical reasons to expect religious tradition to affect what Putnam refers to as the heart of social capital—namely, "connections among individuals." The word "religion" comes from the Latin *religare*, which is variously translated as "to bind," "to tie," "to place an obligation on," and "to connect with." Religion is the most social of institutions. All of the world's major religions involve collective devotional practice. Defining social obligation and the individual's place in the community is central to the doctrines of all the major religions. Even aspects of religious experience that are experienced inwardly, by the individual, have social roots and social implications.[5] If religion is inextricably bound up with social interaction and identity, it is reasonable to expect that different religions may be associated with distinctive patterns of social interaction.

There is a vast literature on social capital. A small subset of writings focuses on Muslim countries.[6] But the literature lacks works that systematically test for whether social capital is particularly abundant (or scarce) among Muslims. So too does the literature lack ideas on why social capital might be more (or less) plentiful in Muslim societies than in others. One might hypothesize that social connections are stronger or weaker in predominantly Muslim countries for a variety of possible reasons. The literature lacks compelling arguments either way. In the absence of debates on the issue, here we will move straight to empirical tests.

Again we will draw upon data from the World Values Survey (WVS), which includes items that assess the frequency with which people enjoy the company of others from various walks of life. These data provide a window on the connections that constitute social capital.

Sociability

Four items in the WVS are particularly useful for assessing sociability. One asks how often people spend time with friends.[7] The second asks how often they spend time with colleagues from work.[8] The third asks how often they spend time with people from their religious organization.[9] The fourth asks how often they spend time with people from sports, voluntary, or service groups.[10] For each question respondents may answer "weekly," "once or twice a month," "only a few times a year," or "not at all." This battery of questions was not asked in the fifth wave (2005–2008) of the WVS, so the following analysis relies on data from the fourth wave (1999–2004) of the survey, which includes responses from 66,214 individuals in 63 countries.[11]

We rescaled each item to fall between 0 and 1, with "0" equal to "not at all" and "1" equal to "weekly." Out of the four items, we constructed a "sociability index," which averages individual scores across the four responses. The end result is a variable that ranges from 0 to 1 in which "0" corresponds to an individual who spends time "not at all" with anyone from any of the four realms of social life (1,202 people in our sample) and "1" corresponds to an individual who spends time weekly with people from all four realms (2,001 people in our sample). Between these two extremes we have a distribution that roughly resembles a bell curve, with a mean of .49.

Table 3.1 shows the average scores on the sociability index for Muslims, non-Muslims, Christians, and nondenominationalists. Overall, there is no meaningful difference between Muslims and non-Muslims with regard to sociability.

As in the previous chapter, here too we must control for the possible effects of socioeconomic development on what we seek to explain. Since material standard of living may influence such a wide range of political, cultural, and psychological outcomes, including the matters we are investigating in this chapter, we must control for it here as well. One might expect social connections to be richer in societies at a higher level of socioeconomic development, as more developed societies may afford people a richer menu of opportunities for interacting with one another. For example, we can hardly expect individuals to spend time with colleagues if they are not employed. On the other hand, one could hypothesize that wealth has an atomizing effect. More prosperous people might find living without the benefit of one another's help and company more feasible, reducing their likely participation in religious or recreational organizations. In any event, we need to control for socioeconomic development in our assessment of the possible difference between Muslims and non-Muslims on sociability. In order to do so, we include country-level

Table 3.1 Mean Scores for Religious Groups on Sociability Index (scored 0–1)

	Muslims	All Non-Muslims[a]	Christians	No Denomination
Sociability Index (average of frequency of time spent with friends, colleagues, people from church, mosque, or synagogue, and people from sports or recreation group)	0.53 (N = 14,293)	0.48 (N = 54,565)	0.50 (N = 37,213)	0.41 (N = 13,098)

[a]Includes all individuals who adhere to a religious denomination other than Islam as well as individuals who did not state adherence to a religious tradition.

controls for GDP per capita and average age at the national level. We also include Freedom House scores to control for any association between sociability and political openness. At the individual level, we control for gender, age, education, and religious denomination.

Table 3.2 presents the results of an HLM analysis that treats the sociability index as the dependent variable. The coefficients in the table tell us the change in the sociability index when the independent variables increase by one unit.[12] When analyzed alone (model 1), the Muslim variable is not statistically significant. In other words, Muslims are no more likely to be more or less sociable than non-Muslims. Once we control for socioeconomic characteristics in model 3, however, the Muslim coefficient becomes statistically significant and positive. Regarding other variables in model 3, gender is statistically significant and negative, while education is statistically significant and positive. Being a female corresponds to a lower sociability score while higher levels of education correspond to a higher score. Although age is statistically significant and negative, the effect on sociability is small. All else being equal, an individual twenty years above the average age in the sample is predicted to have a reduction of .05 in his or her sociability index score.

The country-level variables introduced in model 4 appear to have little influence on how sociable a person is. GDP per capita, average age, Freedom House scores, and the proportion of a country's population that is Muslim are not statistically significant. The proportion of the country's Christian population is statistically significant and positive. According to model 4, the predicted sociability index score for a Muslim man of average age and education, while holding all country-level variables at their means, is .44, while the predicted score for a nondenominationalist man with the same characteristics is .39 and for a Christian man is .46.

These values are largely similar in model 5, in which we also control for religiosity at the individual and country levels. While a country's average level of religiosity is not statistically significant, once we control for it, the proportion Christian variable drops out of statistical significance. At the individual level, however, religiosity is statistically significant and positive, although the effect is slight. Once we control for individual-level religiosity, the Muslim variable is no longer statistically significant. The positive effect of the religiosity control is not surprising, since one of the items in our index is time spent with individuals from a religious organization. It is reasonable to expect that individuals who are not particularly religious will have a score closer to zero for this specific item.[13]

In sum, while it appears that Muslims are slightly more sociable than non-Muslims, the effect is not substantial. Muslims' sociability level is virtually indistinguishable from that of Christians. Furthermore, the religious composition of one's society—whether it be more Muslim or more Christian—does not appear to influence heavily the frequency with which one spends time with others.

Table 3.2 HLM Analysis of Sociability Index [0 = no social interactions, 1 = numerous weekly social interactions]

Predictors	Model 1	Model 2	Model 3	Model 4	Model 5
Intercept	0.48***(.01)	0.48***(.01)	0.48***(.01)	0.48***(.01)	0.48***(.01)
Individual-level[a]					
Female			-0.08***(.01)	-0.08***(.01)	-0.08***(.01)
Age			-0.00***(.00)	-0.00***(.00)	-0.00***(.00)
Education level			0.09***(.01)	0.09***(.01)	0.09***(.01)
Muslim	0.00 (.01)		0.04***(.01)	0.05***(.01)	0.02 (.01)
Christian		0.04***(.01)	0.07***(.01)	0.07***(.01)	0.04***(.01)
Importance of God					0.01***(.00)
Country-level[b]					
GDP per capita (log)				-0.01 (.03)	-0.01 (.04)
Average age				-0.00 (.00)	-0.00 (.00)
Level of democracy				-0.01 (.01)	-0.01 (.01)
Proportion Muslim				0.06 (.07)	0.05 (.06)
Proportion Christian				0.11* (.05)	0.11 (.06)
Average Importance of God					0.00 (.01)

Variance Components[c]

σ^2	0.05	0.05	0.04	0.04	0.04
τ	$u_0 = 0.01$	$u_0 = 0.01$	$u_0 = 0.01$	$u_0 = 0.01$	$u_0 = 0.01$
	$u_M = 0.00$	$u_C = 0.00$	$u_F = 0.01$	$u_F = 0.01$	$u_F = 0.01$
			$u_A = 0.00$	$u_A = 0.00$	$u_A = 0.00$
			$u_E = 0.00$	$u_E = 0.00$	$u_E = 0.00$

Note: For details about the equations used in these and other HLM models throughout the chapter, see appendix 3.B. The base category for the analysis in all HLM/HGLM models is made up of respondents who self-identified with a religion other than Christianity or Islam or did not identify with any religious tradition. Entries are restricted maximum likelihood coefficients with robust standard errors, calculated on HLM 6.06.

$N = 66,214$ individuals in 63 countries.

[a] All individual-level variables are centered at the group mean; all individual-level error terms were treated as random coefficients and were statistically significant at $p < .001$.

[b] All country-level variables are centered at the grand mean.

[c] The variance components for a null model including only the random Level-2 intercept are: $\sigma^2 = 0.05$; $\tau = 0.01$.

$*p < .05$; $**p < .01$; $***p < .001$.

The WVS includes information on organizational memberships. The wording of this item, however, has changed over different waves of the survey. The fifth wave provides us with data from the largest cross section of geographic locations and faith traditions. The question is worded as follows, "I am going to read off a list of voluntary organizations. For each one, could you tell me whether you are an active member, an inactive member or not a member of that type of organization?"[14] This prompt is followed by a list of various organizations. This question provides us with data from forty-nine countries, including eight predominantly Muslim countries—Turkey, Indonesia, Egypt, Morocco, Iran, Jordan, Malaysia, and Mali.[15] Descriptive results on membership frequency from this question are provided in table 3.3.[16]

As we can see, across the board Muslims participate in organizations at a lower rate than non-Muslims (with the exception of the curiously higher percentage for "active" memberships in environmental organizations). In the case of the first organizational group, "church and religious organization," part of the difference may be related to the limits of translation. In both Morocco and Mali, this item was inauspiciously translated word-for-word into the French as "*église ou organisation religieuse*." Offering such a question in largely Muslim Mali and almost uniformly Muslim Morocco would be akin to asking residents of Kansas whether they belong to a "mosque or religious organization." Potential problems are evident in the translation of the question in Muslim Southeast Asia as well. In Malaysia, the question was worded in Malay as "church or religious body (*geraja atau pertubuhan keagamaan*)," and in Indonesia it was translated into Indonesian as "religious organization (*organisasi keagaaman*)."[17] In these translations, Christians would very likely recognize that attending Sunday services constitutes membership in a religious organization, but it is possible that many Muslims would not necessarily see their regular attendance at prayers in the neighborhood mosque as a form of membership. Some Muslim respondents may have assumed that the question was designed for Christians. In Indonesia, the word "church" fortunately was not used in question, but it is likely that the question evoked, at least among Muslims, the idea of membership in one of the country's many Islamic charitable and community organizations, but not necessarily regular attendance at local mosques. Despite these glitches, however, the data may lend insights into organizational membership.

Tables 3.4–3.6 display results from HGLM logistic regression analyses of membership in organizations. We estimated two types of models, one looking at the predictors of "active" membership in an organization, and the other looking at a variable that sums together "active" and "inactive" members in order to observe predictors for membership in an organization more generally. The substantive differences between the two types of models are modest. In the interest of space we present the

Table 3.3 Membership in Formal Organizations (percentages)

Organizational type	Muslims		All Non-Muslims[a]		Christians		No Denomination	
	Active members	Total members[b]	Active members	Total members	Active members	Total members	Active members	Total members
Church or religious organization	16.4% (15,630)[c]	29.9% (15,630)	22.6% (55,065)	44.8% (54,065)	29.4% (34,982)	56.0% (34,982)	2.8% (11,252)	10.5% (11,252)
Humanitarian or charitable organization	7.4% (15,337)	15.3% (15,337)	7.9% (53,723)	18.5% (53,723)	8.1% (34,687)	17.9% (34,687)	6.2% (11,250)	14.4% (11,250)
Sport or recreational organization	9.5% (15,463)	19.3% (15,463)	15.4% (53,965)	28.7% (53,965)	15.2% (34,866)	28.0% (34,866)	17.1% (11,287)	27.7% (11,287)
Art, music, or educational organization	6.9% (15,432)	14.8% (15,432)	10.5% (53,833)	21.3% (53,833)	10.6% (34,765)	20.7% (34,765)	9.6% (11,256)	18.0% (11,256)
Environmental organization	6.1% (15,377)	12.9% (15,377)	4.1% (53,721)	13.3% (53,721)	3.5% (34,679)	11.9% (34,679)	3.9% (11,250)	10.9% (11,250)
Labor union	3.6% (15,331)	10.1% (15,331)	5.9% (53,687)	18.2% (53,687)	5.6% (34,673)	17.3% (34,673)	5.6% (11,231)	16.1% (11,231)
Political party	4.6% (15,392)	13.1% (15,392)	5.8% (53,715)	17.2% (53,715)	5.4% (34,669)	16.7% (34,669)	4.6% (11,248)	11.9% (11,248)
Professional association	5.7% (15,326)	13.5% (15,326)	6.8% (53,580)	16.3% (53,580)	6.6% (34,588)	15.1% (34,588)	6.0% (11,217)	13.3% (11,217)

[a] Includes all individuals who adhere to a religious denomination other than Islam as well as individuals who did not state adherence to a religious tradition.

[b] "Total members" is comprised of the sum of "active" and "inactive" members.

[c] The figures in parentheses are base N for the adjacent percentages.

full results of the total membership models, noting relevant differences between them and the "active" membership models in the notes.

As in the previous model for sociability, we introduce several individual- and country-level socioeconomic controls. The individual-level controls are the same as used in analyses in the previous section on personal sociability. As in the previous analyses, we also include country-level controls for socioeconomic development and level of democracy. One might expect to find broad membership in the full range of organizations in advanced industrialized countries, but sparser membership in some types of organizations, such as professional associations, in poorer countries. Political regime might have an effect as well. More closed regimes might impose heavier restrictions on opportunities for membership in some types of organizations. Yet under some authoritarian regimes, particularly communist-party hegemonies, participation in certain types of organizations is compulsory, and we might expect traces of a legacy of this condition in postcommunist countries.

In order further to minimize the bias that could emerge from the fact that organizational density is not uniform across all countries for reasons that are not necessarily connected to religion, we also add a control for average memberships per country. In order to create this variable we first summed the number of active and inactive memberships for each individual in the data set. We then generated country-level averages based on the active and inactive memberships for respondents in the sample. The end result is a variable that ranges from 0.15 in Jordan to 5.58 in India, with a mean of 1.69. This variable serves a dual role in the model. First, it provides something close to a proxy for organizational density. We cannot readily interpret the point estimate as the effect of organizational density on membership. But inclusion of the average membership variable may reduce bias and provide a more accurate estimate for what interests us, which is how Muslims and non-Muslims differ in terms of membership in organizations. The average memberships variable also helps control for the possible effects of the environment on the individual. In chapter 2, we controlled for national averages in weekly attendance at religious services when we investigated individuals' levels of religiosity. Analogously, in the analyses presented below, we control in some models for national averages on group memberships, under the expectation that living in society in which rates of organizational membership are higher might increase an individual's propensity to join an organization.

Table 3.4 provides HGLM analyses for membership in religious organizations and charitable organizations. When examining participation in religious organizations, we see that Muslim self-identification is not statistically significant when it is the only variable in the model, but becomes significant and positive once we control for other individual- and country-level variables. Being a female, age, education, and self-identification as a Christian are also statistically significant and positive. Model 2 includes the full range of country-level variables. Although GDP per capita is not statistically significant, average age is statistically significant and negative—the older the population in a country, the less likely an individual is to belong to a church or religious organization. Freedom House scores are not statistically significant. Average membership levels, as we anticipated, are statistically significant and positive. The higher the average membership rate in a country as a whole, the more likely an individual living there will belong to a church or religious organization. According to model 2, the proportion of a country that is Christian is statistically significant and positive. Given the translation difficulties raised above, it is not surprising that living in a country with a larger Christian population increases the likelihood that an individual will also belong to a church or religious organization.

How big is the effect of being Muslim on membership in a religious organization? Since logistic regression coefficients do not provide a directly interpretable measure of the size of the independent variables' effects on the outcome of interest, it is useful to calculate predicted probabilities for some hypothetical individuals. According to model 2, a Muslim man of average age and education living in a country with average values on all of the country-level variables has a 39 percent chance of belonging to a religious organization. A Christian man with the same characteristics has a 38 percent chance of belonging. The difference between Muslims and Christians is negligible.

Model 3 excludes Freedom House scores and average membership rates at the country level. Once these variables are dropped from the model, the Christian proportion variable ceases to be statistically significant. The Muslim proportion variable becomes statistically significant and negative. Thus, once we drop the variables that help control for possible bias due to varying organizational density, living in a country with a larger Muslim population reduces the likelihood that an individual will belong to a church or religious organization.

A different dynamic is evident in the models that analyze membership in humanitarian or charitable organizations. Self-identification as a Muslim is not statistically significant in any model specifications. The proportion of the population that is Muslim is also not statistically significant. Neither being Muslim nor the size of the Muslim population in one's country is associated with distinct patterns in membership in charitable or humanitarian organizations. The dynamics of the other variables, however, are broadly similar to what we observed for membership in religious organizations, except that average age is not statistically significant.

Table 3.5 provides the results of the HGLM analysis of membership in sport or recreational organizations; art, music, or educational organizations; and environmental organizations. Although self-identification as a Muslim is statistically significant and negative when it is the only predictor in the model for membership in a sport or recreational organization (model 1), this effect washes away once we introduce other individual- and country-level controls in models 2 and 3. In fact, model

Table 3.4 HGLM Analysis of Membership in Religious and Humanitarian Organizations [1 = member, 0 = non-member]

Predictors	Church or religious organization[37T]			Humanitarian or charitable organization		
	Model 1	*Model 2*	*Model 3*	*Model 1*	*Model 2*	*Model 3*
Intercept	-0.59** (.23)	-0.68*** (.11)	-0.65*** (.19)	-1.80*** (.15)	-1.89*** (.09)	-1.86*** (.15)
Individual-level[a]						
Female		0.17*** (.05)	0.17*** (.05)		0.12** (.04)	0.11* (.04)
Age		0.01*** (.00)	0.01*** (.00)		0.01*** (.00)	0.01*** (.00)
Education level		0.33*** (.10)	0.33** (.10)		1.27*** (.10)	1.27*** (.10)
Muslim	0.05 (.18)	1.22** (.21)	1.24*** (.21)	-0.08 (.15)	0.04 (.15)	0.15 (.15)
Christian		1.81*** (.15)	1.83*** (.15)		0.18*** (.04)	0.22*** (.04)
Country-level[b]						
GDP per capita (log)		0.20 (.39)	-0.25 (.56)		0.61* (.27)	-0.35 (.39)
Average age		-0.11*** (.02)	-0.19*** (.05)		0.00 (.02)	0.00 (.04)
Level of democracy		0.04 (.12)			-0.08 (.09)	
Average memberships		1.05*** (.16)			0.78*** (.12)	
Proportion Muslim		-0.09 (.49)	-2.12* (.88)		-0.22 (.36)	-1.16 (.67)
Proportion Christian		1.67*** (.44)	0.95 (.66)		-0.27 (.38)	-1.20* (.56)

Variance Components^c (τ)	N = 67,855			N = 68,425		
u_0	2.56	0.70	1.97	1.04	0.41	1.17
u_F		0.08	0.08		0.06	0.07
u_A		0.00	0.00		0.00	0.00
u_E		0.35	0.35		0.37	0.37
u_M	0.89	1.46	1.41	0.47	0.54	0.60
u_C		0.93	0.93		0.03	0.04

Note: Entries are restricted maximum likelihood coefficients with robust standard errors for the unit-specific model, calculated on HLM 6.06.

$N = 49$ countries.

[a] All individual-level variables are centered at the group mean; all individual-level error terms were treated as random coefficients and were statistically significant at $p < .001$.

[b] All country-level variables are centered at the grand mean.

[c] The variance components for null models including only the random Level-2 intercept are $\tau = 2.53$ for church or religious organization and $\tau = 1.04$ for charitable or humanitarian organization.

$*p < .05; **p < .01; ***p < .001$.

Table 3.5 HGLM Analysis of Membership in Recreational, Cultural, and Environmental Organizations (1 = member, 0 = non-member)

Predictors	Sport or recreational organization			Art, music, or educational organization[38T,]			Environmental organization[38T,]		
	Model 1	Model 2	Model 3	Model 1	Model 2	Model 3	Model 1	Model 2	Model 3
Intercept	-1.18*** (.14)	-1.34*** (.10)	-1.32*** (.16)	-1.64*** (.14)	-1.77*** (.08)	-1.75*** (.14)	-2.31*** (.16)	-2.38*** (.09)	-2.36*** (.16)
Individual-level[a]									
Female		-0.56*** (.04)	-0.56*** (.05)		0.04 (.04)	0.04 (.04)		-0.12* (.04)	-0.16*** (.04)
Age		-0.02*** (.00)	-0.02*** (.00)		-0.01*** (.00)	-0.01*** (.00)		0.00 (.00)	0.00 (.00)
Education level		1.27*** (.10)	1.28*** (.10)		1.62*** (.10)	1.62*** (.10)		0.95*** (.11)	0.94*** (.11)
Muslim	-0.22* (.11)	-0.07 (.09)	-0.11 (.09)	-0.20 (.14)	-0.01 (.13)	0.02 (.13)	-0.04 (.15)	-0.02 (.15)	-0.05 (.15)
Christian		0.23*** (.04)	0.20*** (.04)		0.19*** (.05)	0.18*** (.05)		-0.02 (.06)	-0.04 (.06)
Country-level[b]									
GDP per capita (log)		0.67 (.36)	0.51 (.34)		0.52 (.28)	0.29 (.41)		0.01 (.29)	-0.27 (.40)
Average age		-0.05* (.02)	-0.09* (.03)		-0.05** (.02)	-0.11* (.04)		-0.02 (.02)	-0.09* (.04)
Level of democracy		0.07 (.09)			0.08 (.09)			0.01 (.10)	
Average memberships		0.60*** (.13)			0.73*** (.12)			0.78*** (.13)	
Proportion Muslim		-0.57 (.30)	-0.53 (.54)		-0.68 (.35)	-1.76* (.73)		-0.67 (.43)	-1.44* (.71)

	-0.24 (.29)	0.20 (.41)	-0.27 (.26)	0.49 (.53)	-0.54 (.37)	-0.75 (.51)
Proportion Christian						
	$N = 68{,}772$		$N = 68{,}613$		$N = 68{,}461$	
Variance	$u_0 = 0.98$	$u_0 = 1.03$		$u_0 = 1.27$		
	$u_M = 0.21$	$u_M = 0.37$		$u_M = 0.45$		
Components[c] (τ)	$u_0 = 0.47$	$u_0 = 1.24$	$u_0 = 0.35$	$u_0 = 1.02$	$u_0 = 0.43$	$u_0 = 1.25$
	$u_F = 0.08$	$u_F = 0.08$	$u_F = 0.05$	$u_F = 0.05$	$u_F = 0.04$	$u_F = 0.04$
	$u_A = 0.00$	$u_A = 0.00$	$u_A = 0.00$	$u_A = 0.00$	$u_A = 0.00$	$u_A = 0.00$
	$u_E = 0.44$	$u_E = 0.44$	$u_E = 0.34$	$u_E = 0.33$	$u_E = 0.39$	$u_E = 0.40$
	$u_M = 0.14$	$u_M = 0.15$	$u_M = 0.28$	$u_M = 0.28$	$u_M = 0.49$	$u_M = 0.48$
	$u_C = 0.03$	$u_C = 0.03$	$u_C = 0.04$	$u_C = 0.05$	$u_C = 0.10$	$u_C = 0.10$

Note: Entries are restricted maximum likelihood coefficients with robust standard errors for the unit-specific model, calculated on HLM 6.06.
$N = 49$ countries.

[a] All individual-level variables are centered at the group mean; all individual-level error terms were treated as random coefficients and were statistically significant at $p < .001$.

[b] All country-level variables are centered at the grand mean.

[c] The variance component for null models including only the random Level-2 intercept are $\tau = 0.98$ for sport or recreational organization, $\tau = 1.03$ for art, music, and educational organization, and $\tau = 1.27$ for environmental organization.

$*p < .05; **p < .01; ***p < .001$.

1 for sport and recreation membership is the only model in table 3.5 in which the variable for being a Muslim is statistically significant. It appears to have no association at all with membership in art, music, or educational organizations or with membership in environmental organizations.

The other individual-level variables that predict membership show some similarities across the models. Education is statistically significant and positive across all three dependent variables. Being a female has a statistically significant and negative effect on membership in sport and recreation organizations and environmental organizations but is not significant for membership in cultural organizations. Age is statistically significant and negative for sport and recreation and cultural organizations but is not significant for environmental organizations. Self-identification as a Christian is statistically significant and positive for sport and recreation and cultural organizations but has no effect on membership in environmental organizations.

How is the size of a country's Muslim population associated with membership? This variable is not statistically significant for membership in sport or recreational organizations. For membership in cultural and environmental organizations, however, we see a trend similar to that observed in the models for membership in church and religious organizations presented in table 3.4: When a countries' average membership numbers are included (in model 2), the proportion of the population that is Muslim is not statistically significant. When average membership is dropped (in model 3), the Muslim proportion variable becomes statistically significant and negative. In other words, there is a negative relationship between the size of the Muslim population and membership in cultural and environmental organizations.

The remaining country-level variables behave similarly across the models. Average membership is always statistically significant and positive, and average age is statistically significant and negative in all of the models in which we exclude average membership. GDP per capita and Freedom House scores are not statistically significant.

The HGLM analyses for membership in the last three organizational types—labor unions, political parties, and professional associations—are listed in table 3.6. The dynamics of these models are very similar to those in the previous tables. Although being a Muslim initially shows a statistically significant and negative relationship to membership in labor unions and professional associations, this correlation washes out once we control for other individual- and country-level variables. The remaining individual-level variables share similar patterns across the three dependent variables: Being a female has a statistically significant and negative relationship with the dependent variable, while age and education are statistically significant and positive. Self-identification as a Christian is a statistically significant and positive predictor for membership in a labor union or professional association but has no statistically significant relationship with membership in a political party.

The country-level effects are also broadly similar across the three organizational types. The only variable that is statistically significant in all three is average memberships. In contrast to some of the models presented in tables 3.4–3.5, when average memberships is dropped, the proportion Muslim variable does not become statistically significant. The one discrepancy in this trend is model 2 for membership in a political party. In this model, the proportion Muslim variable is statistically significant and negative, suggesting that individuals living in countries with larger Muslim populations are less likely to be members of political parties.

In sum, the HGLM analyses presented in tables 3.4–3.6 show several consistent patterns. First, on the whole, self-identification as a Muslim does not appear to have an effect—positive or negative—on membership in organizations. In the only instance in which the variable is found to be statistically significant—membership in a religious organization—the effect is virtually identical to the effect of being a Christian. Second, the proportion of a population that is Muslim also appears to have a minimal effect on organizational membership. With the exception of membership in a political party, the only time this variable was found to be significant was in models that did not include the control for the differences in organizational density across countries. There is no compelling evidence that Muslims are more or less likely to join organizations than non-Muslims.

PERSONAL MORALITY AND TOLERANCE

How tolerant are Muslims? How, if at all, do their opinions differ on "hot-button" issues? Are they more "socially conservative" (or "socially liberal") than non-Muslims? What about their views on behaviors that are generally regarded by all of humanity as unscrupulous? Are Muslims more stringent (or more permissive) in their opposition to bad behavior?

Many writings discuss tolerance in Islam. Some authors hold that Muslims tend to be intolerant. Some such writers locate the seeds of intolerance in the faith itself, or at least in what they see as the long-term historical predominance of traditions that devalue pluralism, openness, and diversity.[18] Many others maintain that Muslims are not prone to intolerance or that whatever signs of intolerance do manifest themselves are attributable to socioeconomic underdevelopment, Western imperialism, or some other factor that is extrinsic to Islam.[19] Still other authors hold that Islam indeed contains the seeds of intolerance but that other major religions do as well. According to such reasoning, contemporary Islam may indeed display signs of intolerance, but they are symptoms of a faith hijacked by its most rigid and backward-looking elements.[20]

Table 3.6 HGLM Analysis of Membership in Labor Unions, Political Parties, and Professional Associations (1 = member, 0 = non-member)

Predictors	Labor union[39T3]			Political party[39T3]			Professional association[39T3]		
	Model 1	Model 2	Model 3	Model 1	Model 2	Model 3	Model 1	Model 2	Model 3
Intercept	−1.83*** (.14)	−1.92*** (.09)	−1.91*** (.14)	−2.00*** (.14)	−2.10*** (.08)	−2.08*** (.14)	−1.91*** (.12)	−2.10*** (.09)	−2.09*** (.13)
Individual-level[a]									
Female		−0.35*** (.05)	−0.36*** (.05)		−0.42*** (.05)	−0.43*** (.05)		−0.24*** (.05)	−0.25*** (.05)
Age		0.01** (.00)	0.01* (.00)		0.01*** (.00)	0.01*** (.00)		0.01*** (.00)	0.01*** (.00)
Education level		1.10*** (.12)	1.11*** (.12)		0.90*** (.11)	0.91*** (.11)		2.23*** (.18)	2.24*** (.18)
Muslim	−0.39** (.13)	−0.22 (.12)	−0.22 (.12)	−0.16 (.14)	−0.02 (.15)	0.05 (.14)	−0.32* (.16)	−0.07 (.15)	−0.05 (.15)
Christian		0.12** (.04)	0.12** (.04)		0.12 (.07)	0.11 (.07)		0.18*** (.05)	0.19*** (.05)
Country-level[b]									
GDP per capita (log)		0.10 (.31)	−0.00 (.39)		−0.27 (.27)	−0.71 (.37)		−0.23 (.30)	−0.13 (.42)
Average age		−0.01 (.03)	−0.03 (.03)		−0.04* (.02)	−0.05 (.03)		0.04 (.02)	−0.01 (.04)
Level of democracy		0.08 (.09)			0.07 (.08)			0.04 (.09)	
Average memberships		0.58*** (.10)			0.67*** (.10)			0.67*** (.13)	
Proportion Muslim		−0.49 (.39)	−1.06 (.62)		−0.62* (.29)	−1.20 (.61)		−0.46 (.28)	−1.16 (.63)

	Labor union			Political party			Professional association		
Proportion Christian		-0.11 (.28)	-0.51 (.43)		-0.20 (.21)	-0.67 (.46)		-0.76** (.27)	-1.01 (.54)
	$N = 68{,}385$			$N = 68{,}463$			$N = 68{,}278$		
Variance									
Components[c] (τ)									
u_0	$u_0 = 0.93$	$u_0 = 0.43$	$u_0 = 0.96$	$u_0 = 1.03$	$u_0 = 0.36$	$u_0 = 1.00$	$u_0 = 0.74$	$u_0 = 0.35$	$u_0 = 0.92$
u_F		$u_F = 0.09$	$u_F = 0.10$		$u_F = 0.09$	$u_F = 0.10$		$u_F = 0.07$	$u_F = 0.07$
u_A		$u_A = 0.00$	$u_A = 0.00$		$u_A = 0.00$	$u_A = 0.00$		$u_A = 0.00$	$u_A = 0.00$
u_E		$u_E = 0.58$	$u_E = 0.57$		$u_E = 0.49$	$u_E = 0.50$		$u_E = 1.49$	$u_E = 1.51$
u_M	$u_M = 0.30$	$u_M = $ fixed to 0	$u_M = $ fixed to 0	$u_M = 0.34$	$u_M = 0.46$	$u_M = 0.37$	$u_M = 0.55$	$u_M = 0.48$	$u_M = 0.48$
u_C		$u_C = $ fixed to 0	$u_C = $ fixed to 0		$u_C = 0.13$	$u_C = 0.13$		$u_C = 0.07$	$u_C = 0.07$

Note: Entries are restricted maximum likelihood coefficients with robust standard errors for the unit-specific model, calculated on HLM 6.06.

N = 49 countries.

[a] All individual-level variables are centered at the group mean; all individual-level error terms were treated as random coefficients and were statistically significant at $p < .001$, except when otherwise noted. Error terms were fixed to zero when necessary in order for the likelihood function to converge.

[b] All country-level variables are centered at the grand mean.

[c] The variance components for null models including only the random Level-2 intercept are $\tau = 0.93$ for labor union, $\tau = 1.03$ for political party, and $\tau = 0.73$ for professional association.

*$p < .05$; **$p < .01$; ***$p < .001$.

The WVS contains many questions that deal with ethical principles. Here we draw on those questions that elicit telling responses on personal morality and tolerance in particular. We divide these questions into two groups. One is about what Americans often call "hot-button issues." These are matters about which people disagree, often hotly and deeply. They touch on personal values. Opinion on them often has implications for public policy. The acceptability of homosexuality is one such issue. The extent to which a person considers homosexuality tolerable is a matter of personal values; those values may be the topic of public debate; and the level of people's tolerance may influence how the law deals with homosexual behavior. The same may be said of having an abortion and getting a divorce. Here we will treat these three matters as the "controversial behaviors" on which people may disagree and which may reflect social values and tolerance.

The reason we may consider these behaviors "controversial" is that, however lopsided public opinion might be on them in this or that society, some people in some places are likely to view them as entirely acceptable. Many might regard one or another (or all) of them as abhorrent, sinful, or distasteful. But some people will regard them as unobjectionable, and the question of whether the behaviors victimize or harm anyone is open to debate. That is what makes them controversial.

Other behaviors, however, are different insofar as we would not expect anyone fully to condone them. The reason is that they are deceitful and antisocial. Stealing, lying, and cheating fit this category. There is no question that someone or something loses as a result of the behavior. Whether one believes that a purely naturalistic psychological impulse or a divinely planted seed of conscience is to credit, human beings universally agree that they are wrong. Yet they can disagree on how bad they are. They may differ on whether these behaviors may, in some circumstances, be more or less justifiable. The matters we will cover are accepting bribes, wrongfully claiming government benefits, and cheating on taxes. The first is a type of stealing, the second a kind of lying, and the third a matter of cheating.

Opinion about the two categories of behaviors—the first of which we may call "controversial," the second "dishonest"—provides a peek at popular tolerance on a substantial range of important issues. Separating controversial and dishonest behaviors, moreover, allows us to treat "tolerance" in a reasonably differentiated way.

It merits note that we are not examining behaviors but rather what people say they think about behaviors. For some advanced industrialized countries, we have plentiful information on matters such as the prevalence of homosexuality and abortion, but for most of the world we lack reliable data. We may use the information we have on opinions about those practices to gauge people's mindsets and values. But we must bear in mind that here we are observing attitudes toward behaviors, not the incidence of the behaviors themselves.

Many behaviors are controversial; here we pick those for which the WVS provides plentiful data and that have some resonance in all or virtually all societies. The first question asks whether homosexuality can be justified.[21] The second asks whether abortion can be justified.[22] The third inquires whether divorce can be justified.[23] Respondents are asked to score each item on a 1–10 scale, with 1 standing for "never justifiable" and 10 for "always justifiable." We also constructed an index that averages responses across all three items. As usual with such scoring, we use the mean values as our indicator.

Table 3.7 shows the averages for Muslims, non-Muslims as a whole, Christians and nondenominationalists. For tolerance of all three behaviors the Muslim average is much lower than the non-Muslim, specifically Christian, and specifically non-denominationalist averages. The disparity is especially dramatic for tolerance of homosexuality. How do these scores withstand hypothesis tests with hierarchical linear models (HLM) that include relevant confounding variables?

Table 3.8 presents HLM models of tolerance for homosexuality. Model 1 shows us that being a Muslim has a statistically significant and negative effect on tolerance

Table 3.7 Mean Scores for Religious Groups on Indicators of Popular Tolerance of Controversial Behavior

Survey Item	Muslims	All Non-Muslims[d]	Christians	No Denomination
Is homosexuality justifiable? (1= never justifiable; 10 = always justifiable)[a]	1.63 (19,649)	3.81 (80,942)	3.66 (53,532)	4.53 (18,153)
Is abortion justifiable? (1= never justifiable; 10 = always justifiable)[b]	2.15 (23,349)	3.76 (82,501)	3.51 (54,489)	4.73 (18,450)
Is divorce justifiable? (1 = never justifiable; 10 = always justifiable)[c]	3.39 (26,351)	4.98 (83,133)	4.85 (54,885)	5.75 (18,667)
Controversial Behavior Index (average of responses to homosexuality justifiable, abortion justifiable, and divorce justifiable)	2.40 (19,148)	4.18 (79,102)	3.99 (52,411)	5.04 (17,593)

Note: The figures in parentheses are Ns.

[a] This question was not asked in Iraq, Morocco, Peru, and Egypt.

[b] This question was not asked in Peru and Egypt.

[c] This question was not asked in Peru.

[d] Includes all individuals who adhere to a religious denomination other than Islam as well as individuals who did not state adherence to a religious tradition.

Table 3.8 HLM Analysis of Tolerance for Homosexuality (1 = never justifiable, 10 = always justifiable)

Predictors	Model 1	Model 2	Model 3	Model 4	Model 5
Intercept	3.51*** (.21)	3.51*** (.21)	3.51*** (.21)	3.45*** (.16)	3.44*** (.15)
Individual-level[a]					
Female			0.40*** (.05)	0.40*** (.05)	0.48*** (.06)
Age			−0.02*** (.00)	−0.02*** (.00)	−0.02*** (.00)
Education level			1.30*** (.13)	1.30*** (.13)	1.24*** (.13)
Muslim	−1.13*** (.15)		−1.51*** (.16)	−1.48*** (.17)	−1.13*** (.14)
Christian		−0.42*** (.07)	−0.46*** (.06)	−0.46*** (.06)	−0.20*** (.05)
Importance of God					−0.14*** (.01)
Country-level[b]					
GDP per capita (log)				0.46 (.27)	0.26 (.25)
Average age				−0.01 (.03)	−0.03 (.02)
Level of democracy				0.22** (.08)	0.23** (.08)
Proportion Muslim				−1.12** (.42)	−0.55 (.51)
Proportion Christian				−0.28 (.44)	0.06 (.46)
Average Importance of God					−0.26** (.09)

Variance Components[c]

σ^2	6.56	6.53	5.89	5.89	5.76
τ	$u_0 = 3.51$	$u_0 = 3.51$	$u_0 = 3.51$	$u_0 = 2.05$	$u_0 = 1.82$
	$u_M = 1.21$	$u_C = 0.37$	$u_F = 0.18$	$u_F = 0.18$	$u_F = 0.23$
			$u_A = 0.00$	$u_A = 0.00$	$u_A = 0.00$
			$u_E = 1.35$	$u_E = 1.34$	$u_E = 1.19$
			$u_M = 1.75$	$u_M = 1.90$	$u_M = 1.20$
			$u_C = 0.22$	$u_C = 0.22$	$u_C = 0.13$
					$u_I = 0.01$

Note: Entries are restricted maximum likelihood coefficients with robust standard errors, calculated on HLM 6.06.

$N = 98,211$ individuals in 79 countries.

[a] All individual-level variables are centered at the group mean; all individual-level error terms were treated as random coefficients and were statistically significant at $p < .001$.

[b] All country-level variables are centered at the grand mean.

[c] The variance components for a null model including only the random Level-2 intercept are: $\sigma^2 = 6.61$; $\tau = 3.51$.

*$p < .05$; **$p < .01$; ***$p < .001$.

for homosexuality. The size of this effect actually increases slightly once individual- and country-level controls are introduced in models 3 and 4. When we control for religiosity in model 5, we find that it is statistically significant and negative and the size of the Muslim coefficient returns to the magnitude it has as the single predictor in model 1. Among individual-level characteristics, gender, age, education, and self-identification are all statistically significant. Being a female and being better educated are positively associated with tolerance for homosexuality, while being older and identifying oneself as a Christian have a negative effect.

According to model 4, the proportion of a country's population that is Muslim is statistically significant and negative. Living in a country with more Muslims decreases one's tolerance for homosexuality. Once we control for both individual- and country-level religiosity in model 5, however, this variable falls out of statistical significance. In other words, the greater a country's average religiosity level, the more intolerant an individual is toward homosexuality, regardless of religious denomination.

The relationship between Muslim self-identification and opposition to homosexuality is quite large. According to model 5 in table 3.8, with all country-level variables held at their means, a Muslim man of average age and education is predicted to have a score of 2.40 on the 1–10 scale, while a Christian man with the same characteristics is predicted to have a score of 3.33 and a nondenominationalist would have a predicted score of 3.53. Even though the variable for being a woman is statistically significant and positive, it corresponds to an increase of just 0.24 on the tolerance scale. The effect of education is also dwarfed by the effect of being a Muslim. Having completed a college degree, for example, corresponds to an increase of 0.62 on the tolerance scale. Though substantial, this figure is smaller than the 1.13 difference we see between the predicted scores for Muslims and nondenominationalists.

Table 3.9 presents the HLM models of tolerance for abortion. The general patterns we observed for the previous models on homosexuality are also present here. Self-identification as a Muslim has a statistically significant and negative association with tolerance for abortion, which persists even after the controls are introduced, although the magnitude of the association weakens a bit once we control for religiosity. Similarly, age and self-identification as a Christian also have a statistically significant and negative effect on tolerance for abortion while education corresponds positively with tolerance for abortion. In contrast to the models that examine homosexuality, gender shows a statistically significant relationship to tolerance for abortion only when we control for religiosity (model 5), which, as above, is negative. Models 4 and 5 show that the proportion of a country's population that is made up of Muslims is not related to individual tolerance for abortion. Individuals living in countries with higher rates of average religiosity are less likely to be tolerant of abortion.

Yet the magnitude of the correlation between being Muslim and opposing abortion is smaller than is the correlation between being Muslim and opposing homosexuality. For example, according to model 5 in table 3.9, if we hold all country-level variables at their means, a Muslim man of average age, education, and religiosity is predicted to have an abortion tolerance score of 3.02, while a Christian man with the same characteristics will have a predicted score of 3.50 and a nondenominational man will have a predicted score of 3.74. All else being equal, Muslim self-identification results in a tolerance score that is 0.48 points lower than that of a Christian and 0.72 points lower than that of a nondenominationalist. If we consider the effects of other variables in the model, being a female corresponds to a 0.15 increase in abortion tolerance compared to being a man and having a college degree corresponds to a 0.38 increase in abortion tolerance over having only a high-school degree.

The HLM models of our third indicator of controversial behaviors, tolerance for divorce, show patterns consistent with the previous two indicators. The models are presented in table 3.10. Self-identification as a Muslim has a statistically significant and negative effect on tolerance for divorce, and this effect is present even when we control for socioeconomic characteristics and religiosity. As with the models that analyze tolerance for homosexuality and abortion, being female and being better educated correspond positively with tolerance, while older age, self-identification as a Christian, and religiosity correspond negatively.

Likewise, models 4 and 5 show that the size of a country's Muslim population is not statistically significant. Yet, in contrast to the previous two sets of models, we see some other differences in country-level predictors. First, GDP per capita is statistically significant and positive. As national income increases, one's tolerance for divorce also increases. Second, once we control for a country's average religiosity (which is statistically significant and negative), the size of the Christian population becomes statistically significant and positive, meaning that living in a country with a larger Christian population increases one's tolerance for divorce.

The difference between Muslims and non-Muslims in terms of tolerance for divorce is slightly smaller than is the difference in terms of tolerance for abortion. According to model 5 in table 3.10, holding all country-level variables at their means, the predicted divorce tolerance score for a Muslim man with average age, education, and religiosity is 4.28. A Christian man with the same characteristics is predicted to have a divorce tolerance score of 4.67 and a nondenominationalist a score of 4.95. Thus, the difference in predicted scores between a Muslim and a Christian man is 0.39 and between a Muslim and a nondenominational man is 0.67. The effect of being a Muslim is greater than the effect of being a female, which adds 0.19 points to one's divorce tolerance score. The effect of education, however, is much greater. An individual with a college degree has a predicted score on the divorce tolerance scale that is 1.94 points higher than an individual with only a high-school degree.

Table 3.9 HLM Analysis of Tolerance for Abortion (1 = never justifiable, 10 = always justifiable)

Predictors	Model 1	Model 2	Model 3	Model 4	Model 5
Intercept	3.58*** (.17)	3.58*** (.17)	3.58*** (.17)	3.57*** (.13)	3.55*** (.09)
Individual-level[a]					
Female			0.04 (.02)	0.04 (.02)	0.15*** (.03)
Age			-0.01*** (.00)	-0.01*** (.00)	-0.01*** (.00)
Education level			1.02*** (.09)	1.02*** (.09)	0.93*** (.08)
Muslim	-0.93*** (.14)		-1.34*** (.14)	-1.31*** (.14)	-0.72*** (.10)
Christian			-0.65*** (.07)	-0.66*** (.07)	-0.24*** (.05)
Importance of God		-0.55*** (.09)			-0.20*** (.01)
Country-level[b]					
GDP per capita (log)				0.30 (.24)	0.02 (.21)
Average age				0.06* (.03)	-0.01 (.02)
Level of democracy				0.06 (.10)	0.17 (.09)
Proportion Muslim				-0.80 (.43)	0.65 (.40)
Proportion Christian				-0.70 (.44)	0.55 (.39)
Average Importance of God					-0.55*** (.06)

Variance Components[c]

σ^2	6.21	6.14	5.88	5.88	5.63
τ	$u_0 = 2.23$	$u_0 = 2.23$	$u_0 = 2.23$	$u_0 = 1.33$	$u_0 = 0.67$
			$u_F = 0.02$	$u_F = 0.02$	$u_F = 0.03$
			$u_A = 0.00$	$u_A = 0.00$	$u_A = 0.00$
			$u_E = 0.58$	$u_E = 0.57$	$u_E = 0.45$
	$u_M = 1.00$	$u_C = 0.51$	$u_M = 1.17$	$u_M = 1.16$	$u_M = 0.44$
			$u_C = 0.29$	$u_C = 0.29$	$u_C = 0.10$
					$u_I = 0.01$

Note: Entries are restricted maximum likelihood coefficients with robust standard errors, calculated on HLM 6.06.

$N = 103,280$ individuals in 81 countries.

[a] All individual-level variables are centered at the group mean; all individual-level error terms were treated as random coefficients and were statistically significant at $p < .001$.

[b] All country-level variables are centered at the grand mean.

[c] The variance components for a null model including only the random Level-2 intercept are: $\sigma^2 = 6.25$; $\tau = 2.23$.

$*p < .05; **p < .01; ***p < .001$.

Table 3.10 HLM Analysis of Tolerance for Divorce (1 = never justifiable, 10 = always justifiable)

Predictors	Model 1	Model 2	Model 3	Model 4	Model 5
Intercept	4.78*** (.17)	4.78*** (.17)	4.78*** (.17)	4.77*** (.11)	4.77*** (.10)
Individual-level[a]					
Female			0.11*** (.03)	0.11*** (.03)	0.19*** (.03)
Age			-0.02** (.00)	-0.02*** (.00)	-0.01*** (.00)
Education level			1.08*** (.08)	1.08*** (.08)	1.02*** (.08)
Muslim	-0.61*** (.17)		-1.05*** (.15)	-1.04*** (.15)	-0.67*** (.14)
Christian		-0.56*** (.08)	-0.58*** (.06)	-0.59*** (.06)	-0.28*** (.05)
Importance of God					-0.13*** (.01)
Country-level[b]					
GDP per capita (log)				1.09*** (.32)	0.95** (.32)
Average age				0.06* (.03)	0.02 (.03)
Level of democracy				0.12 (.09)	0.13 (.09)
Proportion Muslim				0.03 (.51)	0.75 (.57)
Proportion Christian				0.63 (.47)	1.21* (.49)
Average Importance of God					-0.26** (.09)

Variance Components[c]

	7.38	7.35	7.05	7.05	6.93
σ^2					
τ	$u_0 = 2.36$	$u_0 = 2.36$	$u_0 = 2.36$	$u_0 = 1.05$	$u_0 = 0.90$
			$u_F = 0.05$	$u_F = 0.05$	$u_F = 0.07$
			$u_A = 0.00$	$u_A = 0.00$	$u_A = 0.00$
			$u_E = 0.48$	$u_E = 0.48$	$u_E = 0.42$
	$u_M = 1.37$		$u_M = 1.23$	$u_M = 1.25$	$u_M = 0.87$
		$u_C = 0.42$	$u_C = 0.20$	$u_C = 0.20$	$u_C = 0.11$
					$u_I = 0.01$

Note: Entries are restricted maximum likelihood coefficients with robust standard errors, calculated on HLM 6.06.

$N = 106{,}819$ individuals in 82 countries.

[a] All individual-level variables are centered at the group mean; all individual-level error terms were treated as random coefficients and were statistically significant at $p < .001$.

[b] All country-level variables are centered at the grand mean.

[c] The variance components for a null model including only the random Level-2 intercept are: $\sigma^2 = 7.43$; $\tau = 2.36$.

$^*p < .05$; $^{**}p < .01$; $^{***}p < .001$.

We may have a look at how Muslims differ from non-Muslims in terms of overall tolerance for controversial behaviors by analyzing the index that averages the scores for attitudes toward homosexuality, abortion, and divorce. Table 3.11 shows the results. As with the three separate models, self-identification as a Muslim is statistically significant and negative, even when we control for other variables. Being a female and being more highly educated correspond positively with tolerance, while older age and self-identification as a Christian correspond negatively. When country-level variables are introduced in model 4, there is a positive relationship between GDP per capita and tolerance for controversial behaviors, but the remaining country-level variables—including the proportion of a country's population that is Muslim—are not statistically significant. Model 5 includes controls for religiosity. Individual-level religiosity is statistically significant and negative, and its inclusion reduces the size of the Muslim coefficient. A country's average religiosity level is also statistically significant and negative.

What is the magnitude of the effect of self-identification as a Muslim on tolerance for controversial behaviors? If we look at model 5, the predicted tolerance score for a Muslim is 0.63 points lower than that of a Christian and 0.87 points lower than that of a nondenominationalist. Being a Muslim therefore has a considerably larger effect than does being a woman, which is predicted to increase tolerance by 0.28 points compared to being a man, or the effect of having a college versus a high-school education, which corresponds to an increase in tolerance of 0.44 points.

Based on our HLM analyses of tolerance for homosexuality, abortion, and divorce, we can say that self-identification as a Muslim corresponds with greater opposition to these controversial behaviors, even once confounding variables are taken into consideration. The proportion of the national population that is made up of Muslims, however, does not appear to have an effect on attitudes. Across the spectrum of behaviors, Muslims are, relative to non-Muslims, most tolerant of divorce, followed by abortion and then homosexuality. The differences in predicted scores between Muslims and non-Muslims are sizeable for homosexuality and less substantial for the other two indicators.

Popular Tolerance of Dishonest Behavior

Next we examine tolerance of dishonest behaviors. No one considers these behaviors laudable, but people may differ in their views of how unacceptable they are. The WVS asks several keen questions on tolerance for dishonesty. One inquires on whether taking a bribe in the course of one's duties is justifiable.[24] The second solicits opinion about claiming government benefits to which one is not entitled.[25] The third focuses on cheating on one's taxes.[26] As with the questions above, respondents score the items on a 1–10 scale, ranging from "never justifiable" to "always justifiable." Having looked at each of these variables individually, we found little difference between responses to the three items. Therefore, we averaged them together to form a dishonesty tolerance index. Table 3.12 provides the mean scores for Muslims, non-Muslims, Christians, and nondenominationalists on this measure. We see that Muslims are less tolerant of dishonest behavior than are non-Muslims.

Does the finding hold when we control for other potentially influential factors? Table 3.13 shows the results of an HLM analysis of the dishonesty tolerance index. Model 1 finds that self-identification as a Muslim has no statistically significant effect on tolerance for dishonest behaviors. Once we control for individual-and country-level characteristics in models 3 and 4, however, the Muslim variable becomes statistically significant and negative. All else being equal, self-identification as a Muslim corresponds to lower tolerance for dishonest behaviors. The remaining individual-level controls are also statistically significant and negative. Being a female, self-identification as a Christian, older age, and higher education are all associated with lower tolerance for dishonest behavior. The size of the effect of Muslim self-identification is modest. Muslims are 0.04 points less tolerant of dishonest behavior than Christians, and 0.14 points less tolerant than nondenominationalists. As a comparison, the size of the effect of being a woman is to decrease tolerance by 0.14 points, while having a college education versus a high-school education decreases tolerance by 0.08 points.

According to model 4, the proportion of a country's population that is Muslim also has a statistically significant negative effect on tolerance for dishonest behavior. In fact, this is the only statistically significant country-level variable; levels of economic development and democracy do not appear to play a role. All else being equal, living in a country that is 95 percent Muslim decreases an individual's predicted tolerance score by 0.64 points compared to living in a country with an average proportion of Muslims (21 percent), while living in a country that is 5 percent Muslim increases one's predicted tolerance for dishonesty by 0.16 points.

These dynamics change, however, once we control for religiosity in model 5. Individual-level religiosity is statistically significant and negative. When this variable is included in the model, self-identification as a Muslim or Christian both fall out of statistical significance. A country's average religiosity level is also statistically significant and negative, wiping out the statistical significance of the Muslim percentage variable.

In sum, while it appears that Muslims are slightly less tolerant of dishonest behavior than non-Muslims, the differences are not substantial.

In the case of dishonest behaviors we have considered here, even libertines who lean toward a "10" on their answers on the controversial behaviors (homosexuality, abortion, and divorce) would probably concede that there is nothing bigoted about stern disapproval of dishonest behaviors (bribe-taking, taking

Table 3.11 HLM Analysis of Controversial Behaviors Tolerance Index (1 = never justifiable, 10 = always justifiable)

Predictors	Model 1	Model 2	Model 3	Model 4	Model 5
Intercept	3.99*** (.17)	3.99*** (.17)	3.99*** (.17)	3.95*** (.12)	3.88*** (.10)
Individual-level[a]					
Female			0.19*** (.03)	0.19*** (.03)	0.28*** (.03)
Age			−0.02*** (.00)	−0.02*** (.00)	−0.02*** (.00)
Education level			1.16*** (.10)	1.16*** (.10)	1.09*** (.09)
Muslim	−0.97*** (.14)		−1.33** (.14)	−1.30*** (.14)	−0.87*** (.11)
Christian		−0.51*** (.08)	−0.57*** (.06)	−0.58*** (.06)	−0.24*** (.04)
Importance of God					−0.16*** (.01)
Country-level[b]					
GDP per capita (log)				0.68** (.24)	0.31 (.22)
Average age				0.04 (.02)	0.00 (.02)
Level of democracy				0.12 (.08)	0.10 (.07)
Proportion Muslim				−0.50 (.43)	−0.20 (.38)
Proportion Christian				−0.05 (.41)	0.13 (.32)
Average Importance of God					−0.18** (.07)

Variance Components[c]

σ^2	4.44	4.40	4.03	4.03	3.87
τ	$u_0 = 2.42$	$u_0 = 2.42$	$u_0 = 2.42$	$u_0 = 1.18$	$u_0 = 0.89$
			$u_F = 0.05$	$u_F = 0.05$	$u_F = 0.07$
			$u_A = 0.00$	$u_A = 0.00$	$u_A = 0.00$
			$u_E = 0.67$	$u_E = 0.67$	$u_E = 0.55$
	$u_M = 1.02$		$u_M = 1.17$	$u_M = 1.20$	$u_M = 0.64$
		$u_C = 0.38$	$u_C = 0.22$	$u_C = 0.22$	$u_C = 0.10$
					$u_I = 0.01$

Note : Entries are restricted maximum likelihood coefficients with robust standard errors, calculated on HLM 6.06.

$N = 96{,}401$ individuals in 79 countries.

[a] All individual-level variables are centered at the group mean; all individual-level error terms were treated as random coefficients and were statistically significant at $p < .001$.

[b] All country-level variables are centered at the grand mean.

[c] The variance components for a null model including only the random Level-2 intercept are: $\sigma^2 = 4.48$; $\tau = 2.42$.

$*p < .05; **p < .01; ***p < .001$.

Table 3.12 Mean Scores for Religious Groups on Dishonesty Tolerance Index (0–1)

	Muslims	*All Non-Muslims*[a]	*Christians*	*No Denomination*
Dishonesty Tolerance Index (average of scores for rating bribe-taking, cheating on taxes, and accepting benefits not entitled)	2.00 (21,632)	2.29 (80,654)	2.24 (54,197)	2.35 (18,120)

Note: At least one of the three questions was not asked in Iraq, Israel, Peru, and Saudi Arabia, so they are excluded from this analysis. The figures in parentheses are *N*s.

[a] Includes all individuals who adhere to a religious denomination other than Islam as well as individuals who did not state adherence to a religious tradition .

government benefits to which one is not entitled, and cheating on taxes). There is intolerance and there is intolerance. Some types of intolerance might even be admirable. Disaggregating issues as we have done here helps cast "tolerance" in a somewhat different light than it is often seen. There is nothing necessarily wrong with being especially prejudiced against dishonesty. Our findings provide some evidence that Muslims may be at least a bit less inclined to countenance fraud and deceit than non-Muslims, though as noted above, the difference is minor.

Summary

In this section we have had a look at people's views on a variety of behaviors that are often considered deviant. We separated them into controversial and dishonest behaviors. Opinion between Muslims and non-Muslims on the three controversial behaviors we examined, homosexuality, abortion, and divorce, clearly diverged. Muslims are inclined toward greater conservatism. Muslim distinctiveness is particularly evident in opinion on homosexuality.

On dishonest behavior, we found little consistent difference between Muslims and non-Muslims. Muslims are a bit more censorious in their views, but only a bit.

DISCUSSION OF THE FINDINGS

This chapter has investigated social capital (and sociability and organizational membership in particular) and moral attitudes (and tolerance of controversial behaviors and dishonest behaviors in particular). First, let us take stock of the findings.

On social capital, we find no appreciable difference between Muslims and non-Muslims. Muslims are slightly more sociable than non-Muslims, meaning that Muslims are a bit more likely to spend time with other people from various walks of life. But the difference is insubstantial. Much the same may be said of membership in organizations, which is our other indicator of social capital. The empirical evidence suggests that there is nothing about being a Muslim that inclines a person to be appreciably more or less likely to participate in organizational life. When it comes to social connectedness, then, we find little or nothing to distinguish Muslims from non-Muslims.

Our investigation of social attitudes turned up more distinctiveness. Muslims are moderately more opposed to abortion and divorce and strikingly more opposed to homosexuality than non-Muslims are. Muslims are also more inclined to express opposition to dishonest behaviors, but the difference between Muslims and non-Muslims in this area is diminutive.

The only area of clear distinctiveness, then, is in attitudes toward what Americans call "hot-button" issues. Muslims exhibit relatively more "conservative" (or "traditional") attitudes on these matters than do non-Muslims. While divorce is no longer the subject of deep political division in the United States, where over half of marriages end in it, controversy over the legality of abortion and the status of homosexual unions are arguably the central social issues in American politics in the early twenty-first century. They are also in hot dispute in much of Europe and Latin America as well as parts of Africa and Asia among people of many different faith groups. Their salience in politics around the globe makes the possible distinctiveness of the opinions of the people of a particular religious tradition substantively interesting and all the more worthy of discussion.

Muslim attitudes on homosexuality are particularly idiosyncratic. On divorce and abortion, Muslim opinion differs from non-Muslim opinion, but the gap is not dramatic. It is dramatic on homosexuality. We will therefore focus on that issue, after which we will offer some brief ruminations on the others. Is there something about Islam that inclines its adherents to extraordinary distaste for homosexuality?

Many Muslims believe that the Qur'an and the Hadith (the body of reports on the Prophet Muhammad's life and testimony that are second only to the Qur'an in sacredness to most Muslims) condemn homosexuality. Depending on how one counts, there are five to ten passages in the Qur'an that may be interpreted as proscribing homosexuality. The most explicit are found in surahs (chapters) 4, 7, and 26.[27] In 4:16, the Prophet reports the word of God (Allah) as follows, "If two men among you commit a lewd act, punish them both. If they repent and mend their ways, let them be. God is forgiving and merciful." In 7:80–81, the Prophet records that God recounted the story of Sodom, which also appears in the Bible (including Gen. 18 and 19 and Jude 1), and stated, "And Lot, who said to his people: 'Will you persist in these lewd acts which no other nation has committed before you? You lust after men instead of women. Truly, you are a degenerate people.'" In

Table 3.13 HLM Analysis of Tolerance for Dishonest Behaviors (1 = never justifiable, 10 = always justifiable)

Predictors	Model 1	Model 2	Model 3	Model 4	Model 5
Intercept	2.26*** (.08)	2.26*** (.08)	2.26*** (.08)	2.25*** (.07)	2.24*** (.07)
Individual-level [a]					
Female			−0.14*** (.02)	−0.14*** (.02)	−0.12*** (.02)
Age			−0.01*** (.00)	−0.01*** (.00)	−0.01*** (.00)
Education level			−0.20*** (.04)	−0.20*** (.04)	−0.21*** (.04)
Muslim	0.01 (.08)		−0.15* (.07)	−0.14* (.07)	−0.07 (.07)
Christian		−0.12*** (.04)	−0.10*** (.03)	−0.10*** (.03)	−0.03 (.03)
Importance of God					−0.05*** (.01)
Country-level [b]					
GDP per capita (log)				−0.28 (.27)	−0.31 (.26)
Average age				−0.01 (.02)	−0.02 (.02)
Level of democracy				−0.07 (.09)	−0.05 (.09)
Proportion Muslim				−0.86** (.29)	−0.48 (.42)
Proportion Christian				−0.15 (.35)	0.15 (.45)
Average Importance of God					−0.13* (.06)

Variance Components [c]

σ^2	2.51	2.51	2.45	2.45	2.43
τ	$u_0 = 0.47$	$u_0 = 0.47$	$u_0 = 0.47$	$u_0 = 0.46$	$u_0 = 0.46$
	$u_M = 0.22$	$u_C = 0.07$	$u_F = 0.01$	$u_F = 0.01$	$u_F = 0.01$
			$u_A = 0.00$	$u_A = 0.00$	$u_A = 0.00$
			$u_E = 0.10$	$u_E = 0.10$	$u_E = 0.10$
			$u_M = 0.17$	$u_M = 0.17$	$u_M = 0.14$
			$u_C = 0.03$	$u_C = 0.03$	$u_C = 0.04$
					$u_I = 0.00$

Note: Entries are restricted maximum likelihood coefficients with robust standard errors, calculated on HLM 6.06.

$N = 99{,}996$ individuals in 79 countries.

[a] All individual-level variables are centered at the group mean; all individual-level error terms were treated as random coefficients and were statistically significant at $p < .001$.

[b] All country-level variables are centered at the grand mean.

[c] The variance components for a null model including only the random Level-2 intercept are: $\sigma^2 = 2.52$; $\tau = 0.47$.

$*p < .05$; $**p < .01$; $***p < .001$.

26:159–66, God again cites Lot's experience. God states through the Prophet, "Your Lord is the Mighty one, the Merciful. Lot's people, too, disbelieved the apostles. Their kinsman Lot had said to them: 'Will you not fear God? . . . Will you fornicate with males and eschew the wives whom God has created for you? Surely you are great transgressors.'"

Muslims who oppose a stringent reading of these texts make several points. One is that the Qur'an also may suggest that "male youths" are numbered along with the "[female] virgins" whose pleasant company virtuous men will enjoy as their reward in paradise. So too do those who urge a generous reading note that there is no record of a single case of a punishment carried out for homosexuality during the Prophet's lifetime.[28]

Other points may be added as well. First, a multitude of acts meet with Divine opprobrium in the Qur'an and some of them are condemned much more frequently and forcefully than homosexuality. They are accompanied by explicit descriptions of the tortures that the offender will encounter in the afterlife. Such sins include, prominently, acts of injustice against the poor. God denounces homosexual behavior but offers no descriptions of hell for the offender. Furthermore, as the passage from 4:16 quoted above suggests, repentance following earthly (non-lethal) punishment for the offenders will satisfy God.

Now, even these mild and spare injunctions could help explain the especially great opposition among Muslims to homosexuality if the main texts of the other major world religions did not also condemn homosexuality. But the sacred texts of other religions do also revile it. A brief examination of the Bible will suffice.[29] Leviticus 18:22 states, "Do not lie with a man as one lies with a woman; that is detestable." Leviticus 20:13 stipulates the punishment: "If a man lies with a man as one lies with a woman, both of them have done what is detestable. They must be put to death; their blood will be on their own heads."

Since these passages appear in the Old Testament, which Christians generally regard has having been superseded (albeit not annulled) by the New Testament, many regard the harsh judgment as a rule for ancient times. These injunctions would therefore be binding only on Jews (for whom the Christian Old Testament is, of course, the Bible in its entirety) and Christians who do not privilege the authority of the New Testament over the old.

But the New Testament also contains passages that explicitly denounce homosexual behavior as well, albeit without the instruction to punish with death. The apostle Paul, the founder of the Church, states in his letter to the Romans (Rom. 1:26–27), "Even their women exchanged natural sexual relations for unnatural ones. In the same way the men also abandoned natural relations with women and were inflamed with lust for one another. Men committed indecent acts with other men, and received in themselves the due penalty for their error." In his first letter to the church at Corinth (1 Cor. 6:9–10), Paul includes "homosexual offenders" in a list of moral offenders who "will not inherit the kingdom of God."

Some contemporary Christians oppose a severe reading of these passages. Some scholars have claimed that the passages in Leviticus are not about homosexuality specifically but rather anal intercourse and are mere matters of purity ritual. Based on some passages in the book of Samuel (such as 2 Sam. 1:26), some have claimed evidence of a homosexual relationship between King David and his close friend Jonathan.[30] Many other arguments are also possible. One may note that Jesus himself, while condemning a multitude of sins during his ministry, made no mention of homosexuality. So too may one argue that the general tenor of charity and clemency that characterizes the Gospels of Jesus rules out any negative judgment of a behavior that does not contravene the practice of loving one's fellows.

What we find are remarkable parallels between the Qur'an and the Bible. Even the number of mentions of homosexuality—five to ten times per book, depending on how one interprets certain passages—is roughly the same in the two texts. We also find among both contemporary Muslims and Christians some voices who urge a reading of scripture that decriminalizes homosexuality. A small number of commentators of each faith go as far as to find passages that they believe endorse homosexuality.

Thus, explaining why contemporary Muslims are especially averse to homosexuality, and more averse than Christians are, cannot readily be accomplished by plumbing sacred scripture because the holy writ of the two largest world religions points in the same general direction. In both the Qur'an and the Bible homosexuality is denounced in several passages. Neither book contains passages that explicitly condone it, though some contemporary scholars claim to find implicit approval in both. In both books, moreover, homosexuality is mentioned as one among a multitude of sinful behaviors. In neither text is it singled out for sustained criticism or treated as being uniquely or especially wicked.

Our finding does not mean that sacred scripture cannot possibly affect contemporary believers. Many scholars regard any attribution of Christians' attitudes or behavior to the Bible or Muslims' attitudes or behavior to the Qur'an as naïve or simply unthinkable.[31] As Akbar Ahmed notes, "No self-respecting political or social scientist, reared in the secular or liberal tradition of the West, would dream of looking at the Quran for explanations of political behavior." But, as Ahmed adds boldly, referring to his own investigation of culture and politics in the Muslim world, "but that is what we will do here."[32] That is what we are doing here, too, and it is what we must do.

We can and must avoid the incredulous scholars' error. But in the case of attitudes toward homosexuality, scripture comes up short as an explanation. The reason is that the considerable variation we find between Muslims and non-Muslims (including Christians) in contemporary attitudes is not paralleled by a disparity between the Qur'an and the Bible, which treat homosexuality in essentially the same way.

On homosexuality we are left without an explanation of any type. The statistical analyses controlled for socioeconomic status at both the individual and national levels, so greater poverty or lesser educational attainment among Muslims probably does not explanation the distinctiveness of Muslim opinion. We have evidence that Muslims may be especially inclined to disapprove of homosexuality, but we do not know why. It is possible that attitudes toward homosexuality could be tied to mentalities about sex and gender more generally. We will take up the question of gender-based inequality in chapter 6.

A word is in order about the other controversial behaviors investigated here, abortion and divorce. It is noteworthy that many adherents of both Islam and Christianity oppose abortion on religious grounds, though abortion is not mentioned in either the Qur'an or the Bible. Many Muslims and Christians find passages of scripture that they regard as casting censure upon the practice. Muslims can point to statements in the Qur'an that harshly condemn infanticide, which was frequently visited upon newborn girls at the time of the Prophet but thereafter became rarer among Muslims.[33] Some Christians adduce biblical passages that refer to God's work of creating humans in "the womb."[34] Catholic Church doctrine, from the early centuries of the church's existence to the present day, has condemned abortion. Thus, while neither the Qur'an nor the Bible mentions abortion, many Muslims and Christians locate implicit condemnation of the practice in their scriptures.

The question of divorce is also interesting from a scriptural point of view. The voice of God in the Qur'an explicitly condones divorce (initiated by the man) and even prescribes in some detail how it is to be carried out, and Islamic law has always allowed for divorce.[35] In the Bible, Jesus Christ explicitly forbids divorce except in cases of marital infidelity.[36] We would expect much higher support for the justifiability of divorce among Muslims than among Christians if holy writ determined opinion. Yet Muslims exhibit less tolerance for divorce than Christians, all else being equal.

Let us leave behind discussion of controversial behaviors and turn to our findings on dishonest behavior. Why Muslims, once we control for socioeconomic development, have sterner views—albeit only slightly sterner views—than non-Muslims is anyone's guess. The Qur'an, to be sure, is full of injunctions against unjust gain. But so do the sacred texts of all other major religions, including the Bible, overflow with passages that laud honesty and condemn bribery, undeserved gain, and cheating. Thus, we cannot attribute Muslims' lower tolerance of dishonesty to sacred scripture. Nor, for that matter, are any other explanations readily available.

Before we despair, however, we may note that the effect of being a Muslim on attitudes toward dishonest behavior is actually modest. It is possible that we have encountered little more than a very minor difference or an empirical fluke. We will have opportunity for further investigating this matter when we look at actual behavior, as opposed to mere opinion on behavior, in the next chapter.

4 Corruption and Crime

The relationship between Islam and social disorder is a matter of public interest around the world, though surprisingly few studies actually investigate the issue using empirical evidence. This chapter offers some data, basic empirical tests of those data, and discussion of the findings. We seek evidence on whether Muslim societies are more or less corrupt than non-Muslim societies, and on whether Muslims are more or less prone to violent crime than adherents of other religions. In this chapter we stick with investigation of corruption and crime. In chapter 5, our focus will shift to political violence.

In chapters 2 and 3, we focused mainly on people's attitudes and opinions. While we controlled for country-level data, we concentrated mainly on individuals. In the current chapter and subsequent ones, countries, rather than individuals, are the main units of analysis. Accordingly, our methods will shift. Conducting cross-national analysis requires different techniques than we used in the previous two chapters. As always, we will keep our eye on what we intend to understand: How Muslims differ (if at all) from non-Muslims. As always, the statistical analyses are tailored to assessing that question alone.

In this chapter we are concerned with corruption and crime. One section of the chapter is devoted to each matter.

CORRUPTION

We pick up here where we left off in the previous chapter. There we examined survey data to see if there were any discernable differences between Muslim and non-Muslim opinions toward taking bribes, wrongfully claiming government benefits, and cheating on taxes. Here we look beyond what people say about the acceptability of such behaviors and examine the extent to which they engage in them.

Hypotheses on Muslims and Corruption

Corruption is the subject of great interest and vast research. Yet few works address whether corruption varies across societies according to religious tradition. While some observers might suspect that this or that religion promotes behavioral norms that conduce to or circumscribe fraud, few scholars have yet treated such hunches as hypotheses and tested them.[1]

Still, it is not difficult to generate hypotheses. First, we might anticipate that Muslims are less prone to corruption. Perhaps malfeasance is lower among Muslims because they are less tolerant of it. In the previous chapter, we saw that Muslims are a bit sterner than non-Muslims in their disapproval of dishonest behavior. If behavior reflects attitudes, public ethics may be higher among Muslims than non-Muslims.

According to the rival hypothesis, Islam would be associated with higher levels of corruption. A link could be found in tribalism and familism. Some observers have asserted that tribal and family connections are especially strong in Muslim societies. Some scholars implicate Islam itself, while others refer to historical, geographical, or ecological conditions in the regions in which Islam emerged and to which it spread.[2] Whatever the roots of the condition, if tribalism and familism are especially strong in Muslim lands, one might expect corruption to be higher there. Tribalism and familism may serve positive social functions. They may preserve social bonds and foster allegiances that prevent feelings of alienation. But they may also hinder the development of an impersonal ethic of responsibility that eschews favoritism and embraces transparency in public life. Extraordinary loyalty to kin and tribe may retard the universalization of rules and norms for probity in relations with people with whom one has no personal ties. Thus, in modern mass society, tribalism and familism are sometimes considered barriers to curtailing corrupt practices.[3] Another possible cause of greater corruption in Muslim societies might be an unusual degree of intimacy of political and religious institutions. Abdullahi Ahmed An-Na'im states, "The potential problems associated with blending of religious institutions with those of the state often entail hypocrisy and corruption, as illustrated by the additional functions of the *muhtasib* [public inspector] as a tax collector and a guardian of public morality."[4] If the proximity of religious and political institutions is more intimate in Muslim societies, we might expect more opportunities for corruption for that reason.

Measuring Corruption

We human beings are not always honest about our own dishonesty. We therefore lack precise data, based exclusively on people's self-reporting, on the prevalence of deceitful behavior. But we do have surveys of experts and businesspeople about the prevalence of corruption in the countries they know.

There are two such surveys that produce yearly national-level data on corruption. One is conducted by Transparency International (TI), an international NGO dedicated to reducing corrupt practices. It conducts surveys of businesspeople and experts on the extent of malfeasance and uses the results to create an annual Corruption Perceptions Index (CPI). TI adopts a conventional conception of corruption as the use of public office for private gain, which manifests largely as bribe-taking. In recent years TI has expanded its universe to include about 150 countries. TI assigns each country a score on the CPI ranging from 1 (grimy) to 10 (spotless). I use a three-year average of the annual ratings for 2005–2007.[5]

The other major source of data, produced by a team of economists, Daniel Kaufmann, Aart Kraay, and Massimo Mastruzzi, is called the "control of corruption" score. It is one of the six so-called "governance indicators" that the scholars generate in their "Governance Matters" research program.[6] The data cover nearly all of the world's countries and are based on myriad sources. Scores range from about –2.5 (most corrupt) to +2.5 (least corrupt). I recode the scores on a 0–100 scale to facilitate interpretation. I use a three-year average of the annual ratings for 2005–2007 and label it the "KKM score" (for its authors, Kaufmann, Kraay, and Mastruzzi).

Assessing the Link between Muslims and Corruption

We begin by examining corruption as measured by Transparency International's CPI. This is the dependent variable. Table 4.1 presents the average scores on the CPI for Muslim and non-Muslim countries, and table 4.2 shows the raw data for the largest Muslim and Christian countries. In table 4.2, as in subsequent tables that provide data for the largest Muslim and Christian countries, within each group the countries are listed in descending order according to population size. The Christian group runs from the United States, with 301 million inhabitants, to Peru, with 29 million. The Muslim group ranges from Indonesia, with a population of 235 million, to Tunisia, with a population of 10 million.[7]

From review of the numbers in these tables, one would surmise that corruption is more severe in predominantly Muslim countries. Table 4.1 shows that Muslim countries have a mean CPI of 3.2 and non-Muslim countries a mean of 4.4, meaning that Muslim countries on average are moderately more corrupt than non-Muslim countries.[8] Figure 4.1 illustrates the difference using boxplots.[9] As figure 4.1 shows, there is a large difference in the distributions of the CPI in Muslim and non-Muslim countries. In Muslim countries, scores range from less than 2 to about 6, with a median of 2.8, while non-Muslim countries have values ranging from less than 2 to about 10, with a median of 3.4. From the plot, we can also see that there is much more variation in the CPI among non-Muslim countries than among Muslim countries.

Table 4.1 Mean Scores on Corruption Perceptions for Muslim and Non-Muslim Countries

Survey Item	Muslim Countries	Non-Muslim Countries
Transparency International Corruption Perceptions Index (2005–2007 annual average)	3.2 (*N* = 35)	4.4 (*N* = 115)

Table 4.2 Data on Corruption Perceptions in the Largest Muslim and Christian Countries

Muslim Countries		Christian Countries	
Country	Corruption Perceptions Index (10 = cleanest; 1 = most corrupt)	Country	Corruption Perceptions Index (10 = cleanest; 1 = most corrupt)
Indonesia	2.3	United States	7.4
Pakistan	2.2	Brazil	3.5
Bangladesh	1.9	Russia	2.4
Egypt	3.2	Mexico	3.4
Turkey	3.8	Phillipines	2.5
Iran	2.7	Germany	8.0
Sudan	2.0	Dem Rep Congo	2.0
Morocco	3.3	France	7.4
Algeria	3.0	UK	8.5
Afghanistan	NA	Italy	5.0
Uzbekistan	2.0	Ukraine	2.7
Saudi Arabia	3.4	Colombia	3.9
Iraq	1.9	South Africa	4.7
Malaysia	5.1	Spain	6.8
Yemen	2.6	Argentina	2.9
Syria	2.9	Poland	3.8
Niger	2.4	Kenya	2.1
Senegal	3.4	Canada	8.5
Mali	2.8	Uganda	2.7
Tunisia	4.6	Peru	3.4
19-country average	2.9	19-country average	4.6

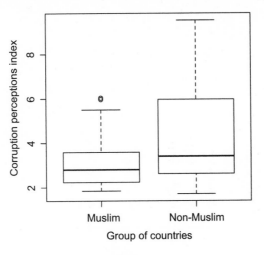

FIGURE 4.1:

Corruption Perceptions

In order to assess the possible link between Muslims and corruption, we must control for other variables that also might influence corruption. There are many hypotheses about what causes corruption. Here we will include those that have received the most attention in the literature.[10] They are socioeconomic development (measured here as Gross National Income [GNI] in the year 2000 and life expectancy in 2000), ethnic diversity, a legacy of Soviet-type communism, extent of economic dependence on hydrocarbons, a British colonial heritage, structure of government (decentralized versus unitary), and political regime (or level of democracy).[11]

In the regressions that follow and subsequent analyses, the proportion of the population made up of Muslims is the independent variable of interest. Data on this variable are drawn from the Association of Religion Data Archives (ARDA).[12] These regressions, like any statistical models using countries as the units of analysis, should be interpreted with caution. Countries constitute a finite population, not a random sample. In some instances, the independence of observations is questionable and heteroskedasticity (when the variance of the error terms differs across observations) presents a potential problem. While the data explored in this book do not meet all of the assumptions of OLS perfectly, regression analysis provides a first cut at understanding a complex set of relationships that cannot be uncovered in basic descriptive statistics.

Table 4.3 contains the output from several specifications of OLS regression models of the CPI on hypothesized predictors.[13] As can be seen in model 1, if no control variables are included in the models, the percentage of the population made up of Muslims in a country is statistically significantly associated with a lower corruption perceptions score. The relationship is not strong; the R^2 is less than .1, suggesting that the percentage of Muslims in a country explains less than 10 percent of the variation in the CPI.

Table 4.3 Regressions of Corruption Perceptions on Hypothesized Predictors

	Model 1	Model 2	Model 3	Model 4	Model 5	Model 6
(Intercept)	4.533*** (0.231)	1.968*** (0.487)	0.644 (0.832)	1.080 (0.707)	1.546** (0.533)	0.840 (0.644)
Percent Muslim	−0.017*** (0.004)	−0.003 (0.002)	0.004 (0.003)	−0.002 (0.003)	0.003 (0.002)	0.005[+] (0.003)
Income per capita		0.207*** (0.019)	0.185*** (0.024)	0.200*** (0.023)	0.186*** (0.021)	0.193*** (0.023)
Life expectancy		0.007 (0.009)	0.005 (0.012)	0.013 (0.013)	0.006 (0.009)	0.000 (0.010)
Ethnic diversity			−0.306 (0.500)		−0.328 (0.355)	
Post-communist country			−0.278 (0.198)	−0.403[+] (0.223)	−0.307[+] (0.181)	
Fuels dependence			−0.002 (0.003)		−0.005* (0.003)	−0.004 (0.003)
Former British colony			0.287 (0.242)		0.159 (0.201)	
Unitarism of state structure			0.114 (0.072)	0.148* (0.073)		0.089 (0.070)
Level of democracy			0.240** (0.087)		0.171* (0.066)	0.244** (0.092)
N	150	150	119	119	150	119
Adjusted R^2	.071	.810	.826	.812	.831	.825

Note: OLS models with robust standard errors in parentheses.

[+] significant at $p < .10$; *$p < .05$; **$p < .01$; ***$p < .001$.

Including the controls for socioeconomic development transforms the picture. The addition of the controls for socioeconomic development alone in model 2 boosts the portion of the variance explained to over 80 percent. Socioeconomic development is widely regarded as the greatest foe of corruption, and the findings support that idea. Higher income per capita is associated with a much better score on the CPI. When the controls for socioeconomic development are included, the coefficient for percentage Muslim shrinks and is not statistically significant. The other models, which include other predictors, raise the possibility that a legacy of Soviet-type rule may create conditions that exacerbate corruption and that fuels-dependent economies may be more prone to corruption. Greater unitarism of state structure is associated, in one model at a statistically significant level, with less corruption. Greater ethnic fractionalization, which is often seen as sowing conditions for corruption, and a heritage of British colonial rule, which is sometimes viewed as having fostered norms that encourage public probity, do not have statistically significant effects. More open polities (that is, those with higher levels of democracy) have lower levels of corruption. Income per capita and level of democracy are clearly the strongest predictors of cross-national variation in the CPI.

In none of the models that include controls is the coefficient for proportion of Muslims negative and statistically significant. In model 6, it is actually positive and statistically significant, albeit not at a highly demanding level. The analysis suggests that corruption very likely has little to do with religion and everything to do with socioeconomic development and, perhaps secondarily, political openness.

The power of wealth is obvious even in the raw numbers in table 4.2. Malaysia and Tunisia, two of the most highly developed Muslim countries, have respectable scores on the CPI. In Christendom, the affluent nations of North America and Western Europe generally have very favorable scores. Wealth does not necessarily buy public integrity. Among Muslim countries, fortunate Saudi Arabia posts a mediocre score. Among Christian countries, Russia's fairly high level of development does not save it from abysmal corruption. But these are exceptions. Money might not buy everything, but it does buy a fighting chance at lower corruption. The statistical analyses, moreover, suggest that Muslim countries on average have lower scores on the CPI because they are poorer, not because they are Muslim.

Let us repeat the analysis using the Kaufmann, Kraay, and Mastruzzi (KKM) score to measure corruption. Like when we use the CPI, when we use the KKM control of corruption score Muslim countries have less favorable ratings when we look only at the country averages, which are presented in table 4.4 and illustrated in figure 4.2.[14] The raw data for the largest Muslim and Christian countries, presented in table 4.5, reinforce the impression of high corruption among Muslims.

Table 4.4 Mean Scores on Control of Corruption for Muslim and Non-Muslim Countries

Survey Item	Muslim Countries	Non-Muslim Countries
Kaufmann, Kraay, and Mastruzzi Control of Corruption Score (2005–2007 annual average)	41.4 ($N = 44$)	51.7 ($N = 128$)

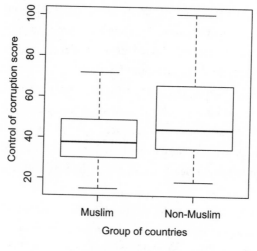

FIGURE 4.2:
Control of Corruption

When we include controls for the other variables that might also affect corruption, the picture changes. Table 4.6 presents the numbers. Income per capita is the strongest predictor of the control of corruption measure. Once this variable is included in the model the coefficient for percentage Muslim goes to almost zero and is no longer statistically significant, as is evident in model 2. And as in the above analyses, the amount of variance explained (shown in the R^2) is very large when we add the controls for development. Richer countries are predictably less corrupt. The other variable that is consistently associated with the control of corruption score is political openness; democracy may help control malfeasance.

Of greatest interest is the effect of the variable for percentage Muslim. Here we have an interesting finding: A higher percentage of Muslims is associated with lower corruption at a statistically significant level in some of the models. Specifically, when we control for level of democracy as well as socioeconomic development (in models 3, 5, and 6), a higher proportion of Muslims in a country is associated with a lower level of corruption and the relationship is statistically significant. In these models, the coefficient for percentage Muslim is statistically significant and positive, though it is not large. This finding suggests that Muslims do reasonably well on control of corruption *for their countries' levels of development and democracy.*[15] We return to the question of democracy in chapter 7.

Table 4.5 Data on Control of Corruption in the Largest Muslim and Christian Countries

Muslim Countries		Christian Countries	
Country	Control of Corruption Score (100 = cleanest; 0 = most corrupt)	Country	Control of Corruption Score (100 = cleanest; 0 = most corrupt)
Indonesia	34.3	United States	78.7
Pakistan	31.4	Brazil	44.3
Bangladesh	26.2	Russia	33.6
Egypt	40.5	Mexico	42.7
Turkey	50.3	Philippines	36.2
Iran	39.0	Germany	86.7
Sudan	24.9	Dem Rep Congo	22.6
Morocco	47.3	France	77.7
Algeria	41.5	UK	87.9
Afghanistan	20.1	Italy	57.8
Uzbekistan	29.1	Ukraine	36.5
Saudi Arabia	52.1	Colombia	45.2
Iraq	22.7	South Africa	59.6
Malaysia	55.5	Spain	74.5
Yemen	37.6	Argentina	41.1
Syria	35.9	Poland	53.0
Niger	32.1	Kenya	30.6
Senegal	42.1	Canada	89.4
Mali	41.0	Uganda	34.4
Tunisia	52.1	Peru	41.9
20-country average	37.8	20-country average	53.8

Summary

By far the most important determinant of cross-national variation in corruption is wealth. Bertrand Russell's injunction that "nothing improves the moral level of a community as much as an increase of wealth, and nothing lowers it so much as a diminution of wealth" is on target.[16] Generally speaking, when people feel less need to steal in order to get by in life, they steal less. Norms that encourage fair play and honest transactions, and institutions needed to enforce rules against fraudulent behavior, find richer soil for growth in richer societies. Other variables might matter as well. Democracy may promote probity.

Table 4.6 Regressions of Control of Corruption on Hypothesized Predictors

	Model 1	Model 2	Model 3	Model 4	Model 5	Model 6
(Intercept)	52.235*** (2.041)	24.921*** (5.139)	8.172 (8.025)	17.415* (7.629)	16.930** (5.820)	11.383[+] (6.002)
Percent Muslim	−0.161*** (0.034)	−0.036[+] (0.020)	0.066* (0.026)	−0.025 (0.026)	0.039[+] (0.022)	0.070** (0.025)
Income per capita		1.831*** (0.165)	1.594*** (0.199)	1.761*** (0.197)	1.579*** (0.175)	1.640*** (0.190)
Life expectancy		0.146 (0.089)	0.093 (0.120)	0.199 (0.126)	0.119 (0.098)	0.046 (0.100)
Ethnic diversity			−0.188 (4.701)		−1.101 (3.272)	
Post-communist country			−1.831 (1.593)	−3.129 (2.019)	−2.985[+] (1.531)	
Fuels dependence			−0.036 (0.034)		−0.048[+] (0.028)	−0.040 (0.031)
Former British colony			1.625 (2.147)		0.633 (1.766)	
Unitarism of state structure			0.856 (0.636)	1.219[+] (0.704)		
Level of democracy			3.477*** (0.790)		2.601*** (0.671)	0.678 (0.609)
N	172	172	124	124	171	3.500*** (0.811)
Adjusted R^2	.077	.767	.832	.795	.807	124
						.834

Note: OLS models with robust standard errors in parentheses.

[+]significant at $p < .10$; *$p < .05$; **$p < .01$; ***$p < .001$.

But there is little substantial evidence of a link between Muslims and corruption. In separate analyses that alternately use Transparency International's CPI and the KKM control of corruption score, we see no evidence of a consistent, robust relationship between the religious composition of societies and level of corruption. When the latter indicator is used, in some statistical models the percentage of Muslims is positively associated with controlling corruption. The relationship is not adequately strong or consistent for us to conclude that Muslims are unusually skilled at controlling fraud, though the intriguing positive relationship found in some models may merit the attention of scholars who study the correlates of corruption. While the positive results are insufficiently clear to enable us to declare that Muslims are better at controlling corruption, we can be more confident of the negative results, which are that Muslims are not unusually prone to corruption.

CRIME

So far we have investigated corruption, a nebulous phenomenon that is difficult to observe and that is measured using data from expert surveys. Let us now turn to real, measurable illicit acts and see how, if at all, Muslims differ.

Hypotheses on Muslims and Crime

First, we may hypothesize that Muslims are more prone to violent crime. Such a perception is not uncommon in non-Muslim countries, including those with substantial Muslim minorities. The recent experiences of a single European country, the Netherlands, show why. Over the course of a short interval in the early 2000s, Theo Van Gogh was slain by Islamists who were offended by the Dutch filmmaker's work, Pim Fortuyn was murdered by an assassin who disliked the politician's opposition to militant Islam, and the Somali-Dutch feminist politician Ayaan Hirsi Ali was hounded into exile under threats of death from Dutch Muslims. These events made headlines around the world. They created, or reinforced, a feeling in the West that Muslims are unusually cavalier in their treatment of human life. Whether such tendencies arise from a prickly sense of honor, scriptural injunctions that appear to justify the murder of religion's enemies, or some other factor, one might expect violent crime to be especially severe among Muslims.

The counterhypothesis is that Muslims are less crime-prone. The previous chapter presented evidence that Muslims may hold stricter-than-average views on some moral matters. In the previous section of the present chapter, moreover, we found some evidence that the percentage of Muslims in a country may be associated, albeit only slightly, with lower corruption. Given these findings, one might expect crime to be lower in Muslim societies. Perhaps there is something about the moral community of Islam or Islam's sacred texts that controls crime.

Measuring Crime

Here we will focus on a single type of crime: murder. For several reasons, this act is a good candidate for investigation. It is the "biggest" crime of all; examining it lends insight into the most acute form of criminal violence. Furthermore, murder universally meets with high opprobrium. While the intensity of feeling across cultures regarding the seriousness of this or that crime against property, morals, or political authority may vary, murder is regarded with great—and, according to some evidence, equally great—revulsion.[17] Additionally, the data on homicide are better and more plentiful than what are available on other criminal acts.[18] Information on assault and property crimes is plentiful for the advanced industrialized countries, but mediocre and sparse for many other countries. Rape is grossly underreported everywhere but is probably even more underreported in societies at lower levels of socioeconomic development. Many developing countries do not even have agencies capable of collecting and publicizing reliable statistics on most crimes. But in most societies, murder is the one crime that is adequately grave that it normally is reported and recorded. Even when a person of inferior social status is murdered, the act typically causes serious loss to someone more powerful—be he (or she) a father, a husband, or an employer.

Here we measure murder rates in typical fashion, as the number of intentional homicides annually per 100,000 people. Most of our data are for an available year in the first half of the first decade of the 2000s.[19]

Assessing the Link between Muslims and Homicide Rates

Homicide rates are our dependent variable and, as always, we seek to uncover the possible effects of adherence to Islam on the dependent variable. Table 4.7 shows the average rates of homicide in Muslim and non-Muslim countries, and table 4.8 presents the numbers for the largest Muslim and Christian countries.

The differences are dramatic. Muslim societies have a much less severe problem with murder than do non-Muslim societies. The difference in averages shown in table 4.7 is stark. The average number of intentional homicides in the Muslim world is 2.4 per 100,000 people per year, while it is 7.5 per 100,000 people per year in non-Muslim countries.[20] And looking at the big countries in table 4.8, we see that the

Table 4.7 Mean Scores on Murder Rates for Muslim and Non-Muslim Countries

Survey Item	Muslim Countries	Non-Muslim Countries
Intentional homicides per 100,000 people	2.4 $(N = 39)$	7.5 $(N = 112)$

Table 4.8 Data on Murder Rates in the Largest Muslim and Christian Countries

Muslim Countries		*Christian Countries*	
Country	*Intentional homicides per 100,000 people*	*Country*	*Intentional homicides per 100,000 people*
Indonesia	1.1	United States	5.6
Pakistan	6.9	Brazil	11.2
Bangladesh	2.8	Russia	19.9
Egypt	0.4	Mexico	13.0
Turkey	3.8	Philippines	4.3
Iran	2.9	Germany	1.0
Sudan	0.3	Dem Rep Congo	NA
Morocco	0.5	France	1.6
Algeria	1.4	UK	2.1
Afghanistan	NA	Italy	1.2
Uzbekistan	3.2	Ukraine	7.4
Saudi Arabia	0.9	Colombia	62.7
Iraq	5.8	South Africa	47.5
Malaysia	2.4	Spain	1.2
Yemen	4.0	Argentina	9.5
Syria	1.1	Poland	1.6
Niger	0.9	Kenya	4.5
Senegal	0.3	Canada	1.9
Mali	0.7	Uganda	7.4
Tunisia	1.2	Peru	5.5
19-country average	2.1	19-country average	11.0

worst murder rate in the Muslim group is far lower than the average rate in the Christian group.

This difference between Muslim and non-Muslim countries is illustrated in figure 4.3. The distribution of murder rates in Muslim countries ranges from about just over 0 to 10 with a median of 1.3, while in the non-Muslim world the figures range from just over 0 to more than 60, with a median of about 3.5. Clearly, there are also several major outliers among the non-Muslim countries.

In order to see whether these differences might have something to do with religious adherence, we need to control for other factors that may affect cross-national variation in homicide rates.[21] Socioeconomic development is widely regarded as a potentially important factor, and as usual we control for it using income per capita and life expectancy. Development may cut either way, however. Higher development

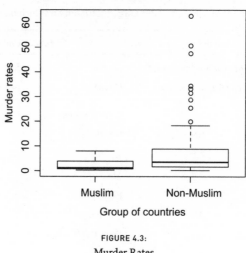

FIGURE 4.3:
Murder Rates

may create more favorable life conditions and thereby reduce the social stress and friction that may breed violent crime. On the other hand, the rigid, confining social hierarchies associated with traditional, less developed societies may check violent crime. Ethnic fractionalization might also contribute to violent crime. Higher heterogeneity may spell less social cohesion and a higher risk of murder. We measure ethnic fractionalization as above. Socioeconomic inequality may also have an effect. Societies where inequalities are greater might have higher murder rates. Cross-class resentments and suspicions and high levels of severe deprivation among the poor may be more acute in more unequal societies and may increase the incidence of murder. Socioeconomic inequalities are measured using the Gini score, which runs from 1 to 100. Higher Gini scores indicate more severe inequalities in income. Finally, the openness of the political system may affect crime rates. Particularly in the wake of the failure of many new democracies to guarantee elementary protections against criminal violence, there is a widespread perception in the world that authoritarian regimes are better than democracies at containing criminal violence. Democracy may have its benefits, but in the minds of many people safer streets is not one of them. Democracies are often seen as softer on violations of all types, and therefore less prone to create strong disincentives (meaning the threat of harsh and certain punishments) for crime. An undesirable side effect of more freedom for all may be more freedom for evildoers and freer rein for people's violent impulses. We measure level of democracy using Freedom House ratings.[22]

While the factors controlled for here cover a broad range of the most important hypothesized determinants of homicide rates, it is impossible to control for all possible determinants. The reason is shortage of data. Scholars who study homicide in the United States have examined the effects of race, family dynamics, and fluctuations in wages, among other factors.[23] While these variables may be important, they are difficult to measure and compare cross-nationally. Some of the factors that have been examined in other cross-national studies must also be left out of the present analysis for lack of data that are comparable in a global contest. For example, Ineke Marshall and Carolyn Block have found a significant correlation between the proportion of young men who are dissatisfied with their income and homicide.[24] It is possible that this factor affects homicide rates. But reliable, comparable data are not available for most of the world. Marshall and Block's study, while helpful for studying homicide's causes in advanced industrialized countries, excludes most of Asia, Africa, and Latin America. In order to make inferences about the possible correlation between Muslims and homicide rates, we must rely on variables for which data are more widely available, which requires sticking with the factors discussed in the previous paragraph.

Table 4.9 presents the output from running negative binomial models of murder rates on hypothesized predictors. These models are used instead of OLS models because the data on homicide are not normally distributed. Negative binomial analysis is commonly used to estimate count models where many cases have very low scores on the dependent variable. We also conducted the analyses using standard OLS models, and the results were very similar to those obtained in the negative binomial models. The findings are presented in appendix 4.[25]

Of greatest importance for our purposes is that the coefficient for percentage of Muslims in a country is negative and highly statistically significant in all the models. Income per capita is negatively associated with murder rates (richer countries have lower murder rates), and income inequality is positively correlated with murder rates (countries with greater socioeconomic inequality have higher murder rates). Neither ethnic diversity nor level of political openness is associated with homicide rates at a statistically significant level.

As figure 4.3 showed, there were some obvious outliers with extraordinarily high murder rates among the non-Muslim countries. To test whether these outliers drive the results, we reran all the models excluding the countries with a murder rate higher than 22.7, which marks the 95th percentile. The alternative models therefore exclude eight countries: Colombia, El Salvador, Guatemala, Honduras, Jamaica, Lesotho, South Africa and Venezuela. Table 4.10 shows the output for the models excluding these outliers. The findings are very similar to those shown in table 4.9, although the size of the coefficients for percentage Muslim is moderately reduced. They are still statistically and substantively significant. In the models excluding the outliers, the coefficients for income inequality are statistically significant at a lower level than in the models shown in table 4.9, perhaps because the excluded cases have very high levels of both income inequality and homicide.

The coefficients of negative binomial models do not lend themselves to straightforward interpretation. Thus, in order better to grasp the substantive implications of the findings, we may rely on graphic depiction of predicted murder rates. Figure 4.4

Table 4.9 Regressions of Murder Rates on Hypothesized Predictors

	Model 1	Model 2	Model 3	Model 4	Model 5
(Intercept)	2.095*** (0.139)	1.942* (0.789)	-0.764 (0.747)	-0.778 (0.689)	1.766[†] (0.923)
Percent Muslim	-0.015*** (0.003)	-0.018*** (0.003)	-0.013*** (0.003)	-0.012*** (0.002)	-0.018*** (0.003)
Income *per capita*		-0.077*** (0.016)	-0.057*** (0.013)	-0.063*** (0.014)	-0.077*** (0.014)
Life expectancy		0.012 (0.013)	0.025* (0.011)	0.021* (0.009)	0.013 (0.016)
Ethnic diversity			0.202 (0.432)		0.211 (0.535)
Income inequality			0.044*** (0.011)	0.044*** (0.011)	
Level of democracy			-0.069 (0.084)		-0.003 (0.083)
N	151	151	132	132	150
AIC	849.300	814.274	720.404	717.611	814.977
BIC	873.438	862.550	801.122	775.267	887.232
log L	-416.650	-391.137	-332.202	-338.805	-383.488

Note: Negative binomial models with robust standard errors in parentheses.

[†]significant at $p < .10$; *$p < .05$; **$p < .01$; ***$p < .001$.

Table 4.10 Regressions of Murder Rates on Hypothesized Predictors Excluding Outliers

	Model 1	Model 2	Model 3	Model 4	Model 5
(Intercept)	1.671*** (0.094)	1.273** (0.405)	0.618 (0.681)	0.694 (0.560)	1.237* (0.614)
Percent Muslim	−0.009*** (0.002)	−0.013*** (0.002)	−0.013*** (0.002)	−0.011*** (0.002)	−0.014*** (0.003)
Income per capita		−0.065*** (0.012)	−0.052*** (0.013)	−0.060*** (0.013)	−0.063*** (0.012)
Life expectancy		0.015* (0.007)	0.022** (0.008)	0.015* (0.007)	0.018* (0.008)
Ethnic diversity			0.273 (0.365)		0.100 (0.343)
Income inequality			0.013+ (0.008)	0.013+ (0.008)	
Level of democracy			−0.113 (0.072)		−0.039 (0.060)
N	143	143	124	124	142
AIC	715.310	683.695	610.041	609.459	684.375
BIC	739.013	731.100	689.009	665.865	755.315
log L	−349.655	−325.847	−277.021	−284.730	−318.188

Note: Negative binomial models with robust standard errors in parentheses.

+significant at $p < .10$; *$p < .05$; **$p < .01$; ***$p < .001$.

provides an illustration of the predicted murder rate in countries with various percentages of Muslims. The two graphs are based on model 3 in table 4.9 and model 3 in table 4.10, respectively. These are the fully specified models (that is, those that include all the independent variables). The predictions are based on holding all the control variables in the models constant at their mean. Using all the available data, the predicted murder rate in a country with no Muslims is about 7 per 100,000 per year, while the predicted murder rate in a country that is all Muslims is 2 per 100,000 per year. The right-hand graph in figure 4.4 shows the predicted values when the outliers in the data are excluded. Here the predicted murder rate in a country with no Muslims is about 5.5 and in a country that is all Muslims is about 2. Even when all the major outliers are excluded from the data, countries with proportionally more Muslims have less homicide.

The findings are consistent with those of Jerome Neapolitan, who also finds a negative relationship between percentage Muslim and murder rates in his cross-national study.[26] They are inconsistent with the findings of Byron Groves, Graeme Newman, and Charles Corrado, who found that when economic development is controlled for, Muslim countries do not differ significantly in homicide rates.[27] There are several possible reasons for the disparity in findings. First, Groves, Newman, and Corrado control for socioeconomic development alone; they do not include the other controls I include here. Second, their data are older than those I use; their numbers are from the early 1970s, while those I use here are for two to three decades later. Third, they analyze just 47 countries; I have the benefit of a larger sample.

Why are Homicide Rates Lower among Muslims?

The analysis allows us, at least tentatively, to rule out as well as rule in some possible links between Muslims and homicide rates. First, the findings suggest that Muslims are not less prone to homicide because they are poorer; lower levels of income are actually associated with higher murder rates, as shown by the negative coefficient for income per capita in the regressions. Second, Muslims are not less prone to homicide because they live in more authoritarian polities, where, at least according to urban legend, punishment for crime is more harsh and swift and the bad guys have more to fear from the authorities. I controlled for level of democracy in the analyses and it is not a good predictor of homicide rates. Even if Muslims disproportionately live in more authoritarian polities (a matter we will take up in chapter 7), murder rates among Muslims are not lower for that reason.

But the analysis also suggests the need to rule in a possible explanation for the favorable effect of Islam on homicide. Income inequality is a statistically significant predictor of homicide rates, and higher inequality is associated with more murder. It is possible that part of what is good about Islam for controlling violence is that lower

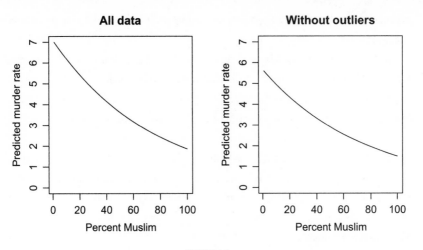

FIGURE 4.4:
Predicted Murder Rates

levels of socioeconomic inequality prevail among Muslims. Islam is negatively associated with homicide at a statistically and substantively significant level even when
we control for income inequality. But part of what is good about large Muslim populations for controlling homicide might be the prevalence of less acute socioeconomic inequalities in Muslim societies. Whether income inequality is really lower
among Muslims, and if so, how much lower, is a topic we will return to in chapter 6.

What other factors might account for the difference? Sacred text alone probably
provides little explanation. In the scriptures of most major world religions, murder
is depicted as the gravest of transgressions. One may plumb the Qur'an and the
Hadith of Islam, as well as the Bible and the writings of the early church fathers of
Christianity, and search for differences in the gravity with which murder is treated.
I have done so, and if there are major differences, they are too subtle for my blunt
mind to discern. Both the Islamic and Christian scriptures unequivocally and
repeatedly condemn murder as a heinous act, and both condemn it ferociously. We
probably need to look elsewhere for explanations for the strikingly low rates of
homicide among Muslims.

Cross-national studies of homicide are not plentiful; most studies focus on a
single country. In the few cross-national studies that are available, however, a
number of variables have been shown to have some predictive power. Generally
speaking, something like what might be called cultural integration emerges as a
leading explanation. Cultural integration is distinct from ethnic homogeneity,
which does not perform well as a predictor of homicide rates in my analysis or in
most other studies. Rather, it is integration in Émile Durkheim's sense, meaning
norms of behavior and styles of life that are well adjusted to those of one's fellows,
that appears to be important. According to Durkheim, individuals' alienation from
the community, which he called "anomie," causes a plethora of social ills. The key to

promoting a well-functioning society, according to Durkheim, is reducing people's sense of anomie.[28]

Some contemporary social scientists have applied Durkheim's ideas to contemporary problems of violent crime. Most notably, Freda Adler found that "synnomie"—the opposite of Durkheim's "anomie"—played a special role in controlling crime. She conceived of synnomie as robust informal institutions of social control that embody and transmit shared values among the population.[29]

Adler, like Durkheim, relied on data drawn from a small set of countries and did not test her hypotheses using statistical analyses. But Durkheim's and Adler's ideas resonate among students of cross-cultural variation in crime. These scholars include those whose work does not include consideration of a religious or specifically Muslim dimension as a causal variable.[30]

The few scholars who do consider religious causes also arrive at conclusions that align with Durkheim's and Adler's theories. Several authors have found a negative correlation between Muslims and violent crime and have offered explanations that are consistent with the cultural integration thesis. Neapolitan holds that traditional cultural norms and values in Muslim societies are to credit for lower crime rates. He argues, "Islamic nations tend to have low crime rates because they have a great emphasis on tradition and shared values, creating a sense of community and informal social controls." He attributes integration and the persistence of traditional values to what he sees as Muslim societies' lesser degree of penetration by the cultures of colonial powers. He holds that Islam predated European colonialism in many areas of the world and provided more continuity in cultural norms and values than where Christianity supplanted indigenous culture and religion. Drawing on Adler's theory of synnomie, Neapolitan concludes, "Christianity in developing nations is an indicator of past conquest, colonization, and violence that resulted in cultural changes conducive to violence. A significant negative association was found between percentage Muslim in nations and homicides. I suggest that this has to do with the cultural integration and traditional values in these nations."[31] Other scholars have also held that Islam promotes sociocultural practices and structures that are, in some senses, synnomie-producing. Adel Helal and Charisse Coston arrive at such a conclusion in their investigation of low crime rates in Bahrain.[32]

What, then, are the possible sources of the synnomie that Islam might foster? One is historical continuity of tradition; this is the argument that Neapolitan offers. Other writers have located other sources. In a bold and intriguing argument, Sam Souryal claims that the application of *sharia* law is to credit. Souryal sets up a seven-country comparison of Saudi Arabia and six other Arab countries. He finds that murder rates are lower in Saudi Arabia, which applies *sharia* code for criminal offenses, than in the other countries, none of which do.[33]

Souryal's findings are consistent with those of the defenders of *sharia* law in Muslim countries, who tout what they regard as the deterrent affect of corporal and mutilating punishments.[34] How much hard evidence do we actually have of such a dynamic?

Souryal himself stops short of claiming that fear of the harsh prescriptions of *sharia* criminal law per se deters crime. Rather, relying on Marcus Felson's theory of social control in tightly knit communities, in which anonymity is difficult and mechanisms for controlling individuals' behavior abound, Souryal states that "the spiritual community established around Shariah law neatly fits Felson's model of a 'tight community.' Members of the extended family serve as primary intimate handlers. The *Sheik* (clergyman) at the mosque keeps tabs on those who fail to appear for prayer and informs family elders." Furthermore, according to Souryal, "Saudi adolescents are virtually in groups at all times, and older men, by virtue of their mandate of piety, can always call their attention to religious duties and communal obligations."[35] Souryal identifies *sharia* law as the means by which faith deters deviant behavior.

Souryal may be on to something important, but his attribution of causal force to *sharia* law as such is tenuous. The close conformity to social norms imposed by the proximity of elders that he finds so pronounced in Saudi Arabia characterizes life in many traditional societies in which *sharia* is not imposed. Indeed, although murder rates are astronomical in South Africa, in many other countries in sub-Saharan Africa, including some of those listed in table 4.8, they are very low. They are also extremely low (0.5 per 100,000) in Japan, which is renowned for group intimacy and informal social control. Senegal, Mali, and Niger are Muslim countries, but they do not apply *sharia* in criminal law, so their low murder rates cannot be attributable to it. Japan, of course, is not a Muslim country. What is common to these societies is the persistence of a high degree of social proximity and mutual restraint among their members, not the presence of *sharia* criminal law.

It is difficult rigorously to test Souryal's hypothesis, since so few countries have consistently applied traditional *sharia* criminal code. Souryal's evidence, while suggestive, is not based on a design that can bear strong conclusions. His universe is limited to eight cases, and he does not control for variables besides *sharia* that might influence murder rates. The evidence from the cases we have, moreover, does not support the *sharia* hypothesis. As Rudolph Peters shows, among major Muslim countries, in addition to Saudi Arabia, only Iran, Pakistan, and Sudan have adopted *sharia* regulations in criminal law in recent decades, and only in Iran have these rules been enacted and consistently applied over a substantial period.[36] As we see in table 4.8, murder rates in Iran and Pakistan are actually higher than average for Muslim countries, so we find little evidence here that the imposition of *sharia* criminal codes has produced unusually low murder rates, though rates are low in Sudan.

The most apt inference we can draw is the summary that Seyed Hossein Serajzadeh offers after reviewing crime rates in two-dozen countries and weighing the influence of *sharia* sanctions. According to Serajzadeh, "If Islamic penal law—as part of *Shari'a*—has had a real prohibitive effect on crime, it is not simply because it is applied as formal penal law. It is mainly because the complex of religious ideas to which it belongs has had a great influence on the mentality of Muslims." Serajzadeh asserts that "regardless of whether the official penal law is based on *Shari'a* or not, public opinion in Muslim countries can be expected to be stricter towards crime, particularly toward those offenses named in the penal law of Islam that are considered to have an especially devastating effect on the moral health of the society." In short, "Islamic penal law has had its prohibitive effect on crime as a normative system respected by Muslims, and not just as a penal law that threatens offenders."[37]

Given the shortage of direct, compelling evidence on the influence of *sharia* per se on murder rates, this is probably the strongest statement that can be made about the effect of *sharia*. In fact, as Serajzadeh suggests, it is not the law itself but rather the "normative system" that it is embedded in which might have some deterrent effect. This conclusion brings us back to the cultural integration theory pioneered by Durkheim and Adler and applied by several of the scholars of the Muslim world discussed above. Muslim societies, on average, may enjoy higher degrees of cultural or social integration. Whether Neapolitan's explanation, which attributes Islam's advantages in integration to global patterns of colonial history, is sound or not must be left to question here, though it undoubtedly provides a plausible hypothesis.

That a higher degree of social integration may check homicide is broadly consistent with our finding that lower socioeconomic inequalities are correlated with lower murder rates. Whether high social integration limits the growth of socioeconomic inequalities and whether lower inequalities promote higher social integration cannot be addressed here, but logically it is not difficult to see an elective affinity between these conditions. As Robert Putnam concludes, based on a cross-state and cross-regional empirical study of the United States, "Inequality and social solidarity are deeply incompatible."[38] We will return to the matter of inequality, and specifically whether it is lower in Muslim lands than elsewhere, in chapter 6.

Summary

In this section we have investigated whether Muslims are distinctive in terms of murder rates. Homicide is markedly rarer in Muslim societies than non-Muslim societies. The proportion of the country that is made up of Muslims is a good predictor of the murder rate, with a larger Muslim population associated with less homicide. This relationship holds when we control for other potentially important determinants of homicide.

Accounting for why murder rates are lower among Muslims is difficult. Several plausible explanations do not stand up to empirical scrutiny. Muslims are not less murder-prone because they are poorer than average, since poverty is associated with higher, not lower, murder rates. Homicide is not rarer among Muslims because Muslims tend to live under more authoritarian political regimes, since authoritarianism is not correlated with lower murder rates. The possibility that the application of *sharia* law in criminal code reduces murder cannot be ruled out, but neither do we have good evidence to support this proposition. We did find evidence that a higher level of socioeconomic inequality may be linked to higher homicide rates. We must consider whether Muslim countries have lower levels of socioeconomic inequality, which we will do in chapter 6. In general, the evidence seems to point to the possibility that the "anomie" that Durkheim regarded as the foe of a well-functioning society, and that some contemporary scholars have considered a contributor to violent crime, might be lower in Muslim societies. Here we do not have hard data but must rely upon admittedly indirect inferences drawn from our findings and opinion among other scholars who have investigated this issue.

This chapter has examined two important aspects of social order, corruption and crime. Both of these problems are important; but neither is political. In the next chapter, we move to investigation of specifically political violence.

5 Large-Scale Political Violence and Terrorism

Few matters in contemporary world politics command more interest than the relationship between Islam and political violence. Are Muslims especially prone to political violence? Office conversation among elites in Kuala Lumpur, Washington, Paris, Delhi, Beijing, and Ankara—as well as kitchen-table talk in Johor Bahru, Kansas City, Marseille, Bangalore, Kunming, and Istanbul—swirls around the issue. Discussion fills airwaves and newspapers, not to mention blogs and electronic correspondence, even as many people hesitate to confront the issue directly.

But the headlines and the polemics—not to mention the fears, accusations, insinuations, and denials—are shrouded in a cloud of unknowing. The task of actually testing whether a relationship between Islam and political violence really exists has hardly been touched. The question of whether Muslims are more prone than non-Muslims to political violence percolates in public and private discussions the world over, but few studies adduce empirical evidence based on tests of theoretically grounded hypotheses.

The weighty question at hand cannot be resolved here. But it is possible to remove it from the arena of polemics and punditry for a moment, treat it as a hypothesis, marshal the available data, see what the data tell us, and try to make sense of the findings.

Hypotheses on Muslims and Large-Scale Political Violence

Over 250 years ago, in his celebrated *Spirit of the Laws*, Montesquieu put forward a thesis that is still widely held in the West. According to Montesquieu, "The gentleness so recommended in the gospel stands opposed to the despotic fury with which a prince would mete out his own justice and exercise his cruelties. . . . The Mohammedan religion, which speaks only with a sword, continues to act on men with the destructive spirit that founded it."[1] Some contemporary authors still regard Montesquieu's assessment as sound.[2] In the most globally influential work of social science of the late twentieth century, *The Clash of Civilizations and the Remaking of World Order*, Samuel Huntington asserts that Muslim societies are especially prone to large-scale political violence. Huntington discusses both "intercivilizational" and "intracivilizational" violence. By the former, he means conflict between Muslim and non-Muslim countries; by the latter, he means conflict within countries. Huntington sees both kinds of strife as especially acute among Muslims. He not only asserts that "Islam's borders are bloody," but adds "and so are its innards."[3]

Its innards are what concern us here. Armed conflict between Muslim and non-Muslim countries lies outside our purview and is best left to specialists in international relations. Here we will stick with assessment of whether the internal politics of predominantly Muslim countries are unusually bloody.

The notion that Islam is conducive to mass political violence is based on a claim about the way Muslims understand jihad, or holy struggle. Jihad has multiple meanings and manifestations. Recent scholarly works have provided sophisticated and useful treatment of the concept.[4] One meaning of jihad is spiritual and refers to the individual's struggle for self-improvement. Another meaning of jihad is armed struggle against the perceived enemies of Islam. Some people, Muslims and non-Muslims alike, read passages of the Qur'an as condoning violence against the enemies of Islam. Many contemporary observers regard the notion of violent jihad as very much alive among contemporary Muslims. Holy war is not, of course, foreign to Christianity, whose Crusader armies struggled mightily (if unsuccessfully) to recover the Holy Land during the eleventh and twelfth centuries. Nor is it alien to other religious traditions. But neither contemporary Christianity nor any other modern major world religion has a concept of jihad—at least not one that is as central to its doctrine as jihad is to Islam. If some modern Muslims take to heart what they perceive as permission—even a prescription—to commit violence, one might expect large-scale political violence to be especially high among Muslims. The religion's perceived enemies may include non-Muslims, Muslims who collaborate with non-Muslims, Muslims who are viewed as lacking in piety, or Muslims who are seen as enforcing a political order that harms the faith. If the concept of jihad has sharp teeth, we might expect large-scale political violence to be greater in societies with larger Muslim populations.

The counterhypothesis is that Islam may help inoculate societies against large-scale political violence. Some writers claim that the vast majority of Muslims properly understand jihad in nonviolent terms, and that the prevalence of the idea among Muslims is no spur to violence.[5] It may even promote personal discipline and social solidarity in a manner that reduces the risk of large-scale violence. Evidence presented in the previous chapter showed that murder rates are lower where Muslims are more numerous. We conjectured that a relatively high degree of cultural integration among Muslims might be to credit. The same factors that maintain low murder rates may also promote lower levels of political violence. Perhaps the social "synnomie" about which Freda Adler wrote, and which some scholars find in abundance in Muslim societies, reduces the risk of mass political violence as well as personal crime.

These hypotheses may guide our inquiry, but there is no extensive body of literature that actually tests them. Despite immense interest in Islam and violence around the world, there have been surprisingly few efforts to assess empirically whether Muslims are especially prone to mass political violence. Assertions and commentary abound, but empirical tests are virtually nonexistent. The findings offered below may provide a starting point for bringing evidence to bear on questions that are of great significance and public interest.

Measuring Large-Scale Political Violence

There are several sources of data on large-scale political violence in the world. The compilation authored and regularly updated by Monty Marshall stands out for its comprehensiveness and quality. I draw on it here. Marshall's "Major Episodes of Political Violence" data set provides a complete list of events in the postwar period that produced 500 or more deaths. The most recently updated version, as of this writing, covers the period from 1946 to early 2007, and I rely on this version here.[6]

According to Marshall, during the period under consideration, there were 326 episodes of large-scale political violence. Some of these events were international (or interstate) in character; others were domestic. I am concerned with domestic (meaning intrastate) conflict. I exclude international conflicts, which include independence struggles against foreign (often colonial) domination. Marshall helpfully includes his own coding of types of conflict, which facilitates the task of distinguishing between interstate and intrastate violence.

Most episodes—by my count, 235—were domestic (intrastate) in nature. This is the universe we will examine here. A complete list of these episodes, including the relevant data about them used in this chapter, is found in appendix 5.A. As this list shows, the episodes include protracted civil wars, relatively short-lived rebellions, cases of large-scale repression by governments, and instances of interethnic conflict.

From this list we may extract several valuable pieces of data. One is how many episodes occurred in Muslim countries and how many took place elsewhere. These numbers provide only a starting point, however. The severity of the episodes varies widely, and we need to consider the toll each episode took in terms of human life. Marshall provides estimates on the number of deaths that each episode produced. His figures are necessarily rough and round, since we lack precise body counts for many major civil conflagrations.

Assessing the Link between Muslims and Large-Scale Political Violence

How much mass political violence has occurred among Muslims and how much among people of other creeds? First, let us have a look at the raw numbers.

We may start with a rudimentary classification of the world's countries and examination of the distribution of conflicts. Of the 171 countries in the world with populations of one-quarter million or more inhabitants, 43 (25 percent) are predominantly Muslim.[7] Now, of the 235 major episodes of intrastate political violence, 76 (32 percent) happened in Muslim countries. Thus, Muslim countries have experienced a mildly disproportionate share of episodes.

We can cut into the data more deeply by looking at lives lost. If we sum up the body count in all 235 major episodes of political violence, the (sobering and stunning) statistic is 21,011,400. Of these, 5,586,150 people, or 27 percent of the total, perished in Muslim countries. So 27 percent of the loss of life in major episodes of political violence occurred in the 25 percent of the world's countries that are predominantly Muslim. In order to produce figures on deaths that are comparable across countries and useful for comparative analysis, we need to take the size of countries' populations into account. Thus, I divide the total number of deaths in each country by the country's population in 1990.[8]

The resulting figures reveal what portion of each country's people was consumed in political conflagrations. In Muslim countries, on average, 0.65 percent of the population (about two-thirds of 1 percent) perished in major political violence. In non-Muslim countries, 0.72 percent (or between seven-tens and three-quarters of 1 percent) died in such episodes on average. Muslim countries have, on average, suffered slightly less severely from loss of life in major episodes of political violence than have non-Muslim countries.

Table 5.1 summarizes the information on deaths as a percentage of the population. Table 5.2 provides the numbers for the largest Muslim and Christian countries, listed in descending order of population size.

The data in table 5.1 show that there have been fewer deaths per capita related to political violence in Muslim countries than in non-Muslim countries, but this difference is not statistically significant.[9] In figure 5.1, the variation in the number of

Table 5.1 Mean Scores on the Indicators of Large-Scale Political Violence for Muslim and Non-Muslim Countries

Survey item	Muslim Countries	Non-Muslim Countries
Deaths in major episodes of political violence, 1946–2007, as a percentage of the total population	0.65 ($N = 43$)	0.72 ($N = 128$)

Table 5.2 Data on Large-Scale Political Violence in the Largest Muslim and Christian Countries, Number of Deaths as a Percentage of the Population

Muslim Countries		Christian Countries	
Country	Deaths	Country	Deaths
Indonesia	0.43	United States	0.00
Pakistan	0.90	Brazil	0.00
Bangladesh	0.02	Russia	0.05
Egypt	0.01	Mexico	0.01
Turkey	0.10	Phillipines	0.16
Iran	0.16	Germany	0.00
Sudan	6.92	DR Congo	4.34
Morocco	0.00	France	0.01
Algeria	0.25	UK	0.00
Afghanistan	5.66	Italy	0.00
Uzbekistan	0.00	Ukraine	0.00
Saudi Arabia	0.00	Colombia	0.92
Iraq	1.00	South Africa	0.06
Malaysia	0.16	Spain	0.00
Yemen	0.54	Argentina	0.07
Syria	0.20	Poland	0.00
Niger	0.01	Kenya	0.02
Senegal	0.04	Canada	0.00
Mali	0.01	Uganda	2.19
Tunisia	0.00	Peru	0.14
20-country average	0.82	20-country average	0.40

deaths per capita within the Muslim and non-Muslim groups is presented. As can be seen, not only is the mean higher in non-Muslim countries, but the highest number of deaths per capita also occurred in non-Muslim countries.

Several other facts are worthy of note. An overwhelming amount of the carnage took place in a fairly small set of countries. Roughly three-quarters of all deaths

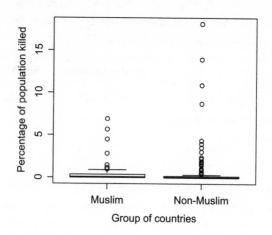

Percentage of Population Killed in Episodes of Large-Scale Political Violence

occurred in just nine countries. In descending order of the number of deaths, those countries are China, Vietnam, Sudan, Cambodia, the DRC (Democratic Republic of Congo, formerly called Zaire), Korea (North and South, mostly during the war of the early 1950s), Pakistan, Angola, and Afghanistan. Three of those countries are predominantly Muslim (Sudan, Pakistan, and Afghanistan), two are predominantly Christian (the DRC and Angola), and in four neither Christianity nor Islam predominates (China, Vietnam, Cambodia, and Korea).

When we consider total deaths as a percentage of the population, the worst-off countries again represent a mélange of religious traditions. In twelve countries, 3 percent or more of the national population died in large-scale political violence. In descending order of percentage that perished, those countries are Cambodia, Equatorial Guinea, Angola, Rwanda, Sudan, Afghanistan, Bosnia, the DRC, Burundi, Mozambique, Korea, and Vietnam. These are the countries that, in per capita terms, suffered the most severely from mass intrastate political violence. Three of them are Muslim (Sudan, Afghanistan, and Bosnia) and five are Christian (Equatorial Guinea, Angola, Rwanda, the DRC, and Burundi). The other four (Cambodia, Mozambique, Korea, and Vietnam) are neither predominately Muslim nor predominantly Christian.

In order to assess whether there is a link between Islam and mass political violence, we need statistical analyses that control for the possible impact of variables other than religion. As usual, we measure Islam as the percentage of the population that is made up of Muslims. Here we encounter a potential measurement problem that we did not face earlier, since the data on percentage Muslim is drawn from a survey of conditions in recent decades, and our dependent variable, mass political violence, covers episodes reaching back to 1946. We do not have good cross-national data on religious composition of countries in 1946, however, so we must rely on the data we have for later years. Doing so probably causes little distortion, since the religious composition of societies normally changes slowly if at all, and the correlation between conditions in, say, 1950 and 1990 is probably very high. Thus, we use the data for more recent decades as a proxy for conditions throughout the postwar period, while bearing in mind that the data are imperfect.

As always, we must control for socioeconomic development. One might expect richer societies to be less conflict-prone than poorer societies. Where want is greater and more widespread, mass violence may be more likely. Ethnic fractionalization may also be important. Higher fractionalization may be conducive to greater intercommunal tension and more mass political violence. Socioeconomic inequality may threaten civil peace as well. Higher inequality might be associated with more violence. The level of democracy might also exert influence. Here the effect could cut either way. It is possible to imagine that more open government might furnish channels for the peaceful resolution of differences among groups and thereby reduce the risk of large-scale violence. But a rival hypothesis is also plausible. Authoritarian regimes, by virtue of their greater harshness and commitment to imposed stability, may be better than democracies at staving off mass political violence. The robustness of the state apparatus is another potentially important variable. Weak states may be more vulnerable to mass political violence than stronger ones.

This is by no means a complete set of possible determinants of large-scale intrastate violence. But it does cover a good deal of what have often been considered the main explanatory variables. Controlling even for the variables outlined here, however, is difficult. The main problem is that we are examining events that cover a substantial period of time (about sixty years, starting with the first year after the end of World War II). It would be ideal to have data for each country for our control variables for 1946, which we could treat as the starting point of the period, or for each year starting from 1945 or 1946, which might allow for time-series analysis. But we lack such data. We lack good information on level of socioeconomic development, measured as income per capita and life expectancy (as we have measured development thus far in this book) for the early postwar years. We do have some numbers, but prior to the 1970s data for many countries are missing and what we have is often of dubious reliability. The further we move back in history, the sketchier the data become. Even the most complete sources lack data for many countries for the indicators that best measure development, including income per capita, fertility rate, life expectancy, infant mortality, and the proportion of the population engaged in agriculture.[10] Our best hope is to rely upon data on fertility for a midpoint in the interval of time we are considering. Here we measure socioeconomic development as total fertility rate (births per woman) during 1970–75, as reported by the United Nations Development Programme (UNDP) in a recent report.[11] Lower fertility rates indicate higher socioeconomic development. Thus, if higher levels of development promote civil peace, we would expect to find a positive relationship between fertility rates and deaths per capita in large-scale political violence.

We lack data on ethnic fractionalization for the immediate postwar period. The data we have were gathered over the past several decades. Yet, since ethnic composition rarely changes rapidly, we may consider those numbers rough estimates of conditions throughout the postwar years. We would expect greater fractionalization to cause more political violence.

Data on socioeconomic inequality, which is measured using the Gini score, are too sparse and unreliable for decades preceding the 1990s to be used here. This variable must be omitted.

We do have some data for the openness of political regime, and those scores will be used here. Freedom House ratings, which we use elsewhere in the book to capture level of political openness (or democracy), began appearing only in 1973. Here we use data for Freedom House scores in 1975.[12] Scores range from 1 (most open polity) to 7 (least open polity). As usual, I flip the scores such that 7 represents most open and 1 least open, to provide more intuitive presentation. For the countries of the former USSR, I use the USSR's score in 1975; for those of the former Yugoslavia, Yugoslavia's score in that same year; for the Czech Republic and Slovakia, Czechoslovakia's score in that year.[13]

Including a control for the robustness of the state apparatus, which may affect the risk of large-scale political violence, would be desirable, but it is not practicable. We have several good sources of quantitative data based on expert surveys, but they apply only to the past decade or so.[14] We may, however, use a dichotomous variable for when countries received their independence. Countries that did not enjoy independent statehood as of the beginning of the previous century may be more likely to have weak state structures than those that obtained statehood earlier. Countries that were not independent by the year 1900 include those that were constituents of empires and that were under colonial rule. Here we control for that factor using a dichotomous (dummy) variable, with 1 standing for countries whose history of independent statehood postdates the beginning of the twentieth century and 0 for those that did enjoy independent statehood before 1900. If late national independence is associated with weaker state structures and thus with a higher propensity to suffer large-scale political violence over the past six decades, we would expect a positive relationship between the dummy variable for late statehood and deaths due to political violence.

If we were attempting definitively to assess the causes of large-scale political violence in a cross-national framework, the data available to us and the methods used here would be barely adequate at best. But we have no such pretension. We seek only to ascertain the correlation between a single factor, the Muslim proportion of the population, and mass political violence. The other independent variables are merely controls. Thus, the shortage of stellar data, while suboptimal, need not derail our investigation.

Deaths as a percentage of the population in major episodes of political violence constitute our dependent variable. If Muslims are more prone to mass political violence, we should see a positive relationship between percentage of the population made up of Muslims and the dependent variable; if Muslims are less prone to mass political violence, the relationship should be negative. Table 5.3 shows the results of the statistical analyses.

Here we rely upon negative binomial regression, which is commonly used to estimate count models where many cases have very low scores on the dependent variable. We also conducted the analyses using standard OLS models, which are presented in appendix 5.B. In the negative binomial models presented here in tables 5.3 and 5.4, the coefficients are log odds ratios. The coefficient we are interested in is the percent Muslims in the country. As can be seen in table 5.3, this coefficient is weakly negative but not statistically significant at conventional levels.

As was clear in figure 5.1, while most countries had no or a very small portion of the population destroyed in episodes of large-scale political violence, a few countries have very high numbers. To what extent are these outliers driving the results? In table 5.4 we run the same models as in table 5.3, but exclude the six countries with the highest number of deaths per capita: Afghanistan, Angola, Cambodia, Equatorial Guinea, Rwanda, and Sudan. These countries have abnormally high values for deaths related to political violence. As we can see in table 5.4, excluding the extreme cases does not dramatically change the results. In fact, the percent Muslim in the population still has a weak, negative effect which is not statistically significant.

The relationship between percentage Muslim and predicted deaths per capita in major episodes of political violence may be illustrated graphically. The plots in figure 5.2 display the relationships. The left-hand plot in figure 5.2 shows the relationship between the percentage Muslims in a country and the predicted percentage of the population that will die due to political violence. The prediction is based on model 3 presented in table 5.3, holding fertility rate and level of democracy to their mean value and late national independence to 1. Moving from being 0 percent Muslim to 100 percent Muslim is associated with a 0.36 reduction in the predicted percentage of the population killed in episodes of large-scale political violence. Yet, as was reported in table 5.3, this reduction is not statistically significant, meaning that we cannot be confident that the percentage of Muslims has an effect. The right-hand plot shows the relationship without outliers, as predicted by model 3 in table 5.4. Moving from a country with 0 percent to 100 percent Muslims is associated with a 0.17 reduction in the percentage of the population destroyed in mass political violence, but again this reduction is not statistically distinguishable from zero.

To sum up the findings of this section: People who inhabit countries with proportionally larger Muslims populations are less likely to perish in large-scale political violence, but the Muslim effect is small and not statistically distinguishable from zero. The safest and soundest conclusion we can draw is that we find no evidence that Muslims are more inclined than non-Muslims to large-scale political violence.

Table 5.3 Regressions of Deaths in Major Episodes of Political Violence on Hypothesized Predictors

	Model 1	Model 2	Model 3	Model 4	Model 5	Model 6	Model 7
(Intercept)	−0.249 (0.309)	−2.320*** (0.643)	−0.441 (0.694)	−0.500 (0.685)	−3.065*** (0.654)	−3.012*** (0.645)	−0.276 (0.685)
Percent Muslim	−0.004 (0.006)	−0.009 (0.008)	−0.009 (0.007)	−0.010 (0.007)	−0.011 (0.007)	−0.010 (0.008)	−0.010 (0.007)
Fertility rate		0.392** (0.132)	0.281+ (0.145)	0.248* (0.118)	0.339** (0.127)	0.370* (0.166)	0.248* (0.118)
Ethnic diversity			−0.624 (0.888)			−0.549 (0.991)	
Level of democracy			−0.460*** (0.112)	−0.462*** (0.118)			−0.485*** (0.128)
Late independence			0.229 (0.407)	0.204 (0.400)	1.273** (0.468)	1.279** (0.482)	
N	171	171	171	171	171	170	171
AIC	354.738	343.101	330.542	329.637	339.275	340.078	327.745
BIC	379.871	380.801	405.801	392.470	389.541	402.794	378.012
log L	−169.369	−159.551	−141.271	−144.818	−153.637	−150.039	−147.873

Note: Negative binomial models with robust standard errors in parentheses.

+significant at $p < .10$; *$p < .05$; **$p < .01$; ***$p < .001$.

Table 5.4 Regressions of Deaths in Major Episodes of Political Violence on Hypothesized Predictors, Excluding the Major Outliers in the Data

	Model 1	Model 2	Model 3	Model 4	Model 5	Model 6	Model 7
(Intercept)	−1.026*** (0.227)	−2.074** (0.715)	−0.794 (0.679)	−0.809 (0.726)	−2.394*** (0.673)	−2.394*** (0.652)	−0.789 (0.763)
Percent Muslim	−0.002 (0.004)	−0.006 (0.007)	−0.008 (0.007)	−0.008 (0.006)	−0.008 (0.007)	−0.007 (0.007)	−0.008 (0.007)
Fertility rate		0.219 (0.146)	0.153 (0.163)	0.141 (0.137)	0.197 (0.150)	0.200 (0.178)	0.141 (0.135)
Ethnic diversity			−0.211 (0.940)			−0.041 (0.982)	−0.291** (0.102)
Level of democracy			−0.289** (0.092)	−0.289** (0.096)	0.589 (0.455)	0.590 (0.451)	
Late independence			0.039 (0.423)	0.019 (0.416)			
N	165	165	165	165	165	164	165
AIC	255.575	252.227	249.781	248.203	252.513	253.994	246.205
BIC	280.422	289.499	324.177	310.322	302.208	315.991	295.900
log L	−119.787	−114.114	−100.890	−104.102	−110.256	−106.997	−107.102

Note: Negative binomial models with robust standard errors.

†significant at $p < .10$; *$p < .05$; **$p < .01$; ***$p < .001$

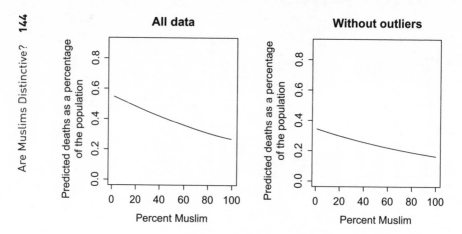

FIGURE 5.2:

Predicted Deaths as Percentage of the Population in Large-Scale Episodes
of Political Violence

Islamism and Large-Scale Political Violence

So far we have examined the relationship between Muslims and mass political violence. But what about the impact of radical Islamism, as opposed to Muslims?
Above, we found that countries with larger shares of Muslims in the population do
not have higher death rates from mass political violence. But it still is possible that
Islamists are responsible for a grossly disproportionate amount of the world's mass
political violence. I conceive of Islamists as people who seek to advance religious
claims in the political sphere. The defining goals of Islamism are often regarded as
establishing Islam as a state religion and implementing Islamic law. Islamism is
sometimes identified with rigid conservatism in moral matters, insistence upon
literal interpretation of the sacred scriptures, and/or antagonism toward other
faiths. Some variants of Islamism, however, may seek to inject Islamic religious
values into the political sphere, sometimes in opposition to oppressive secularist
regimes, without necessarily embracing puritanical or intolerant approaches to doctrine. The concepts of "Islamism" and "Islamist" are controversial and are defined
in a multiplicity of ways, and there is enormous diversity among those who self-
identify as Islamists. The common trait that unites various strains of what is often
referred to as Islamism is the impulse in one way or another to politicize Islam or to
Islamicize politics.[15]

Are Islamists responsible for a highly disproportionate share of mass political carnage? The findings of some writers might lead one to such a conclusion. Monica
Duffy Toft finds that in the 42 religious civil wars that took place between 1940 and
2000, incumbent governments and rebels who identify with Islam were involved in
a far greater percentage of wars than were governments and rebels who identified
with other religions. Toft explains her finding in terms of numerous factors, including

the historical absence in the Muslim world of an internecine religious war analogous to Europe's Thirty Years' War in the seventeenth century, the spatial proximity of Islam's holiest sites to Israel and to large oil reserves, and the concept of jihad.[16] Toft's findings are noteworthy. They may help explain why Islamists are more frequently involved in religious civil wars than are partisans of other religions. Here, however, our main question and our data differ substantially from Toft's. She focuses specifically on religious wars, while here we are looking at all large-scale episodes of political violence and asking how much of a role Islamists had in the making of those conflicts.

In order to answer the question, I have coded all episodes of large-scale political violence in terms of whether or not Islamists were involved in instigating the conflict. In making this judgment, I have relied on press reports, secondary sources, personal communication with country specialists, and (most importantly) talented and diligent research assistants.[17] I identify Islamists in terms of actors' self-identification as well as the way they are perceived by governments and observers. Assessing whether or not Islamists were culpable is, for the vast majority of cases, unproblematic. Little sleuthing is required. Most of the episodes are protracted conflicts, not one-time events perpetrated by actors who operated clandestinely. Still, in some cases, coding requires judgment calls. In order to maximize transparency, I present the coding in the table in appendix 5.A. I ask whether or not the conflict was "instigated in whole or in part by Islamists." The answer (yes or no) is shown in the right-most column of the table.

Cases are coded "yes" even if Islamists were only *partially* responsible. Sometimes Islamists were only one of several instigators, and perhaps not the main one. For example, the genocide against communists and ethnic Chinese that took place as the Suharto regime consolidated power in Indonesia in 1965–66 is coded as "yes," even though Islamists were only one of several culprits. In this case, Islamists were arguably more tools of Suharto's—decidedly secularist—military than prime movers. In another genre of episode, Islamists were partially involved in instigating violence but did more dying than killing over the course of the conflict. Thus, Islamists are coded as being "in whole or in part" responsible for the instigation of the civil violence that took 2,000 lives in Egypt during 1992–99, though agents of the secularist government may have killed more of their Islamist foes than the other way around.

Of the 235 major episodes of intrastate political violence, Islamists participated in instigating 27, or 11 percent of the total. Of the 21,011,400 deaths in all episodes, 3,402,700, or 16 percent, occurred in the episodes in which Islamists were involved in instigation.

We may compare the numbers on Islamist-instigated violence with those on episodes that actors other than Islamists instigated. The brief accounts provided in the "description" column in the table in appendix 5.A contain the needed information.

Ten episodes (4 percent of the global total), accounting for 3,069,020 deaths (15 percent of the global total), occurred in China and Taiwan in revolutionary and postrevolutionary violence stemming from the Chinese Communist Party's capture and consolidation of power. Thus, these episodes exacted approximately the same number of deaths as all episodes in which Islamists were wholly or partly responsible for the commencement of conflict. Twenty-six episodes, accounting for 3,830,300 deaths (18 percent of the global total), occurred in the six Middle and East African nations of Angola, Burundi, Congo-Brazzaville, the DRC, Rwanda, and Uganda. Government forces and partisans of rival ethnic groups bear responsibility for these conflicts, whose total frequency and death toll were roughly equivalent to those of the conflicts in which Islamists bore some responsibility. None of these countries is primarily Islamic, nor were the instigators of any of these conflicts Islamists.

Is Islamist-instigated conflict responsible for a disproportionate amount of violence? Are the 11 percent of episodes and 16 percent of deaths for which Islamists bear some responsibility a grossly disproportionate amount or not? Here the reader must make her or his own judgment. We have no base rate or objective standard against which to judge. Our assessments are further complicated when we consider that some of the conflicts that Islamists participated in igniting were also instigated by other actors who bear joint responsibility. All we can say with certainty is that Islamists do bear some responsibility for major episodes of political violence in the postwar world, but non-Islamist actors, including the revolutionary movement and government in China and partisans of ethnic strife in Middle and East Africa, have been responsible for roughly as much carnage as Islamists have.

Summary

This section investigated the possible link between Muslims and large-scale political violence. Controlling for other potentially influential variables, we found a negative correlation between the proportion of society made up of Muslims and the fraction of society killed in intrastate political conflict. The relationship, however, is not strong. We therefore lack the evidence necessary to conclude that Muslims are less prone to political violence than are non-Muslims. But the findings do show, in contradistinction to Huntington's famous thesis, that countries with larger Muslim populations are not more susceptible to mass political bloodletting than are countries with smaller Muslim populations.

On the question of whether Islamists, as opposed to Muslims, participated in initiating a disproportionate amount of large-scale political violence, our conclusions must be more equivocal, since there is no baseline to judge how much violence counts as disproportionate. Islamists were at least partially responsible for the initiation of 11 percent of the episodes of large-scale political violence, which accounted for 16 percent of the total deaths. Islamists are, therefore, significant culprits for major political conflict in the modern world. Yet the gravity and extent of their culpability depends on how one reads the evidence.

The following section shifts our focus from major episodes of intrastate political strife to terrorism. Here the picture changes dramatically.

TERRORISM

Hypotheses on Muslims and Terrorism

The hypotheses presented above on why Muslims might be more or less prone to large-scale political violence may also apply to terrorism. The concept of jihad and the violent militancy that it may contain could breed terrorism. The counterhypothesis is that the sociocultural integration (or "synnomie") to which we tentatively attributed the low murder rate in Muslim societies in the previous chapter might curb the hazard of terrorism.

In the previous section, I noted that writings on the effect of Islam on mass political violence are sparse. Not so with the literature on Islam's influence on terrorism. On this subject we find an outpouring of writings in recent years.[18] Most works focus on particular terrorist networks or acts of terrorism in a specific country or set of countries. Some works offer arguments about the causes of terrorism; I will discuss those arguments below in a section that grapples with how Islam may affect the incidence of terrorism.

Defining and Measuring Terrorism

Defining terrorism can be difficult. Many authors have noted the possibility of bias. One observer's terrorism might be another's heroic act. There may be no neutral, objective way of pinpointing precisely what constitutes terrorism.

Most definitions use several criteria. First, they examine the target of the attack. Attacks on unarmed civilians are classified as terrorism; this much is uncontroversial. Violent acts against nonmilitary political targets (such as embassies) are usually considered terrorism, though some analysts resist calling any attack on a political target terrorism. Attacks against armed political targets (such as police stations or training facilities) are often considered terrorism as well, though here the distinction between terrorism and guerilla action becomes less clear. The distinction becomes yet blurrier when we consider attacks on armed occupiers or foreign military forces. Here many analysts refrain from labeling the attack an act of terrorism. I share this viewpoint and do not regard attacks on armed occupiers or foreign military forces as terrorism. My concept of terrorism is limited to attacks on civilians, nonmilitary political targets, and armed political targets.

A second criterion used for defining terrorism is the duration of the event. Most analysts do not consider sustained, major episodes of mass political violence to be terrorism. Thus, the episodes that we investigated in the previous section of this chapter do not count as terrorism. These episodes had a sustained character— typically months or years, but even in the briefest episodes, days or weeks. They were not single events, but rather series of events that stretched over time. Terrorist episodes, by contrast, are brief, one-off affairs.

Not all authors share this definitional distinction. Some conceive of certain major episodes of mass political violence as protracted, slow-motion terrorist acts. For example, Mahmood Mamdani labels the civil war that beset Nicaragua during the 1980s an act of state terrorism perpetrated by the United States, since the U.S. government sustained a counterrevolutionary group that was responsible for what Mamdani sees as a long series of terrorist acts. Mamdani also applies the concept of state terrorism to the civil war in Angola between 1975 and 2002, and again he fixes blame on the U.S. government, which helped finance the UNITA fighters who constituted one side in the conflict.[19] Mamdani focuses on cases in which he regards the U.S. government as culpable. But one could apply his concept to other conflicts as well. The rolling massacres of civilians under the Pol Pot regime, in which Khmer Rouge government forces slaughtered one-and-a-half million people between 1975 and 1978, could be seen as an instance of state terrorism (in this case, perpetrated by the government of Cambodia, backed by the government of China).

Mamdani's view may provide a needed corrective to notions of terrorism that whitewash the actions of actors that pose as opponents of terrorism, and specifically governments. He rightly shows that terror is in the eye of the beholder—or of the terrorized, who may live in African or Central American forests as well as in North American or European cities.

Still, for our purposes, such a notion of terrorism is deficient. The atrocities— including those against civilians—committed by the U.S.-backed Contras in Nicaragua and UNITA forces in Angola, while very real, were embedded in larger civil wars. Without denying American culpability, we must acknowledge that such conflicts had the quality of civil wars. Mass violence was committed by both insurgents and government forces, and the U.S.-backed opponents of sitting governments drew on domestic sources of support. Not all violence in these struggles, moreover, was aimed against civilians. Much of it targeted other armed fighters. Insurgents aimed to topple governments and governments tried to quell insurgencies. In cases such as the Khmer Rouge's repression of what it considered class enemies, the violence was for the most part unidirectional (the state's agencies of coercion against the civilian population). But even here it is difficult to identify discrete events that readily fit an operational definition of terrorism. Furthermore, we have already accounted for such mass carnage in the discussion of major episodes of political violence. Here I will stick with a more conventional definition of terrorism as a one-time attack, rather than a protracted conflict. Attacks on civilians, nonmilitary political targets, and armed political targets are all considered acts of terrorism. Attacks on armed occupiers or foreign military forces are not.

For data, Monty Marshall's "High Casualty Terrorist Bombings" list provides an excellent starting point. Marshall has assembled a list of all terrorist bombings that took fifteen or more lives between September 1994 and, as of this writing, September 2008.[20] This data set does not cover as long a period as Marshall's list of major episodes of political violence that we used in the previous section to assess mass political conflict. But it does give us a good list for the past fifteen years. Marshall provides information on the date, location, and number of deaths for each terrorist act.

The database is not without its shortcomings. It is limited to terrorist bombings, meaning that other methods of carrying out attacks are not included in the list. Still, this is only a mild drawback. As I found in conducting my own research, the vast majority of incidents that qualify as terrorism and that claimed fifteen or more lives took the form of bombings. Perhaps the greatest drawback of the database is the cutoff that it establishes at fifteen deaths. Many acts of terrorism claim fewer than fifteen lives. An act of terrorism that kills two people is not, of course, any less "terrorist" than one that slays twenty. Some terrorist acts take no lives, either because the planned attack was botched or because the perpetrators intended to induce fear or destroy property without killing people. Including all terrorist acts, regardless of their human toll, would have advantages. The data would be more complete. Yet Marshall chose to set a threshold at fifteen deaths, and after carrying out extensive research of our own, my research assistant and I could readily see why. Assembling data on every act of terrorism, regardless of means and regardless of number of casualties, would be a daunting task. Low-casualty episodes sometimes escape international intention; one would have to plumb the newspapers of virtually all of the world's countries, in scores or hundreds of languages, in order to have confidence in the comprehensiveness of the database. If the type of terrorism we were interested in cataloguing were limited to a specific type—say, suicide terrorism or terrorism in a specific region—perhaps drawing up a list of acts that included a small number of casualties would be feasible. But the goal of our inquiry requires us, to the extent possible, to cover the globe and to avoid restricting our data to particular types of acts or perpetrators.

While we found Marshall's list to be remarkably accurate as we verified and coded each incident, my research assistant and I did find some mistakes in the number of casualties, dates, and location of the events. We make the needed corrections here. For four events, we found that Marshall inadvertently overstated the number of deaths and that fewer than fifteen people were actually killed. We exclude those events from our list. Where we found discrepancies in numbers of deaths between Marshall's data and our own findings, but where the body count still totaled at least fifteen, we note what we regard as the correct numbers without brackets, place

Marshall's numbers in brackets, and leave these events in the list of incidents. These data are included in our list of terrorist bombings in appendix 5.C. Errors in Marshall's data set are not pervasive and do not diminish the overall utility of his remarkably useful list.

Marshall's list provides only raw data; it does not specify the target of the attack or if Islamists were responsible. Since we are concerned with these matters, we researched each event and coded it in terms of the target of the attack and whether it was perpetrated by Islamists.

Assessing the Link between Muslims and Terrorism

To assemble our list of cases, we divide the events in Marshall's list into categories depending on target. The first target is civilians. Many attacks on civilians aimed simply to wreak havoc by destroying people in a spectacular manner. Some were more specifically targeted and went after civilians of a particular type—for example, members of a particular national or ethnic group. The second type is unarmed political targets. These include public officials, the offices of political parties, public demonstrations held by political parties or movements, and embassies. The third is armed political targets, which may be military housing complexes, gatherings of military personnel or police officers, military parades, police stations, or police and military training centers. I consider attacks on all three of these types of targets to be acts of terrorism.

The fourth target is occupiers and foreign military forces. These include representatives of occupation forces and the armed forces of foreign occupiers. I do not consider attacks on such targets to be terrorism. Thus, items that we coded as aimed at such targets were deleted. There are nine such incidents in Marshall's list that we excluded on these grounds.

We further exclude all incidents that occurred in Iraq following the U.S. invasion in March 2003. Inclusion of these incidents would more than double the total number of attacks and completely transform the profile that the data create. Coding many of these incidents in terms of their targets is impossible. A great number are aimed at foreign occupiers and would on those grounds alone be excluded. Many acts that appeared have a sectarian cast were perpetrated by forces that claimed to be striking foreign occupation. Coding many of the events in Iraq, at least given our state of knowledge as of the present time, would be extraordinarily difficult. Excluding incidents that occurred in post-invasion Iraq improves the clarity and utility of the data for our purposes. As of this writing, there have been 307 high-casualty terrorist bombings in post-invasion Iraq, all of which we exclude.

We also exclude incidents on Marshall's list for which we can turn up no corroborating information on the occurrence of the attack, as well as incidents for which we find strong evidence that the event was accidental rather than intentional. For these cases, we are uncertain of the reliability of the data and are unable to code the events. There are eleven such incidents in Marshall's list, and we eliminate them.

In sum, we begin with Marshall's list of high-casualty terrorist bombings but use only a subset of that list. Eliminating the 307 incidents that took place in post-invasion Iraq reduces the total number from 535 to 228. We then exclude the four attacks for which we found that the death count was lower than fifteen, the nine attacks that targeted occupiers and that we therefore do not consider terrorism, and the eleven cases for which we can find no corroborating data that enable us to confirm the event's occurrence and code it. The process of elimination leaves a total of 204 events. This is our universe of cases.

Within this universe, we code the incidents in terms of whether they were perpetrated by Islamists. We define "Islamist" in strict, rather than permissive, terms. Only groups that identify themselves, and are widely identified by others, as Islamists are counted as such. Such groups claim to act in the name of Islamic principles and the Muslim community. They act against non-Muslim communities or Muslims regarded as collaborators with non-Muslim governments, forces, or causes.

Identifying the perpetrator, whether Islamist or not, is not difficult in most cases. Usually the culprit claims responsibility and there is general agreement among the inhabitants and authorities in the affected area about the culprit's identity. We identify a responsible party only where two or more sources agree on it and where we find general consensus on the matter. If evidence on responsibility is murky, thin, or highly contested, we do not attribute responsibility for the act at all. All events that we classify as having an Islamist perpetrator were (1) carried out by groups that fit our restrictive definition of Islamist; and (2) carried out by groups we can readily identify using the criteria just spelled out. We prefer to err on the side of caution. Where we cannot establish the identity of the terrorists, we assume a non-Islamist culprit and treat the incidents as such in the statistics. We benefited from consultations with country experts that we undertook to improve the reliability of the coding. The complete list of terrorist incidents under examination, including information on the coding of each case, is provided in appendix 5.C.[21]

Table 5.5 sorts the terrorist bombings into the relevant categories. The top portion of the table shows the totals, with cases classified according to the target. As the numbers show, two-thirds of attacks were carried out against civilians. Roughly one-sixth of attacks struck unarmed political targets and another one-sixth hit armed political targets. The second and third portions of the table separate the acts by perpetrator and specifically whether or not Islamists were the culprits. The second part shows the numbers excluding the attack of September 11, 2001 on the United States, which was the highest-casualty attack of the period, and the third portion shows the numbers with that attack included.

Islamists were responsible for 125 of 204, or 61 percent, of the high-casualty terrorist bombings that took place between late 1994 and late 2008. These attacks, if

Table 5.5 Descriptive Summary of High-Casualty Terrorist Bombings, by Target and
Perpetrator

Target	Number of Incidents (percentage of total)
Civilians	136 (66.7%)
Unarmed political target	36 (17.6%)
Armed political target	32 (15.7%)
Total	204 (100%)

Perpetrator	Number of Incidents (percentage of total)	Number of Deaths (percentage of total)
Islamists	124 (61.1%)	4786 (58.5%)
Not Islamists	79 (38.9%)	3399 (41.5%)
Total	203 (100%)	8185 (100%)

Note: These figures do not include the attack on the United States of September 11, 2001.

Perpetrator	Number of Incidents (percentage of total)	Number of Deaths (percentage of total)
Islamists	125 (61.3%)	7768 (69.6%)
Not Islamists	79 (38.7%)	3399 (30.4%)
Total	204 (100%)	11,167 (100%)

Note: These figures include the attack on the United States of September 11, 2001.

we include 9/11, caused 69.6 percent of all deaths; if we exclude 9/11, 58.5 percent of all deaths. If we focus exclusively on attacks on civilians, Islamists were responsible for 74 of 136, or 54 percent, of the incidents, which accounted for 68 percent of total deaths if we include 9/11 and 51 percent of deaths if we do not.

Thus, Islamists have been responsible for the bulk of global terrorism over the past fifteen years. We have no baseline to establish expectations about what percentage of terrorist acts or deaths would constitute a "disproportionate" amount. Furthermore, statistical analyses of the type that we conduct on many other matters in this book would be less useful here. Here our units are neither people nor countries nor country-specific events, and it would be difficult to control for factors that may influence the incidence of terrorist bombings.

Yet, even without the benefit of baseline expectations or statistical analysis, the conclusion is obvious. If 10 or 20 percent of terrorist bombings in the world were carried out by Islamists, another 10 or 20 percent by extremists claiming to represent some other religion or ideology, and the remainder by partisans of other causes, it would be difficult to say whether terrorism is disproportionately an Islamist tactic.

This is the situation we encountered above in our investigation of the involvement of Islamists in major episodes of intrastate political violence. It was hard to judge whether Islamism was a particularly common culprit. But in our examination of terrorism the data tell a different story. Here, self-proclaimed Islamists have been responsible for over three-fifths of all incidents and nearly seven-tenths of all deaths. Terrorism is not a uniquely Muslim disease, but its perpetrators in recent times are disproportionately Islamists.

Yet terrorist acts are concentrated in geographical terms. They tend to occur frequently in a handful of countries and rarely or not at all in the rest of the world. Figure 5.3 shows the geographical locations of all high-casualty terrorist bombings. Seven countries suffered from ten or more such attacks, and the attacks in these countries accounted for nearly three-quarters of the global total. Afghanistan, Algeria, India, Israel, Pakistan, Russia, and Sri Lanka alone were the sites of 73 percent of all incidents. Terrorism is extremely rare in the West; Europe (excluding Russia) and North America suffered only five incidents over the fifteen-year period. All of Latin America experienced only six attacks, five of which happened in Colombia. Thus, Algeria alone, with a population of 33 million, suffered as many terrorist bombings as did the entire Western Hemisphere and Europe combined, whose population totals one-and-a-half billion.

Geographical concentration is even more evident when we examine the locations of terrorist acts perpetrated by Islamists. Figure 5.4 graphs these incidents. Three countries—Pakistan, Israel, and Afghanistan—were the sites of nearly half the attacks. Besides these three countries, only India, Algeria, and the Philippines suffered five or more attacks. Pakistan is the site of many attacks perpetrated by Islamists and non-Islamists alike. This much is evident in figure 5.4 and in figure 5.5, which shows the location of acts of terrorism not committed by Islamists.

Each of these six countries has been the site of major political upheaval. Afghanistan has been a failed state during much of its tumultuous national history. The same may be said, albeit to a lesser degree, of Pakistan. India cannot be considered a failed state, but several of its provinces suffer chronic tensions between Hindus and Muslims. In Algeria, after an Islamist party won the first round of parliamentary elections in 1991, the government annulled the contest, sparking a gruesome conflict that has been punctuated by acts of terrorism by Islamist groups. The Philippines has long endured a low-intensity civil war over separatist demands emanating from a Muslim-majority portion of Mindanao, the country's large southern island. The terrorist acts committed in the Philippines, which have been staged by the Moro Islamic Liberation Front or the Abu Sayyaf Group, are linked to that conflict. Israel is the object of the sustained hostility of its Arab neighbors, and it has occupied adjacent lands inhabited by several million Palestinian Muslims for much of the past four decades. Since most Arabs, and indeed Muslims worldwide, do not regard the existence of Israel as legitimate, from their point of view the attacks in Israel would

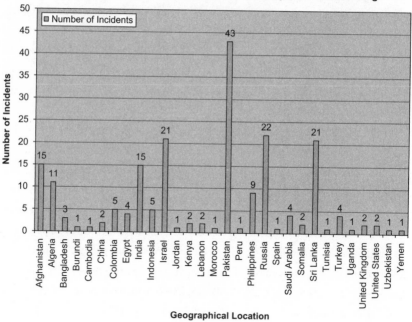

FIGURE 5.3:

Sites of All High-Casualty Terrorist Bombings

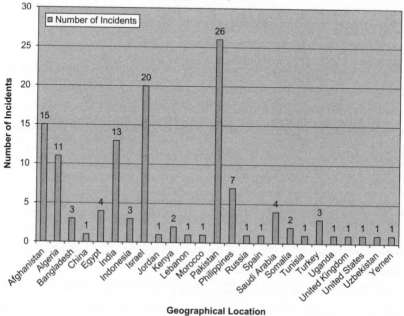

FIGURE 5.4:

Sites of High-Casualty Terrorist Bombings Perpetrated by Islamists

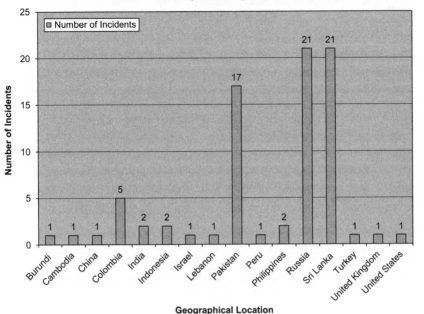

FIGURE 5.5:
Sites of High-Casualty Terrorist Bombings Not Perpetrated by Islamists

not qualify as terrorism as I define it, but rather as assaults on armed occupiers or foreign military forces. As my coding shows, I do not share that stance. It bears note, however, that many Muslims have a view that differs from my own.

Furthermore, most Islamist attacks occurred in Muslim countries. Fifteen of the twenty-five countries in which Islamists committed terrorist bombings are predominantly Muslim. Seventy-seven of the 125 attacks, or 62 percent of the total, were carried out in these lands. Another forty attacks, or 32 percent of the total, were carried out in Israel, India, and the Philippines. We lack data on the religious identity of the victims of terrorism. But it is safe to assume that, if we exclude the attack of September 11, 2001, in the United States, most of the victims of Islamist attacks have been Muslims.

Only four of the 125 acts of Islamist terrorism happened in the Western Hemisphere, Europe, and the non-Muslim countries of the former USSR. One took place in Russia, one in Spain, one in the United Kingdom, and one in the United States. These attacks were ghastly and dramatic. In terms of frequency, however, what may be regarded as the core lands of Christendom, which account for over three-quarters of the world's Christian population, endured on average only about one terrorist attack by Islamists every four years. There was a total of thirty-three terrorist acts, or about two per year, in these lands, but twenty-nine of them were not committed by Islamists. Most were perpetrated by separatists in Russia and "narcoterrorists" in Colombia's cocaine-fueled civil conflicts. The conflict in Russia indeed pits separatists from a mainly Muslim region, Chechnya, against the central government in a largely Christian society, but most of the terrorist attacks were arguably ethnonational in character. We hold that they were carried out by forces that neither identified themselves, nor were identified by the Russian or other governments, as Islamists. Some analysts might disagree with our coding on this item, arguing that what began as a secular separatist conflict had become part of a global Islamist jihad by the beginning of the twentieth century, and that the terrorist bombings in Chechnya should be considered the work of Islamists. Given the contested—and perhaps multifaceted—identities of the perpetrators of the bombings, we favor a conservative call in coding and classify the culpable forces as ethnonationalists rather than Islamists.[22]

Outside countries that are predominantly Christian or predominantly Muslim, Sri Lanka was by far the most badly afflicted nation. It endured twenty-one bombings, none committed by Islamists. Most were carried out by the Liberation Tigers of Tamil Eelam, the armed force that aims to separate the predominately Hindu, Tamil-speaking lands of the north from the largely Buddhist, Sinhalese-speaking remainder of the country.

What can we make of all this information? Several patterns emerge. One is that Islamists are responsible for a disproportionate share of terrorist bombings in the contemporary world. The second is that there is considerable national concentration of the sites of terrorism, with a large portion of attacks occurring in a handful of countries. Third, most attacks are embedded in larger conflicts. Terrorist attacks can be distinguished and analyzed separately from episodes of large-scale political violence, as we do in this chapter. But terrorist attacks are much more likely to happen in places beset by civil wars or insurgencies than in places that are not. Fourth, those places are mostly developing countries. While the terrorist events that happened in the West have received much public attention, only a small fraction of all terrorism occurs there. All but a handful of terrorist bombings carried out by Islamists occurred in Muslim countries or in Israel, India, or the Philippines.

The finding of greatest interest is that Islamists have been responsible for a very large share of the world's terrorism. They committed roughly three-fifths of all high-casualty terrorist bombings, which account for about seven-tens of all deaths. We arrive at these numbers despite the use a restrictive conception of "Islamist." As noted above, we classify as Islamists only those who identify themselves and are identified by others as such. For example, we do not code attacks by Chechen fighters against Russian targets as Islamist. The Chechen fighters are mostly Muslims and they seek independence from a predominantly Christian country, but we conceive of the Chechen fighters as ethnonational separatists, not Islamists. Furthermore, as noted above, we attribute responsibility to Islamists—or to groups of any other type—only if multiple sources agree on the responsible party. In the vast majority of incidents, the perpetrators identified themselves publicly. If evidence on responsibility is thin or highly contested, we do not attribute responsibility for the act. Even with our restrictive definition of "Islamist" and high bar for attributing responsibility to any particular actor, we still find that terrorism in the late twentieth and early twenty-first century is an overwhelmingly Islamist tactic.

How Might Islam Influence the Incidence of Terrorism? Some Ideas

Why are the self-styled representatives of one particular religion so prominent among terrorists in recent years? Most Muslims oppose terrorism.[23] Still, the clamor of Muslim protest against Islamist terrorism is often less than deafening. Following the attacks of September 11, 2001, in the United States, in which Islamists slaughtered nearly 3,000 civilians, Hamzah Haz, the vice president of Indonesia, warned the United States not to "scapegoat" Muslims and added that he believed the attacks might help the United States "cleanse" itself of its iniquities. The president of Indonesia, Megawati Sukarnoputri, while showing a bit more concern than her vice president, offered little more than wan words of consolation. Neither leader, to say the least, displayed outrage that their own religion, and that of the vast majority of their countrymen, was being invoked to justify the attacks.[24]

Hamzah and Megawati were not dictators who were unmindful of public opinion. They spoke as the elected leaders of a country that was undergoing a vibrant push toward democracy and were as conscious of public opinion as any politician in an open polity must be. Nor were they the leaders of a country that was hostile to the United States. Indonesia has typically been a U.S. ally or a neutral power; it is no Iran, Libya, or Syria, and anti-Americanism has traditionally been pale in Indonesia. Nor did they hold office in an insignificant country; Indonesia is the world's largest Muslim-majority polity. That Hamzah and Megawati could react as they did speaks to why so many non-Muslims suspect that many Muslims, even if not supportive of terrorism, are not quite as staunchly opposed to it as one would hope. Indeed, in the wake of September 11, 2001, many Indonesians expressed approval of Osama bin Laden, the perceived leader of al-Qaeda, the organization responsible for the attack. In a major poll of Indonesians conducted in 2003, when asked "How much confidence do you have in Osama bin Laden to do the right thing regarding world affairs?" 58 percent expressed "a lot of confidence" or "some confidence," while only 36 percent expressed "not too much confidence" or "no confidence at all."[25]

Is there a link between Islam itself and terrorism? If there is, what is its source? Writings on Islamism and terror offer a host of answers. Here I will consider the most prominent.

Some writers see acceptance of terrorism as innate to Islamic doctrine. According to Robert Spencer, Muslims believe that murdering non-Muslims, even unarmed civilians, can be laudable. He asks, "In slaying infidels, are the terrorists not acting as pious Muslims? They believe they are, and the letter of the Qur'an seems to back them up." For textual support for violence, Spencer alludes to the Qur'an 9:5, which states, "Slay the idolaters wherever you find them." It is true, Spencer says, that parts of the Christian Bible seem to endorse violence against those who are outside the community of faith. But he notes that "for Christians, the New Testament supersedes the Old and corrects its violent tendencies, as in Jesus's celebrated admonition, 'You have heard it said, "An eye for an eye and a tooth for a tooth" [Lev. 24:20]. But I say to you, Do not resist one who is evil' [Matt. 5:38–39]." Spencer states that "Muslims have no such tradition, and nothing akin to the New Testament corrective of the gospel of mercy."[26] Similarly, Mark Gabriel sees modern Islamist terrorists as acting in a manner consistent with Qur'anic injunction and the example set by Muhammad.[27]

An alternative argument concedes that modern Islam contains a violent strain but claims that this tendency defies mainstream tradition and sound Qur'anic reasoning. Khaled Abou El Fadl articulates this view. He argues that fanatical groups, including terrorist networks such as al-Qaeda and al-Jihad organizations, "derive their theological premises from the intolerant Puritanism of the Wahhabi and Salafi creeds." Neither creed has deep roots. Wahhabism was founded in the eighteenth century and had little appeal outside the Arabian Peninsula until the twentieth century. Salafism began in the early twentieth century as a modernist reform movement but was hijacked by Wahhabism, whose diffusion depended on Saudi oil money. Abou El Fadl suggests that the extreme intolerance and even endorsement of terrorism manifest in Wahhabism and Salafism, salient as they may have become in present times, represent a deviation from Muslim historical traditions, which offer no more theological cover for violent extremism than do the traditions of any other world religion. According to Abou El Fadl, even the concept of jihad as "holy war" lacks depth. He states, "Islamic tradition does not have a notion of holy war. Jihad simply means to strive hard or struggle in pursuit of a just cause, and according to the Prophet of Islam, the highest form of jihad is the struggle waged to cleanse oneself from the vices of the heart."[28]

According to Abou El Fadl, terrorism also lacks Qur'anic justification. He notes, "Holy war (al-harb al-muqaddasah) is not an expression used by the Qur'anic text or by Muslim theologians. In Islamic theology, war is never holy; it is either justified or not. . . . The Qur'anic text does not recognize the idea of unlimited warfare, and does not consider the simple fact of the belligerent's Muslim identity to be sufficient to establish the justness of his cause." Arguing that scripture imposes on Muslims a requirement of proportionality and moderation, Abou El Fadl cites the Qur'an 2:194, "Mandated is the law of equality, so that who transgresses against you, respond in kind, and fear God, and know that God is with those who exercise restraint."[29] What is more, Abou El Fadl notes, the Qur'an "legitimizes a multiplicity of religious convictions and laws," as in 5:49, where God's word may readily be interpreted as providing for multiple paths to Himself. Abou El Fadl also cites 5:69 and 2:62, which contain the passages: "Those who believe, those who follow Jewish scriptures, the Christians, the Sabians, and any who believe in God and the Final Day, and do good, all shall have their reward with their Lord and they will not come to fear or grief." While "the Qur'an clearly claims that Islam is the divine truth," its spirit, expressed in passages such as those just cited, provides ample justification for religious tolerance.[30] Abou El Fadl acknowledges that scripture does contain passages that "offer possibilities of intolerant interpretation," and he sees that "these possibilities are exploited by the contemporary puritans and supremacists." Yet, he asserts, "The text does not command such intolerant readings." On the contrary, "the Qur'anic message of tolerance and openness to the other," as well as the "moral trajectory" of the history of Islamic civilization, speak emphatically against the fanaticism and disregard for humanity expressed in terrorism.[31]

In contrast with the two views examined above, which trace Islamist terrorism to holy scripture or flawed interpretations of scripture, some other writers find explanations in long-standing political tradition. Efraim Karsh, for example, locates an acceptance of terrorism in Islamic imperial practice that is as old as the religion itself.[32] In his view, Islam's millenarianism and universalism and its birth as a conquering faith created an urge to global mastery that justified the use of any means necessary to expanding the realm of Islam's ascendancy. Karsh holds that in the historical imagination of many contemporary Muslims, Osama bin Laden represents a modern version of Saladin, the twelfth-century conqueror who seized Palestine from European Christian Crusaders and reigned over Egypt, Syria, Iraq, and the Arabian Peninsula. Both, after all, sought to expel the infidel from Muslim lands and expand the realm of Islam's dominion. The Prophet's leadership, according to this view, included a vision of political conquest, which was realized with the dramatic spread of the faith and founding of the Abbasid and Umayyad caliphates during the early centuries after the Prophet's death. Indeed, by the early ninth century, conquering armies had established the Dar al-Islam (House of Islam) from Spain and Morocco in the West to the area of present-day Uzbekistan and Pakistan in the East. Since the dawn of Islam, imperialism and conquest have been intertwined with faith, and when the political ascendancy of Islam is challenged, by apostates or non-Muslims, any manner of force is seen as justifiable. Thus, in Karsh's view, terrorism is hardly foreign to Islam. But the religion's political impulses, passions, and ingrained patterns of behavior provide a surer basis for comprehending contemporary terrorism than does the Qur'an. Scripture may be invoked instrumentally to justify violence. But the faith's millennium-and-a-half-old political project, rather than the sacred texts, furnishes the key to understanding Islamist terrorism and the tolerance of it by many modern Muslims.

An alternative view also finds historical rather than scriptural cause for contemporary terrorism but casts Muslims as victims of aggression rather than authors of their own imperial tradition. Some scholars who hold such a view find the roots of Islamist militancy in the Crusades of the eleventh and twelfth centuries. Karen Armstrong, for example, states, "I now believe that the Crusades were one of the direct causes of the conflict in the Middle East today."[33] Armstrong holds that there is nothing intrinsic to Islam that disposes contemporary Muslims to commit or countenance acts of terror. She sees the roots of terror in reaction against injustice that began with, and continues to be symbolized by, the time when Christian fighters attempted to take the Holy Land from its Muslim custodians a millennium ago. Some authors hold that the feeling of grievance is intensified by memories of Islamic ascendancy in the eighth to twelfth centuries, when Muslim culture, learning, and political prowess excelled the achievements of Christendom. In short, this view regards contemporary Islamist terrorism as growing out of deep historical grievance, rooted in the Crusades, rather than an Islamic imperial impulse or anything innate to Islamic scriptures or doctrine.[34]

Still another theory locates the link between Islam and terrorism in a particular aspect of sociocultural life: namely, the social and sexual frustration of young males. The perpetrators of terrorism, most of whom are young men, may seek to affirm their bravery and masculinity and achieve sexual reward. Such a dynamic is not necessarily specific to Muslim communities. But the religiously sanctioned practice of polygyny and promise of sexual bliss in the afterlife for the fighter for the faith are, among major world religions, unique to Islam. And the segregation of the sexes, normative proscriptions against premarital sex, and high economic costs of obtaining a bride may be especially pronounced among Muslims.[35]

Other theories of terrorism look to factors that are not specific to the doctrine or history of Islam. Poverty is one such factor. In the aftermath of 9/11, the director of the World Bank, James Wolfensohn, called for a new fight against poverty for the sake of reducing the risk of terrorism. While noting that "poverty in itself does not immediately and directly lead to conflict, let alone to terrorism," Wolfensohn argued that eradicating poverty would greatly reduce the risk of future terrorist acts.[36] Marc Sageman, in his in-depth investigation of terrorist networks, finds that people join militant organizations neither out of poverty nor religious devotion but out of a yearning to belong to a tight-knit social group. Personal alienation underlies the growth of terrorist networks.[37] Leaving aside deep history and religious doctrine as well as economic and psychological factors, Barry Rubin focuses on the proximate political matter of state sponsorship. He argues that many acts that appear to be the work of fanatical believers can be traced to cold-eyed governments that use terrorism as a weapon against their adversaries. According to Rubin, "While Islamist groups often seem to be a threat to the state, they are more often, in practice, tools of the state."[38] Rubin traces terrorism to the governments of Saudi Arabia, Iraq, Syria, and Libya. Dore Gold also blames states and specifically investigates the Saudi state's culpability.[39] In an empirical study that focuses specifically on suicide terrorism, Robert Pape assigns primary causal weight to nationalism as a reaction to occupation by foreign forces. Most acts of suicide terror, Pape finds, are responses to foreign occupation.[40]

How Might Islam Influence the Incidence of Terrorism? Weighing the Arguments

There may be value in many of these arguments, and some are not mutually exclusive. But none provides a full understanding of why Islamists figure so prominently in contemporary terrorist activity and why many Muslims are less than strident in their criticism of Islamist terrorism. We may begin with the ideas summarized in the previous paragraph, which attribute terrorism to nonreligious causes. All of these arguments may have merit. But none explains the predominance of Islamism in acts of terrorism. The notion that poverty fuels terrorism may carry some weight if we look across whole societies, but empirical evidence has shown that the portrait of the terrorist as a desperate young man with nothing to lose is largely inaccurate. Both Pape and Sageman, who have done extensive research on the identity of terrorists, find that terrorists are not disproportionately poor or undereducated.[41]

Yet Pape's and Sageman's own arguments do not provide us with keys to explanation, either. Let us begin with Pape's argument.

Pape uses different data than I do, which might explain why he largely overlooks Islamism and highlights foreign occupation in his explanation. He includes acts in which no one or only one or a handful of people were killed, while I include only bombings in which there were fifteen or more deaths. His data cover 1983–2005, while mine cover 1995–2008. He focuses on suicide bombings alone, whereas I include bombings that did not take the lives of their perpetrators. Perhaps most importantly, Pape includes post-invasion Iraq, which accounts for over one-third of his cases. I exclude all cases in post-invasion Iraq. Finally, since my definition of terrorism does not include attacks on armed occupiers, many of the events that Pape regards as terrorism I do not. Yet, even when we exclude those events, as I do here, I find that Islamists have been disproportionately responsible for terrorism.

The frequency of suicide bombings in Iraq, Sri Lanka, Russia, and Israel drives Pape's findings. Given the U.S. occupation of Iraq, the view of the Tamil separatists that their land is occupied by a foreign power (the government of Sri Lanka), the Chechen belief that their land is under Russian occupation, and the common Palestinian view of Israel as occupied Palestinian territory as well as an occupying power, Pape's finding that foreign occupation is responsible for suicide terrorism is unsurprising. His findings may have merit. Yet they do not tell us why such a large proportion of terrorist bombings occur at the hands of Islamists. Pape's findings could help solve that question if most of the bombings committed by Islamists took place in occupied territories, or if a grossly disproportionate number of Muslim countries were under occupation. Yet neither is the case. When we exclude post-invasion Iraq, as I do, in only Israel and perhaps Afghanistan do we find a large number of Islamist-instigated bombings that may be attributed to rebellion against occupiers. And in these countries as in all others, I excluded any attacks carried out against foreign military forces. As figure 5.4 shows, moreover, only 36 of the 125 bombings that Islamists carried out occurred in Israel, Afghanistan, or Russia. Furthermore, all of the bombings in Sri Lanka and all but one of the bombings in Russia I code as not instigated by Islamists. Still, Islamists carried out the bulk of all terrorist bombings in our data set.

Pape's work may unearth something important, and he presents convincing evidence that lands under foreign occupation are fertile grounds for the growth of suicide terrorism. Yet he leaves us without an answer to why Islamists have been such frequent perpetrators. He does not tell us why so many bombings against targets other than armed occupiers are perpetrated by Islamists rather than partisans of some other cause.

Sageman's findings are similarly interesting and revealing but also fail to answer our main question. They might do so if anomie were especially high among Muslims, since a desire to escape feelings of alienation is what Sageman says drives people into the company of groups that commit terrorist acts. But Sageman does not argue for a correlation between Islam and alienation, and to the best of my knowledge no scholar has yet provided evidence of such a relationship. In fact, it runs contrary to what we found in the previous chapter, where we saw that anomie may be lower in Muslim social contexts, which may help explain the low murder rates in Muslim countries. Sageman may well be right to argue that personal alienation, more than intense religiosity, poverty, or some other factor, drives people into militant groups. But that conclusion does not explain why Islamists are disproportionately culpable for terrorism.

Rubin's and Gold's argument that governments often finance and manipulate terrorists may be true, but it too fails to account for the predominance of Islamists among terrorists. If Islamist terrorists relied mostly upon the governments of non-Muslim countries, we could say that the name of Islam was being exploited by non-Muslims to advance their own political ends. But most of the states that back terrorism are found in the Muslim world. State support for terrorism is not limited to Muslim countries. The governments of North Korea, Russia, and the United States may have a role in backing terrorists as well. But the governmental supporters of Islamist-instigated terrorism are found in predominantly Muslim countries such as Saudi Arabia, Iran, Syria, and Libya. Why would such governments sponsor terrorism?

The question leads us back to why Hamzah Haz, the vice president of Indonesia at the time of the attacks on the United States of September 11, 2001, refrained from condemning the perpetrators of the atrocities. Hamzah, like most politicians, was ever on the hunt for popular support. He held office in a new democracy. But the rulers of Saudi Arabia and other dictatorships also hope to please or appease their subjects—or at least distract them from misrule. Why would political leaders in Muslim countries find advantage in backing, or at least not strongly condemning, Islamist terrorism? Might they expect their support or tolerance of terrorism to boost their legitimacy or at least buy some quiescence? This possibility leads us away from officialdom and back to the people, and specifically Muslims. It again raises the question of whether Muslims may be prone to tolerate terrorism in the name of their religion—which in turn points our attention to explanations for Islamist terrorism that have a religious dimension.

In short, arguments that attribute terrorism to causes other than religion may have merit. But they do not begin to tell us why Islamists instigate so great a proportion of terrorist acts. Let us now consider the arguments that do see religious adherence as relevant to terrorism.

The first argument discussed above, associated with Robert Spencer and others, claims that Islamist terrorism flows logically from injunctions in the Qur'an. There are several reasons to regard this argument as untenable. First, as we saw in chapter 3, both the Qur'an and the Bible are subject to myriad interpretations, and interpretation tends to determine people's attitudes and practices. Locating statements in the Qur'an that appear to justify violence against outsiders is not difficult. But finding such passages in the Bible is just as easy. The book of Joshua, for example, provides an extensive narrative of Joshua's conquering armies slaughtering entire captured cities—putting wailing children (along with everyone else) to the sword, hanging people by trees, and carrying off the plunder and booty—all under God's holy orders. Joshua, "totally destroyed all who breathed, just as the Lord, the God of Israel, had commanded" (Josh. 10:40). In terms of prolixity, gory detail, ferocity, and divine enthusiasm for the slaughter of innocents, the Qur'an contains nothing analogous to the account in Joshua 10–11.

The New Testament does take precedence over the Old in the thinking of some Christians. But many other Christians see the Bible as a seamless web of infallible truths and deny any contradictions in the text. Contemporary Christians widely celebrate Joshua, the slaying conqueror of the Old Testament book named after him, as a model of bravery and unflinching commitment to God. "Joshua" has been one of the five most common names given to baby boys born in the United States each year over the past quarter century.[42]

Furthermore, Spencer's contention that Muslims have in their holy scriptures "nothing akin to the New Testament corrective of the gospel of mercy" is strained, given the multitude of passages in the Qur'an in which God describes himself as "the Merciful One." Each chapter of the Qur'an begins with "In the Name of God, the Compassionate, the Merciful," a phrase with which religious Muslims today preface their speeches, sermons, and public statements. Mercy, moreover, is not

God's alone. God enjoins His followers to show goodness and mercy to others as He shows them to his creation, as in the Qur'an 42:43, where God declares that "to endure with fortitude and to forgive is a duty incumbent on all." Similarly, in 25:70–76, God both declares His own mercy and demands mercy on the part of his people: "God is forgiving and merciful: he that repents and does good works shall truly return to God; who do not bear false witness, and who maintain their dignity when listening to profane abuse. . . . These shall be rewarded for their fortitude with the loftiest abode in Paradise." Since there is ample justification for both horrific violence and abundant grace in the Bible and the Qur'an alike, holy scripture provides a weak reed on which to base causal arguments about the prevalence of Islamist terrorism in the modern world.

Abou El Fadl's argument that modern Islamism contains a violent tendency but that this tendency is at odds with mainstream Muslim tradition may be more credible. Abou El Fadl enjoys intimate knowledge of Islam's sacred scriptures and history. He grasps how the Qur'an and the Hadith, like any sacred texts, may be used and abused in the service of a virtually limitless variety of ends. While arguing that violence in the name of Islam is deplorable and anti-Qur'anic, he does not deny the virulence of some strains of Islamism or blame terrorism on a tiny handful of rotten characters. While holding that "it would be wrong to say that fanatic supremacist groups such as al-Qaeda or al-Jihad organizations now fill the vacuum of authority in contemporary Islam," Abou El Fadl concedes, "Still, they are extreme manifestations of more prevalent intellectual and theological currents in modern Islam."[43] He does not engage in quantitative empirical analysis, but even without the numbers Abou El Fadl is aware that contemporary Islam has a terrorism problem. Abou El Fadl provides incisive reasoning, but his insights still do not provide a full explanation for why Islamism is responsible for so much of the world's terrorism.

Karsh's argument that terrorism is inherent in Islam's universalism, millenarianism, and imperial tradition may also contribute to our understanding, but falls short of answering our question. Islam is unquestionably a millenarian and universalistic religion. Most religious Muslims believe that all people can and should be Muslims, and that in the end of days, God will show His favor to those whose lives demonstrated adherence to His word as revealed uniquely and authoritatively to the Prophet Muhammad and recorded in the Qur'an. And Islam does, as Karsh claims, have a long history of foisting the faith upon conquered peoples.

Yet precisely the same things may be said of Christians and Christianity. Christians are millenarians and universalists; they look forward to the day when every knee will bow toward Jesus Christ and every tongue will proclaim His Lordship. They regard the Bible much the way Muslims regard the Qur'an: as the unique and authoritative revelation of God's will. The adherents of each confession regard their faith as properly the faith of all people, even as many adherents of each faith urge tolerance toward those who do not (yet) grasp the truth. Furthermore, Christianity is no less of an outbound, conquering faith than Islam is. European colonial expansion to the New World, Africa, and Asia was heavily influenced by religious-ideological purpose and justification; colonial conquerors and missionaries are central to Christianity's political history. In short, everything Karsh says of Islam may be said of Christianity as well. And yet Islamists, not zealots claiming to speak for Jesus Christ, have been responsible for the bulk of terrorist bombings in recent years. Karsh's arguments are not necessarily wrong, but they fail to answer our main question.

The same is true of Armstrong's argument. She and like-minded authors are undoubtedly right to point out that the Crusades left a deeper imprint on Muslims' consciousness than on Christians' thinking. Many contemporary Muslims, including Islamist terrorists, refer frequently to what they regard as the perfidies of the Crusades, while most Christians, if pressed, probably could not say whether the Crusades happened in the 6th, 11th, or 16th centuries. In fact, most Christians probably do not even know precisely what the Crusades were. Yet Armstrong's attribution of causal force to events that occurred a millennium ago is debatable. After all, the Muslims, under Saladin, actually won the wars against the Christian invaders. They ultimately rebuffed Christian incursions and recaptured the Holy Land. Why do Christians care so little about this defeat? Why do most Christians pay the Crusades so little heed, while many Muslims continue to remember them with bitterness? For that matter, why do so few Christians harbor bitterness at the initial loss of the Holy Land, which Arab Muslim invaders took from Christians in the seventh century, shortly after Muhammad's death?

Surely contemporary conditions shape the salience of historical memories. Historians' arguments about the primacy of the Crusades cannot be disproven. But nor do historians such as Armstrong demonstrate a causal connection between these distant events and contemporary problems. Perhaps Muslims do nurse historical grudges against Christians to a greater extent than the reverse, and the Crusades may be an especially salient symbol of Christian imperialism. But would Muslims care so much about the Crusades if Muslims had come out on top over the past century or two?

Finally, we may consider the argument that sexual and social frustration on the part of young males produces Islamist terrorism. This explanation may have some promise. Some of the countries that have substantial problems with terrorism, including Afghanistan, Algeria, India, Pakistan, and Saudi Arabia, do have strict norms regarding premarital sexual relations and contain massive reservoirs of young men with dim marriage prospects. Still, we lack the data on the personal attributes of terrorists needed to make definitive statements. The notion that feelings of frustration and sensitivity to affronts to personal honor would be especially acute among marginalized young men, as well as the hypothesis that such individuals might be particularly susceptible to the lure of violence, are sensible. But in the absence of detailed information about the frequency and intensity of frustration among terrorists compared to people who do not engage in terrorism, we cannot know how important this factor is. What is more, some of what little information we have casts doubt on the hypothesis. In his sample of terrorists on which he obtained family status information, Sageman found that most of the terrorists were married men who had children.[44] This finding is based on a limited sample and does not rule out the possibility that sexual and social deprivation may motivate some terrorist acts. But we do not yet have strong empirical evidence supporting the sexual-and-social-frustration hypothesis.

Thinking about Why Terrorism Happens

Frustration and humiliation may well have a great deal to do with the causes of terrorism. Yet that frustration and humiliation may be more collective than individual, more national than specifically religious, and more political than sexual.

Let us begin with a few simple facts: People in predominantly Christian countries account for one-third of the world's population and control roughly two-thirds of its material production and nine-tenths of its military power. If Muslims now found themselves in such a position in the world, how much would the Crusades matter to them? If the G-8 group of leading industrial powers were composed not of seven predominantly Christian countries (Canada, France, Germany, Italy, Russia, the United Kingdom, and the United States) plus Japan, but rather of seven predominantly Muslim countries plus Japan, or for that matter, of four Christian countries and three Muslim countries plus Japan, how much would the incursions of a millennium ago bother Muslims today?

Let us now shift from hard facts to some counterfactual, extravagant futuristic thinking. Let us imagine that, over the next half-century, predominantly Christian countries decline in power and prestige. The United States, due to overspending on international commitments as well as its people's inability voluntarily to endure even a modest, temporary reduction in personal consumption, wanes as a world power. It attempts, belatedly, to shift resources to investment in human capital at home, but crushing debt as well as fear and risk-aversion leave Americans a position that resembles that of the present-day Japanese. Americans continue to enjoy a relatively high standard of living, but their country is nevertheless stuck in long-term regression relative to rising powers. Western Europe's gradual, relative decline continues. A fall in hydrocarbons prices and limitless greed for lucre on the part of Russia's rulers and their cronies, coupled with popular xenophobia and chronic conflict in the post-Soviet neighborhood, leave Russia and its predominantly Christian neighbors in a position of fading influence as well. Latin America's yawning socio-economic inequalities and internal strife persist, producing stagnation in the central and southern portions of the Western hemisphere. Overwhelmed by disease, war, and intractable problems of governance, much of Christian southern and central Africa continues its descent into poverty and turmoil.

As Christendom declines, non-Christian nations rise. The spectacular growth of China's economy and international influence, already visible today, continues apace. China replaces the United States as the world's most influential country. In an effort to secure control over mineral wealth, expand foreign markets to absorb its exports, extend its geopolitical reach, and resist competition from a declining West, China undertakes a bold, long-term program of economic and political investment in the Arab world, Iran, and parts of Muslim West Africa. This policy pays off handsomely for both investor and recipients. Parts of the Middle East and Muslim Africa grow in economic power and global political influence. (Incidentally, in our hypothetical scenario, China's external investments—in their scope, motivation, and results— bear a marked resemblance to U.S. investments in Western Europe and parts of East Asia in the second half of the twentieth century.)

Turkey and Turkic Muslim Central Asia, spurned by Europe and pressured by Russia, turn south and east. They embrace Chinese tutelage in exchange for security guarantees and Chinese acquiescence in a leadership role in the political management of the rising Middle East. Arabs and Persians, many of whom associate Turkish military leadership with the long centuries of caliphal glory and resistance to Christian encroachment, welcome the Turks into the fold.

In Southeast Asia, Indonesia and Malaysia move from the medium-high tempo of economic growth that they have experienced in recent decades to Chinese-style expansion. They easily assume regional leadership. Their influence increases as that of the other major countries of the region, notably the Philippines, Thailand, and Burma, which are already beset by chronic political instability, declines. Indonesia and Malaysia, with their Muslim majorities and Chinese minorities, embody and bolster the ties between China and the Muslim world that are central to our hypothetical scenario. Singapore, with its Chinese majority and Malay-Muslim minority, is closely aligned with China, Indonesia and Malaysia. In South Asia, India ascends in economic power and political influence, although it is balanced by an equally rapidly growing Pakistan, which enjoys close ties with the rest of the Muslim world and with China.

In this world of Sino-Muslim ascendancy, things happen that do not appeal to people in predominantly Christian countries. The stresses arising from the erosion of Western hegemony drive Americans and Europeans apart. The rift further weakens the appeal of Western culture and models of politics. Indeed, Americans and Europeans find their ways of living, producing, and thinking less charming to people outside the West than they were in previous centuries. In order to participate in global commerce, finance, technological innovation, scholarly discourse, and cultural production, Americans, Frenchmen, and Russians must master Mandarin Chinese and Modern Standard Arabic—with Turkish and Indonesian strongly recommended. Arab countries and Iran, now in possession of formidable economic, organizational, and military assets as well as security guarantees from China, easily dismantle the state of Israel. The occasional invasion and occupation of parts of Russia, Southeastern Europe, and the Philippines by China, Turkey, Iran, or united Arab military forces at moments when China or the Muslim countries believe they detect a security threat from those Christian lands becomes part of the rhythm of global politics. Such actions spark outrage in Christendom. But they do not prompt concerted counteractions, since the governments of predominantly Christian countries do not have the wherewithal to resist the encroachments. What is more, many politicians in Europe, Latin America, and the United States, who naturally need substantial resources to finance their electoral campaigns and personal consumption, do not always refuse the financial inducements offered by the governments of China, Turkey, and the Arab states. Accepting help from such quarters, which of course is done quietly, cools politicians' passions for resisting what at any rate seem like inexorable trends in world politics.

Would everyone in Christendom accept these developments with equanimity? Some might not. They might even regard the world as a house of injustice. Disregard for their cultural achievements, languages, products, services, and security concerns may even ignite a hard, slow-burning rage. The inability or unwillingness of their governments to set right a world of injustice might exacerbate people's frustration. The suspicion that even some of their own leaders were complicit in their countries' degradation might be the final straw.

The final straw, that is, that broke a healthy human abhorrence of deadly violence against innocents and a normal human capacity for distinguishing between innocents and oppressors. Under such conditions, is it difficult to imagine that some self-proclaimed soldiers of Christianity would lash out by committing terrorist acts? Is it possible that individuals such as Paul Hill, the Presbyterian pastor and affiliate of the Army of God antiabortion movement who murdered a physician and his assistant who performed abortions in 1994, might engage in terrorism against what he regarded as Christianity's enemies in the Muslim world? What of Timothy McVeigh, who bombed the federal building in Oklahoma City in 1995 to protest what he regarded as the tyranny of the federal government? Might he be tempted to target Muslim overlords rather than the Feds? What about Eric Robert Rudolph, a member of the Christian Identity movement who carried out the Centennial Park bombing in Atlanta during the 1996 Olympics as well as a string of other bombings to protest abortion and homosexuality, and James Charles Kopp, an affiliate of The Lambs of Christ antiabortion movement who murdered a physician who performed abortions in 1998? Might such people turn their ire on those whom they regard as enemies of their country and faith?

And might some Christians countenance such acts? In fact, each of the killers just mentioned enjoyed vocal support among some extremist Christian organizations as well as quieter, more diffuse sympathy among conservative Christians or, in McVeigh's case, antigovernment extremists. Rudolph was feted in popular music and lore and shielded by local communities in North Carolina where he hid during his years as a fugitive prior to his arrest in 2003. In the hypothetical scenario portrayed above, in which Christian countries are reduced to second-rate status, is it possible that many people would sympathize with, or at least fail to condemn, terrorism against those seen as subordinating Christians? Might terrorism against Muslims abroad, Muslims at home, or non-Muslim leaders who are seen as collaborators, be greeted with something other than universal condemnation in predominantly Christian societies?

The realism or likelihood of the scenario sketched above is of little importance. What matters are two things. The first is recognizing that the hypothetical scenario simply flips the power relationship between Christians and Muslims that actually exists in today's world. The second is pondering what Christians' reaction to a reversal of fortunes might be.

Assigning blame for terrorism and tolerance of it, and specifically judging whether or not Western (or Christian) imperialism and abuse of power are at fault for the resentments that fuel Islamist terrorism, is a pointless exercise. Determining whether Western arrogance or Muslim overreaction to disempowerment is to blame is impossible. No nation or group of nations has ever apologized for coming out on top in a given historical epoch, or refrained from regarding its own virtues as to credit for its accomplishments. It is hardly surprising that most non-Muslims and Westerners in particular do not reproach themselves for Muslim frustration. It is equally unremarkable that so many Muslims feel deeply aggrieved. The Western world's lack of appreciation of their circumstances only fuels such sentiment.

I intend to justify neither contemporary Islamist terrorism nor terrorism by Christian fanatics in some future scenario. There is no justification for slaying and maiming innocents, which is what terrorist bombings do. The aim of this section has not been to justify or to even understand terrorism; rather, it has been merely to explain it.

The onset of cancer cannot be justified. Nor can we fully understand why it happens in one person and not another. But we can, at least partially, explain the causes of cancer. Terrorism is like that.

Further Thoughts on the Causes of Islamist Terrorism

A profound sense of grievance among Muslims is not the only plausible explanation for the prominence of Islamism in contemporary terrorism. The opportunities for engaging in terrorism, and especially the rapid spread of internet technologies as well as technologies and materials needed to make powerful man-portable bombs, at just the time when Islamism became a predominant source of resistance to the hegemony of Western liberalism, may matter as well. The incentives to move from traditional guerilla warfare to spectacular attacks on "soft" targets, moreover, may be enhanced by the recent revolution in mass communication, which ensures that terrorism reverberates instantly around the world—indeed, that attacks take on the aura of Hollywood theatrics as they are broadcast again and again over the airwaves and online by international networks such as CNN and Al Jazeera. What is more, Muslims' sense of grievance may have been aggravated in recent decades by the appearance of a certain hauteur in the rhetoric and foreign policy of the world's dominant non-Muslim powers. The United States under the administration of George W. Bush was the exemplar of triumphalism. Twenty-first-century Russia, France, and China, with their growing global assertiveness and less-than-hospitable policies toward Muslim religiosity at home, have exhibited this tendency as well.

Indeed, consideration of these matters reminds us that we are dealing with a time-bound phenomenon. The data analyzed above cover only a fifteen-year period in the recent past. If we had good data for the past century or so and could analyze them instead, our results might be different. During the Cold War, communism rather than Islamism posed the most powerful ideological challenge to predominant Western models. Communist terrorism committed by the likes of Peru's Shining Path, Italy's Red Brigades, and the German Red Army Faction was common. If we were to focus instead on the nineteenth century, forces other than Islamists or communists might emerge as key perpetrators. Perhaps anarchists or the bearers of other principles or programs would predominate.

Contemporary conditions matter the most to most of us, so our findings are relevant and important. But we cannot generalize our findings to long stretches of history. At the very least, we need to continue to ask ourselves how conditions in the contemporary world explain the prominence of Islamism in terrorism. As with the other findings presented in this book, we may not simply assume that what is true of our times necessarily holds throughout history.

OVERVIEW OF THE FINDINGS

We have covered a lot of territory in this chapter. But the findings do not allow a clear-cut conclusion on whether Muslims are especially prone to political violence. We found that major episodes of political violence are not disproportionately common in Muslim lands. More precisely, when we control for other possible predictors, a higher percentage of Muslims was associated with a bit less carnage in major episodes of intrastate political violence. But the effect is small and tenuous. The most we can say for sure is that we turned up no evidence that countries with a larger share of Muslims have experienced a disproportionate share of carnage in political strife. Our finding of a nonrelationship contradicts widespread perceptions, including arguments that Samuel Huntington offers in his celebrated study, *The*

Clash of Civilizations and the Remaking of World Order, which portrays Muslim lands as especially strife-ridden.

Whether Islamist political forces, as opposed to Muslims per se, are responsible for a great deal of the world's large-scale political violence is a separate question. That question is difficult to answer. We generated reasonably good data to probe the matter. But whether the share of conflicts that Islamists had some hand in initiating is disproportionate or not is in the eye of the observer. Islamists had some responsibility for instigating 11 percent of all major episodes of political violence, which account for 16 percent of all deaths. In the view of this author, these numbers are not negligible, but nor are they overwhelming. Non-Islamist actors, such as revolutionary forces in China and partisans of interethnic struggles in Middle and East Africa, had a hand in instigating roughly as much strife and loss of life as Islamists did.

When we shifted our attention to terrorism, the picture changed dramatically. Here our data cover only the fifteen years leading up to late 2008, but the data show unequivocally that at least during that particular period, Islam had a terrorism problem. Islamists were responsible for more than 60 percent of high-casualty terrorist bombings, which accounted for nearly 70 percent of all deaths. Even with no baseline of expectations or preestablished notion of what counts as a disproportionate number of attacks and casualties, we may conclude that Islamists are culpable for a great deal of the world's terrorism.

Yet Islamist terrorism is geographically concentrated. Nearly three-quarters of terrorist acts carried out by Islamists occurred in just seven countries, none located in the West. In fact, Islamist terrorism is extremely rare in the West, which has suffered only a handful of attacks. Those attacks captured much public attention. They created the impression that terrorism is disproportionately an Islamist disease and that the West is highly vulnerable to Islamist terrorism. Our investigation shows that the first of these assumptions is correct, while the second is not.

Accounting for the salience of Islamism in contemporary terrorist activity is exceedingly difficult. None of the explanations found in the literature is entirely satisfactory. Nor did I offer an adequate explanation. I nevertheless attempted, using a counterfactual thought experiment, to supply some insights. I emphasized the grievance that some Muslims may feel as a result of their subordinate political, cultural, and economic status in the contemporary world.

Our conclusions on the relationship between Islam and violence grow even more ambivalent when we recall the material presented in chapter 4. There we found that homicide rates are substantially lower among Muslims than non-Muslims.

Thus, in the contemporary world, Muslims do well on avoiding murder, neither better nor worse on mass political violence, and worse on terrorism. These decidedly mixed findings do not allow us the satisfaction of an up or down verdict on whether Muslims are more or less violence-prone than non-Muslims, but they are what the evidence shows.

6 Social Inequality

Inequality has long fascinated social scientists. A passion for depicting, explaining, and overcoming it motivated Mary Wollstonecraft, Alexis de Tocqueville, Karl Marx, Max Weber, W. E. B. Du Bois, and Amartya Sen. Unearthing the sources of inequality remains one of the great pursuits of people who study people.

This chapter investigates whether a particular religious tradition is linked to social inequality. Is social inequality among Muslims higher, lower, or about the same as among non-Muslims?

Race, gender, and class are the main loci of social inequality in the contemporary world. Ideally we could investigate each of them. But assessing racial inequality is beyond our reach. There is no generally accepted metric for assessing racial inequality across societies, and there are no cross-national data that rate the level of racial inequality in a comparative framework. Thus, a study such as this book, which relies on cross-national comparison and comparison among individuals around the world, cannot investigate racial equality. We know that some religious traditions contain sacred exhortation to full equality. Among humanity's holy scriptures, the Qur'an arguably contains the most explicit and poetic injunction against racial inequality and discrimination. In 30:20–22, God, speaking in the third person, goes so far as to depict racial and linguistic diversity as marks of His lordship and His goodness to man: "By one of His signs He created you from dust; and behold, you became humans and multiplied throughout the earth. . . . Among his other signs are the creation of the heavens and the earth and the diversity of your tongues and colours.

Surely there are signs in this for all mankind." The Bible depicts God's coming in Jesus Christ as rendering racial difference irrelevant. Referring to the rebirth of creation that Jesus has wrought, the apostle Paul writes, "In that renewal there is no longer Greek and Jew, circumcised and uncircumcised, barbarian, Scythian, slave, and free; but Christ is all and in all!" (Col. 3:11). We also know, however, that racial slavery, with Muslims and Christians in the role of slave owners as well as slaves, is part of Muslim and Christian history. Thus, while we cannot empirically test whether Muslims are more or less prone to racial discrimination and inequality than adherents of other faiths, we may note that Islam, like Christianity, contains both a sacred ban on racism and historical practice that defies injunctions in its central texts.

Inequality between the genders and between classes may be investigated, since we do have data on them. On gender-based inequality, there is a plethora of quantitative data. I will use a variety of indicators covering the status of women in public life, popular attitudes toward gender-based inequality, and structural inequalities in well-being. Data on class inequality are much less plentiful. Measuring class inequality is more difficult, and only one statistic, the Gini score, is widely used. I will use it here.

We begin with consideration of gender-based inequality, then investigate class inequality. The main question is: Do Muslims and non-Muslims differ from one another in terms of general patterns of social inequality?

GENDER-BASED INEQUALITY

In the minds of many Muslims and non-Muslims, inequality between the genders is a salient characteristic of Muslim societies. Some writers, even while resisting stereotypes that reflexively cast women as victims, still hold that special challenges face women and girls in Muslim societies. Sometimes this problem is said to be much more pronounced among Arabs than non-Arabs. Many writings take the form of scholarly or semischolarly studies.[1] Others are personal accounts, sometimes written by or about women who have emigrated from predominantly Muslim societies to the West.[2] Yet few works have systematically compared the status of women and girls in Muslim and non-Muslim communities.[3] Case studies, polemics, and personal accounts may provide valuable insights, but we need to supplement them with systematic comparative work based on broad, large-N statistical analysis.

Muslims and Gender-Based Inequality: Hypotheses and Measurement

Some writers, including some of those cited in note 1, hold that inequality between men and women is particularly acute in Muslim communities. They highlight, among other things, segregation of the sexes, which is undoubtedly more conventional in Muslim than non-Muslim societies. Some also often point to the headscarf and other accoutrements of personal modesty that are common among women in Muslim communities but unusual elsewhere. Writers who maintain that inequality between the genders is greater in the Muslim world point to a variety of causes. Some see the Qur'an and the Hadith as providing explicit sanction for an unusual degree of inequality. Others point to factors such as the greater degree of tribalism that is sometimes said to obtain in Muslim societies due to the supposedly strong influence of Arabian culture on Muslim thinking. In desert and mountainous cultures, tribalism may, for demographic reasons, be more pronounced than in other settings. Since political alliances in sparsely populated tribal societies depend vitally on blood ties, any question regarding the paternity of children poses an existential threat to the social and political order. These circumstances may create conditions in which men are especially eager to cloister and control the movement of women and girls.

A rival viewpoint holds that the status of females is not inferior among Muslims—or, at the very least, that non-Muslim observers often misread the meaning of institutions such as the headscarf or sexual segregation.[4] According to such a view, the notion that women have it worse under Islam is based on misunderstanding and superficial evidence. The segregation of the sexes, according to this argument, does not necessarily imply poorer treatment for females. It might even promote better conditions for females than mixed-sex environments do, as some graduates of Wellesley College who do not lack feminist credentials would claim. Furthermore, the headscarf may be regarded as a normal symbol of religious commitment, much the way Orthodox Jewish men regard the yarmulke. Innumerable Muslim women don the headscarf even in settings in which governments do not mandate its use. While we lack global data on the matter, it is possible that most women who wear it feel no more oppressed than American or Japanese men do by wearing a necktie. As with the necktie, the headscarf might not be one's choice on a warm day if physical comfort were one's sole criterion for dressing; and, as with the necktie, only one sex feels obliged to wear it. But, as with the necktie, it would be a mistake to assume that wearers feel like victims of sexual discrimination. Most may simply regard it as a normal part of dressing for appearance in public.

Unfortunately, much of what little evidence is adduced on one side or another in debates over the status of women in Muslim societies is about attire or segregation. Critics of treating the headscarf as a sign of subordination are undoubtedly right to say that observers often misconstrue its real meaning to those who wear it. We need better indicators than dress habits. Segregation of the sexes may also be overrated as an indicator; certainly, its meaning and consequences are not straightforward or easy for outsiders to interpret. Ideally, our indicators should reflect phenomena that have largely the same meaning across societies.

Here I will investigate the relative status of females using a variety of indicators. The first set of indicators measures the status of women in public life. The second measures public opinion on gender-based inequality. The third assesses structural conditions of personal well-being. Using a variety of indicators that cover a broad set of phenomena gives us a reasonably good view of the evidence on inequality between the genders.

The Status of Women in Public Life

In order to assess the status of women in public life, we may have a look at data on women in the workplace and positions of political leadership. To measure the first, I use earned income ratio. The data are from a year during the second half of the 1990s or the first half of the first decade of the 2000s.[5] This statistic captures female workforce participation, which refers to the proportion of women who work outside the home, as well as women's earnings relative to men's earnings among people in the workforce. Even in what we often regard as highly egalitarian societies, the earned income ratio is not equal (which would be reflected in a score of 1, indicating parity in earnings) because almost everywhere, more women than men of working age remain outside the workforce for the purpose of bearing and raising children. Yet low earned income ratios may reflect lower status for women. So too might they *cause* lower status by making financial independence for women who seek it harder to achieve. I also consider the representation of women in high politics. To do so, I use two measures. One is the share of seats in the national legislature held by women as of 2008.[6] The second is the percentage of personnel at the ministerial level of government who are women. Our data for this variable are for 2005.[7]

Table 6.1 presents the averages for predominantly Muslim and other countries. Table 6.2 shows the data for the largest Muslim and Christian countries.[8]

Table 6.1 Mean Scores on Indicators of the Status of Women in Public Life for Muslim and Non-Muslim Countries

Survey Item	Muslim Countries	Non-Muslim Countries
Ratio of female-to-male earned income, 2005	.42 ($N = 39$)	.56 ($N = 121$)
Percentage of members of parliament who are women, 2008	11.6 ($N = 42$)	19.6 ($N = 125$)
Percentage of officials at the ministerial level who are women, 2005	9.2 ($N = 40$)	16.7 ($N = 123$)

Figure 6.1 presents boxplots that illustrate the differences between predominantly Muslim and non-Muslim countries for the indicators of the status of women in public life. Figure 6.1, like tables 6.1 and 6.2, reveals substantial differences. The plot on the left shows that in Muslim countries the ratio of female-to-male earned income varies from less than 20 percent to about 70 percent, with a median of about 40 percent, while in non-Muslim countries it ranges from about 30 percent to about 80 percent with a median of roughly 55 percent. The second plot shows that in Muslim countries the percentage of parliamentarians who are women ranges from 0 to a little

Table 6.2 Data on the Status of Women in Public Life in the Largest Muslim and Christian Countries

	Muslim Countries		
Country	Ratio of female-to-male earned income, 2005	Percentage of members of parliament who are women, 2008	Percentage of officials at the ministerial level who are women, 2005
Indonesia	.46	11.6	10.8
Pakistan	.29	22.5	5.6
Bangladesh	.46	13.0	8.3
Egypt	.23	1.8	5.9
Turkey	.35	9.1	4.3
Iran	.39	2.8	6.7
Sudan	.25	18.1	2.6
Morocco	.25	10.5	5.9
Algeria	.34	7.7	10.5
Afghanistan	NA	27.7	10.0
Uzbekistan	.60	17.5	3.6
Saudi Arabia	.16	0.0	0.0
Iraq	NA	25.5	18.8
Malaysia	.36	10.8	9.1
Yemen	.30	0.3	2.9
Syria	.34	12.4	6.3
Niger	.57	12.4	23.1
Senegal	.54	22.0	20.6
Mali	.68	10.2	18.5
Tunisia	.29	22.8	7.1
18/20/20-country average	.38	12.9	9.0

continued

Table 6.2 *Continued*

	Christian Countries		
Country	Ratio of female-to-male earned income, 2005	Percentage of members of parliament who are women, 2008	Percentage of officials at the ministerial level who are women, 2005
United States	.63	16.8	14.3
Brazil	.58	9.0	11.4
Russia	.62	14.0	0.0
Mexico	.39	23.2	9.4
Philippines	.61	20.5	25.0
Germany	.58	31.6	46.2
DRC	.52	8.4	12.5
France	.64	18.2	17.6
UK	.66	19.5	28.6
Italy	.47	21.3	8.3
Ukraine	.55	8.2	5.6
Colombia	.63	8.4	35.7
South Africa	.45	33.0	41.4
Spain	.50	36.3	50.0
Argentina	.54	40.0	8.3
Poland	.60	20.2	5.9
Kenya	.83	9.8	10.3
Canada	.64	22.1	23.1
Uganda	.70	30.7	23.4
Peru	.55	29.2	11.8
20-country average	.58	21.0	19.4

less than 30, with a median of a little more than 10, while in non-Muslim countries it extends from 0 to more than 50, with a median of almost 20. The plot on the right shows that in Muslim countries the percentage of ministers who are women ranges from none to about a quarter, with a median of less than 10, while in non-Muslim countries it ranges from none to more than half, with a median of about 15.

Let us have a closer look at the relationship between Islam and status difference between the genders. Doing so requires controlling for other possible determinants of the status of women relative to men in public life.[9]

Table 6.3 presents the regression output for OLS models that investigate the relationship between the percentage of Muslims in a country and the female-to-male earned income ratio. Three specifications are presented. The

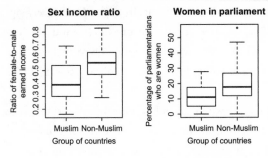

FIGURE 6.1:

The Status of Women in Public Life

Table 6.3 Regressions of Female-to-Male Earned Income Ratio on Hypothesized Predictors

	Model 1	*Model 2*	*Model 3*
(Intercept)	56.83*** (1.20)	79.09*** (7.50)	77.57*** (7.63)
Percent Muslim	–0.17*** (0.03)	–0.17*** (0.03)	–0.13*** (0.03)
GDP per capita		0.39* (0.17)	0.35* (0.17)
Life expectancy		–0.38** (0.12)	–0.41** (0.13)
Level of democracy			0.73 (0.89)
Fuels dependence			–0.05 (0.04)
N	160	160	160
Adjusted R^2	.17	.22	.23

Note: OLS models with robust standard errors in parentheses.

†significant at $p < .10$; *$p < .05$; **$p < .01$; ***$p < .001$

first model shows the simple bivariate relationship between the proportion of the population made up of Muslims and the female-to-male earned income ratio. The second model controls for indicators of socioeconomic development (income per capita and life expectancy). We would expect higher levels of economic development to be associated with higher status for women and thus higher female-to-male earned income ratio. The third model adds controls for level of democracy and fuels dependence, since these variables are sometimes also regarded as predictors of status inequality between the genders. One might expect the status of women to be higher in more democratic polities, and at least one recent study has found evidence that the public status of women may be lower in countries whose economies are highly reliant upon oil.[10]

The coefficient for percentage Muslim is statistically and substantively significant in all the models. The negative coefficient of 0.13 in model 3 suggests that a country that is all Muslims will have a female-to-male earned income ratio that is 13 percentage points lower than a country that is 0 percent Muslims.

The second indicator of the status of women in public life is the proportion of the national legislature that is made up of women. As noted above, that figure for predominantly Muslim countries is, on average, just over one-tenth; for other countries, it is just under one-fifth. The first column in table 6.4 presents the results of an OLS model of the association between the percentage of Muslims in a country and the proportion of parliamentarians who are women. The coefficient suggests that a 1 percentage-point increase in the Muslim population is associated with a 0.09 reduction in the proportion of parliament made up of women. The model predicts that a country with 0 percent Muslims has 9 percent more female parliamentarians than a country with 100 percent Muslims. In models 2 and 3, other predictors of the number of female parliamentarians are included. GDP per capita is positively correlated with women's representation in legislatures, with wealthier countries generally having more female parliamentarians. While wealth matters, controlling for it, as well as for other possible predictors, does not substantially diminish the statistical or substantive significance of the coefficient for the percentage of Muslims.

The third indicator of the status of women in public life is the percentage of ministerial positions occupied by women. In this case the raw data show a difference of approximately 7.5 percentage points between Muslim and non-Muslim countries. The OLS model that regresses women at ministerial levels on percentage Muslim,

Table 6.4 Regressions of the Percentage of Parliamentarians Who Are Women on Hypothesized Predictors

	Model 1	Model 2	Model 3
(Intercept)	20.15*** (1.03)	27.04*** (6.39)	28.81*** (6.78)
Percent Muslim	–0.09*** (0.02)	–0.08*** (0.02)	–0.08** (0.03)
GDP per capita		0.41** (0.14)	0.50** (0.16)
Life expectancy		–0.15 (0.10)	–0.14 (0.10)
Level of democracy			–0.67 (0.69)
Fuels dependence			–0.05 (0.03)
N	167	167	166
Adjusted R^2	.10	.14	.15

Note: OLS models with robust standard errors in parentheses.

†significant at $p < .10$; *$p < .05$; **$p < .01$; ***$p < .001$

Table 6.5 Regressions of the Percentage of Women at the Ministerial Level on Hypothesized Predictors

	Model 1	Model 2	Model 3
(Intercept)	17.23*** (1.11)	27.22*** (4.91)	23.49*** (4.95)
Percent Muslim	−0.09*** (0.02)	−0.08*** (0.02)	−0.02 (0.02)
GDP per capita		0.51** (0.16)	0.38* (0.16)
Life expectancy		−0.22* (0.08)	−0.28*** (0.08)
Level of democracy			1.86** (0.57)
Fuels dependence			−0.01 (0.02)
N	163	163	162
Adjusted R^2	.08	.15	.19

Note: OLS models with tobust standard errors in parentheses.

†significant at $p < .10$; *$p < .05$; **$p < .01$; ***$p < .001$

presented in model 1 in table 6.5, shows that a 1 percentage-point increase in the proportion of Muslims in a country is associated with a 0.09 percentage-point reduction in women at the ministerial level. This means that the model predicts that a country with 0 percent Muslims should have 9 percent more women in ministerial positions than a country with 100 percent Muslims. This difference remains statistically significant when we control for socioeconomic development, as we see in model 2. Yet when level of democracy is included, as it is in model 3, the coefficient for the percent Muslim variable becomes much smaller and is no longer statistically significant. Both greater wealth and more democracy are associated with more women in ministerial positions, but the proportion of Muslims in society may not have a substantial independent correlation.

Popular Attitudes toward Gender-Based Inequality

What about popular attitudes on questions pertaining to the status of women and girls? The World Values Survey (WVS) contains three items that address the matter directly. The first asks respondents whether they believe that "a university education is more important for a boy than for a girl."[11] The second asks whether the respondent thinks that "when jobs are scarce, men should have more right to a job than women."[12] The third item queries respondents on whether "men make better political leaders than women do."[13]

As table 6.6 shows, Muslims express more traditional views toward gender-based inequality than non-Muslims do. This pattern holds even once we separate out Christians and nondenominationalists. The percentage of Muslims who agree or strongly agree that a university education is more important for a boy than a girl is

Table 6.6 Mean Scores on Indicators of Attitudes toward Gender-Based Inequality for Muslims and Non-Muslims

Survey Item	Muslims	All Non-Muslims[a]	Christians	No Denomination
Percentage who "agree strongly" or "agree" that "a university education is more important for a boy than for a girl"[b]	38.4% (26,103)	17.7% (64,411)	16.7% (42,657)	15.2% (13,440)
Percentage who "agree" that "when jobs are scarce, men should have more right to a job than women"[c]	68.2% (25,079)	29.0% (78,019)	28.7% (51,657)	25.1% (17,634)
Percentage who "agree strongly" or "agree" that "on the whole, men make better political leaders than women do"[d]	70.9% (25,987)	40.3% (63,264)	39.7% (41,926)	35.8% (13,089)

Note: Figures in parentheses are base *N*s for the adjacent percentage.

[a]Includes all individuals who adhere to a religious denomination other than Islam as well as individuals who did not state adherence to a religious tradition.

[b]This question was not asked in Austria, Belgium, Belarus, Croatia, Czech Republic, Denmark, Estonia, Greece, Hungary, Iceland, Ireland, Israel, Latvia, Lithuania, Luxembourg, Malta, Portugal, and Slovakia.

[c]This question was not asked in Colombia and Israel.

[d]This question was not asked in Austria, Belgium, Belarus, Croatia, Czech Republic, Denmark, Estonia, Greece, Hungary, Iceland, Ireland, Israel, Latvia, Lithuania, Luxembourg, Malta, Portugal, and Slovakia.

double the percentage of Christians agreeing with the statement, and the percentage of Muslims who agree that when jobs are scarce men should have more right to a job than women is more than double the percentage of Christians who agree with the statement. Do these differences hold when we consider level of socioeconomic development?

Let us begin with analysis of the first of the three questions. The models in table 6.7 analyze agreement with the statement "a university education is more important for a boy than a girl" using hierarchical generalized linear models (HGLM). HGLM is the appropriate technique for this question, which has four ordered response categories from "strongly agree" to "strongly disagree." The coefficients in table 6.7 can be viewed as the log odds for a cumulative logit model. While these coefficients are not directly interpretable, they provide us with useful information about the statistical significance of a variable and the direction of the effect. All models show that self-identification as a Muslim has a statistically significant and positive effect on the likelihood of agreeing with the statement. Even when we control for individual-level and country-level variables, the effect of being a Muslim is still statistically significant.[14] Regarding other individual-level variables, being a female has a negative effect on the likelihood of agreeing that a university education is more important for a boy than a girl. Likewise, the relationship between education and agreement is also negative; the greater one's education level, the lower the likelihood of agreement with the statement. Age is statistically significant and positive: As age increases, the likelihood of agreement also becomes higher. While self-identification as a Muslim has a positive effect on agreeing with the statement, the percentage of a country's population that is Muslim does not have a statistically significant effect. Individuals who live in a country that is predominantly Muslim have no greater likelihood of agreeing with the statement than those living in a country that has no Muslims.[15]

In order better to understand the magnitude of differences between Muslims and non-Muslims according to the models estimated in table 6.7, it is useful to calculate several predicted probabilities for hypothetical individuals. As table 6.8 shows, when we look only at individual-level characteristics, Muslim men have the highest predicted probability of agreement, followed by Christian men, Muslim women, and Christian women. The difference in predicted probabilities between Muslim and Christian males is not very large, however. Rather, gender appears to have a greater impact on responses than does religious identification. A Muslim woman of average age and education has a predicted probability of agreeing with the statement that is 8 percentage points lower than the predicted probability for her male counterpart. Our HGLM analysis shows that even though there is an independent effect of being Muslim on agreement with the statement, the effect of gender is actually greater. In other words, being a Muslim per se has moderate effect on the probability of adopting a traditionalist attitude about gender-based inequality, but

Table 6.7 HGLM Analysis of Statement: "A University Education is More Important for a Boy Than for a Girl"[72t]

Predictors	Model 1	Model 2	Model 3	Model 4	Model 5
Intercept	-2.65*** (.16)	-2.65*** (.16)	-2.75*** (.16)	-2.83*** (.14)	-2.86*** (.14)
Individual-level[a]					
Female			-0.61*** (.03)	-0.61*** (.03)	-0.61*** (.03)
Age			0.01*** (.00)	0.01*** (.00)	0.00*** (.00)
Education level			-1.00*** (.05)	-1.00*** (.05)	-0.99*** (.05)
Muslim	0.29*** (.08)		0.20** (.07)	0.21** (.07)	0.18** (.06)
Christian		-0.11* (.05)	-0.01 (.04)	0.02 (.04)	0.00 (.03)
Importance of God					-0.02 (.01)
Country-level[b]					
GDP per capita (log)				-0.13 (.22)	-0.16 (.22)
Average age				-0.02 (.02)	-0.01 (.02)
Proportion Muslim				0.37 (.31)	0.01 (.36)
Proportion Christian				-0.67** (.23)	-0.99*** (.26)
Average Importance of God					0.10 (.06)

	Model 1	Model 2	Model 3	Model 4	Model 5
Thresholds	$\delta_1 = 1.27$	$\delta_1 = 1.27$	$\delta_1 = 1.31$	$\delta_1 = 1.31$	$\delta_1 = 1.32$
	$\delta_2 = 3.44$	$\delta_2 = 3.44$	$\delta_2 = 3.57$	$\delta_2 = 3.57$	$\delta_2 = 3.58$
Variance Components[c] (τ)	$u_0 = 0.53$	$u_0 = 0.53$	$u_0 = 0.57$	$u_0 = 0.38$	$u_0 = 0.37$
	$u_M = 0.20$	$u_C = 0.14$	$u_F = 0.07$	$u_F = 0.07$	$u_F = 0.07$
			$u_A = 0.00$	$u_A = 0.00$	$u_A = 0.00$
			$u_E = 0.17$	$u_E = 0.17$	$u_E = 0.16$
			$u_M = 0.12$	$u_M = 0.12$	$u_M = 0.10$
			$u_C = 0.05$	$u_C = 0.05$	$u_C = 0.03$
					$u_I = 0.01$

Note: Dependent variable includes four response categories, ranging from "strongly agree" to "strongly disagree." In the HGLM analysis, "strongly agree" is "1" and "strongly disagree" is "4." For details about the equations used in these and other HGLM models in the chapter, see appendix 6. The base category for the analysis in all HLM/HGLM models is made up of respondents who self-identified with a religion other than Christianity or Islam or did not identify with any religious tradition. Entries are restricted maximum likelihood coefficients for an ordered logit model using robust standard errors for the unit-specific model, calculated on HLM 6.06.

$N = 88{,}542$ in 65 countries.

[a] All individual-level variables are centered at the group mean.

[b] All country-level variables are centered at the grand mean.

[c] The variance component for a null model including only the random Level-2 intercept is $\tau = 0.53$.

$*p < .05; **p < .01; ***p < .00.$

Table 6.8 Predicted Probabilities of "Agreeing" or "Strongly Agreeing" with the Statement: "A University Education is More Important for a Boy Than for a Girl" (model 4 from table 6.7)

	Muslim Man	Christian Man	Muslim Woman	Christian Woman
Living in country that is 95% Christian, 5% Muslim	.20	.17	.12	.10
Living in country that is 5% Christian, 95% Muslim	.39	.34	.25	.22

being a Muslim *man* corresponds to a considerably stronger probability of traditional attitudes.

Let us turn to the second question. Table 6.9 analyzes agreement with the statement, "When jobs are scarce, men should have more right to a job than women." The coefficients in the table are for ordered logit response models. As with the statement about university education, self-identification as a Muslim has a statistically significant and positive effect on one's likelihood of agreement that is still evident when we control for other individual-level and country-level factors.[16] As with the previous models in table 6.7, gender and education have a statistically significant and negative effect on agreement, while age has a statistically significant and positive effect. In other words, women and more educated individuals are more likely to not agree that men should have more right to a job than women, while older individuals are more likely to agree with it.[17]

In contrast to the question about university education, the size of a country's Muslim population has a statistically significant and positive effect on the likelihood of agreeing with the statement about preferential treatment under job scarcity. Living in a country with a larger Muslim population increases the likelihood that one will agree with the statement. In model 5, a country's level of religiosity, measured by its average score on the importance-of-God scale, is also statistically significant and positive. While this variable was not statistically significant in table 6.7, living in a more religious country increases the likelihood that one will agree with the statement analyzed in table 6.9.

In order to aid substantive interpretation, we again may calculate several predicted probabilities for individuals, holding all factors other than gender, religious identification, and the denominational composition of a country at their means. The probabilities are shown in table 6.10.[18] These predicted probabilities display similar trends to the findings for the statement about university education. The predicted probability of agreement with the statement is highest for Muslim men,

Table 6.9 HGLM Analysis of Statement: "When Jobs are Scarce, Men Should Have More Right to a Job Than Women" [1 = agree, 0 = neither agree or disagree/ disagree]

Predictors	Model 1	Model 2	Model 3	Model 4	Model 5
Intercept	-0.72*** (.13)	-0.72*** (.13)	-0.78*** (.14)	-0.78*** (.09)	-0.78*** (.09)
Individual-level [a]					
Female			-0.55*** (.04)	-0.56*** (.04)	-0.59*** (.04)
Age			0.01*** (.00)	0.01*** (.00)	0.01*** (.00)
Education level			-1.34*** (.08)	-1.33*** (.08)	-1.30*** (.08)
Muslim	0.44*** (.07)		0.56*** (.08)	0.54*** (.08)	0.40*** (.07)
Christian		0.02 (.06)	0.12** (.04)	0.10* (.04)	0.01 (.04)
Importance of God					0.04*** (.01)
Country-level [b]					
GDP per capita (log)				-0.20 (.22)	-0.01 (.24)
Average age				-0.05* (.02)	0.00 (.02)
Proportion Muslim				1.61*** (.39)	1.02* (.44)
Proportion Christian				-0.56 (.31)	-1.12** (.37)

Average Importance of God   0.23** (.08)

Variance Components [c] (τ)				
$u_o = 1.31$	$u_o = 1.31$	$u_o = 1.52$	$u_o = 0.70$	$u_o = 0.62$
$u_M = 0.14$	$u_C = 0.19$	$u_F = 0.14$	$u_F = 0.13$	$u_F = 0.12$
		$u_A = 0.00$	$u_A = 0.00$	$u_A = 0.00$
		$u_E = 0.39$	$u_E = 0.38$	$u_E = 0.37$
		$u_M = 0.22$	$u_M = 0.26$	$u_M = 0.12$
		$u_C = 0.06$	$u_C = 0.07$	$u_C = 0.04$
				$u_I = 0.00$

Note: In the fourth-wave data this question was given two response options, "agree" and "disagree." In the fifth wave, the question had three possible responses, "agree," "neither," and "disagree." In order to compare data from both waves, the "neither" and "disagree" categories were combined into the "0" category. Entries are restricted maximum likelihood coefficients with robust standard errors for the unit-specific model, calculated on HLM 6.06.

$N = 100,428$ in 81 countries.

[a] All individual-level variables are centered at the group mean.

[b] All country-level variables are centered at the grand mean.

[c] The variance component for a null model including only the random Level-2 intercept is $\tau = 1.30$.

$*p < .05$; $**p < .01$; $***p < .001$.

Table 6.10 Predicted Probabilities of "Agreeing" that "When Jobs Are Scarce, Men Should Have More Right to a Job than Women" (model 5 from table 6.9)

	Muslim Man	Christian Man	Muslim Woman	Christian Woman
Living in country that is 95% Christian, 5% Muslim	.31	.24	.20	.15
Living in country that is 5% Christian, 95% Muslim	.75	.68	.63	.54

lower for Christian men, lower again for Muslim women, and lowest for Christian women. We also see that the differences between men and women are greater than the differences between Muslims and Christians. On average, a Muslim man is 11–12 percentage points more likely than a Muslim woman to agree with the statement that when jobs are scarce, men should have more right to a job than women. When we vary the size of the Muslim and Christian populations, we see that living in a country with a large Muslim population greatly increases the predicted probability of agreement. A Muslim man living in a country that is 5 percent Christian and 95 percent Muslim has a 75 percent likelihood of agreeing with the statement, while a Muslim man with the same characteristics living in a country that is 5 percent Muslim and 95 percent Christian has a mere 31 percent chance of agreement. The variation in the size of the Muslim population plays a greater role in the likelihood of agreeing with the statement than do individual-level characteristics.

Table 6.11 presents an HGLM analysis of the final indicator of attitudes toward gender-based inequality, agreement with the statement, "On the whole, men make better political leaders than women do." In general, table 6.11 shows broad similarities with the previous two indicators.[19] Self-identification as a Muslim has a statistically significant and positive effect on the likelihood of agreeing with the statement. This effect holds even when we control for other individual- and country-level socioeconomic characteristics.[20] Other individual-level factors display the same pattern: Being female and having a higher level of education have a negative effect on agreement with the statement while older age slightly increases the likelihood of agreement.

The effect of the size of a country's Muslim population on agreement with the statement is less definitive. According to model 4, the percent of a country's population that is Muslim has a statistically significant and positive effect, while the percent of the population that is Christian is not statistically significant. Once individual- and country-level controls for religiosity are introduced in model 5,

Table 6.11 HGLM Analysis of Statement: "On the Whole, Men Make Better Political Leaders than Women Do"[73T]

Predictors	Model 1	Model 2	Model 3	Model 4	Model 5
Intercept	−1.87*** (.14)	−1.87*** (.14)	−1.94*** (.15)	−2.07*** (.10)	−2.11*** (.10)
Individual-level[a]					
Female			−0.67*** (.03)	−0.67*** (.03)	−0.68*** (.03)
Age			0.00*** (.00)	0.00*** (.00)	0.00*** (.00)
Education level			−0.72*** (.06)	−0.71*** (.06)	−0.70*** (.06)
Muslim	0.33*** (.06)		0.36*** (.06)	0.35*** (.06)	0.32*** (.06)
Christian		−0.07 (.04)			
Importance of God			0.14*** (.03)	0.11** (.03)	0.08* (.03)
Country-level[b]					
GDP per capita (log)				−0.48* (.23)	−0.55* (.23)
Average age				−0.02 (.02)	−0.01 (.02)
Proportion Muslim				0.98** (.33)	0.31 (.33)
Proportion Christian				−0.45 (.24)	−0.95*** (.28)
Average Importance of God					0.16* (.07)

Thresholds	$\delta_1 = 1.73$	$\delta_1 = 1.73$	$\delta_1 = 1.79$	$\delta_1 = 1.79$	$\delta_1 = 1.79$
	$\delta_2 = 3.85$	$\delta_2 = 3.85$	$\delta_2 = 3.99$	$\delta_2 = 3.99$	$\delta_2 = 4.00$
Variance Components[c] (τ)	$u_0 = 0.98$	$u_0 = 0.98$	$u_0 = 1.04$	$u_0 = 0.49$	$u_0 = 0.45$
	$u_M = 0.10$	$u_C = 0.10$	$u_F = 0.09$	$u_F = 0.09$	$u_F = 0.09$
			$u_A = 0.00$	$u_A = 0.00$	$u_A = 0.00$
			$u_E = 0.16$	$u_E = 0.16$	$u_E = 0.16$
			$u_M = 0.09$	$u_M = 0.09$	$u_M = 0.07$
			$u_C = \text{fixed to } 0$	$u_C = 0.04$	$u_C = 0.03$
					$u_I = 0.00$

Note: Dependent variable includes four response categories, ranging from "strongly agree" to "strongly disagree." In the HGLM analysis, "strongly agree" is "1" and "strongly disagree" is "4." Entries are restricted maximum likelihood coefficients for an ordered logit model using robust standard errors for the unit-specific model, calculated on HLM 6.06.

$N = 87{,}346$ in 65 countries.

[a] All individual-level variables are centered at the group mean.

[b] All country-level variables are centered at the grand mean.

[c] The variance component for a null model including only the random Level-2 intercept is $\tau = 0.97$.

$*p < .05; **p < .01; ***p < .001.$

the percent of the population that is Muslim ceases to be statistically significant. Religiosity has a statistically significant and positive effect on the likelihood of agreement.

Again we calculated predicted probabilities for several scenarios. The probabilities are shown in table 6.12.[21] As with the previous two indicators of attitudes toward gender-based inequality, the differences in predicted probabilities between Muslim and Christian men are moderate (here, approximately 5 percentage points) while the differences between Muslim men and Muslim women are substantial (about 15 percentage points). The size of a country's Muslim and Christian population also has a strong effect on an individual's likelihood of agreeing that men make better political leaders than women, as is obvious when comparing the numbers in the top and bottom rows in table 6.12.

What do these findings tell us? Taken together, the data for the three questions produce some clear trends. In all three cases, being a Muslim increased the likelihood that one would agree with statements that favor a more traditional—meaning male-superior—view of gender-based inequality. Yet in all three questions gender itself stood out as an important predictor as well. Men—both Muslim and Christian—were more likely to agree with the statements than were women. In fact, the findings suggest that support for gender-based inequality may be less an attribute of Muslims in general than of Muslim men.[22]

The religious composition of one's society, independent of one's own personal religious identification, may matter in important ways. While the percent of a country's population that is Muslim was not statistically significant in the statement about university education, it played a substantial role in the analyses that use the other two indicators. The greater the Muslim population, the more likely individuals were to agree with statements supporting traditional gender roles.

Parceling out the different effects for Muslim individuals and societies with predominantly Muslim populations, as we have done with the above models, is a task that can only be accomplished using multilevel modeling such as HGLM. Preliminary analyses of the pooled individual-level data without attention to country-level characteristics gave us somewhat different results. Namely, the Christian variable was always statistically significant and negative, resulting in an overestimation of the differences between Muslims and Christians. In some models the magnitude of the Muslim variable was far greater than the effect of gender. This divergence from the HGLM models is a consequence of omitting country-level effects and neglecting to take into consideration different sample sizes for each country. Although we cannot make the WVS representative of the world's population, HGLM allows us more precisely to separate out country- and individual-level effects and compare individuals across countries.

Table 6.12 Predicted Probabilities of "agreeing" or "strongly agreeing" that, "On the whole, men make better political leaders than women do"

| | Model 4 (Table 6.11) | | | | Model 5 (Table 6.11) | | | |
	Muslim Man	Christian Man	Muslim Woman	Christian Woman	Muslim Man	Christian Man	Muslim Woman	Christian Woman
Living in country that is 95% Christian, 5% Muslim	.47	.42	.31	.27	.45	.39	.29	.24
Living in country that is 5% Christian, 95% Muslim	.77	.73	.63	.58	.72	.67	.56	.50

While the analyses just conducted focused on attitudes, our next set of indicators captures deeper structural conditions. The first indicator is the female-to-male literacy ratio. It is measured as the female adult literacy rate divided by the male adult literacy rate.[23] These numbers reflect the value that people assign to the education of their girls relative to that of their boys. Literacy rates also influence people's life chances. Table 6.13 shows the averages for Muslim and non-Muslim countries and table 6.14 compares the biggest Muslim and Christian countries.[24]

Figure 6.2 presents a boxplot that shows the female literacy rate as a percentage of the male literacy rate in Muslim and non-Muslim countries in the year 2005. The number 100 represents parity, meaning that the female literacy rate is 100 percent of the male rate and literacy rates between the genders are identical. As can be seen in the figure, the rate in Muslim countries varies from about 30 to 100, with a median slightly above 80. It ranges from a little less than 40 to more than 120, with a median that approaches 100, in non-Muslim countries. The female-to-male literacy ratio is generally lower in Muslim countries than elsewhere.

The differences shown in the tables and illustrated by the boxplot are large. In order to assess whether they are due to religion per se or something else, we must control for other variables. As usual, it is necessary to control for socioeconomic development, which is measured as GDP per capita. Another important control in this analysis is overall literacy rates, which are highly correlated with the female-to-male literacy ratio. Lower overall literacy is associated with lower female-to-male literacy ratios.[25] We would expect this variable also to be highly correlated with socioeconomic development. In fact, some studies use overall literacy rates to measure socioeconomic development. I also control for level of democracy and fuels dependence, measured as above. I further add a dichotomous (dummy) variable for members of the Arab League, since structural inequalities between the genders are sometimes seen as especially—and perhaps uniquely—acute in Arab countries.

Table 6.15 shows the results of the OLS regressions that examine the relationship between the proportion of Muslims in society and the female-to-male literacy ratio. In model 1, the coefficient for percent Muslim is –0.21, meaning that the expected female literacy rate as a percent of the male rate is reduced by .21 for every 1 percentage-point increase in the proportion of Muslims in the population. Thus, the expected female literacy rate as a percentage of the male rate is 21 percentage points higher in a country with 0 percent Muslims than it is in a country that is all Muslims. The coefficient falls to –0.05 when we control for the overall literacy rate as well as other predictors, as is shown in models 3–5. Countries with high overall rates of literacy have higher female-to-male literacy ratios; gender-based inequality is less

Table 6.13 Mean Scores on Female-to-Male Literacy Ratio for Muslim and Non-Muslim Countries

Survey Item	Muslim Countries	Non-Muslim Countries
Female literacy rate as a percentage of male rate, 2005	78 ($N = 44$)	91 ($N = 125$)

Table 6.14 Data on Female-to-Male Literacy Ratio in the Largest Muslim and Christian Countries

Muslim Countries		Christian Countries	
Country	Female Literacy Rate as a Percentage of Male Rate	Country	Female Literacy Rate as a Percentage of Male Rate
Indonesia	92	United States	100
Pakistan	55	Brazil	100
Bangladesh	76	Russia	100
Egypt	72	Mexico	97
Turkey	84	Phillipines	102
Iran	87	Germany	100
Sudan	73	Dem Rep Congo	67
Morocco	60	France	100
Algeria	76	UK	100
Afghanistan	29	Italy	99
Uzbekistan	100	Ukraine	100
Saudi Arabia	87	Colombia	100
Iraq	76	South Africa	96
Malaysia	93	Spain	100
Yemen	47	Argentina	100
Syria	84	Poland	100
Niger	35	Kenya	90
Senegal	57	Canada	100
Mali	49	Uganda	75
Tunisia	78	Peru	88
20-country average	71	20-country average	96

acute in more literate societies. According to models 2–5, however, there is still a negative and statistically significant relationship between the female-to-male literacy ratio and percent Muslims in a country, even when we control for overall literacy rate and other predictors of gender-based inequality. The models provide

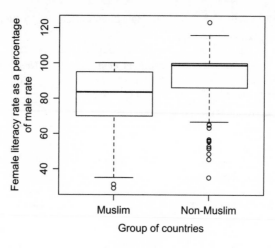

FIGURE 6.2:
Female-to-Male Literacy Ratio

evidence that the female-to-male literacy ratio is lower among Muslims than it is among non-Muslims.

The second indicator of structural inequality is difference in life expectancy. Female life expectancy naturally exceeds male life expectancy. By how much, however, depends on life conditions and varies from society to society. Differential access to health care that favors boys and men over girls and women, as well as particularly onerous life conditions for females, can compress the life expectancy gap.

An especially useful measure is the "healthy life expectancy" statistic devised by the World Health Organization (WHO). Healthy life expectancy, dubbed the "HALE" by its creators, is defined as the "average number of years that a person can expect to live in 'full health' by taking into account years lived in less than full health due to disease and/or injury."[26] The statistic provides valuable information on the status and life conditions of females relative to males. Here we examine the difference in the HALE, measured as the female rate minus the male rate.

The average difference in the HALE is shown in table 6.16.[27] The numbers for the biggest Muslim and Christian countries appear in table 6.17. There is a pronounced disparity. The average gap between men and women is only about half as large in Muslim as in non-Muslim countries, as table 6.16 shows. In two of the three largest Muslim countries, Pakistan and Bangladesh, the HALE is actually lower—substantially lower—for females than for males. Part of the problem here might be poor conditions for females in the South Asian region in general. But even there, Pakistan and Bangladesh stand out. The gap in India is 0.3 years (in favor of females). This number is a red flag in terms of the life conditions of females, but it is still not as bad as the analogous figures for Pakistan and Bangladesh. In none of the largest twenty predominantly Christian countries do males exceed females in healthy life

Table 6.15 Regressions of the Female-to-Male Literacy Ratio on Hypothesized Predictors

	Model 1	Model 2	Model 3	Model 4	Model 5
(Intercept)	93.11*** (1.26)	19.68* (8.43)	23.58*** (4.70)	23.23*** (4.76)	24.23*** (4.60)
Percent Muslim	−0.21*** (0.04)	−0.16*** (0.03)	−0.05** (0.02)	−0.05† (0.03)	−0.05* (0.03)
GDP per capita		−0.17 (0.11)	−0.12 (0.08)	−0.16† (0.09)	−0.11 (0.08)
Life expectancy		1.12*** (0.13)	0.08 (0.11)	0.04 (0.11)	0.06 (0.11)
Literacy rate			0.75*** (0.06)	0.77*** (0.06)	0.76*** (0.06)
Level of democracy				0.45 (0.42)	
Fuels dependence				−0.02 (0.02)	−0.02 (0.02)
Arab country				2.42 (2.11)	2.15 (2.10)
N	169	169	169	169	169
Adjusted R^2	.17	.59	.84	.84	.84

Note: OLS models with robust standard errors in parentheses.

†significant at $p < .10$; *$p < .05$; **$p < .01$; ***$p < .001$

Table 6.16 Mean Scores on Sex Difference in Healthy Life Expectancy (HALE) for Muslim and Non-Muslim Countries

Survey Item	Muslim Countries	Non-Muslim Countries
Sex difference in healthy life expectancy (female rate minus male rate, in years), 2002	1.8 (N = 43)	3.5 (N = 127)

Table 6.17 Data on Sex Difference in Healthy Life Expectancy (HALE) in the Largest Muslim and Christian Countries

Muslim Countries		Christian Countries	
Country	Healthy Life Expectancy, Female Rate Minus Male Rate (in years), 2002	Country	Healthy Life Expectancy, Female Rate Minus Male Rate (in years), 2002
Indonesia	1.5	United States	4.1
Pakistan	−1.9	Brazil	5.2
Bangladesh	−2.0	Russia	11.5
Egypt	2.4	Mexico	4.2
Turkey	1.6	Phillipines	4.4
Iran	3.0	Germany	4.4
Sudan	2.7	Dem Rep Congo	4.1
Morocco	1.4	France	5.4
Algeria	1.9	UK	3.0
Afghanistan	0.5	Italy	4.0
Uzbekistan	3.0	Ukraine	8.7
Saudi Arabia	3.1	Colombia	8.5
Iraq	2.3	South Africa	2.0
Malaysia	3.2	Spain	5.4
Yemen	2.7	Argentina	5.6
Syria	2.7	Poland	5.4
Niger	−0.6	Kenya	0.7
Senegal	1.8	Canada	3.9
Mali	0.8	Uganda	2.0
Tunisia	2.3	Peru	2.8
20-country average	1.6	20-country average	4.8

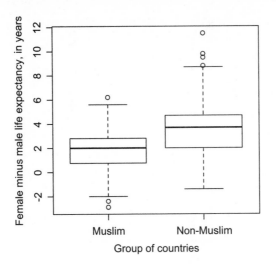

FIGURE 6.3:

Sex Difference in Healthy Life Expectancy

expectancy. In only one, Kenya, is the gap favoring females smaller than two years. Even if we exclude Russia, which has the world's broadest gap, the average among the remaining nineteen largest predominantly Christian countries is 4.2 years—two-and-a-half times larger than the average for the twenty largest predominantly Muslim countries.

Figure 6.3 illustrates what the numbers in tables 6.16 and 6.17 reveal: Females in Muslim countries have a substantially smaller healthy life expectancy advantage than they do in non-Muslim countries. In Muslim countries females have healthy life expectancies that range between three years shorter and six years longer than those of males; the median is a female advantage of about two years. In non-Muslim countries females live between one year less and almost twelve years longer than males; the median is a female advantage of almost four years.

Until we control for other possible determinants of the gender gap in healthy life expectancy, however, we do not know whether religion matters. Perhaps level of socioeconomic development alone determines the gap, and the lower overall level of development in predominantly Muslim countries is to blame. We would expect societies with higher levels of socioeconomic development to have relatively better conditions for women. We must also control for the overall HALE for both genders, which itself may be treated as indicator of socioeconomic development. As in analysis of the female-to-male literacy ratio, I also include a control for Arab countries. We need to control for several other variables that may affect the HALE as well. One is a legacy of communist rule. I use a dichotomous variable for countries that have a legacy of Soviet-type socialism. For reasons that are not yet well understood, postcommunist countries have large, female-favoring gaps in healthy life expectancy. The final control is the proportion of the population that is infected

Table 6.18 Regressions of Sex Difference in Healthy Life Expectancy (HALE) on Hypothesized Predictors

	Model 1	Model 2	Model 3	Model 4	Model 5
(Intercept)	3.759*** (0.209)	-1.764* (0.787)	1.885 (1.208)	0.013 (0.844)	1.736 (1.006)
Percent Muslim	-0.025*** (0.004)	-0.022*** (0.004)	-0.028*** (0.006)	-0.026*** (0.005)	-0.024*** (0.004)
GDP per capita		-0.087*** (0.025)	-0.026 (0.027)	-0.027 (0.025)	-0.009 (0.024)
Healthy life expectancy		0.107*** (0.016)	0.015 (0.020)	0.060*** (0.017)	0.032† (0.019)
Arab country			1.014† (0.542)	0.761 (0.546)	
Level of democracy			0.207* (0.100)		
Fuels dependence			0.006 (0.004)		
Post communist country			2.687*** (0.460)	2.678*** (0.483)	2.555*** (0.453)
Percent HIV infected			-0.085** (0.030)		-0.071* (0.029)
N	170	170	168	170	168
Adjusted R^2	.150	.295	.473	.447	.459

Note: OLS models with robust standard errors in parentheses.

†significant at $p < .10$; *$p < .05$; **$p < .01$; ***$p < .001$.

with HIV.[28] This figure ranges from negligible in many countries to roughly one-fifth of the adult population in much of southern Africa. High HIV/AIDS rates not only slash overall healthy life expectancy but also tend to compress differences between males and females. Whether sex discrimination in access to health care is to blame is not yet fully understood by scholars who study the epidemic. But we know from examining the data that life expectancy differentials favoring women tend to fall with an increase in HIV/AIDS, so a control is included for the proportion of the population that is infected with the virus.

Table 6.18 shows the regressions. Model 1 estimates that a 1 percent increase in the proportion of Muslims in a country's population is associated with a reduced life-expectancy advantage for females of 0.025 years. Thus, females in a country with 0 percent Muslims are expected to have a life expectancy advantage that is 2.5 years greater than do females in a country that is 100 percent Muslims. This difference remains constant when we control for other predictors of gender difference in healthy life expectancy, as can be seen in models 2–5.

Some Reflections on the Findings

All the findings point in the same direction. Whether we focus on status in public life, popular attitudes, or structural inequities in well-being, females tend to fare relatively poorly in places where Muslims predominate. In none of the results is Islam associated with better status for females relative to males, and in most of the analyses it is clearly correlated with inferior conditions for females.

The findings should be treated with caution. First, it is noteworthy that not all of the findings are robust or point unequivocally to large gaps between Muslims and non-Muslims. Of the three indicators for the status of women in public life, the measures for the female-to-male earned income ratio and for women in parliament showed a clear, robust Muslim disadvantage, but the finding on the proportion of ministerial positions occupied by women did not. The investigation of opinion on the status of women relative to men revealed that Muslims generally hold less egalitarian views, though it also uncovered evidence that support for gender-based inequality may be less an attribute of Muslims in general than of Muslim men specifically. In the investigation of structural inequalities between the genders, a Muslim disadvantage was evident in both the female-to-male literacy ratio and the gap in healthy life expectancy.

Some of the indicators may be culture-bound, in the sense that people in different settings attach different meanings or values to them. Let us start with the indicators for the status of women in public life. Europeans and Americans generally regard earned income ratio as a good indicator. Yet such a view is not necessarily universal. In some societies, most women may regard the opportunity to exit the workplace (or never enter it) as desirable. Even among upper-middle-class women in the West, some writers have noted what appears to be a trend toward opting out of the work-force in favor of greater dedication of time to family.[29]

Some cultures may also assign greater significance than others to the presence of women in high office. What people in some societies find irksome, others may find acceptable. When I was living in Russia in 1996, I recall seeing an interview on television with a presidential candidate, Aleksandr Lebed, that made a much greater impression on me, an American observer, than it made on the general audience. During the interview, Lebed, a grizzled but charming former army general, was asked if he thought that a woman could be president of Russia. Lebed shook his head. He said that a woman's job was to transmit the nation's cultural riches to the next generation. A woman's place was at home, with the children, not in the office of the presidency. I watched the interview with a group of highly educated Russian friends, none of whom were Muslims, including several young women. Lebed's remark prompted no hint of a stir in the room. After the program, I asked a woman who had watched the interview with me what she thought of the remark. She was a bright, ambitious young professional who was moving up quickly in the brave new world of Russian finance. She shrugged and said, "Who knows, maybe he's right."

The next day I scoured the press for coverage of Lebed's statement about women. I searched in vain; the remark did not even make news. Russians found it unremark-able. It had no effect on Lebed's campaign. Lebed went on to finish a strong third in the balloting for president. Among my American friends, particularly educated young women, I would expect a different reaction. Coming from a presidential can-didate in the United States, a statement such as Lebed's might be a campaign-ender, even a political career-ender, for the man who uttered it.

The point here is not that Russian women are less enlightened than American women; nothing of the sort may be inferred from the anecdote. It is rather that the significance of a woman serving as president (or, for that matter, as a minis-ter or a member of parliament) may vary in people's minds and values across societies.

We need also to account for the possibility that in our consideration of popular attitudes on gender-based inequality, people's responses to the survey questions might reflect their positive evaluations (meaning their take on the way things are) rather than normative evaluations (meaning their opinion on the way things should be). For example, a Saudi Arabian who agrees with the statement that "a university education is more important for a boy than for a girl" may simply be confirming what he or she understands to be a fact in his or her society, rather than what he or she regards as desirable. The same might hold for a Brazilian or a respondent from any other country. The large difference between the way Saudi Arabians and Brazil-ians respond to this survey item, with twice as many Saudis as Brazilians agreeing with the statement, may indicate what people in these two societies see as reality, not necessarily what they would like to be the case. So we cannot reflexively infer from the data that "sexist attitudes" are vastly more prevalent in Saudi Arabia than in Brazil.

Still, even if people's answers reflect what they think is, as opposed to what they feel should be, those answers are telling. There must be some reason why so many more Saudi Arabians than Brazilians feel that a university education is more important for a boy than for a girl. People's answers on the survey question, if not due to what would be considered sexism in the West, must reflect real differences in the actual post-graduation opportunities faced by young women as opposed to young men. If the questions fail to tap people's normative evaluations, they must elicit positive evaluations. In either case, the data reveal something of consequence.

Examination of structural inequalities in well-being, moreover, showed that actual social conditions for females are worse in countries where a larger proportion of the population is Muslim. Here we departed from subjective evaluations and entered the realm of rock-hard facts. It is impossible to account for strikingly small gaps in healthy life expectancy in terms of benign cultural diversity. Unless one is prepared to argue that inferior health care and education for females is justifiable in cultural terms, Muslims have an especially acute problem with gender-based inequality.

Why Is Gender-Based Inequality Higher among Muslims? The Possible Role of Sacred Scripture

What, then, is the basis for that inequality? Is it rooted in religion itself?

In order to argue that social practices that deny equality between the genders are innate to Islam, one would need to locate the bases for those practices in the scriptures that constituted the religion's genetic code and that continue to provide its textual foundation. Thus, we must ask: Is gender-based inequality inscribed in the Qur'an and/or the Hadith of Islam?

There are many passages in the Qur'an and the Hadith that do appear to endorse inequality. The Qur'an prescribes that males shall inherit twice as much as females (4:11), and this injunction undergirds inheritance law in many predominantly Muslim countries today. Some Hadith reports contain statements that can be construed as endorsements of gender-based inequality. For example, the *Sahih al-Bukhari*, the reports collected by Muhammad ibn Ismail al-Bukhari purporting to be statements of the Prophet that Sunni Muslims typically regard as the most reliable source of Hadith, contains the following passage: "The Messenger of Allah 'Allah's blessing and peace be upon him' answered: 'Do not you see that the two women's witness is considered to be equal only to one man's witness?' [the women] replied: 'Yes.' He said: 'Then, this is the woman's deficiency of intelligence.'"[30]

Some contemporary authors consider the social implications of living by such injunctions and statements to be clearly inegalitarian. Such writers, including Ibn Warraq, a vocal critic of Islam, identify bases for gender disparities in Muslim societies in the scriptures.[31] Other writers display agnosticism about what the sacred texts of Islam really teach about gender-based inequality, but regard the social practices of Muslims in this area as so unjust as to render the question of Qur'anic authority of secondary importance. Ayaan Hirsi Ali, a Somali-born former member of the Dutch parliament who left the Netherlands under death threats from Muslims, is such a figure.[32]

Some contemporary authors have taken a different approach. They have reconsidered the sacred texts and found them to be far more sexually egalitarian than they have often appeared to be. Most such authors have not argued that Islam, in contemporary practice, is sexually egalitarian. Amina Wadud, a leading force in reinterpreting the scriptures, states plainly, "Because women are not deemed as important as men in most Muslim majority or minority communities, Muslim women do not enjoy a status equal to men. If the definitive basis for what Islam means is determined by what Muslims do, then women and men are not equal." But Wadud's research on the Qur'an led her to believe that "in Islam a female person was intended to be . . . a morally full human being, equal to all who accepted Allah as Lord, Muhammad as prophet, and Islam as *din* [the faith]."[33] Wadud is only one of a number of authors who have offered a spirited reinterpretation of the sacred texts from an antipatriarchal point of view.[34]

Such authors hold that the Qur'an contains passages that appear to justify male supremacy but also includes others that affirm equality between the genders. They hold that the latter passages best capture the overall spirit of the Book and therefore should be regarded as authoritative. According to such reasoning, the Qur'an retains its infallibility and logical coherence as God's revelation, but fallible human beings cannot fully grasp the mind of God. They therefore should not pounce on this or that passage to justify what is contrary to the merciful and egalitarian spirit of the text as a whole. Thus, while it is true the Qur'an states in 4:34 that "men have authority over women because God has made the one superior to the other, and because they spend their wealth to maintain them," it also portrays women and men as equally capable of virtue and equally entitled to eternal reward for upright lives. What is more, God does not distinguish, in broad terms, between what is virtuous for men and what is virtuous for women; right action is right action. Thus, God states in 33:35, "Those who submit to God and accept the true Faith; who are devout, sincere, patient, humble, charitable, and chaste; who fast and are ever mindful of God—on these, both men and women, God will bestow forgiveness and a rich recompense."

The same logic may be applied to the passages on polygyny. The Qur'an 4:3 states, "If you fear you cannot treat orphans with fairness, then you may marry other women who seem good to you: two, three, or four of them. But if you fear that you cannot maintain equality among them, marry only one or any slave-girls you may own. This will make it easier for you to avoid injustice." Yet 4:128 reveals, "Try as you may, you cannot treat all your wives impartially." These passages, respectively, (1) allow men to take multiple wives, if they can treat them equally, but (2) state that men cannot possibly treat multiple wives equally. When viewed from this perspective, the mention of the care of orphans comes to the forefront of the reader's attention. Only the necessity of saving orphans can explain why God would apparently allow for multiple wives in the first place (in 4:3), but then deny that men are able to fulfill His injunction to equal treatment required to justify taking multiple wives (in 4:128). When the passages are taken together, polygyny appears strictly as an expedient to ensure the survival of orphaned children. When there exists an alternative to polygyny to ensure that orphans will not be left to die, the justification for taking multiple wives evaporates and God's intended plan for monogamous marriage can be realized.

A like-minded approach is possible to injunctions about life inside marriage. In one of the most challenging (and chilling) passages in the Qur'an (4:34), God enjoins men to beat women whom they suspect of insubordination: "As for those from whom you fear disobedience, admonish them and send them to beds apart and beat them. Then if they obey you, take no further action against them. Surely God is high, supreme." Yet many other passages order men to treat their wives with kindness. Even when a man has decided to divorce a woman, he is urged to take her back after a waiting period if the wife desires reconciliation (2:228). Whether he takes her back or not, he is to treat her with respect, "When you have renounced your wives and they have reached the end of their waiting period, either retain them in honour or let them go with kindness. But you shall not retain them in order to harm them or to wrong them. Whoever does this wrongs his own soul" (2:231).

According to authors who resist what they regard as unjust and inaccurate readings of the Qur'an, advocates of patriarchy have essentially enshrined passages such as those found in 4:34 and 4:3 while ignoring or, at best, failing to grasp those found in 4:128, 33:35, 2:228, and 2:231. Such selective reading amounts to abuse of the scriptures for the purpose of justifying male superiority.

How did this happen? According to Asma Barlas, the main problem has been that the classical exegesis (tafsir in Arabic) of the Qur'an as well as the Hadith were written and compiled in Islam's early centuries. Since male domination characterized life in those times, exegesis and the Hadith naturally were infused with a patriarchal tone and understanding. Now, none of this would necessarily block movement toward greater equality if contemporary exegeses were lively and influential, and if Muslims consistently considered the Qur'an superior to the Hadith. But, Barlas holds, the classical exegesis of the earliest centuries, as well as the Hadith, have long enjoyed, and continued to enjoy, supreme authority among Muslims. Indeed, she argues, these companion texts have come to have more influence on Muslims' thinking than the Qur'an itself. Barlas holds that the classical exegeses and the Hadith "have come to eclipse the Qur'an's influence in most Muslim societies today, exemplifying the triumph not only of some texts over others in Muslim religious discourse but also of history, politics, and culture over sacred text, and thus also of the cross-cultural, transnational, and nondenominational ideologies on women and gender in vogue in the Middle Ages over the teachings of the Qur'an."[35]

What may we say of the passages in the Qur'an itself that sound unequivocally misogynistic, such as the injunction to beat one's wife found in 4:34? This passage poses a special challenge to modern writers who claim that the Qur'an prescribes equality and mutual respect between the genders. Barlas and Wadud, like several other writers, emphasize several points. They hold that context must be taken into account when reading the Holy Book. Given the hyperpatriarchal nature of social relations in Arabia at the time that the Prophet received God's revelation, the passage is best read as a limitation on male authority rather than a prescription to engage in wife-beating. At the time, men could do as they pleased with women. This passage, and others that modern readers may see as enshrining male dominance, actually restricted the circumstances under which men could exercise their authority. It thereby granted women protection that they previously did not enjoy. Furthermore, the content of the passage is open to multiple interpretations. The verb *daraba*, meaning "to strike," can also mean "to set an example" and is to be distinguished from *darraba*, which is translated as "to strike repeatedly or intensely." The verb *daraba* is used elsewhere in sacred scripture in a symbolic sense, meaning "beating" with a sprig of leaves. The "beating" referred to in 4:34 may be regarded as a symbolic gesture, not an act that would cause bodily harm to a woman.[36] Finally, the authors return to the spirit of the Qur'an as a whole, which they regard as egalitarian and nonviolent. According to Barlas, given the ambiguity and room for multiple interpretations, "We should be able to admit that reading this Āyah [verse] as a license to batter wives, or to compel obedience upon them, is not acceptable in that it is not the best meaning we can derive from the Qur'ān. Moreover, it contradicts the Qur'ān's view of sexual equality and its teaching that marriages should be based in love, forgiveness, harmony, and *sukūn* [tranquility]."[37]

Writers such as Barlas and Wadud do not claim that any interpretations other than their own are illegitimate. Rather, they argue that readings such as their own have not even been given a chance, due to the supremacy that contemporary Muslims assign to the early exegeses on the Qur'an and reports on the Prophet's life offered in the Hadith. Barlas, Wadud, and others intend to give voice to a nonpatriarchal reading of the Qur'an. They also seek to elevate the Qur'an above the Hadith and the early commentaries on the Qur'an, both of which they see as more heavily influenced by patriarchal contexts than was the Holy Book itself.

To these arguments, several others could be added. Some writers, most notably Barlas, claim that the Hadith is far more problematic than the Qur'an. The Hadith is voluminous, and some quotations and actions attributed to the Prophet do appear to justify inequality. The passage from al-Bukhari's Hadith quoted above, in which the Prophet refers to women's "deficiency in intelligence," is an example.

Yet, to this author, the Hadith reports also seem to contain abundant fodder for justifying gender-based equality and kind treatment of women. As one who cannot read the texts in Arabic and must rely upon English translations, I cannot claim a shred of authority in matters of scriptural interpretation. Still, I have read (in English) a large body of Bukhari's Hadith and the Hadith of other reporters, and I have been shocked by the portrait of the Prophet's community that emerges. Al-Bukhari's reports are replete with passages that depict women as leaders and spiritual counselors,[38] that recount women without embarrassment asking the Prophet for advice on the most intimate sexual matters and invariably receiving from him serious, specific (even graphic) answers,[39] and that demonstrate that the Prophet worshiped with women and explicitly allowed women to worship with men at the mosque.[40] The Prophet mixed with women other than his wives openly and regularly. He heeded women's requests and even obeyed their orders. Al-Bukhari recounts, "Anas ibn Malik reported that: 'Any common woman of Madinah could have caught hold of the hands of the Holy Prophet S.A.W. [may Allah bless him and grant him peace] and taken him where she needed him to help her.'" Furthermore, "Anas ibn Malik reported that a woman was mentally ill. Once she came to the Holy Prophet S.A.W. and said: *Verily I have got some work to be done by you.* The Holy Prophet S.A.W. said: 'O Mother of so and so! Tell me where you want me to go with you and I will finish your work.' Then the Holy Prophet S.A.W. went with her and completed the work she gave to him" [emphasis in the original translation].[41]

Other reports that Muslims widely consider authentic (even if not as reliable as those of al-Bukhari, who is seen as uniquely dependable) also contain many quotations from the Prophet and accounts of his actions that place heavy burdens on men to treat women justly. Al-Tirmidhi's Hadith includes a quotation from the Prophet saying, "The most perfect Believer in his faith is he whose conduct is best, and the best among you is he who behaves best towards his wife."[42] A Hadith of Abu Da'ud recounts that Aisha, a wife of the Prophet late in his life, recalled, "Once I went with the Holy Prophet S.A.W. [may Allah bless him and grant him peace] on a journey and raced him on foot and beat him. Later, when I got plump, I raced him again and he beat me.

In the mind of this author—again, a non-Muslim who can make no claim to authoritative understanding of Islamic scriptures—the portrait that emerges from the reports of al-Bukhari and others is remarkable. In al-Bukhari's depiction of the Prophet's community, rigorous segregation of the sexes in daily life, reflexive female subordination to male authority, and sexual puritanism are simply absent. After reading how the Hadith was used to justify hyperpatriarchal practices in relations between the genders in the modern world, I have been surprised to encounter Muhammad's wife whipping him in foot races and receiving from him a challenge to a rematch after she had put on some weight; to see Muhammad engaging in all manner of social interaction with women of every station; to see Muhammad following a mentally ill old woman's orders to finish some (probably manual) work for her; and to hear Muhammad tell men that the very measure of their faith was how well they treated their wives.

So too have I found that the Qur'an is no more heavily laden with misogynistic passages than is the Bible, the book I was raised with, read regularly, and know well. In fact, parts of the Bible and the Qur'an address topics regarding women in parallel, and the Qur'an's injunctions are sometimes more liberal, in the contemporary sense, than their counterparts in the Bible.

Divine injunction on how to deal with male jealousy provides an example. In the book of Numbers in the Bible, God tells Moses that the Israelites are to handle a husband's suspicions in the following way:

[I]f feelings of jealousy come over her husband and he suspects she is impure—or if he is jealous and suspects her even though she is not impure—then he is to take his wife to the priest. . ... The priest shall bring her and have her stand before the Lord. Then he shall take some holy water in a clay jar and put some dust from the tabernacle floor into the water. . .. He shall have the woman drink the bitter water that brings a curse, and this water will enter her and cause bitter suffering. . ... If she has defiled herself and been unfaithful to her husband, then when she is made to drink the water that brings a curse, it will go into her and cause bitter suffering; her abdomen will swell and her thigh will waste away, and she will become accursed among her people. If, however, the woman has not defiled herself and is free from impurity, she will be cleared of guilt and will be able to have children. . ... The husband will be innocent of any wrongdoing, but the woman will bear the consequences of her sin. (Num. 5:14–16, 24, 27–28, 31)

The analogous passage in the Qur'an is the following:

If a man accuses his wife but has no witnesses except himself, he shall swear four times by God that his charge is true, calling down upon himself the curse of God if he is lying. But if his wife swears four times by God that his charge is false and calls down His curse upon herself if it be true, she shall receive no punishment. (24:6–8)

In the Bible, a husband's jealousy alone is enough to lead to his wife being forced to drink a mix of holy water and whatever the priest sweeps off the ground. If she is not guilty, the water will not do her in; if she is guilty, it will. Even by ancient standards this is, of course, pure sorcery. The modern reader might say that the woman's bodily reaction to the elixir would ultimately depend on hygienic conditions on the temple floor. In any event, a husband's jealousy subjects his wife to an ordeal, whether or not she is guilty of any wrongdoing. In contrast, her husband "will be innocent of any wrongdoing" regardless of whether or not his jealousy was justified. In the Qur'an, the entire matter is to be handled between husband and wife, with no intermediation by a religious authority. The suspicious husband has the right to level his accusation. But if his wife denies wrongdoing under a sacred oath she swears herself, the matter is settled. She is innocent. Her word is final.

The reader may put himself or herself in the place of the wife of a jealous husband and decide whether he or she would prefer be under Biblical or Qur'anic authority in this instance.

As discussed in previous chapters, the Bible contains a break-point that the Qur'an does not, namely the coming of God into the world in the form of Jesus Christ. This event, according to many Christians, renders the law of the Old Testament, from which the above-cited passage was drawn, null. The Qur'an lacks such a dualist structure. Muslims widely regard the Qur'an in its entirety to be evenly binding. Thus, if the New Testament of the Bible lacked material that could be used to justify male superiority, we might find a crucial difference between the Islamic and Christian scriptures that could help explain why Muslims in the contemporary world have a relatively bleak record on gender-based inequality.

But the New Testament does contain passages that assert male superiority. For example, in his first letter to the Christians of Corinth, Paul states:

Now I want you to realize that the head of every man is Christ, and the head of the woman is man, and the head of Christ is God. Every man who prays or prophesies with his head covered dishonors his head. And every woman who prays or prophesies with her head uncovered dishonors her head—it is just as though her head were shaved. If a woman does not cover her head, she should have her hair cut off; and if it is a disgrace for a woman to have her hair cut or shaved off, she should cover her head. A man ought not to cover his head, since he is the image and glory of God, but the woman is the glory of man. For man did not come from woman, but woman from man; neither was man created for woman, but woman for man. (1 Cor. 11:3–9)

In addition to establishing greater distance of women than men from God and justifying women's subordination to men, the Bible, it is also interesting to note, enjoins women to cover their heads.

It would be misguided to state that the Bible is inherently "sexist." Some of Paul's other statements sound like endorsements of gender equality and urgent calls to mutual love and commitment between husbands and wives. The four books that comprise the Gospels, moreover, may be regarded as in tune even with modern feminism. Jesus engaged in all manner of social interaction, including close friendship, with women. He treated women as the equals of men, in defiance of the social norms of his time. The personages in his parables and the beneficiaries of his healing miracles are as frequently female as male. The original witnesses to his resurrection were all women—this in a cultural setting that did not even regard women's testimony as valid. Many passages in the Gospels and other books of the Bible may be read as commands to each sex to esteem the other or as statements of complete equality of all humans in God's eyes. The point is that the same can be said about the Qur'an and the Hadith—and, further, that the Bible, like the Qur'an and the Hadith, also contains passages that can readily be deployed to justify inequality between the genders.

We thus arrive at a difficult place. If we examine the Islamic scriptures in isolation, we see that a broad range of interpretations is possible. If we place the Islamic scriptures in comparative perspective and hold them side-by-side with the Christian Bible, we see that both sets of scriptures contain material that can be used to authorize either gross inequality or full equality between the genders. Muslims could just as easily use their texts to require integration of the sexes, equality in educational opportunities, and severe punishment of men who abuse women, as they could to require segregation of the sexes, disparity in educational opportunities, and laxity in treatment of men who abuse women. Exactly the same can be said of Christians and their holy texts. Thus, Islam's foundational texts cannot readily explain the relatively poor record of Muslims in the contemporary world on the status and treatment of women and girls.

Yet, as our discussion has suggested, interpretation of the texts may influence social practice. This matter begs another question: Is there something in Islam's tradition of textual interpretation that encourages gender inequality? Scholars such as Barlas and Wadud argue that Muslims have long accepted patriarchal interpretations of the sacred texts that were formulated in the earliest centuries of Islam. Why might this be the case? While we cannot answer this question with certainty, it merits note that some scholars have pointed to the possible importance of the institution of *fiqh*, or Islamic jurisprudence. *Fiqh* is not the same as *sharia*, which is considered a legal framework that is fully part of the divine revelation of the Qur'an. *Fiqh* represents an expansion of *sharia* law and is made up of a compilation of legal rulings produced by Muslim jurists based on both the *sharia* and the *sunnah*, which is best translated as the way of the Prophet, much of which is known from the Hadith. *Fiqh*, unlike *sharia*, is drawn from a variety of sources and considered subject to change.

Yet the classic *fiqh* texts of the early centuries enjoy a prestige that derives in part from the proximity of their authors to the time of the Prophet, and they have remained the touchstones of Islamic jurisprudential thinking down to the present day. In some Islamic societies, such as post-1979 Iran, *fiqh* is the basis of the entire legal structure. In other countries, it influences the law and may shape social thought and practice, even if it is not formally the basis for all legal code. It is, in any event, often legally or socially influential in Muslim societies; and it is based in large part on decisions made a millennium ago. According to Ziba Mir-Hosseini, "In the classic fiqh texts, gender inequality is taken for granted, a priori, as a principle. It reflects the world in which the authors of these texts lived, a world in which inequality between men and women was the natural order of things, the only known way to regulate the relations between them."[44] The world in which the jurists lived, as Mir-Hosseini rightly points out, shaped their reasoning and their decisions. Regardless of how powerful the early jurists' intellects and imaginations may have been—and they were often formidable—their reasoning and writings were naturally products of their times. And since most problems of jurisprudence are not settled in the Qur'an itself, the jurists who established the classics of *fiqh* naturally relied upon their own powers of reasoning. Abdulaziz Sachedina states, "The Muslim jurists, by exercise of their rational faculty to the utmost degree, recorded their reactions to the experiences of the community: they created, rather than discovered, God's law."[45]

What emerges as a possible religious basis for gender-based inequality, then, if such a basis exists at all, is the very existence of a legal tradition rooted in religion itself, combined with the matchless prestige of the early, classical writings within that jurisprudential tradition. Perhaps if Christianity had its own body of jurisprudence, based on opinion issued by the early church fathers during the first half-millennium of the faith's existence, gender-based inequality might be more severe than it is in fact in predominantly Christian societies. Hassidic and ultraorthodox Judaism, like Islam but unlike Christianity, do have a jurisprudential tradition rooted in holy scriptures and other ancient texts; and rigidity in gender roles, sexual segregation, puritanical sexual mores, and generally inferior status for women is arguably a feature of these types of Judaism in the modern world. Perhaps the very existence of a jurisprudential tradition rooted in religion and especially in ancient texts provides an institutional locus for the persistence of practices that retard change in the direction of equality between the genders.

The ruminations provided here are merely speculative. They are based on counterfactual reasoning and cannot readily be tested. They merit mention, however, and might deserve the attention of scholars who seek to grasp—and, in some cases, loosen—the link between a religious tradition and gender-based inequality.

Accounts that are based in the scriptures and interpretation of them do not exhaust possible explanations. Let us briefly consider several other possible causes.

Why Is Gender-based Inequality Higher among Muslims? Other Hypotheses

One theory begins with the observation that in sparsely populated desert societies, ties of blood and tribe tend to be especially strong. At least until recent times, vast distances made lines of communication and administration attenuated and precarious. In the absence of the administrative and communicative structures found in more densely populated societies, kin ties constituted the social cement for government and political alliances. Ties based on anything thinner than blood could not reliably sustain political arrangements in such demographic circumstances. The same dynamic may prevail in mountainous areas, where population density may be higher than in the desert but distances measured in travel time and communication capacity still daunting. Under such conditions, in which intermarriages among far-flung tribes constituted the sinews of power and administration, certainty of the legitimacy of progeny was so important that cloistering women was often felt to be necessary to preserve social order and group survival. Nikki Keddie argues that "especially in the heavily tribal Near and Middle East, men's concern about the assured paternity of their offspring and the purity of their lineage led to increasing control over women's public actions and movements and to seclusion of at least upper class women."[46]

Now, Islam was born in the Arabian Peninsula, in the lands of what is present-day Saudi Arabia. It was carried from there in all directions by the desert Arabs in whose language the text was revealed. Even if the Qur'an itself is not genetically inegalitarian, the people to whom it was revealed, and who subsequently spread the faith— as conquering warriors, merchants, and proselytizers—sprung from tribal desert societies in which the station of women was low to begin with. The lifestyles they imparted to newly converted Muslims as they fanned out from Morocco to South Asia during Islam's expansive early centuries may have been especially sexually inegalitarian. Thus, according to the logic of this view, the Arabian origins of Islam could have left the imprint of inequality on the religion. It could have influenced how even converts in sedentary, more densely populated areas outside the original Arabic-speaking desert communities appropriated the cultural package they received and imbibed as "Islam."[47]

This explanation may have merit. The association between tribalism and patriarchy has not been firmly established empirically in social science, perhaps because defining and measuring tribalism is so difficult. But many areas in which tribalism is strong, from Afghanistan to indigenous communities in the Americas, exhibit marked patterns of male dominance. Islam originated in a society in which tribe was the key unit of social organization. To this day, tribal affiliation is an especially salient aspect of social identity in the Arabian Peninsula and, according to some accounts, the Arab world more broadly. The enduring strength of tribalism and the low status of women in Arab countries are discussed in several sources, most notably the *Arab Human Development Report*, published by the UNDP in 2005. The *Report* not only notes these conditions but also suggests a possible causal link between them. It holds that tribalism might be at least partially to blame for gender-based inequality in the Arab world.[48]

Still, while this explanation is plausible and potentially compelling, we do not yet have strong evidence to support it. If tribalism were to blame for the negative relationship between the status of women and Islam, one might expect the variable for Arab countries to have a strong, negative, statistically significant effect in the analyses shown in tables 6.15 and 6.18, but it does not. Furthermore, while measuring "tribalism" directly is difficult, some efforts have been made to measure the conditions that promote it, and they do not appear to be decisive. In an innovative study, Michele Penner Angrist has gathered cross-national data on the percentage of the land that is barren, meaning not covered by arable land, permanent crops, or forest. Angrist put together her data to test the possible effects of tribalism on the status of women in political life in Muslim countries, which makes her research particularly interesting to us. Angrist does not find that the percentage of the land that is barren is a good predictor of women's status, or that it accounts for variation among Muslim countries in women's representation in office.[49] Following Angrist, I assembled my own data for this indicator. While she focuses on variation among Muslim countries and is especially interested in how Arab countries might differ from others, I compare Muslim countries with non-Muslim countries in a global framework. In my analyses on the determinants of cross-national variation in the female-to-male literacy ratio and gender difference in healthy life expectancy, I included a control for the percentage of land that is barren. I do not show the results in tables 6.15 and 6.18, but I can report that the percentage of land that is barren is not a statistically significant predictor of either the female-to-male literacy ratio or gender difference in healthy life expectancy. Furthermore, inclusion of the variable does not substantially affect the regression coefficients for the Islam variable.

It must be admitted that even if we were able to define and measure "tribalism" precisely, our efforts to assess its impact might fall short. After all, what might be important is the extent of tribalism generations or centuries ago. Tribalism at some earlier period might have created cultural "lock-in" effects that persist to the present day. These effects might be more substantial than anything we could measure today using demographic indicators. One can hope that future investigations of particular societies undertaken by historians will focus on the possible influence of tribalism on gender-based inequality, and that such studies will shed light on the problem as it presents itself in the contemporary world.

In short, tribalism, which may largely be a product of geography, might be associated with gender-based inequality, but we lack direct evidence for its effects. Nor does Arab culture, which is widely regarded as especially deeply influenced by tribalism, appear to be decisive. These factors might be of some importance, and their potential impact certainly merits deeper investigation. For now, though, the evidence does not point to them as the crucial factors linking Muslims and gender-based inequality.

Another hypothesis, advanced by Michael Ross, posits that economic reliance on oil explains the low status of females in Muslim societies.[50] There is indeed a correlation between Islam and oil; nearly two-thirds of the world's oil exports originate from the roughly one-quarter of countries that are predominantly Muslim. That correlation is not causal, unless one believes that God has blessed (or cursed) Muslims with a surfeit of oil beneath the lands they inhabit. Tracing geological and demographic circumstances back to Divine intent probably does not get us very far, so let us go with the commonsensical assumption that the correlation between the location of oil and the global distribution of people by religious affiliation is accidental.

Taking female participation in parliament and in ministerial positions as his dependent variable, Ross finds that including oil rents as an independent variable renders the variable for Islam, which he measures as I do as the percentage of the population that is Muslim, statistically insignificant. In his analyses, oil, which he measures as oil rents per capita, is a statistically significant predictor of the status of women in high politics. The relationship is negative; more oil lowers the status of women. Ross spells out a theory of modernization and workforce participation that provides the causal link. He argues that oil production involves an unusually small amount of female employment, and that fewer women in the workforce reduces women's political influence. Oil-producing countries consequently have especially strong patriarchal social norms.

Ross may be onto something. But it is unlikely that oil really explains the status of women in Muslim societies. The regressions presented above in tables 6.3, 6.4, and 6.5, which treat as dependent variables the female-to-male earned income ratio, the percentage of parliamentarians who are women, and the percentage of ministerial positions occupied by women, respectively, include a variable for hydrocarbons as a percentage of national exports. In none of the analyses is the variable for fuels statistically significant, and only in the third set of regressions is the variable for Islam not statistically significant. The control for fuels dependence is also included in the analyses that treat structural inequalities (the female-to-male literacy ratio and the difference in healthy life expectancy) as the dependent variables, and the fuels variable again fails statistical significance, while the variable for percentage Muslim is statistically and substantively significant.

Ross and I use different sources of data and somewhat different controls, which may explain the divergence in our findings. Furthermore, Ross includes in all of the results he presents in print a dichotomous variable for "Middle East," which he defines as including Djibouti and excluding Israel and Turkey. This variable may be simply masking the effect of the variable for Islam in Ross's analysis, since every one of the seventeen countries that Ross classifies as part of the Middle East is predominantly Muslim and the correlation between percentage Muslim and the regional variable is overwhelming. Ross also looks only at what I treat here as the status of women in public life. He does not examine the possible influence of Islam on structural variables, such as female-to-male literacy ratio and the gap in healthy life expectancy. In fact, Ross's causal scheme treats the structural condition of women as an intervening variable that affects women's status in public life. Ross examines the effect of oil dependence, but not the percentage of the population that is Muslim, on the structural variables. In sum, Ross offers a fresh perspective and a bold hypothesis but does not explain why the status of women is generally inferior in predominantly Muslim societies.[51]

We are left without a clear, compelling explanation for one of the weightiest global problems of our time. Why the station of women in Muslim communities is unusually low is a question of great practical importance. No doubt it will be the topic of more investigation in coming years. Ideally, understanding causes will pave the way for remedies.

One crucial step that must precede all others is an end to denial of the problem. Addressing the matter is often painful. Investigating it openly is not a way to win plaudits for political sensitivity, especially in the academy. But the fact that the gender difference in healthy life expectancy in non-Muslim countries is twice what it is in Muslim countries—in the latter, on average, a paltry 1.8 years—is just that. It is a fact. To ignore or gloss over it and others like it, or to engage in methodological tricks in order to obscure such facts, does not defend the honor of a religious tradition. The opposite is true.

CLASS INEQUALITY

Inequality between the genders is only one major basis of injustice in the modern world. We know two others: race and class. As discussed in the introduction to this chapter, we lack the data needed to test for racial inequalities across countries, so we must leave aside whether Muslims are more or less prone to racial inequality than non-Muslims. We are therefore left with one more type of inequality to investigate, that based on class.

Muslims and Class Inequality: Hypotheses and Measurement

The question of whether Muslim societies tend to be more or less egalitarian in class terms than non-Muslim societies are has not been the subject of extensive scholarly debate or empirical investigation. Some works have studied the ethics of socioeconomic justice in Muslim communities, just as other works have examined these matters in non-Muslim settings.[52] But these writings do not explicitly compare Muslim and non-Muslim societies or focus on whether Islam, in a comparative context, may be a force promoting greater or lesser socioeconomic equality. Some economists and political scientists have recently launched potentially fruitful lines of inquiry on the possible influence of religion on redistribution. Yet most such studies focus on religiosity rather than religious denomination and on attitudes toward redistribution rather than on outcomes in terms of socioeconomic inequality. Studies that do examine outcomes focus mostly on advanced industrialized countries.[53]

While the literature does not offer us an extensive debate, we may readily generate hypotheses. One might expect class inequities to be higher among Muslims. We saw in the previous section that gender inequalities are greater among Muslims. Perhaps the same holds for class inequalities, following some general pattern of social hierarchy. Contrariwise, one might expect class inequities to be less severe among Muslims. Perhaps the tradition of *zakat*, or almsgiving, which stands as one of the five pillars of Islam and which Muslims are obliged to observe, fosters a sense of obligation to the poor. So too might it provide a stimulus to generating and sustaining institutions that look after the needs of the poor. Such dynamics might restrict inequalities between social strata.

Testing these hypotheses is problematic. The main obstacle is shortage of data. In the previous section, we saw that an abundance of data is available for assessing inequality between the genders. We do not face such favorable conditions for gauging inequalities between social classes. In fact, we really have only one measure that is usable for cross-national analysis, the Gini coefficient. The Gini coefficient runs from 0 to 1, with 0 representing perfect equality and 1 perfect inequality. A Gini coefficient of 1 would indicate that one citizen received all income and everyone else got nothing; a coefficient of 0 would indicate that everyone's income is identical. Thus, lower coefficients represent lower levels of inequality. The information used to calculate Gini coefficients is normally inequality in income, though some surveys use consumption instead. The Gini

Table 6.19 Mean Scores on Socioeconomic Inequality for Muslim and Non-Muslim Countries

Survey Item	*Muslim Countries*	*Non-Muslim Countries*
Gini score, most recent available year 1990–2006	38.0 ($N = 26$)	41.1 ($N = 114$)

score (or index) is simply the Gini coefficient times 100. Thus, Gini scores run between 0 (perfect equality) and 100 (perfect inequality). Here I will use the Gini score (or index). The data are drawn from the UNDP, which reports the most recent Gini score available for roughly three-quarters of the world's polities. Most of the data are for some year during the first decade of the twenty-first century; for a smaller number of countries, the most recent data are from the 1990s.[54]

No society approaches perfect equality or inequality. The actual empirical range is only about half the hypothetical range. Thus, while scores may range from 0 to 100, in practice they extend from about 25 in relatively classless Denmark, Sweden, Iceland, and Japan, to about 74 in extremely inegalitarian Namibia.

Assessing the Link between Muslims and Class Inequality

Is there a link between religious adherence and Gini scores? Table 6.19 shows the average scores for the Muslim and non-Muslim countries for which we have data. Predominantly Muslim countries have moderately lower average scores than countries where non-Muslims predominate.[55] Table 6.20 displays the numbers for the largest Muslim and Christian countries. Figure 6.4 illustrates the distributions of the Gini score in Muslim and non-Muslim countries. In Muslim countries it ranges from about 25 to 50, while in the non-Muslim countries it ranges from 25 to 74. These numbers and the figure all show a mild advantage for Muslim countries.

In order to probe more deeply, we must control for other factors that may affect socioeconomic inequality. Level of socioeconomic development is one such factor. Typically, higher development is associated with lower income inequalities. I control for socioeconomic development using the usual indicators. I also control for level of democracy, guided by the hypothesis that more open political regimes may promote greater socioeconomic equality than more closed political regimes. Since the most recent available data for the Gini scores for some countries are from the mid-1990s, in order to avoid temporal endogeneity I use data for the controls that are from earlier years. The data for GDP per capita and life expectancy are for 1990 and for democracy are a three-year average of Freedom House scores for 1992–94.

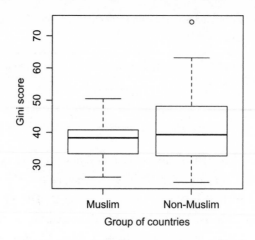

FIGURE 6.4:

Socioeconomic Inequality

Table 6.20 Data on Socioeconomic Inequality in the Largest Muslim and Christian
Countries

Muslim Countries		Christian Countries	
Country	*Gini Score*	*Country*	*Gini Score*
Indonesia	34.3	United States	45.0
Pakistan	30.6	Brazil	57.0
Bangladesh	33.4	Russia	39.9
Egypt	34.4	Mexico	46.1
Turkey	43.6	Philippines	44.5
Iran	43.0	Germany	28.3
Sudan	NA	Dem Rep Congo	NA
Morocco	39.5	France	32.7
Algeria	35.3	UK	36.0
Afghanistan	NA	Italy	36.0
Uzbekistan	36.8	Ukraine	28.1
Saudi Arabia	NA	Colombia	58.6
Iraq	NA	South Africa	57.8
Malaysia	49.2	Spain	34.7
Yemen	33.4	Argentina	51.3
Syria	NA	Poland	34.5
Niger	50.5	Kenya	42.5
Senegal	41.3	Canada	32.6
Mali	40.1	Uganda	45.7
Tunisia	39.8	Peru	52.0
15-country average	39.0	19-country average	42.3

Table 6.21 Regressions of Income Inequality on Hypothesized Predictors

	Model 1	Model 2	Model 3	Model 4
(Intercept)	41.23*** (1.11)	66.59*** (5.70)	68.29*** (5.58)	56.81*** (5.89)
Percent Muslim	-0.03[†] (0.02)	-0.09*** (0.02)	-0.08*** (0.02)	-0.08*** (0.02)
GDP per capita		-0.33*** (0.09)	-0.42*** (0.11)	-0.60*** (0.11)
Life expectancy		-0.34*** (0.09)	-0.46*** (0.09)	-0.20[†] (0.11)
Level of democracy			1.41* (0.62)	0.86 (0.66)
Post communist country				-10.67*** (1.56)
N	140	140	139	139
Adjusted R^2	.00	.28	.30	.44

Note: OLS models with robust standard errors in parentheses.

[†] significant at $p < .10$; *$p < .05$; **$p < .01$; ***$p < .001$.

I also control for a communist heritage. Postcommunist countries are often considered to have lower socioeconomic inequalities. Some analysts argue that Soviet-style socialism did what it intended to do: destroy classes. Some people had more than others, of course, and those with political power often had a great deal more. But Sovietism crushed traditional upper classes and compressed income differentials. One might hypothesize that a legacy of communist rule would be associated with lower inequalities. As usual, I use a dummy variable for countries from the postcommunist region.

Table 6.21 contains the output from regression models of the Gini score on hypothesized predictors. According to model 1, a 1 percentage-point increase in the proportion of Muslims in a country is associated with a 0.03 point decrease in the Gini score. Thus, a country with 0 percent Muslims is predicted to have a Gini score that is three points higher than a country with 100 percent Muslims.

This coefficient increases greatly and becomes highly statistically significant when the controls are added. Income per capita and life expectancy are both negatively correlated with the Gini score, showing that more developed countries generally have lower levels of socioeconomic inequality. When these variables are added to the regression in model 2, the size of the coefficient for percent Muslim is –0.09. This coefficient remains largely stable as other predictors are added to the model. As expected, postcommunist countries have especially low levels of income inequality. The variable for percent Muslim remains large and highly statistically significant when the control for postcommunist countries is included in model 4.

Why Is Class Inequality Lower among Muslims?

Amy Singer states, "Read the Qur'an. Talk to Muslims about their religion. Surf the World Wide Web for sites that explain Islam. In every case, you will encounter zakat, obligatory almsgiving."[56] Singer is right. *Zakat* is one of the five mandatory acts prescribed for Muslims, the others being profession of faith (*shahadah*), prayer (*salah*), fasting during Ramadan (*sawm*), and pilgrimage to Mecca (*hajj*). Almsgiving is prominent in the Qur'an (for example, 2:177, 58:12–13). Furthermore, the Qur'an is replete with calls to the faithful to give over and above the obligation of *zakat*. The poor are portrayed as having a claim on the resources of the rich, and poverty in the community is seen as a problem that calls for amelioration by those who are able (51:18–19; 70:22–24). The wealthy are depicted as especially vulnerable to the conceit of regarding themselves as the authors of their own existence, above the need for God's aid and mercy (63:9, 104:1–3).[57] Singer is undoubtedly right to say that almsgiving is common fodder in discussion among contemporary Muslims about the very meaning of being a member of the faith community.

Are the textual foundations of Islam uniquely unequivocal in their commands to care for the poor and their condemnation of gross socioeconomic inequality? As Jonathan Benthall and Jérôme Bellion-Jourdan rightly point out, "All the great religions lay stress on almsgiving."[58] Indeed, the Hebrew Scriptures and the Christian Bible are also full of commands to relieve the poor (in the book of Proverbs, for example, 3:28, 19:17, 21:13). In the Gospels, Jesus is quoted three times as excluding the rich from the kingdom of God (Matt. 19:23–24; Mark 10:23–24; Luke 18:24–25) and twice as commanding a rich man who seeks to follow him to forfeit his possessions as a prerequisite for discipleship (Matt. 19:21; Mark 10:21–22). Jesus warns that the rich are especially in danger of arrogance and disregard of their own need for God (Luke 12:13–21). In other places in the New Testament, the leaders of the early church similarly eschew material wealth and starkly portray social justice as those who have sacrificing for those who do not (for example, James 2:5–7, 5:1–6).

Do we therefore encounter another case, as we did in our examination of gender-based inequality, where there is not enough differentiation among the sacred texts to attribute variation in contemporary circumstances to differences in the foundational tenets of the faiths?

Perhaps, but not necessarily. There is a noteworthy dissimilarity in the foundational texts. It is found not in the exaltation of sacrifice, the hostility to greed, the exhortations to share wealth, and the treatment of the poor as full partners in God's plan. These things figure as prominently in the Bible as they do in the Qur'an, and they are found in the teachings of Buddhism and other world religions as well. Where Islam's scriptures differ is in the specificity of the prescription. Neither Jesus nor any other authority in the New Testament spells out the obligation of almsgiving in terms as specific as those found in the Qur'an and the Hadith (and particularly the Hadith of al-Bukhari). One could argue that Jesus's command to give up all one has for the poor and his exclusion of the rich from the kingdom of God are more radical than anything found in the Islamic texts. Yet it is possible that Jesus's injunctions are actually too demanding for most ordinary mortals to treat as practical prescriptions. They are, therefore, readily regarded by Christians as a metaphor for giving all of oneself to God (as opposed to all of one's stuff to other people). The specific and less totalistic material obligation set down in the Islamic scriptures makes the duty harder for the faithful to overlook or treat as metaphor. The injunctions in the Qur'an and the Hadith also lend themselves to ready codification. Specifically, Muslims are required to give away 2.5 percent of accumulated wealth annually for poor relief. While one can give to charitable organizations, many Muslims continue to abide by the long-standing custom of giving money directly to needy people. One-fortieth is the minimum; many Muslims regard themselves (and their fellows) as lax if they do not give at a considerably higher rate. A set obligation may create good habits, which in turn may create (or reinforce) good morals—in this case, a principled commitment to poverty alleviation.

Indeed, when one talks to Muslims about their religion, as Amy Singer asserts in the quote that began this section, one is often struck by how consistently almsgiving comes up. We do not have the data to test whether contemporary Muslims are unusually scrupulous about charitable giving or more prone to view socioeconomic inequality as unacceptable. But several generalizations and observations are possible.

Justice occupies pride of place in Muslim moral thinking. In broadest general terms, it is the essence of the Muslim ideal and message, much as the essence of the Christian ideal and message is love. The Buddhist equivalent is more difficult to capture in a word or phrase, but one may venture to say that it is the oneness, or transcendental unity, of all things. Throughout the centuries, justice has been understood by Muslims very largely in terms of socioeconomic obligation.

Some behaviors that the Qur'an prescribes and proscribes exact a real economic cost on individuals, but are nevertheless actually observed. Formal almsgiving is very widely practiced by Muslims; Islam is virtually unimaginable without it. Usury is condemned in the Qur'an. It is proscribed in the same passages that almsgiving is prescribed, and the purpose is to prevent unjust profiteering and exploitation of the poor (2:273–76). The prohibition of usury, like the command to engage in almsgiving, actually affects the way Muslims live. While banks in Muslim societies engage in arithmetical gymnastics to soften the ban on paying or receiving interest, they nevertheless operate differently than do banks in other settings. Holy injunction affects business.[59]

It would be difficult to imagine a practice that has a serious economic cost being ritually and habitually observed on a broad scale by contemporary Christians. While many Christians give money to their churches, most who are not regular churchgoers do not feel under religious obligation to give to a church. Nor, despite Jesus's teachings, does Christianity require giving to the poor, though some churches do prescribe obligatory contribution to the church.

One may also observe that the appeal of ideologies of production and prosperity do not resonate among Muslims with the same vigor that they do in, say, Protestant and Chinese societies. Muslims may be as materialistic as anyone else. An "Islamic ethic of capitalism" based on hard work and thrift that mirrors what Max Weber found among Protestants is not hard to imagine. It may exist and affect the economic practices of many Muslims.[60] Yet the motivation for such an ethic would very likely differ from what Weber found among Protestants. According to Weber, Protestants sought material gain in order to reassure themselves that they were part of God's elect, that portion of humanity that He had predestined for salvation. Prosperity was seen as a sign of God's favor.[61] This view waxes mightily among present-day Christians. Some Christian thinkers and activists urge what they regard as a return to Jesus's call for radical personal economic sacrifice.[62] Yet many others have continued to pursue the Calvinist logic that Weber noted. One of the most politically influential religious leaders in the United States of the postwar period, Jerry Falwell, once declared that "material wealth is God's way of blessing people who put him first."[63] Such thinking has evolved into an optimistic doctrine widely known as the "prosperity gospel," which holds, to use the title of a bestselling book in this genre, that "God wants you to be rich."[64] This notion is by no means universally embraced by Christians; Catholicism, for example, has nothing like a prosperity gospel. Still, it does pervade the thinking and preaching of many of Christianity's most influential thinkers and activists. As evangelical Protestantism has spread across Latin America, Africa, and Asia in recent decades, the sway of the prosperity gospel has grown around the globe.

Just as Deng Xiaoping asserted that "to get rich is glorious" as he embarked upon his economic reforms in China in the 1970s, adherents of the prosperity gospel contend that to get rich is godly. The acquisition of wealth is a sign of God's blessing and one's own goodness as well as service to a God who desires material abundance for humanity.

Such principles are about production and consumption, not distribution. According to these principles, greater production and higher levels of consumption create a world that is better in tune with God's purposes. The logic underlying such a belief is a notion of just deserts. Those who work to become rich are justly rewarded by God for their efforts; those who do not naturally must make do with less.

It is hard to imagine Muslims, on a large scale, embracing such a view. They may desire material wealth as much as anyone else. But an ideology rooted in religion that is divorced from a notion of distributive justice, or that equates distributive justice with the outcome of self-interested individuals seeking gain in the marketplace, is not prominent in Muslim thinking. It never has been. Muslim social and economic thought, even in all its panoramic richness, includes no equivalent of a prosperity gospel.

It would be difficult readily to identify such things as "Islamic economics" or "Christian economics." Still, to the extent that we can discern general tendencies, it seems obvious that Islamic economics is about distribution rather than production or consumption. The same cannot be said of Christian economics.

Indeed, in predominantly Muslim countries it is difficult to find major political organizations that place economic individualism and free markets at the center of their programs. Social justice, understood as just distribution, figures prominently in virtually every successful organization's agenda. In the Muslim world's relatively open polities, where voters' preferences affect who governs and how they govern, this generalization is at least as true as in closed polities where popular opinion has little effect on government. Turkey's governing Justice and Development Party (AKP), led by the Prime Minister, Recep Tayyip Erdoğan, guided Turkey away from economic statism and toward a more open economy during the first decade of the twenty-first century. Still, the party's stated principles and rhetoric, as well as some of its policies, are about just distribution and fairness. Parties that resemble Mexico's

National Action Party (PAN), the Liberal Party of the Philippines, the Republican Party of the United States, Chile's National Renewal (RN), and Italy's Forward Italy (FI), all of which tout freedom and refrain from defining justice in terms of material distribution, are notable by their absence in Turkey. The same is true for the Muslim world's other major open polity, Indonesia, where even the most liberal (in the European sense) major parties, such as the National Mandate Party (PAN), emphasize just distribution rather than individualism and freedom of the marketplace. Indeed, I noted in my many interviews with political party leaders in Indonesia in 2007 that interviewees across the political spectrum consistently emphasized fair distribution and care for the poor as a top priority. Even representatives of the relatively liberal parties, which obviously had an interest in carving out a niche among the growing urban middle class and leaving appeals to social justice to the well-established populist and clientelist parties, the Democratic Party of Indonesia-Struggle (PDI-P) and Golkar, invariably claimed that just distribution was of supreme importance. To a Westerner, the simultaneous emphasis on economic freedom and egalitarian distribution may sound a bit contradictory, or like an expression of the politician's habit of championing all good things. But I never sensed that any interviewee was ready to sacrifice fairness for openness or the welfare of the poor for growth.

The only political figure in Indonesia I ever heard openly defend classical economic liberalism was a leader of the Liberal Islamic Network (JIL), a forum for discussing and disseminating liberal ideas. That leader, Hamid Basyaib, admits that "liberalism is a dirty word in Indonesia" and that "we are the only organization in the country that extols liberalism openly." As he rightly notes, "We're pioneers, and do not have much political influence. There are no liberal parties." Indonesia certainly suffers no shortage of democrats who esteem popular rule and human rights. It is economic liberals who are in short supply. Basyaib states, "We are hand-in-hand with many others against religious fundamentalists; but then economics comes up, and we find ourselves alone again. We try to argue that freedom is good in all realms of life, even in the economy." The idea that freedom should come before fairness and rapid development before just distribution is, in Basyaib's estimation, still foreign to Indonesian Muslims and rare among Muslims more generally.[65]

Another potentially germane observation is also drawn from my field research in Indonesia. In addition to interviewing politicians, I also interviewed many leaders of major religious groups, most notably the Nahdlatul Ulama and Muhammadiyah. These are Indonesia's two major Islamic organizations. Each has deep roots in society and comprises tens of millions of members. I interviewed some dozen heads of regional organizations from around the country. One was the head of the Nahdlatul Ulama for East Java, Ali Maschan Musa, who invited me to his residence for the meeting.[66] East Java is a regional stronghold for Nahdlatul Ulama; by some estimates, half of the province's 35 million people are active members. Ali himself is widely regarded as a potential future governor of East

Java. Upon being invited to the interview, I expected to be met in an expansive home in an upscale neighborhood. I was surprised to find the regional chairman living in a house about the size of my own, covering perhaps 2,000 square feet. The house also resembled my own in that it was stuffed with books, countless varieties of tea, young children, and little else. It was tastefully appointed but hardly lavish. It was located in one of central Surabaya's teeming residential neighborhoods; Ali lives cheek-by-jowl with the poor. Surabaya does not lack glittering, upscale districts. But the chairman of East Java's largest mass organization does not live in one of them.

I interviewed Ali early in my time in Indonesia and thought that his circumstances might be exceptional. I was disabused of that notion over the succeeding months. Shortly after my interview with Ali, Salahuddin Wahid, Director of Pondok Pesantren Tebuireng Jombang, an Islamic boarding school in Jombang, East Java, graciously granted me an interview.[67] Salahuddin Wahid, the brother of Abdurrahman Wahid, the first democratically elected president of Indonesia, himself stood for vice president on the third-place ticket in 2004. He is a figure of national renown. But Wahid's surroundings were every bit as unpretentious as Ali Maschan Musa's in Surabaya. In moral terms, Wahid's prestige was unmistakable. My colleagues who introduced me to Wahid and accompanied me to the interview, themselves Muslims and distinguished academic figures, displayed great deference. The group of Wahid's subordinates from the school who sat with us during the interview, and the stream of students and apprentices who flowed through the room during the hours Wahid spoke with me, also showed him extraordinary reverence.

What by my own standards seemed to be the mismatch between moral authority and economic status of religious leaders continued in full display as I went from one interview to the next throughout the country. I was fortunate enough to interview Salahuddin Wahid's older brother, the former president, Abdurrahman Wahid, known in Indonesia as Gus Dur, in Jakarta.[68] Prior to his death at the end of 2009, Gus Dur was Indonesia's best-known and best-loved living public figure. Before becoming the first president of postauthoritarian Indonesia, a post he held from 1999 to 2001, he was the head of the national organization of the Nahdlatul Ulama. His grandfather, Hasyim Asy'ari, founded the Nahdlatul Ulama in 1926, and Gus Dur partook of his family's charisma. His rough equivalent in the United States, in terms of fame and public esteem, would be Bill Clinton (with whom Gus Dur enjoyed warm relations during the time that the two overlapped in their service as their countries' respective presidents). Gus Dur's office was a circus, often crammed with prominent political, religious, and cultural figures from Indonesia and around the globe. It was just a couple times larger than my own modest professor's office at Berkeley, though the ceiling was a bit lower. The furnishings, like those in my own office, were sturdy, decent-quality government-issue stuff.

All of the leaders just mentioned, as well as many of the other political and religious leaders I interviewed in Indonesia, may possess formidable wealth. But if they do, they do not show it.

When the mystery finally grew to be too much for me, I started posing intrusive and impolitic questions. I asked one leader, Muhammad Adnan, the chairman of the NU for Central Java and then a candidate for vice governor of the province, whether he knew of the contrast between his own material circumstances and those of his counterparts in my own country.[69] With grace and good humor, he stated that he was aware that there was a bit of a cultural as well as a material gap. He explained that to live large would simply be socially unacceptable to the members of his organization. It would also be politically unwise. A Muslim leader who flaunted personal prosperity would be considered arrogant, boorish, and remiss in his obligations to the poor. He further stated that a man who was ostentatiously acquisitive would be considered lacking in personal fortitude. He attributed the decline in the legitimacy of President Suharto during the 1990s to Suharto's shift from quiet acquisition to ostentatious opulence. The problem in the minds of ordinary Muslims, according to Adnan, was not just the injustice of Suharto's theft of state assets. It was also the erosion of his reputation for what people had regarded as his "true personal power, his self-discipline."

While some might attribute such thinking to Javanese or Indonesian culture, it is not unknown elsewhere in the Muslim the world. The outrageous opulence of the sheiks of the oil-soaked countries of the Gulf region is well known. But these figures are widely despised and their religious credentials ever under suspicion. More popular and legitimate among his own people and Muslims worldwide is Iran's Ayatollah Ruhollah Khomeini, who lived in a modest house bereft of furnishings.

It is difficult to imagine political or religious leaders in the United States, Brazil, Russia, or South Africa living such lifestyles or amassing moral authority among ordinary Christians and Jews for doing so. The masses of the faithful generally do not question the sincerity of the faith of political or religious leaders who hold great wealth and inhabit expansive residences. Nor do they necessarily esteem their leaders for living modestly. Few Americans even know that the former president, Jimmy Carter, still lives in the unpretentious home in rural Georgia that he inhabited even before he served as president between 1977 and 1981. Those who do know are more likely to regard Carter's lifestyle as eccentric than as exemplary. Carter does not receive great credit from fellow Christians for donating most of his substantial income as a former president and Nobel Prize recipient to his charitable foundation rather than using it for personal consumption. Carter's attitude toward money and his lifestyle are, in fact, inspired by his Christian faith. But most Christians neither expect him to behave the way he does nor exalt him for it. Nor is there much evidence that most American Christians regarded Ronald Reagan as a less faithful Christian for retiring to a mansion in southern California after his presidency and using his income for personal consumption.[70]

In sum, we cannot say with certainty whether there is something about Islam itself that explains the relatively low level of class inequality found in the Muslim world. It is possible that Muslims place an unusually high premium on avoiding gross inequalities in wealth and income. Whether or not social practices are rooted in scriptural traditions is difficult to determine, but our discussion provides some speculative ideas that connect the two. Whatever the explanation for the phenomenon, we do have some evidence that it exists; countries with a higher proportion of Muslims tend to have lower socioeconomic inequalities.

Of course one encounters gross inequalities in Muslim societies, as in all others. I have seen the posh limousines with darkly tinted windows winding through the sprawling slums of Cairo, the ostentatious nouveaux riches showing off their German roadsters and sparkling trinkets in hardscrabble Tashkent, and the glistening skyscrapers standing against the background of tin-scrap lean-tos in Jakarta. Muslim societies are not immune from gross class inequality.

Still, everything is relative. Indonesia and the Philippines are both large, lower-middle income, polyglot nations that were colonized in the seventeenth century. They are neighbors whose people for centuries have pursued similar modes of survival in rice-based subsistence agriculture and small-scale maritime trade. They have occupied common economic space in the vast, tropical archipelago that rings the southern and eastern edges of Asia. Their cultures are distinguished mainly by the predominance of Islam in Indonesia and Christianity in the Philippines. Yet there is a major societal difference that is evident to any traveler. In Indonesia, poverty is everywhere but hunger is not rife. In the Philippines, whose average income per capita is slightly higher than Indonesia's, the poverty of the poorest seems deeper; real desperation is widespread. Available data bear out the obvious. According to the UNDP, 6 percent of Indonesians are undernourished, compared to 18 percent of Filipinos. In Indonesia about 8 percent of the population lives on a dollar a day or less, compared to roughly 15 percent in the Philippines.[71] In Indonesia, the government and private organizations alike habitually respond with alarm and alacrity (even if not always with skill) when rice prices rise above a level that threatens subsistence; in the Philippines, deprivation is more taken for granted. Indonesia's Gini score is 34.3; the Philippines' is 44.5.

OVERVIEW OF THE FINDINGS

Social inequality takes many forms and can divide people along many lines. In the modern world, we usually think of race, gender, and class as the main fault lines. In this chapter, we did not investigate racial inequality. It would be extremely interesting to know whether inequality according to race, understood as skin color or some other criterion, is more or less acute among Muslims than non-Muslims. But we lack the data to make such an assessment. We do have some data for testing hypotheses about gender and class inequalities, however, and we used those data to arrive at some assessments.

Gender-based inequality is more acute and class inequality less acute among Muslims. The data to test the hypothesis on gender-based inequality are abundant, and I tapped multiple sources and measured several dimensions of gender-based inequality. Muslims generally exhibit lower levels of equity between the genders. The data to test the class inequality hypothesis are much less plentiful. According to the evidence that is available, class disparities are lower in societies where Muslims constitute a larger fraction of the population. The findings therefore cut in opposite directions. On gender-based equality, Muslims lag; on class equality, they lead.

These are the findings on the descriptive, "whether" questions—that is, on whether Muslims are distinctive. The answers on both of the "whether" questions are affirmative. In terms of both gender and class inequalities, Muslims and non-Muslims differ significantly from each other.

Answering the "why" and "how" questions is exceptionally difficult, however. In investigation of why gender inequalities are especially high among Muslims, I came up with only the most tentative ideas. I could not find anything special about the sacred texts of Islam that explains gender-based inequality in contemporary circumstances, though I did speculate that the enduring influence of religio-juridical institutions based largely on texts written over a millennium ago may sustain a culture of inequality. The discussion, while inconclusive, may help provide a starting point for those who seek to plumb the matter more deeply than I could do here.

Explaining why class inequalities are especially low among Muslims poses an equally challenging problem. Here again I offered just the beginning of a tentative answer to the "why" question. I focused on how the specificity of Islam's sacred scriptures on matters of almsgiving may promote a culture of distributive justice and intolerance of class disparities. This insight, if it qualifies as such, is strictly provisional. I was able to adduce only anecdotal evidence to support it, and my observations and reasoning are open to question. But since the question has not, to the best of my knowledge, even been addressed in other writings, the discussion offered here may be of some value. In fact, in social scientists' investigations of the causes of socioeconomic inequality across societies, religion is not even taken into account. The analysis presented here, plain and unsophisticated as it is, provides some evidence that adherents of a particular faith may partake of traditions and engage in practices that circumscribe inequality. Perhaps scholars should at least consider the possibility that religion affects socioeconomic structure.

7 Democracy

To this point, we have focused on individual attitudes as well as social life. We have dabbled in politics, as in chapter 2, when we considered the extent to which Muslims regard the fusion of religious and political authority as legitimate. But we have not yet paid attention to political institutions. In this chapter, the focus shifts in that direction. Specifically, we are interested in the relationship between Islam and a major, large-scale political institution, namely democracy. Are Muslims particularly inclined to, or resistant to, democracy?

The question is widely regarded as of paramount significance. Khaled Abou El Fadl writes, "The issue of whether Islam can support and bolster a democratic order that respects individual rights is by far the most important challenge confronting Muslims today."[1]

The debate over the compatibility of Islam and self-government is not new. It has been raging for over a century, among Muslim thinkers and non-Muslim observers.[2] Among contemporary writers, some see tensions between Islam and democracy.[3] Others hold that Islam is not incompatible with free government.[4] Indeed, a burgeoning literature addresses the possible relationship between Islam and political regime.

While some writings have enriched our understanding, only a few have sought to establish empirically whether there is a relationship between Islam and political regime. Several works examine public attitudes and opinion toward democracy in Muslim countries.[5] A handful of writings use cross-national analysis to gauge whether levels of democracy are higher or lower in the Muslim world.[6] Still, most writings on Islam and political regime are historical, philosophical, or polemical; only a smattering offer systematic tests of hypotheses. Our grasp of the relationship between Islam and democracy is still in its infancy. This chapter aims to advance our understanding.

WHAT IS DEMOCRACY?

Defining Democracy

Any practical discussion of levels of democracy within and across countries immediately forces us to address the fundamental theoretical question of what we mean by democracy. Our choice of definitions shapes our characterization of real-life cases.

Political science and philosophy furnish many conceptions and definitions. Here I adopt the mainstream definition put forward by Juan Linz and embraced by many political scientists. According to Linz, the "criteria for democracy" are "legal freedom to formulate and advocate political alternatives with the concomitant rights to free association, free speech, and other basic freedoms of the person; free and nonviolent competition among leaders with periodic validation of their claim to rule; inclusion of all effective political offices in the democratic process; and provision for the participation of all members of the political community, whatever their political preferences."[7] Linz sees democracy largely in terms of popular control over the state. This condition is ensured by free elections as well the rights needed to ensure that people can organize and express themselves freely during electoral campaigns as well as between elections. Also important is the stipulation that elected rather than nonelected officials actually do the governing; elections for offices in which little power is vested do not generate popular control over the state. Furthermore, all or almost all adults must have the right to participate in politics, unhindered by fear of retribution. Linz's definition and the conceptions of other leading contemporary theorists converge on these basic principles.[8]

In real life, of course, none of these conditions is met perfectly in any polity. We must therefore speak of democracy in terms of the degree to which these conditions are met. We may think in terms of degrees of "democraticness" and examine differences across countries on this score. Yet "democraticness" is an awkward term, and I prefer the label "political openness." After all, openness is what democracy is all about: Political competition between candidates for election and among elected officials is open, people may associate openly for political ends, political communication flows openly, government operations are open to scrutiny, political participation is open to everyone, and so on. The opposite of openness is closure, which is associated with authoritarian regimes. A political regime may be considered more or less open/closed given the extent to which it meets the basic criteria that Linz spells out.

Measuring Democracy

There are multiple measures of political openness/closure that assign numerical scores to countries. Freedom House's Freedom in the World reports rate all countries of the world on a yearly basis. They are widely used.[9] The Economist Intelligence Unit and the Polity project issue their own assessments as well.[10]

Each of these sources offers useful data. Perhaps the best measure of political openness, however, is the "Voice and Accountability" indicator created by Daniel Kaufmann, Aart Kraay, and Massimo Mastruzzi.[11] The scores are one of the six "governance indicators" that Kaufmann and colleagues devised. Scores range from about −2.5 (least open/democratic polity) to +2.5 (most open/democratic polity). The Voice and Accountability scores (hereafter "VA scores") are based on criteria that fit the conventional conception of democracy I outlined above. In recent years, the authors have offered annual assessments for almost all countries of the world. Here I will use country averages for the most recent five years for which scores are available as of this writing, which cover 2002–2006. The VA scores are based on extensive, multiple surveys. They arguably furnish the most fine-grained and useful data for measuring level of political openness.[12] For ease of interpretation, I recode the scores on a 0–100 scale.

ASSESSING THE LINK BETWEEN MUSLIMS AND DEMOCRACY

Table 7.1 summarizes the data on political openness for Muslim and non-Muslim countries. Table 7.2 shows the numbers for the largest Muslim and Christian countries. The numbers reveal divergence between predominantly Muslim countries and others; the gap favors non-Muslim countries.[13]

Figure 7.1 illustrates the distributions of the VA scores for Muslim and non-Muslim countries. Although there are a few non-Muslim countries that have lower VA scores than all Muslim countries, the highest value for Muslim countries is less than 60, while for non-Muslim countries it is more than 80. We can also see from the figure that not only the mean but also the median value of VA scores is about 20 points higher for the non-Muslim countries.

As always, the country averages and raw data provide only a rough first cut. We must control for other possibly influential variables. There is no standard set of variables that scholars universally consider determinants of political openness, but

Table 7.1 Mean Scores on Indicator of Political Openness

Survey Item	Muslim Countries	Non-Muslim Countries
Voice and Accountability score, 2002–2006 (five-year ave)	32.4 ($N = 44$)	51.9 ($N = 128$)

Table 7.2 Data on Political Openness in the Largest Muslim and Christian Countries

Muslim Countries		Christian Countries	
Country	VA Score	Country	VA Score
Indonesia	43.0	United States	74.8
Pakistan	26.4	Brazil	57.1
Bangladesh	38.7	Russia	37.9
Egypt	29.8	Mexico	54.0
Turkey	47.0	Phillipines	49.7
Iran	25.2	Germany	80.0
Sudan	16.4	Dem Rep Congo	15.0
Morocco	39.2	France	76.2
Algeria	31.9	UK	78.5
Afghanistan	21.6	Italy	71.6
Uzbekistan	15.5	Ukraine	40.7
Saudi Arabia	20.6	Colombia	42.2
Iraq	16.0	South Africa	63.8
Malaysia	44.7	Spain	74.0
Yemen	30.0	Argentina	55.3
Syria	18.3	Poland	71.0
Niger	43.3	Kenya	43.1
Senegal	51.2	Canada	80.8
Mali	55.7	Uganda	34.9
Tunisia	32.0	Peru	50.6
20-country average	32.3	20-country average	57.6

Note: VA score 5-year average 2002–06.

there is some agreement on what factors are likely to matter. We control for them here.[14] As always, we cannot overlook socioeconomic development. As previously, I control for it using income per capita and life expectancy. We would expect higher levels of development (meaning higher incomes and higher life expectancy) to be associated with higher VA scores. Authors differ on whether the process of socio-economic development per se strongly influences the probability of democratization within countries, but there is consensus that in a cross-national framework, richer countries are more likely to have democratic regimes.[15] Ethnic fractionalization may also influence democratization. Some scholars regard democracy as more difficult in more diverse societies.[16] Economic dependence on hydrocarbons is another potentially important factor. A substantial literature has emerged in recent years linking reliance on oil and natural gas with authoritarianism. Resource abundance

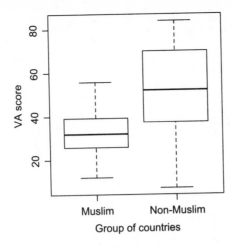

FIGURE 7.1:
Voice and Accountability Scores

may distort modernization, finance a large coercive apparatus, enable the government to buy off society with low taxation and high public spending and thereby
blunt demands for self-government, and otherwise countervail open politics.[17] I
also include a control for when countries achieved statehood. A long history
of independent statehood may be associated with a sturdier state apparatus, less
problematic national unity, and less damage from recent colonization. I use a
dichotomous (dummy) variable for countries that received their national independence only after the year 1900. Countries that enjoyed national independence prior
to the onset of the previous century are coded as "0" and those that did not as "1." I
also include a dummy variable for Arab countries. Some analysts have insisted that
evidence that Islam may pose problems for democracy is driven by a democratic
deficit in the Arab world alone. According to this argument, Arab, but not Muslim,
culture is inimical to open government.[18] I also control for gender-based inequality,
relying on the measure for female-to-male literacy ratio used in chapter 6. In previous work, I have found a link between greater gender-based inequality and more
authoritarian politics, so I control for gender-based inequality here.[19] Finally, I
include a control for population size. Thinkers from the ancient Greeks onwards
have ruminated on the link between political regime and the size of the community.
Montesquieu regarded republican government as sustainable only in a relatively
small polity. Some contemporary scholars have also emphasized the advantages of
small population size for open government, while others have found no correlation
between population and political regime.[20] Here I include a control for the size of
the population in the year 2000.

Do countries with a higher proportion of Muslims generally have more or less
open polities when we control for other predictors? Table 7.3 presents the results of
the statistical analyses, treating the five-year average of the VA scores (2002–2006)

Table 7.3 Regressions of Political Openness on Hypothesized Predictors

	Model 1	Model 2	Model 3	Model 4	Model 5	Model 6	Model 7
(Intercept)	54.14*** (1.90)	21.21*** (6.73)	22.81* (9.23)	23.15* (9.26)	26.89** (9.96)	20.61** (6.78)	21.35** (6.40)
Percent Muslim	−0.27*** (0.03)	−0.19*** (0.03)	−0.09* (0.04)	−0.12*** (0.03)	−0.18*** (0.03)	−0.13** (0.04)	−0.12*** (0.02)
GDP per capita		1.31*** (0.16)	1.37*** (0.16)	1.34*** (0.15)	1.28*** (0.16)	1.36*** (0.17)	1.39*** (0.16)
Life expectancy		0.33** (0.11)	0.36* (0.17)	0.34** (0.12)	0.29* (0.13)	0.43** (0.16)	0.34** (0.11)
Population size		−0.01 (0.01)	−0.01 (0.01)	−0.01 (0.01)	−0.01 (0.01)		
Ethnic diversity			−0.94 (4.41)	0.17 (4.45)	−2.79 (4.64)		
Fuels dependence			−0.17*** (0.03)	−0.19*** (0.03)			
Late independence			−1.47 (2.01)	−1.87 (1.93)	−1.89 (2.21)		−0.19*** (0.03)
Arab country			−5.96† (3.08)			−9.61** (3.68)	
Sex literacy ratio			−1.18 (8.92)			−7.70 (9.00)	
N	172	172	168	171	171	169	172
Adjusted R^2	.23	.61	.67	.67	.60	.62	.67

Note: OLS regression models with robust standard errors in parentheses.

†significant at $p < .10$; *$p < .05$; **$p < .01$; ***$p < .001$.

as the dependent variable. There is a clear, negative relationship between the proportion of Muslims in the population and level of political openness. Model 1, which presents a simple bivariate estimate of the relationship, shows that for every 1 percent increase in the number of Muslims in a country, the VA score decreases by 0.27 (on a scale of 0–100). Thus, controlling for no other variables, the expected score of a country that is 0 percent Muslims is 54, while the expected score of a country that is 100 percent Muslims is 27. In models 2–7, we see that the negative, statistically significant relationship between the proportion of Muslims and political openness is robust to the inclusion of the other predictors. Controlling for other variables, and particularly socioeconomic development and fuels dependence, reduces the coefficient for the percentage Muslim variable. But the latter retains statistical and substantive significance in all models. The estimated difference in VA scores between a country with 0 percent Muslims and one that is all Muslims ranges from 9 to 19 percent in the various models that control for other predictors besides percentage Muslim, and in all specifications the percentage Muslim variable is statistically significant.

Given the complexity and controversial nature of measuring political openness, I reran the regression models presented in table 7.3 using the three other major measures for the dependent variable, which are Freedom House scores, the Economist Intelligence Unit Index, and Polity scores. The results are presented in appendix 7.A. Use of the alternative measures does not change the findings, as the variable for percentage Muslim remains statistically and substantively significant.

WHY IS DEMOCRACY RARER AMONG MUSLIMS?

Structural Conditions

What is the basis for the strong negative correlation we find in the analysis? We cannot hope to establish a firm causal argument here. My main aim is descriptive; I seek to answer the "whether" questions. In this chapter, whether there is a link between Muslims and political regime is the main issue. With the "why" and "how" questions, which are about causation, I hope, as elsewhere in the book, only to lay out a menu of options and offer some hunches.

We may start by considering the possible role of structural conditions that could cause the appearance of a correlation between Islam and authoritarianism but that have little or nothing to do with Islam. One possibility is that predominantly Muslim countries are poorer than average, and that socioeconomic underdevelopment explains the link between Islam and a deficit of democracy. In this case, Muslims might lag on democracy, but the reason would be that they happen to live in poorer countries. The empirical analyses showed that adding the controls for socioeconomic development did reduce the regression coefficient for the percentage Muslim variable, raising the possibility that underdevelopment is part of the story linking Muslims and authoritarianism. But the analyses also suggested that underdevelopment is only part of the story, since the percentage Muslim variable remained large and statistically significant even when we included the controls for socioeconomic development.

The same may be said of fuels dependence. A substantial literature attests to oil's poisonous effects on democracy's prospects, and our findings reinforce that idea. Economic dependence on hydrocarbons, like underdevelopment, is associated with lower levels of political openness. By dint of historical accident, Muslims tend disproportionately to inhabit lands that are particularly rich in oil, which does create a potential barrier to democracy in Muslim lands that has nothing to do with religion. In our data, in predominantly Muslim countries oil accounts for 34 percent of export income on average; the analogous figure in non-Muslim countries is 11 percent. Still, even after we have taken fuels dependence into account, the variable for percentage Muslim is statistically significant. Oil may be a special bane to democracy in Muslim countries, given the surfeit of the poison there. But oil does not account for more than a part of why democracy is scarce in Muslim countries.

The other major structural conditions we included do not have any statistically significant effect on political openness, and we can say with some confidence that they do not explain the negative correlation between Muslims and democracy. Ethnic fractionalization is not markedly higher in predominantly Muslim countries than others, and this factor in any event is not a statistically significant predictor of political openness. With late national independence, there is a difference between Muslim and non-Muslim countries. Of the forty-four Muslim countries, only two, Turkey and Iran, have a history of independent statehood that predates the twentieth century, while 30 percent of non-Muslim countries enjoy such a history. We cannot rule out entirely the possibility that this structural-historical factor disproportionately disadvantages Muslim countries, but our analysis does not show a history of late national independence to be a statistically significant predictor of political openness.

In short, we controlled for the major structural factors that might create a spurious correlation between Islam and authoritarianism, and while several of these factors may explain part of the correlation, they do not account for all of it.

Sociopolitical Conditions in Muslim Societies

What, then, of possible causal links that are not necessarily incidental to Islam? Religion may have little to do with how ethnically fractionalized a county is or how much oil lies in its soil, but other traits of societies may be influenced by religion, and those features, in turn, might affect democracy's prospects. One such feature is the level of corruption. In practice, corruption may be a consequence of political regime. Many analysts would argue that less democratic regimes, by shielding power holders from public scrutiny, furnish more fertile breeding grounds for corruption than more democratic regimes do. But the causal arrow may point the other way as well. Corruption may undermine open politics. Engaging in corrupt practices raises elites' interest in blocking public scrutiny of governmental operations. It also may stoke popular resentment toward the governors, thereby making voters—especially in new or unconsolidated democracies—more susceptible to the appeals of demagogues who promise to humble the rascals in power by any means (including extraconstitutional means, if necessary).[21] Thus, if Muslims had a particularly acute problem with corruption, we might be able to attribute some of the negative correlation between Muslims and democracy to corruption.

But as chapter 4 revealed, there is no compelling evidence that Muslims are especially corruption-prone. Once we controlled for other possibly influential variables, there is no substantial correlation between Muslims and corruption. Thus, Muslim societies are not less likely to be democratic because they suffer more corruption.

What of the possible effect of violent crime? It is conceivable that high crime rates turn people away from democracy, perhaps out of fear of disorder and concern for physical security. Yet, if there is any merit in this argument, the deficit of democracy in the Muslim world is even more paradoxical, since Muslim countries have unusually low murder rates, as was shown in chapter 4.

Mass political violence may pose an even greater challenge to open politics than do corruption or ordinary crime. Such violence may empower the agencies of coercion, undermine the civilian-led institutions that are crucial to democracy, and elevate the value that people attach to security relative to liberty. Political violence is widely and rightly regarded as democracy's foe. If Muslims are markedly more prone to large-scale political violence, we might have an explanation for the link between Muslims and authoritarianism.

Yet, as chapter 5 shows, mass political violence is no more acute among Muslims than among non-Muslims. We located no support for Samuel Huntington's thesis that Muslim societies are unusually "bloody." We even found a modest negative correlation between the percentage of the population that is Muslim and deaths in episodes of large-scale political violence. Muslims are not less democratic because they are more prone to mass political violence, since they are not so prone.

On the question of terrorism, however, the picture changed; Islamists are responsible for the bulk of terrorism in the contemporary world. If terrorist threats may undermine democracy, then we might find in them a link between Islam and authoritarianism. Indeed, many governments in predominantly Muslim countries—those of North African and Central Asian countries provide pronounced examples—constantly invoke the threat of terrorism to justify their repression of opposition, restrictions on the media and association, and other authoritarian tactics. It is conceivable that the violent nature of opposition in some Muslim countries encourages governments to restrict rights and leads citizens to acquiesce in those restrictions.

Yet several facts counsel skepticism toward this thesis. Governments' claims about the danger of terrorism may, in fact, be pretexts for authoritarianism rather than genuine causes of it. First, about two-thirds (29 of 44) of all predominantly Muslim countries experienced no acts of terror at all during the period we considered (1994–2008). This group includes many of the world's least democratic polities, including Iran, Kazakhstan, Libya, Qatar, Syria, and Turkmenistan. While it is conceivable to imagine that there would have been terrorism in the countries that did not experience it had political regimes been more open, such reasoning strains credulity. More sensible is the notion that dictators would have had one less excuse for their despotic ways had they not been able to point to a terrorist threat. The countries that sustained five or more terrorist incidents—Afghanistan, Algeria, Colombia, India, Indonesia, Israel, Pakistan, the Philippines, Russia, and Sri Lanka—run the gamut of regime types, from the democracies (which happen to begin with the letter "I") to the autocracies (which happen to begin with the letter "A"). There is no correlation between the frequency of terrorist acts and political regime type within countries. While more robust state apparatuses may help deter terrorism, there is little evidence that greater authoritarianism does. During the first decade of the twenty-first century, increasingly democratic Indonesia methodically and skillfully shattered terrorist networks, while Pakistan under military rule became the world's playground for terrorists. Between 1994 and 2008, Pakistan experienced as many terrorist acts (43) as the second and third most badly affected countries (Russia, with 22, and Sri Lanka, with 21) combined.[22] That said, given the often transnational nature of terrorism, we should avoid assigning too much meaning to the location of terrorist acts. Perceived terrorist threats emanating from halfway around the world may affect democracy, a fact with which Americans have become well acquainted. We should also refrain from making blanket statements about how governments deal with terrorism and to what ends. Some may adopt sincere but democracy-damaging policies in order to thwart the danger of terrorism launched from abroad. Others may fear no terrorism at all, either imported or homegrown, while rhetorically trotting out the threat of terror as a ruse to justify their own despotism. Some may pursue terrorists with minimal damage to the rights and freedoms that are crucial to democracy. Finally, even if one could establish a causal relationship between terrorism and political regime, it would be difficult to ascertain the direction of the causal arrow, and we cannot do so here. While it is conceivable that the threat of terrorism breeds authoritarianism, it is no less plausible that authoritarianism breeds terrorism by precluding the peaceful expression of dissent and the nonviolent replacement of rulers.

In short, we cannot say with certainty whether the prevalence of Islamists as perpetrators of terrorism takes a disproportionate toll on democracy's prospects in

Muslim societies. The available evidence, however, suggests that the democratic deficit in predominantly Muslim countries is not readily attributable to the threat of terrorism.

Another condition that might link Islam and authoritarianism is social inequality. Gender-based inequality may reduce democracy's prospects. Differentials between males and females in matters such as literacy rates reflect social conditions in families and the immediate community, and these relations might reproduce themselves at higher levels. Some writers have argued that male dominance in basic social relations replicates itself in broader society, creating a culture of domination and dependency in political life.[23] Social marginalization of women, moreover, may exclude distinctive voices from politics. Some scholars have found that women are superior to men in some aspects of building consensus—an essential part of the functioning of any open polity.[24] Other studies have found that women generally are less comfortable than men with hierarchy and subordination, and that women tend to be more averse to extremism in politics.[25] If these findings are valid, the relegation of women to the sidelines of social and political life may dim democracy's prospects.

In chapter 6, we found that the status of females is unusually low among Muslims. Thus, gender-based inequality may provide a key to understanding the relationship between Islam and authoritarianism.

Yet there are reasons to doubt its power as an explanation. In the regression analysis shown in table 7.3, the variable for female-to-male literacy ratio was not statistically significant. In chapter 6, we used this indicator, among others, to assess the status of females relative to males and found an unusually low (female disfavoring) literacy ratio among Muslims. Yet, if literacy ratio is not a good predictor of the level of political openness—and it is not a good predictor in the findings presented in table 7.3—we cannot say that it accounts for the deficit of democracy in the Muslim world. What is more, in regressions that I do not present here, I used other indicators of female status and did not find a stable relationship between them and political openness. This finding represents a departure from an article I published in 2002, in which I argued that predominantly Muslim countries may suffer a shortage of open politics due in part to disparities between the genders.[26] Using more varied and differentiated data, I now find less support for that hypothesis than I did earlier. The possibility that gender-based inequality provides some explanation for the prevalence of authoritarianism in the Muslim world cannot be ruled out, but we do not have adequate evidence to say that the causal path exists.

Gender-based inequality is not the only type of inequity that may affect democracy's prospects. Class differences may also have an effect. A thoroughly marginalized lower class may create a constant threat to open politics by leaving many people so desperate that they are ready to follow even leaders who are not committed to popular rule, if those leaders promise to alleviate suffering and humble the wealthy. Particularly in settings where the rich enjoy life conditions that are vastly better than those of their poor countrymen, resentment among the latter may render robust open politics a poor prospect. Yawning class inequities may also keep the upper classes in a state of anxiety. It may make them less likely to make what Guillermo O'Donnell calls the "democratic wager," which involves entrusting the fate of the polity to the people as a whole—including those whom the better off may regard as unfit for participation, by virtue of their degraded life conditions and lack of basic education.[27] Under such conditions, powerful upper classes may have an especially keen interest in keeping the poor in check and excluding their voices.[28]

In this case, however, Muslims should enjoy an advantage in democracy. As shown in chapter 6, there is a positive correlation between Muslims as a proportion of the population and socioeconomic equality. Gini scores, which are higher in countries with higher inequalities, are generally lower where Muslims make up a larger portion of the population. Socioeconomic inequality does not connect Muslims and authoritarianism.

In sum, sociopolitical conditions that may be related to Islam probably do not account for the deficit of political openness in polities in which Muslims live. Corruption, crime, mass political violence, and class inequalities, each of which may undermine democracy or hinder its nascence, are not especially bad among Muslims. In fact, on some of these matters conditions are unusually favorable among Muslims. Muslims are at a disadvantage on terrorism and gender-based inequality. Yet we do not have strong evidence that either of these problems hinders advancement to or maintenance of open politics.

Public Opinion and Individual Attitudes among Muslims

Perhaps individual-level differences between Muslims and non-Muslims account for the democracy gap. Here we may move away from conditions that manifest at the level of whole societies and consider those that are observable among individuals. Doing so brings us back to issues we investigated in chapters 2 and 3.

Among the matters we investigated, perhaps the most relevant for democracy is whether people regard the fusion of religious and political authority as legitimate. If people believe that the sacred should dominate the temporal in public life, they are likely to regard the separation of religious and political authority as illegitimate. Such a mindset may create problems for open politics. Preeminent among such problems is that modern democracy requires rule by officials elected by the people as a whole. Religious leaders do not fit that description; they always hold their positions by virtue of charisma, inheritance, or selection by a circumscribed, sectarian group. Herein lies the reason why theocracy is incompatible with democracy. Control of the state by clerics would be consonant with democracy if the people as a whole elected the clerics to their religious offices. The problem here is that nowhere do religious organizations allow all members of the political community to participate in selection of the leaders of the religious body. Thus, to regard political authority as logically growing out of religious authority is to reject full political equality, since those who are closer to God are naturally seen as enjoying greater rights. What is more, those who do not share the faith of the leaders, or who the religious leaders regard as impious, logically are deprived of basic political rights. In the extreme case, a single body that holds religious authority is also the custodian of supreme political authority. Such a system obtains in post-1979 Iran, where the Guardian Council acts as the final arbiter on political decisions, including who may run for office. This, in fact, is what theocracy looks like: a small, insular circle whose composition is not determined by the political community as a whole has final say in government. Whether one speaks of postrevolutionary Iran or John Calvin's Geneva, theocracy has never been consonant with democracy.

The more people believe that religious and political authority should be fused, the greater the popular support for a particular institutional setting that is inconsistent with democracy. Thus, if Muslims are distinctly more prone to favor combining religious and political authority, and if popular attitudes have an effect on political regime, we might have a partial explanation for the prevalence of authoritarian rule among Muslims.

Yet, as we saw in chapter 2, Muslims are not especially friendly to religious leaders swaying voters. In contradistinction to conventional wisdom, we did not find evidence that Muslims oppose separating religious and political authority. They are only slightly more likely than non-Muslims to endorse religious leaders influencing how citizens behave in elections. Muslims partake in the global consensus of opposition to religious leaders influencing people's behavior at the polls.

Another possible explanation for the democratic deficit among Muslims might be found in a lower level of social capital. Theorists such as Alexis de Tocqueville and, among contemporary thinkers, Robert Putnam, have held that individuals who are more active in groups are more likely to make good democrats.[29] Experience in social interaction acclimates people to compromise, inclines them to pragmatism, teaches them to lead and to follow, and generally trains them in the citizenship tasks that are required in a free polity. Where individuals associate for mutual benefit less frequently and intently, the arts of association are less well developed, and the polity is more likely to lack the social oil and cement needed to make democracy work.

If social capital were lower among Muslims than non-Muslims, perhaps we would be onto something. But as chapter 3 revealed, we have no evidence of such a deficit. In terms of both time spent in the company of one's fellows from various walks of life and membership in formal organizations, Muslims do not differ appreciably from non-Muslims.

There is still another matter of individuals' orientations that might help explain the shortage of democracy in the Muslim world. That is the simple question of whether Muslims value democracy as much as non-Muslims do. Addressing that question requires delving into some survey data that we have not yet examined. We do so in the following section.

Attitudes toward Democracy among Muslims

Are Muslims less likely to favor democracy as a form of political regime? Authors differ on the extent to which public opinion on democracy affects whether people actually get democracy. But it is plausible to expect authoritarianism to be more fragile, democratization to be more likely, and open politics to be more robust in settings where the people generally think more highly of democracy. Whether Muslims tend to be more or less favorable to democracy is therefore potentially consequential.[30]

One might expect Muslims to be less enamored of democracy than non-Muslims. Democracy is often identified with Western, non-Muslim settings. Based on extensive interviews with Muslim leaders, Anthony Shadid notes, "Some would argue, too, that democracy's very heritage makes it an illegitimate model for the Islamic world." Shadid quotes a leading Egyptian Muslim intellectual, Tariq al-Bishri, who supports Islamists' participation in democratic political competition, but who nevertheless states, "The Western democratic ideal is based on the development of the secular ideal in the West and relies on a secular frame of reference. Democracy was seen as an organization and a system of Western thought."[31] I heard much the same from an Indonesian leader of the global Islamist organization, Hizb ut-Tahrir, which seeks to reestablish the caliphate and draw a clear distinction between Islamic and non-Islamic forms of governance. The leader, Yoyok Tindyo Prasetyo, states plainly, "Democracy is democracy; Islam is Islam. Democracy was born in the West and is opposed to revelation. Bacon, Montesquieu, and other fathers of democracy were secularists. Democracy was born to fight religion. Democracy and Islam are totally different; they have different starting points. Where Muslims adopted democracy, we did so due to imperialism."[32] Even if most Muslims do not draw such stark distinctions, it is possible that many do regard democracy as a Western invention and, in their own lands, a foreign import. If many do hold such a view, they might be less likely than non-Muslims to hold democracy in high esteem. Some authors, however, find little support for the notion that Muslims are less likely to support democracy than non-Muslims. They locate evidence of attitudes among Muslims that are broadly supportive of, or at least not unusually opposed to, popular rule.[33]

Testing this hypothesis means again turning to data from the World Values Survey (WVS). The WVS asks respondents to evaluate types of political systems. The question is worded as follows: "I'm going to describe various types of political systems and ask what you think about each as a way of governing this country. For each one, would you say it is a very good, fairly good, fairly bad or very bad way of governing this country?" The four systems individuals are asked to evaluate are "a strong leader who does not have to bother with parliament and elections"; "having experts, not government, make decisions according to what they think is best for the country"; "having the army rule"; and "having a democratic political system."[34]

This question provides an imperfect measure of support for democracy. When evaluating responses to the item "a democratic political system," we have no way of knowing whether respondents are considering democracy as an abstract form of political organization, a system of government they have heard about in other countries but do not associate with their own country, or their own political system, which of course may fall short of democratic ideals in practice. Furthermore, the question does not ask respondents to rank democracy against the alternatives. An individual can evaluate all four of the options identically. In fact, 4,554 respondents in our sample did just that. It is possible that the responses of at least some of these individuals do not reflect their actual opinions but are rather a product of "response set"—that is, a tendency to answer questions in a systematic way regardless of the questions' content. Questions formed in a list with identical response options, such as these, are vulnerable to biased responses. Finally, the four systems respondents are asked to evaluate do not constitute an exhaustive set of possible regime types, and they are not necessarily mutually exclusive. For example, one can conceive of a government in which the army rules as also being a government with a strong leader who does not have to bother with elections.

Bearing in mind these drawbacks, however, these questions are the best available for constructing a measure of attitudes toward political regime and assessing whether Muslims are less inclined to support democracy. In order to reduce possible bias in analyses of these data that could result from the shortcomings just mentioned, we adopt a measure that includes support for democracy together with rejection of nondemocratic alternatives. We created an index of the four response items, reversing the direction of responses for the "democratic system" and averaging across all responses. The result is an index ranging from 1 to 4, in which 1 indicates least support for democracy and most support for nondemocratic alternatives and 4 represents highest support for democracy and lowest support for nondemocratic alternatives.[35] A person with a score of "1" considered having a strong leader, experts decide, and military rule all as "very good" forms of government and having a democratic system as a "very bad" way of governing. An individual with a score of "4" evaluated all three nondemocratic alternatives as "very bad" and having a democratic system as "very good." Individuals with scores between these two endpoints gave mixed evaluations, some in a more pro-democratic direction and others in a more antidemocratic direction. The overall result of the index is a set of responses with a distribution that roughly resembles a bell curve, with staunch democrats and antidemocrats in the two opposite tails.[36]

As table 7.4 shows, Muslims and non-Muslims alike have mean scores that are closer to the pro-democracy end of the index than to the antidemocracy end. Muslims

Table 7.4 Mean Scores on Democracy Support Index for Muslims and Non-Muslims (1–4)

	Muslims	All Non-Muslims[a]	Christians	No Denomination
Democracy support index	2.83 (21,123)	3.01 (70,795)	3.02 (47,688)	3.04 (15,690)

Note: This question was not asked in Israel, Rwanda, and Saudi Arabia. Figures in parentheses are *N*s.

[a]Includes all individuals who adhere to a religious denomination other than Islam as well as individuals who did not state adherence to a religious tradition.

have a mean score on the democracy support index that is slightly lower than the score for non-Muslims. Does this difference hold once we consider other factors?

Table 7.5 presents HLM analyses that treat the democracy support index as the dependent variable. The coefficients in the table tell us the change in one's democracy "score" when the independent variables increase by one unit. The first two models look at the Muslim and Christian variables as the only predictors of one's score on the democracy support index. According to model 1, self-identification as a Muslim decreases support for democracy. Once we control for other individual-level socioeconomic characteristics in model 3, the Muslim variable weakens in both magnitude and statistical significance. Age and education level are both positively associated with attitudes that are supportive of democracy. Gender and self-identification as a Christian are not statistically significant. Country-level factors are introduced in model 4.[37] National-level socioeconomic factors—measured by GDP per capita and average age—are not statistically significant. The religious composition of one's environment—measured by the proportion of the Muslim and Christian population in a country—is also not statistically significant. The only variable to pass the low threshold of statistical significance is political openness. Living in a more democratic country leads to a slight increase in one's democratic support score. Once we control for these possible influences on support for democracy, self-identification as a Muslim is still statistically significant and negative, but the effect is very small. All else being equal, a Muslim man of average age and education, living in a country with average values on the country-level variables, is predicted to have a democracy support score of 2.94, 0.04 points lower than a non-Muslim is predicted to have.

What about Muslims living in more or less democratic countries? As model 4 shows, Freedom House scores have a slight positive effect on support for democracy. For every one-point increase in a country's Freedom House score, an individual's predicted score on the democracy support index increases by 0.04. With other variables held at their means, a Muslim living in a country with the lowest possible

Freedom House score would have a predicted score on the democracy index of 2.78, while a Muslim living in a country with the highest possible Freedom House score would have a predicted score of 3.02. Their non-Muslim counterparts would have predicted scores of 2.82 and 3.06, respectively. The level of democracy in a country appears to have some effect, and individuals living in a more democratic country are more likely to express prodemocratic sentiments. The size of this effect, however, is not large. In moving from the most authoritarian to the most democratic polity, one's predicted score on the democracy index changes by an amount equal to roughly one-sixteenth of the full scale.

What can we conclude about Muslim attitudes toward democracy? It appears that living in a country with a large Muslim population does not have any discernable statistically significant effect on one's support for democracy. Self-identification as a Muslim does have a statistically significant negative effect on attitudes, and this effect is still evident even after we control for individual and country-level socioeconomic characteristics. Yet the size of this effect is miniscule—0.04 points on a scale that ranges from 1 to 4. Thus, being a Muslim has no meaningful substantive effect on attitudes toward democracy; the scores of Muslim and non-Muslim respondents in the survey are virtually identical. The level of statistical significance, moreover, is low; it would not be surprising if slightly different measures or changes in our sample size would alter the result.

The Arab Effect

Finally, we need to consider whether one particular slice of the Muslim world is responsible for the shortage of democracy. Some authors have acknowledged a deficit of democracy in Muslim countries but argued that the problem is limited to the Arab world. According to these authors, there is no Muslim problem in the realm of democracy; rather, there is an Arab problem. Something about Arab culture, rather than the religion that originated with the Arabs in the seventh century, is to blame.[38]

What that something could be is not specified by the authors who make the claim, but we may offer some speculations. In chapter 6, we considered aspects of Arab culture that might exacerbate gender-based inequality. Analysts of gender-based inequality have also cited what they regard as an Arab problem in that realm as well, as discussed in chapter 6. In fact, "Arab culture" is really a composite of traits that are widely seen as being particularly common among Arabs, perhaps due to their origins as inhabitants of sparsely populated, infertile lands. Such demography may have bred tribalism and patterns of hierarchical, patriarchal authority that made Arab lands resistant to democracy. The particularly close proximity of Arab countries to Israel, the perception of an Israeli threat, and the humiliations inflicted by Israel's occupation of Palestinian territories may pose additional obstacles to democratization among Arabs. Perhaps the Israeli threat is real and justifies maintenance of

Table 7.5 HLM Analysis of the Democracy Support Index (1 = most antidemocracy, 4 = most pro-democracy)

Predictors	Model 1	Model 2	Model 3	Model 4
Intercept	2.99*** (.03)	2.99*** (.03)	2.99*** (.03)	2.98*** (.03)
Individual-level [a]				
Female			-0.01 (.01)	-0.01 (.01)
Age			0.00*** (.00)	0.00*** (.00)
Education level			0.25*** (.02)	0.25*** (.02)
Muslim	-0.07*** (.02)		-0.05* (.02)	-0.04* (.02)
Christian		0.01 (.01)	0.00 (.01)	0.00 (.01)
Country-level [b]				
GDP per capita (log)				0.11 (.10)
Average age				-0.00 (.01)
Level of democracy				0.04* (.02)
Proportion Muslim				-0.01 (.13)
Proportion Christian				0.12 (.12)

Variance Components [c]

σ^2	0.26	0.26	0.26	0.26
τ	$u_0 = 0.07$	$u_0 = 0.07$	$u_0 = 0.07$	$u_0 = 0.06$
	$u_M = 0.01$	$u_C = 0.01$	$u_F = 0.00$	$u_F = 0.00$
			$u_A = 0.00$	$u_A = 0.00$
			$u_E = 0.03$	$u_E = 0.03$
			$u_M = 0.01$	$u_M = 0.01$
			$u_C = 0.01$	$u_C = 0.01$

Note: The base category for the analysis is made up of respondents who self-identified with a religion other than Christianity or Islam or did not identify with any religious tradition. Entries are restricted maximum likelihood coefficients with robust standard errors, calculated on HLM 6.06.

$N = 91{,}122$ individuals in 80 countries.

[a] All individual-level variables are centered at the group mean; all individual-level error terms were treated as random coefficients and were statistically significant at $p < .001$.

[b] All country-level variables are centered at the grand mean.

[c] The variance components for a null model including only the random Level-2 intercept are: $\sigma^2 = 0.27$; $\tau = 0.07$.

$^*p < .05$; $^{**}p < .01$; $^{***}p < .001$.

the massive police state apparatuses found in many Arab countries. On the other hand, the Israeli threat might be a ruse used by Arab leaders to distract their people from the despotism they suffer at home. Either way, one can see how Israel's military and political power, and even mere existence, might create obstacles to democratization in Arab countries that are absent or more weakly present elsewhere in the Muslim world.

Yet there is little evidence in the data that an Arab effect accounts for the link between Muslims and political regime. As table 7.3 shows, the variable for percentage Muslim remains statistically significant when the dummy variable for whether or not a country is part of the Arab League is included in the analyses. The dummy variable for Arab countries is statistically significant and negative, indicating that Arab countries do have lower VA scores. It is, in any event, problematic to include the dummy variable for Arab countries in the models because it is highly correlated with the variable for percentage Muslim (they are correlated at .66), and we get artificially large standard errors due to multicollinearity. Indeed, it is impossible to test precisely whether there is an "Arab" effect that is independent of a "Muslim" effect because there is no non-Muslim Arab country. Multicollinearity makes it impossible to estimate valid results for these two predictors. This fact is often neglected in statistical analyses that include variables for percentage Muslim and a dummy variable for Arab countries (or for the Middle East and North Africa region when that region is defined essentially as the Arab world plus Iran). This methodologically questionable move may be what scholars who claim that there is a regional or Arab—but no Muslim—effect on democracy (or, for that matter, other phenomena) do to generate empirical results that support their argument. While the question of whether the democratic deficit in the Muslim world is due to an Arab effect rather than a Muslim effect is legitimate, there is no methodologically sound way to solve this problem using regression analysis on cross-national data sets.

Given that this matter has received considerable attention in writings about Islam and democracy, it is worth probing further. Here we may set aside regression analysis and simply have a look at mean scores for groups of countries. Table 7.6 presents average VA scores for groups of countries, with an eye to detecting whether the Arab effect might be causing the Muslim effect. If the Arab variable is driving the

Table 7.6 Mean Level of Political Openness for Arab and Muslim Countries

	Non-Arab	*Arab*	*Marginal Means*
Non-Muslim	51.9 (128)	NA (0)	51.9 (128)
Muslim	34.6 (22)	30.2 (22)	32.4 (44)
Marginal means	49.4 (150)	30.2 (22)	46.9 (172)

Note: Political openness is measured on a 0–100 scale, number of countries in parentheses.

difference between Muslim and non-Muslim countries, there should be no or only a modest difference in the VA scores for the non-Arab Muslim countries and the non-Arab non-Muslim countries. Yet the data show something else. The mean VA score for all countries in the data set is 46.9 (on a 0–100 scale). For non-Muslim countries it is 51.9; for non-Arab Muslim countries it is 34.6; and for Arab Muslim countries it is 30.2. Thus, Muslim countries—both Arab and non-Arab—have much lower scores than do non-Muslim countries. The difference in mean level of VA scores between the non-Muslim and the non-Arab Muslim countries is statistically significant, while the difference in means between the non-Arab Muslim and Arab Muslim countries is not.[39]

Summary on How Islam Might Influence the Prospects for Democracy

Our discussion leaves us with, at best, fragments of explanations for the link between Islam and authoritarianism. Relatively low levels of economic development and high endowments of hydrocarbons, factors that happen to be correlated with higher concentrations of Muslim populations but that probably have little to do with religious adherence, may explain part of the correlation between Muslims and authoritarianism. But they certainly do not explain the entirety of the link. The prevalence of Islamism as a motivation for terrorism may matter, but we cannot really test this factor's influence and it probably does not, in any event, provide much explanatory punch. Gender-based inequality, while more acute in societies with higher concentrations of Muslims, does not appear to be a good predictor of political openness. It probably does not explain the link between Muslims and authoritarianism. Muslims are less inclined than non-Muslims to express prodemocratic attitudes in the relevant survey questions, but the difference between Muslims and non-Muslims, while statistically significant, is miniscule. Muslims, like non-Muslims, tend toward support for democratic institutions, at least in the abstract. The other factors we considered very likely supply even less explanatory power.

We are, therefore, left without a key. There is a clear, robust correlation between the proportion of the population that is Muslim and more authoritarian political regimes. But we find little about Islam or Muslims that necessarily countervails democracy, leaving us without a satisfying causal explanation. No doubt other scholars will take up the issue and provide better answers. One can only hope that their efforts, whether they rely upon quantitative or qualitative methods, will include a commitment to formulating clear hypotheses and engaging in real investigation of empirical facts, rather than on the rhetorical fireworks and selective use of evidence that heretofore has figured so prominently in discussions of the link between Islam and democracy.

8 Conclusion

As I completed work on this book, I grew more curious to know whether my hunch about the gravity of the matters I had addressed was as formidable as I had grown to suspect. I had come to think that the questions investigated in this volume are of the greatest importance and that they were at least as crucial for day-to-day, real-world political and social life as for academic analysis. But after investing a great deal of labor in a project, who would not think that it is of vital significance?

GRAVITY OF THE ISSUES

Some Soft Evidence

In an admittedly less-than-scientific endeavor, I decided to check how often the subjects of this book made the front page of the *New York Times*. I picked an eighteen-month period from 2008 to the midpoint of 2009, which was roughly the interval during which this book was written. A talented research assistant, as usual, provided indispensable aid. To our consternation, my colleague and I quickly realized that doing a headline-scan for the word "Islam" would not suffice; many articles that addressed the relevant issues were buried in stories whose headlines did not mention Islam or Muslims. So the effort required actually reading the stories—a lot of them. After learning more than we had ever wanted to know about the events of 2008 and the first half of 2009, we had some answers to our query. Of the 3,282 stories that appeared on the front page of the *New York Times*, 263 dealt with the issues raised in this volume. Thus, during the time of an especially dramatic election campaign for the presidency of the United States and the inauguration of the new president, fully 8 percent (or roughly one in twelve) of all stories dealt with the matters addressed in this book— and this in the newspaper of a country whose population is just 1.6 percent Muslims.

Unsurprisingly, many pieces were about war, insurgencies, and terrorism, particularly in Afghanistan, Pakistan, Iraq, and Palestinian lands. Many stories were also about other topics. Pieces from 2008 included "Turkish Schools Offer Pakistan a Gentler Islam" (May 4); "Young Saudis, Vexed and Entranced by Love's Rules" (May 12); "Global Classrooms: Recruiters for 'Sisters' College See a Bounty in the Middle East" (June 3); "In Algeria, a Tug of War for Young Minds" (June 23); "A Veil Closes France's Door to Citizenship" (July 19); "Wary of Islam, China Tightens a Vise of Rules" (October 19); "Britain Grapples with Role for Islamic Justice" (November 19); "Al-Qaeda Offers Obama Insults and Warning" (November 20); "To Fuel Quest, Hezbollah Harnesses Youth Piety" (November 21); and "As Taboos Ease, Saudi Girl Group Dares to Rock" (November 24). The month of April 2009 featured, among other relevant pieces, stories with the following headlines: "America Seeks Bonds to Islam, Obama Insists" (April 7); "Iraq's Newly Open Gays Face Scorn and Murder" (April 8); "United Militants Threaten Pakistan's Populous Heart" (April 14); "Afghan Women Defy Convention, and Crowds, to Protest New Law on Home Life" (April 16); "Indonesia's Voters Retreat from Radical Islam" (April 25); and "Credentials Challenged, Radical Quotes West Point" (April 29).

As such coverage suggests, how Muslims are distinctive is one of the central questions of our time. Each of the stories just cited potentially raises the question in the reader's mind. A non-Muslim might ask: How do they differ from us? A Muslim might ask the same question. Many of the big questions we have about war and peace, alienation and sociability, bias and justice, and oppression and freedom in the modern world rest on assumptions and convictions about how members of the world's second-largest faith group differ from adherents of other creeds. It is little wonder that the issues addressed in this book are the stuff of everyday conversation and heated controversy around the world. Curiosity about these questions, a conviction that they matter, and a shortage of studies that investigate them rigorously and impartially motivated me to write this book. How well non-Muslims and Muslims alike understand Muslims may have as much influence on the trajectory of human history during the twenty-first century as will the pace of medical innovation, the rate of economic growth, and the responsiveness of governments to climate change.

Why the Issues Are Vital

Understanding members of other faiths, and comprehending one's own religion in a comparative context, is particularly important for Muslims and Christians.

Islam and Christianity are by far the world's largest faiths. According to a recent Pew Forum survey, of the world's 6.8 billion people, 1.57 billion are Muslims and 2.25 billion are Christians.[1] Thus, 23 percent of humanity is Muslim and 33 percent is Christian; well over half of all people adhere to either Islam or Christianity. In strictly structural terms of the type that orient the thinking of specialists in international relations, one would expect relations between the two largest groups or camps, whatever their identity or specific situation, to be competitive and conflict-prone.

Structural conditions that may produce friction are accompanied by doctrines that may aggravate it. The hazard of antagonism arises not out of what differs between the faiths, but from what is common to them. To a far greater extent than the other major Abrahamic creed, Judaism, and the leading Dharmic traditions, Buddhism and Hinduism, Islam and Christianity are proselytizing religions. Neither Islam nor Christianity has an ethnic, tribal, or regional basis. Muslims and Christians seek converts in all corners of the Earth. Both regard their own religion as the path to radical improvement of the human condition on Earth and personal salvation after death. Both believe in an end of times when God will put all things right and take adherents of the truth faith—and only the true faith—to His heaven. For both Muslims and Christians, everything is at stake—for the world as a whole and for each individual—in whether people choose the proper path.

This aspect of Islam and Christianity is not going to change, at least not anytime soon. It is intrinsic to each religion. Islam would not be Islam and Christianity would not be Christianity without a universalizing project. No one should expect a Muslim to accept the Christian route to salvation or a Christian to accept the Muslim path.

To be sure, many people in predominantly Muslim and predominantly Christian societies favor harmonious relations. According to my own informal observational survey, the white-on-blue "COEXIST" bumper sticker, which stylizes each letter into a symbol of a world religion (the "C" into the crescent moon of Islam, the "T" into the Christian cross, and so on) is the most widely sported bumper sticker in the San Francisco Bay Area. This is no mean accomplishment: The Volvos, Volkswagens, and Priuses that crowd the streets of the region do not want for political messages; bumper space is scarce.

But most of the people who bear such messages are not religious Christians or Muslims. Many are not religious at all and know little about those they implore to "coexist." And it is interesting to note that the message is not expressed with the word "coexistence," which would exalt a particular condition. Instead, the message is conveyed as an infinitive verb, in imperative form. The message does not merely hold out a peaceful state of affairs as desirable; it instructs the adherents of all faiths to get along with one another forthwith. Indeed, the secular intellectuals who predominate in the author's city of residence adore the idea of religious harmony and are pleased when religious people—if they *must* be religious—avoid provoking conflicts.

From such a viewpoint, how Muslims and Christians (or for that matter Buddhists and Hindus) differ from one another is of little consequence. The important thing is that they all get along, whatever their beliefs and practices. If everyone thought that way, perhaps the need for mutual understanding would be less pressing. Better understanding of one's own faith would certainly be less urgent, since there would be little to understand.

But secular humanists, numerous as they may be in the major metropolitan areas of North America and Western Europe, make up only a small portion of mankind. Most people—some more strongly, some more loosely—are committed to a particular faith tradition. They often really do want to know how they are distinctive and how others differ from them. Many Christians care if Muslims are averse to separating religious and political authority, and the answer will affect the way Christians think of Muslims' orientation toward politics. Many Muslims want to know if Christians are generally irreligious, and the answer will shape how Muslims think of Christians' morality and worldview.

At our best, adherents of a religion want to know what we can learn from members of other faiths. After completing work on chapter 6, I want to know more about the possible Muslim advantage on class equality. I would like to know more about why Muslims create societies that are on average more egalitarian in socioeconomic terms than Christian societies are. I want to know what I can learn from Muslims. Even many secularists are interested in how adherents of this or that religion actually differ from one another and what can be learned from members of a given religion. Nonreligious people may be interested in what their own society can learn from others. And some bearers of the bumper sticker mentioned above, of course, may even be religious themselves.

Becoming more inquisitive about how members of our own religion fare in matters such as social equality and proneness to violence would be a good thing for our own faith traditions, whatever they are. Better understanding of the beliefs, opinions, and practices of adherents of any faith may be useful to anyone, including people who subscribe to no religion.

Productive inquisitiveness, however, demands not only open-mindedness and introspection. It also requires a comparative perspective (since we do not know how we are doing except in relation to others) and reliable data on members of other faiths (since we cannot know what we have to learn from others unless we have good information about them).

Yet we are still short on even the most rudimentary facts about how members of this or that faith differ (or not) from one another. The doctrines, prescriptions, and injunctions of the major religions are the subjects of innumerable volumes penned through the centuries, and production of works in these areas has only accelerated in recent years. But the richness of theology, philosophy, historiography, and jurisprudence is matched by poverty in social science. We have a great deal of knowledge about the principles and ideas and histories of the great faiths. But what do we know, concretely and on a global scale, about the *people* of the great religions—as individuals and as members of specific national societies—at the present moment? Not much.

This book has attempted to begin alleviating that problem. It has produced a bit of the information we need to begin forming more intelligent opinions about members of a particular faith group. What have we turned up?

SUMMARY OF THE BOOK'S FINDINGS

Table 8.1 summarizes the findings. The first column lists the matters probed in this book. Where investigation did not turn up evidence of substantial dissimilarity between Muslims and non-Muslims, an "x" appears in the next column over; if evidence of difference was found, an "x" is placed in the next column further to the right. The right-most column in the table briefly spells out how Muslims and non-Muslims differ in the cases where evidence of divergence was found.

Table 8.1 Summary of Findings

Variable	Little or No Evidence of Substantial Difference between Muslims and Non-Muslims	Evidence of Substantial Difference between Muslims and Non-Muslims	Substantive Finding (in matters in which Muslims and non-Muslims differ)
Level of personal religiosity	x		
Attitude toward religious leaders being involved in politics	x		
Attitude toward the need for political leaders to be religious		x	Muslims are more averse to atheism among political leaders
Level of personal sociability	x		
Level of membership in formal organizations	x		

continued

Table 8.1 continued

Variable	Little or No Evidence of Substantial Difference between Muslims and Non-Muslims	Evidence of Substantial Difference between Muslims and Non-Muslims	Substantive Finding (in matters in which Muslims and non-Muslims differ)
Tolerance of controversial behavior		x	Muslims are more averse to homosexuality and, to a lesser extent, abortion and divorce
Tolerance of dishonest behavior	x		
Level of corruption	x		
Level of violent crime		x	Murder rates are lower in societies with proportionally larger Muslim populations
Level of large-scale political violence	x		
Level of terrorist activity		x	Muslims are disproportionately responsible for recent acts of terrorism
Gender-based inequality		x	Gender-based inequality is greater in societies with proportionally larger Muslim populations
Class inequality		x	Socioeconomic inequality is lower in societies with proportionally larger Muslim populations
Political regime		x	Democracy is rarer in societies with proportionally larger Muslim populations

Some of our most noteworthy findings are about how different Muslims are not. As reported in chapter 2, we found little or no evidence of substantial Muslim distinctiveness in some areas in which it is commonly assumed that Muslims are atypical. We found only mild and patchy evidence to support the widely held notion that Muslims are exceptionally religious. Furthermore, investigation turned up little support for the folk wisdom that Muslims are unusually inclined to reject the legitimacy of separating religious and political authority. If Muslims are just as or almost as strongly inclined as Christians to say that religious leaders should not influence voters, the thesis that sacred and temporal authority are fused in the Muslim imagination may be a chimera. In fact, Muslims partake of a global consensus on keeping those who convey God's word and ways away from the people in the realm of political decision-making.

We also found little or no evidence of marked Muslim distinctiveness in the world of social interaction. As reported in chapter 3, personal sociability is slightly higher among Muslims than non-Muslims, but only slightly. Levels of membership in formal organizations do not differ appreciably.

Tolerance of dishonest behavior does not diverge markedly, either. As we saw in chapter 3, Muslims express less tolerance of lying, cheating, and stealing than non-Muslims do, but the difference is diminutive.

Absence of disparity between Muslims and non-Muslims extends from the expression of opinion on dishonest behavior, investigated in chapter 3, to actual dishonest behavior, examined in chapter 4. No evidence of substantial difference in proneness to corruption was found. When we control for other relevant factors, countries with proportionally greater numbers of Muslims do not have a markedly more or less acute problem with corruption.

Muslim societies are also unremarkable in terms of large-scale political violence. As shown in chapter 5, contrary to assertions made in some celebrated studies, a close look at the evidence suggests that Muslims are not especially prone to mass violence. Nor are they substantially less inclined to it.

Areas of Substantial Muslim Distinctiveness

We also found areas of divergence. While Muslims are not extraordinarily religious or inclined to favor the involvement of clerical figures in politics, they are especially opposed to atheism in their political leaders, as shown in chapter 2.

As we saw in chapter 3, Muslims' attitudes are also distinctive on a set of controversial behaviors. Being a Muslim is generally associated with stronger opposition to homosexuality, abortion, and divorce. The gap between Muslims and non-Muslims on attitudes toward homosexuality is particularly pronounced.

We found differences in behaviors as well as attitudes. In the examination of violent crime in chapter 4, a large gap in murder rates was evident. Homicide is much less common in societies with proportionally larger numbers of Muslim inhabitants.

But there is also some less good news in terms of Muslims and violence. As shown in chapter 5, the bulk of terrorist acts over the past fifteen years have been committed by Islamists in the name of religion. The vast majority of incidents of Islamist terrorism have occurred outside the West, where fear of Islamist terrorism is strong. This fact raises the possibility that people in the West may sometimes exaggerate the danger of Islamist terrorism in their own lands. Still, Islamists are responsible for most of the terrorist incidents that occur in the world and most of the deaths suffered in acts of terrorism. Most Muslims may oppose terrorism and regard it as incompatible with their religion, but most terrorists are Islamists.

Social inequality furnishes another area where we find a gap that suggests a Muslim disadvantage. In the relative status of the sexes, females have it particularly bad in Muslim society, as we saw in chapter 6. Not all of the numerous analyses used to assess gender-based inequality turned up a Muslim disadvantage, but a preponderance of evidence suggests that an unusually large deficit in equity prevails among Muslims.

In the other area of inequality we investigated, however, we found evidence of a Muslim advantage. Socioeconomic inequality is lower in societies with proportionally larger Muslim populations. Thus, while the gap between the sexes is larger among Muslims, the gap between the rich and the poor is smaller.

Finally, we found that Muslims tend to live in less open polities than do non-Muslims. Democracy is less common in societies with proportionally larger Muslim populations.

A Mixed Picture

We are left with a deeply mixed picture. The evidence certainly does not allow anything like a bottom-line statement on whether Muslims in the contemporary world are generally ahead of, behind, or on par with non-Muslims. In some areas, including those in which standard thinking assumes difference, we found little or no difference. For example, while conventional thinking (among Muslims and non-Muslims alike) holds that Muslims are particularly inclined to regard the separation of religious and political authority as illegitimate, we did not find support for this idea. Similarly, while many people regard Muslims as especially prone to large-scale political violence, we found no evidence to back this claim.

On some questions where conventional wisdom assumes difference we turned up evidence that favors the conventional wisdom. Three areas stand out. The first is terrorism. Terrorism is, in fact, disproportionately a Muslim problem, at least at the present moment. The second is gender-based inequality. The evidence supports what many observers have long suspected: Gender-based inequality is particularly acute among Muslims. The third major issue is political regime. Our findings substantiate the commonly held view that the Muslim world suffers from a deficit of popular rule.

Some of the topics investigated in this book have been the subjects of little or no prior research or debate. Here there is no conventional wisdom to confirm or disconfirm. In some such areas we turned up no signs of Muslim distinctiveness. For example, while some observers may have wondered whether Muslim societies suffer from a deficit of social capital, until now no one has posed the question as a hypothesis and tested it. We did so here, and found no signs of a substantial shortage (or surplus) of social capital among Muslims.

In other areas where there has been little or no prior research, the current investigation turned up evidence of difference between Muslims and non-Muslims. While a handful of criminologists have noted low crime rates in Muslim societies, few if any major works in social science have considered that religion may affect criminal violence and broader problems of public order. Numerous sociologists, political scientists, and economists have grappled with matters such as how drugs trade or natural resource abundance affects levels of public violence and the quality of political life. Yet few if any scholars have even included a control for the confessional orientation of the population. The findings presented here, which revealed a dramatic disparity between Muslims and non-Muslims in murder rates, suggest the need to take religion into account. Similarly, while comprehending and explaining socioeconomic inequality has occupied the minds of many social scientists, few have considered the possible significance of religion. If class inequalities are less severe among Muslims than non-Muslims, as we found evidence for here, scholars who study socioeconomic inequality may wish to consider including religious tradition in their analyses.

USING AND EXTENDING THE FINDINGS

Some Avenues for Future Research

The areas discussed in the previous paragraph present especially fertile grounds for future research. Here we found evidence of Muslim distinctiveness on issues in which religious adherence has rarely or never even been considered a potentially important factor. These matters concern social order and inequality, which are of great interest to social scientists across disciplines and many observers outside academia.

Investigation of possible relationships *between* some of the variables considered in this book may also lead to productive inquiry. Let us take the two areas just mentioned, socioeconomic inequality and homicide rates. Is there a link between them? Is greater socioeconomic inequality conducive to higher rates of criminal violence? In this volume we have not taken up such matters of causation. We have stuck with the largely descriptive task of assessing differences between members of a particular faith group and other people. But our findings have implications that beg some larger causal questions. They also suggest the advantages of taking religion into account. If, for example, scholars were to find that lower socioeconomic inequality favors lower rates of violent crime, they might also ask whether members of some faith traditions are more inclined to curtail socioeconomic inequality than are adherents of other faiths. The findings presented in chapters 4 and 6, while being descriptive rather than causal in nature, suggest the wisdom of bringing people's religious adherence into causal analysis involving criminal violence and socioeconomic inequality. Ignoring religion—which is what most social scientists do on questions regarding class inequality and civil violence—might circumscribe the incisiveness of analysis.

Other questions arise out of our findings as well. Chapter 6 showed that the status of women relative to men tends to be worse in societies with proportionally larger Muslim populations. In chapter 7, we saw that democracy tends to be rarer in those same societies. Is there a link? In an article published in 2002, I presented some evidence that a reason why predominantly Muslim societies lag on democratization is the inferior status of women.[2] I did not pursue that argument at length in this volume, which focused more on describing differences between Muslims and non-Muslims than on explaining the reasons for those differences. I did include a control for female-to-male literacy ratio in the analyses that treated democracy as the outcome variable in chapter 7 and did not find that it was statistically significant. It is possible that the status of females relative to males is not a good predictor of democracy. But this matter obviously presents an intriguing area for future inquiry.

The findings presented in this volume, in addition to illuminating issues concerning religion and Islam in particular, also prompt questions that do not necessarily pertain to creed. One regards the relationship between the individual and his or her broader environment. Ever since people started studying people, we have pondered the relationship between the individual and the group. How much influence does the broader social milieu have on individuals? The notion that individuals are very much the product of their social environment is perhaps most closely associated in modern social science with Émile Durkheim, who was also a pioneer in studying the effect of religion on behavior.[3] Writing in the late nineteenth and early twentieth century, Durkheim offered an especially cogent exposition of what may be termed a "societalist" version of human existence. According to Durkheim, virtually all traits of individuals are molded by society, and society has a life of its own that is distinct from the individuals who compose it. The societal units that Durkheim focused on, at least in his investigations that dealt with his fellow Europeans, were for the most part national societies, or countries.

Our investigations that used hierarchical linear modeling (HLM) and hierarchical generalized linear modeling (HGLM) lent an opportunity to test Durkheim's proposition using some interesting case material. Multilevel modeling such as HLM and HGLM arguably offers the best method available for assessing interactions among macro (here, country-level) and micro (individual-level) factors. The findings suggest the advantages of taking Durkheim seriously and, where possible, analyzing both individuals and aggregates. In a fine tour of the horizon on trends in political science, Robert Huckfeldt argues that the history of political analysis over the past half-century can be understood as a movement from the aggregate to the individual, with multileveled treatments that attempt to take both individuals and aggregates into account now coming to the fore in some works.[4] The portions of our study that lent themselves to HLM and HGLM represented an exercise in doing what Huckfeldt recommends, which is using multilevel analysis to bridge the micro–macro divide.

In some of our analyses that used such modeling, we found strong support for Durkheim's general propositions. For example, as reported in chapter 2, *countries' overall levels* of religiosity appear to have an important effect on *individuals'* religiosity. We turned up evidence that living in an environment with people who are more religious makes an individual more religious. For some questions, the confessional makeup of the environment, not just level of religiosity, affected individuals' orientations. We may pick an example from the investigation of gender-based inequality in chapter 6. As we saw when analyzing individuals' responses on whether men should receive preference in employment when jobs are scarce, living in a country with a proportionally larger Muslim population substantially boosted the predicted probably of respondents *across faith groups* agreeing that men should receive preferential treatment. Variation in the size of the Muslim population plays an even larger part than individual-level characteristics in predicting the likelihood of a person's endorsing preferential treatment for men.

These findings are not necessarily counterintuitive. They will not surprise social scientists who already share Durkheim's cast of mind. But they nonetheless are of considerable moment. A great deal of contemporary social science begins and ends with the individual as the basic unit of analysis. Thus, some scholars would assume that knowledge of individual-level traits, such as gender, level of education, and income would be adequate to predict individuals' religiosity. Society's overall level of religiosity would not necessarily be considered a potentially important predictor. The problem of joining the individual and the broader social environment is often considered mainly a matter of understanding individuals' traits and calculations and then aggregating those traits or considering what the collective outcome of individuals' actions is likely to be under a specific set of constraints.

The possibility that the whole is more and different than the sum of its parts and that the traits of the sum (society) fashion the traits of the parts (individuals) is not always recognized, particularly in works that rely upon microeconomic reasoning. Our findings suggest the desirability of taking into account both macro- and micro-level factors.

Practical Implications

The book's findings have practical implications as well. For example, the discovery that Muslims are not more prone to mass political violence counters conventional thinking and suggests that we should not expect countries that are predominantly Muslim to be especially likely to experience civil conflagration. The finding also raises the possibility that in predominantly Muslim societies that do experience chronic large-scale violence (such as Sudan or Iraq), the inhabitants' religion per se might have little to do with the carnage.

The discovery that Muslims are not substantially more likely to favor fusion of secular and sacred power represents yet another finding of the "it ain't necessarily so" variety. The notion that Muslims regard religious and temporal authority as properly joined is widespread. Yet upon close examination of real evidence, the assumption stumbles. What is commonly accepted as a fact is shown quite possibly to be a fiction.

Why are these two findings important? Taken together, they actually have weighty policy implications. Let us briefly examine why.

Leaders in long-standing democracies who generally back democratization in developing countries often lose their fervor for free elections in Muslim contexts. Autocrats in Muslim countries, like autocrats everywhere, are also unenthusiastic about free elections. The combination of lack of external pressure for open politics and autocrats' (predictable) preference for avoiding real elections may create permissive conditions for the endurance of authoritarianism in Muslim countries.[5]

The claims of autocrats and the feebleness of Western eagerness for free elections in Muslim countries are based on a pair of assumptions. Neither of these assumptions is normally voiced publicly or mentioned in polite company, but both are real and both are widely held. Together they shape policy. The first assumption is that Muslims are unusually prone to favor the fusion of religious and political authority. Thus, goes the logic, if Muslims are allowed to control their own political fates at the ballot box, most (or a large portion) of them will favor candidates who, once in power, will reject pluralism and propound an exclusionary form of rule based on the assertion of the absolute truths of their religion. The second assumption is that Muslims are prone to mass political violence. A firm hand is needed to prevent bloody chaos.

These assumptions create the expectation of a "democratic paradox" among Muslims. The democratic paradox refers to the danger that democracy may undermine democracy—that the people may use the ballot and their freedom to bury the prospects for robust open politics and civil peace. If the assumptions that Muslims are especially prone to endorse fusing religious and political authority and to engage in large-scale political violence are well founded, we would indeed expect Muslims to vote for heaven on earth and to raise hell in the streets. We would therefore presume the dangers of the democratic paradox to be especially acute among Muslims.

Officials in leading Western governments certainly see things this way. When the Tunisian president, Zine al-Abidine Ben Ali, who presides over one of the world's most repressive autocracies, was reelected to a fifth term with 90 percent of the vote in October 2009, the U.S. State Department spokesman stated that "we were concerned about the recent elections," but added that the Obama administration was committed to working with Ben Ali to "advance the partnership between Tunisia and the United States." The Reuters report on the election summed up the mentality of North American and European leaders perfectly: "Ben Ali has established Tunisia as a moderate voice in the Arab world and Western governments view it as a bulwark against Islamist extremism—despite the reservations some of them have about its record on democracy."[6] Autocrats in Muslim countries are happy to reinforce the notion, among leaders abroad and as well as among some of their own subjects, that religious fanatics are the only alternative to themselves and that the people, if entrusted with control of the state, would muck up the business of orderly, secular administration.

But what if Muslims neither want to combine sacred and temporal authority nor incline to large-scale political violence? In this event, the idea of an Islamic democratic paradox rests on phantom foundations. Our findings suggest precisely that. While the democratic paradox may pose a real danger, it is no more likely to arise in Muslim societies than elsewhere. The rationalizations of the Tunisia's Ben Ali—or, for that matter, Egypt's Hosni Mubarak, Jordan's King Abdullah II, Kazakhstan's Nursultan Nazarbayev, and Uzbekistan's Islam Karimov—fall flat. They carry no more force than do the claims of autocrats in non-Muslim societies, such as Zimbabwe's Robert Mugabe, North Korea's Kim Jong-il, or Burma's ruling junta. The fears of Western governments are shown to be poorly founded.

AN AFTERTHOUGHT

In a recent story on international rankings on educational attainment, several experts weighed in with conflicting opinions. One claimed that studies that purport to show that the United States is falling behind on college attainment are flawed and are used for "propaganda" purposes. Other experts embraced the data that cast a negative light on American education. At the conclusion of the piece, one expert was quoted by the reporter as saying: "People pick and choose statistics based on the case they're making. Welcome to the world."[7]

Welcome to the world, indeed. To what kind of world, one might ask? To a world in which social inquiry is often biased at its creation or hijacked shortly thereafter by prejudice, political correctness, policy agendas, political expediency, ossified commitments to scholarly paradigms, or the quest for profit. Is it therefore really surprising that the general public often eyes scientific findings with skepticism? Mark Twain famously quipped: "There are three kinds of lies: lies, damned lies, and statistics." Should we be surprised that so many members of the modern mass public, while better educated and better able to grasp the fruits of science than their ancestors were, regard this quip as a statement of fact rather than a wisecrack? We scholars, particularly in the United States, often bemoan the apparent decline of public respect for science. Yet, while we cannot control what others do with our findings after they are published, are we consistently doing all we can to promote judicious use of our findings? And what if we ourselves, in the course of producing our research and data analysis, engage in cherry-picking data to support a pet argument?

However readers choose to use the information this volume provides, they may know that the findings presented here are based on the author's best shot at unearthing the facts.[8] In the opening chapter, I pledged to present the facts as I found them, without selecting data or picking findings to support a preestablished viewpoint, pet theory, or political purpose. As the book shows, that commitment produced a thoroughly mixed picture. A commitment to showing Muslims' "bright side" might have treated murder rates as the sole aspect of violence and socioeconomic inequality as the only measure of social inequality. Highlighting the "dark side" could have been readily accomplished by focusing on terrorism alone in the investigation of violence and on gender-based inequality alone in the examination of social inequality. Showing that Muslims are distinctive in their political attitudes could have been done by emphasizing attitudes toward the need for political leaders to be religious. Ignoring the data on this question and focusing on attitudes toward religious leaders being involved in politics could have been done to create the impression that Muslims are not distinctive.

Social scientists can do better than that. If we are to help make a better world, we must first and foremost tell the truth and the whole truth as we find it—and do so without tailoring our analyses and presentations of findings to serving *what we think* will make a better world. Perhaps ironically, we cannot place the facts in service of a higher cause without undermining our own potential for contributing to a higher cause. Partisans of particular causes and points of view in the worlds of policy advocacy and punditry may, in the words of the analyst quoted above, "pick and choose statistics based on the case they're making." If social scientists do so, we discredit our enterprise and forfeit our chance to deliver on our highest calling:

discovering and presenting social facts. We can and should offer our findings clearly and plainly and with an eye to capturing the big picture, but we must be willing to live with the facts as they present themselves and resist fitting them to preestablished paradigms or political projects, worthy as those paradigms or projects may be. Fact-finding and map-drawing may be mundane, but they are also indispensable—all the more when exploring deep, turbulent, lightly charted waters that cover large portions of the earth.

Appendix 2.A
World Values Survey: List of Countries and Information on Religious Denominations

List of Countries (survey year)*

Albania (**2002**)

Argentina (**1999**, 2006)

Australia (2005)

Austria (**1999**)

Bangladesh (**2002**)

Belarus (**2000**)

Belgium (**1999**)

Bosnia and Herzegovina (**2001**)

Brazil (2006)

Bulgaria (**1999**, 2006)

Burkina Faso (2007)

Canada (**2000**)

Chile (**2000**, 2006)

China (**2001**, 2007)

Colombia (2005)

Croatia (**1999**)

Cyprus (2006)

Czech Republic (**1999**)

Denmark (**1999**)

Egypt (**2000**, 2008)

Estonia (**1999**)

Ethiopia (2007)

Finland (**2000**, 2005)

France (**1999**, 2006)

Germany (**1999**, 2006)

Ghana (2007)

Great Britain (**1999**, 2006)

Greece (**1999**)

Hungary (**1999**)

Iceland (**1999**)

India (**2001**, 2006)

Indonesia (**2001**, 2006)

Iran (**2000**, 2005)

Iraq (**2004**, 2006)

Ireland (**1999**)

Israel (**2001**)

Italy (**1999**, 2005)

Japan (**2000**, 2005)

Jordan (**2001**, 2007)

Kyrgyzstan (**2003**)

Latvia (**1999**)

Lithuania (**1999**)

Luxembourg (**1999**)

Macedonia (**2001**)

Malaysia (2006)

Mali (2007)

Malta (**1999**)

Mexico (**2000**, 2005)

Moldova (**2002**, 2006)

Morocco (**2001**, 2007)

Netherlands (**1999**, 2006)

New Zealand (2004)

Nigeria (**2000**)

Pakistan (**2001**)

Peru (**2001**, 2006)

Philippines (**2001**)

Poland (**1999**, 2005)

Portugal (**1999**)

Romania (**1999**, 2005)

Russia (**1999**, 2006)

Rwanda (2007)

Saudi Arabia (**2003**)

continued

Serbia (**2001**, 2006)

Singapore (**2002**)

Slovakia (**1999**)

Slovenia (**1999**, 2005)

South Africa (**2001**, 2007)

South Korea (**2001**, 2005)

Spain (**2000**, 2007)

Sweden (**1999**, 2006)

Switzerland (2007)

Taiwan (2006)

Tanzania (**2001**)

Thailand (2007)

Trinidad and Tobago (2006)

Turkey (**2001**, 2007)

Uganda (**2001**)

Ukraine (**1999**, 2006)

United States (**1999**, 2006)

Venezuela (**2000**)

Vietnam (**2001**, 2006)

Zambia (2007)

Zimbabwe (**2001**)

*****Bold** years are fourth-wave surveys (1999–2004). For countries included in both the fourth and fifth waves, fifth-wave data are used in all cases except tables 2.8–2.11.

Religious Denomination Recodes: The response categories for the question on religious denomination were not uniform across all countries in the survey. Each country provided its own response categories. Below is a description of how the authors coded the various WVS responses into denominational categories.

Muslim: Muslim, Al-Hadis, Shia, Sunni, and Druze

Catholic: Roman Catholic, Aglipayan, Brgy Sang Birhen, el Shaddi, Filipinista, and Greek Catholic; and respondents selecting "Christian" in India in the 2006 survey

Orthodox: Orthodox; and Egyptians selecting "Christian" response

Protestant: Protestant, Alliance, Anglican, Assembly of God, Baptist, Born Again, Charismatic, Christian Fellowship, Christian Reform, Church of Christ, Evangelical, Faith in God, Free Church, Independent African Church, Israelita Nuevo Pacto Universal, Jesus is Lord, Jesus Miracle Crusade, Lutheran, Mennonite, Methodist, Pentecostal, Presbyterian, Salvation Army, Seven Day Adventist, Worldwide Church of God, Unitarian, United, United Church of Philippines, and New Testament/Christ Bibleist

Other Christian: Armenian Apostolic, Iglesia ni Cristo, Jehovah's Witness, Mormon; respondents selecting "Christian" in Canada, Saudi Arabia, and Iraq in the fourth wave; respondents selecting "Christian" in Britain, Netherlands, Australia, and Iraq in the fifth wave

Buddhist: Buddhist and Hoa-hao

Other: "other," Cao Dai, Self-realization, Theosofist, Bahai, Jain, Zoroastrian, Sisewiss, Ka-elica

Pagan/Spiritist: ancestral worshiping; Espirit, Candomblé, and Umbanda in Brazil; native in Canada; paganism, Ratana, Shenism, Spiritista, Spiritualist, Taoist, Wicca, Yiguan dao

Hindu: Hindu

Jewish: Jewish

Sikh: Sikh

Appendix 2.B
Model Equations and Summary Statistics for Chapter 2

HIERARCHICAL LEVEL MODELS FOR TABLES 2.6–2.18

Below are the equations for the hierarchical level models presented throughout the chapter. In the interest of space we are only providing the equation for the most saturated models from each table. Simpler models follow the same structure, only with fewer variables.

Table 2.6. Dependent Variable: Importance of God in Life (1 = least importance, 10 = greatest importance)

Model 4:

$$Y_{ij} = \beta_{0j} + \beta_{1j}(\text{female})_{ij} + \beta_{2j}(\text{age})_{ij} + \beta_{3j}(\text{education level})_{ij} + \beta_{4j}(\text{Muslim})_{ij} + \beta_{5j}(\text{Christian})_{ij} + r_{ij}$$

$$\beta_{0j} = \gamma_{00} + \gamma_{01}(\text{GDP per capita})_{ij} + \gamma_{02}(\text{average age})_{ij} + \gamma_{03}(\text{average importance of God})_{ij} + \gamma_{04}(\text{proportion Muslim})_{ij} + \gamma_{05}(\text{proportion Christian})_{ij}$$

$$\beta_{1j} = \gamma_{10} + u_{1j}$$
$$\beta_{2j} = \gamma_{20} + u_{2j}$$
$$\beta_{3j} = \gamma_{30} + u_{3j}$$
$$\beta_{4j} = \gamma_{40} + u_{4j}$$
$$\beta_{5j} = \gamma_{50} + u_{5j}$$

Table 2.7. Dependent Variable: "Are you a religious person?" (1 = yes, 0 = not religious or "convinced atheist")

Model 4:

$$\varphi_{ij} = \frac{1}{1 + \exp\{-\eta_{ij}\}}$$

$$\eta_{ij} = \beta_{0j} + \beta_{1j}(\text{female})_{ij} + \beta_{2j}(\text{age})_{ij} + \beta_{3j}(\text{education level})_{ij} + \beta_{4j}(\text{Muslim})_{ij} + \beta_{5j}(\text{Christian})_{ij}$$

$$\beta_{0j} = \gamma_{00} + \gamma_{01}(\text{GDP per capita})_{ij} + \gamma_{02}(\text{average age})_{ij} + \gamma_{03}(\text{proportion religious persons})_{ij} + \gamma_{04}(\text{proportion Muslim})_{ij} + \gamma_{05}(\text{proportion Christian})_{ij} + u_{0j}$$

$$\beta_{1j} = \gamma_{10} + u_{1j}$$
$$\beta_{2j} = \gamma_{20} + u_{2j}$$
$$\beta_{3j} = \gamma_{30} + u_{3j}$$
$$\beta_{4j} = \gamma_{40} + u_{4j}$$
$$\beta_{5j} = \gamma_{50} + u_{5j}$$

Table 2.8. Dependent Variable: Attendance at Religious Services at Least Once a Week (1 = attends at least once per week, 0 = attends less regularly/never attends)

Model 4:

$$\varphi_{ij} = \frac{1}{1 + \exp\{-\eta_{ij}\}}$$

$$\eta_{ij} = \beta_{0j} + \beta_{1j}(\text{female})_{ij} + \beta_{2j}(\text{age})_{ij} + \beta_{3j}(\text{education level})_{ij} + \beta_{4j}(\text{Muslim})_{ij} + \beta_{5j}(\text{Christian})_{ij}$$

$$\beta_{0j} = \gamma_{00} + \gamma_{01}(\text{GDP per capita})_{ij} + \gamma_{02}(\text{average age})_{ij} + \gamma_{03}(\text{proportion attending services weekly})_{ij} + \gamma_{04}(\text{proportion Muslim})_{ij} + \gamma_{05}(\text{proportion Christian})_{ij} + \gamma_{06}(\text{level of democracy})_{ij} + u_{0j}$$

$$\beta_{1j} = \gamma_{10} + u_{1j}$$
$$\beta_{2j} = \gamma_{20} + u_{2j}$$
$$\beta_{3j} = \gamma_{30} + u_{3j}$$
$$\beta_{4j} = \gamma_{40} + u_{4j}$$
$$\beta_{5j} = \gamma_{50} + u_{5j}$$
$$\beta_{6j} = \gamma_{60} + u_{6j}$$

Table 2.10. Analysis of Attendance at Religious Services by Religious Subgroups

Model 2: Muslim Sample

$$\varphi_{ij} = \frac{1}{1 + \exp\{-\eta_{ij}\}}$$

$$\eta_{ij} = \beta_{0j} + \beta_{1j}(\text{female})_{ij} + \beta_{2j}(\text{age})_{ij} + \beta_{3j}(\text{education level})_{ij}$$

$$\beta_{0j} = \gamma_{00} + \gamma_{01}(\text{GDP per capita})_{ij} + \gamma_{02}(\text{average age})_{ij} + \gamma_{03}(\text{proportion attending services weekly})_{ij} + \gamma_{04}(\text{proportion Muslim})_{ij} + \gamma_{05}(\text{level of democracy})_{ij} + u_{0j}$$

$$\beta_{1j} = \gamma_{10} + u_{1j}$$
$$\beta_{2j} = \gamma_{20} + u_{2j}$$
$$\beta_{3j} = \gamma_{30} + u_{3j}$$

Model 2: Christian Sample

$$\varphi_{ij} = \frac{1}{1 + \exp\{-\eta_{ij}\}}$$

$$\eta_{ij} = \beta_{0j} + \beta_{1j}(\text{female})_{ij} + \beta_{2j}(\text{age})_{ij} + \beta_{3j}(\text{education level})_{ij}$$

$$\beta_{0j} = \gamma_{00} + \gamma_{01}(\text{GDP per capita})_{ij} + \gamma_{02}(\text{average age})_{ij} + \gamma_{03}(\text{proportion attending services weekly})_{ij} + \gamma_{04}(\text{proportion Christian})_{ij} + \gamma_{05}(\text{level of democracy})_{ij} + u_{0j}$$

$$\beta_{1j} = \gamma_{10} + u_{1j}$$
$$\beta_{2j} = \gamma_{20} + u_{2j}$$
$$\beta_{3j} = \gamma_{30} + u_{3j}$$

Table 2.13. Dependent Variable: Responses to Statement, "Religious leaders should not influence how people vote"

Model 6:

$$\eta_{mij} = \beta_{0j} + \sum_{q=1}^{Q} \beta_{qj} X_{qj} + \sum_{m=2}^{M-1} D_{mij} \delta_m$$

$$\eta_{mij} = \beta_{0j} + \beta_{1j}(\text{female})_{ij} + \beta_{2j}(\text{age})_{ij} + \beta_{3j}(\text{education level})_{ij} + \beta_{4j}(\text{Muslim})_{ij} + \beta_{5j}(\text{Christian})_{ij}$$
$$+ \beta_{6j}(\text{importance of God})_{ij} + D_{mij} \delta_m$$

$$\beta_{0j} = \gamma_{00} + \gamma_{01}(\text{GDP per capita})_{ij} + \gamma_{02}(\text{level of democracy})_{ij} + \gamma_{03}(\text{average importance of God})_{ij} + \gamma_{04}(\text{proportion Muslim})_{ij} + \gamma_{05}(\text{proportion Christian})_{ij}$$

$$\beta_{1j} = \gamma_{10}$$
$$\beta_{2j} = \gamma_{20}$$
$$\beta_{3j} = \gamma_{30} + u_{3j}$$
$$\beta_{4j} = \gamma_{40} + u_{4j}$$
$$\beta_{5j} = \gamma_{50} + u_{5j}$$
$$\beta_{6j} = \gamma_{60}$$

Table 2.16. Dependent Variable: Responses to Statement, "It would be better if more people with strong religious beliefs held public office"

Model 5:

$$\eta_{mij} = \beta_{0j} + \sum_{q=1}^{Q} \beta_{qj} X_{qj} + \sum_{m=2}^{M-1} D_{mij} \delta_m$$

$$\eta_{mij} = \beta_{0j} + \beta_{1j}(\text{female})_{ij} + \beta_{2j}(\text{age})_{ij} + \beta_{3j}(\text{education level})_{ij} + \beta_{4j}(\text{Muslim})_{ij} + \beta_{5j}(\text{Christian})_{ij}$$
$$+ \beta_{6j}(\text{importance of God})_{ij} + D_{mij} \delta_m$$

$$\beta_{0j} = \gamma_{00} + \gamma_{01}(\text{GDP per capita})_{ij} + \gamma_{02}(\text{average age})_{ij} + \gamma_{03}(\text{level of democracy})_{ij} + \gamma_{04}(\text{proportion Muslim})_{ij} + \gamma_{05}(\text{proportion Christian})_{ij} + \gamma_{06}(\text{average importance of God})_{ij} + u_{0j}$$

$$\beta_{1j} = \gamma_{10} + u_{1j}$$
$$\beta_{2j} = \gamma_{20} + u_{2j}$$
$$\beta_{3j} = \gamma_{30} + u_{3j}$$
$$\beta_{4j} = \gamma_{40} + u_{4j}$$
$$\beta_{5j} = \gamma_{50} + u_{5j}$$
$$\beta_{6j} = \gamma_{60} + u_{6j}$$

Table 2.18. Dependent Variable: Responses to Statement, "Politicians who do not believe in God are unfit for public office"

Model 5:

$$\eta_{mij} = \beta_{0j} + \sum_{q=1}^{Q} \beta_{qj} X_{qj} + \sum_{m=2}^{M-1} D_{mij} \delta_m$$

$$\eta_{mij} = \beta_{0j} + \beta_{1j}(\text{female})_{ij} + \beta_{2j}(\text{age})_{ij} + \beta_{3j}(\text{education level})_{ij} + \beta_{4j}(\text{Muslim})_{ij} + \beta_{5j}(\text{Christian})_{ij} + \beta_{6j}(\text{importance of God})_{ij} + D_{mij}\,\delta_m$$

$$\beta_{0j} = \gamma_{00} + \gamma_{01}(\text{GDP per capita})_{ij} + \gamma_{02}(\text{average age})_{ij} + \gamma_{03}(\text{level of democracy})_{ij} + \gamma_{04}(\text{proportion Muslim})_{ij} + \gamma_{05}(\text{proportion Christian})_{ij} + \gamma_{06}(\text{average importance of God})_{ij} + u_{0j}$$

$$\beta_{1j} = \gamma_{10} + u_{1j}$$
$$\beta_{2j} = \gamma_{20} + u_{2j}$$
$$\beta_{3j} = \gamma_{30} + u_{3j}$$
$$\beta_{4j} = \gamma_{40} + u_{4j}$$
$$\beta_{5j} = \gamma_{50}$$
$$\beta_{6j} = \gamma_{60} + u_{6j}$$

SUMMARY STATISTICS

Individual-level variables	Mean (min, max)
Age	40.92 (15, 101)
Education	0.49 (0, 1)

Country-level variables	
GDP per capita (logged)	3.81 (2.68, 4.53)
Freedom House Average (1994–98)	4.92 (1, 7)
Average age	41.43 (29.79, 52.45)
Average importance of God level	7.54 (3.58, 10)
Proportion Muslim	0.20 (0, 0.99)
Proportion Christian	0.54 (0, 0.99)
Proportion "religious persons"	0.72 (0.22, 0.98)
Proportion attending religious services at least once a week	0.31 (0.02, 0.92)

Appendix 2.C
Female and Male Attendance at Religious Services among Muslims in Countries with a Muslim Population of 25 Percent or Greater

Country	Percent of Muslim women who attend services one or more times per week	Percent of Muslim men who attend services one or more times per week
Albania	20.2	20.8
Bangladesh	49.6	63.3
Bosnia and Herzegovina	38.4	34.9
Egypt	42.3	42.6
Indonesia	63.4	64.4
Iran	24.3	29.2
Iraq	8.0	58.6
Jordan	6.5	81.7
Kyrgyzstan	17.2	28.8
Macedonia	34.2	71.0
Morocco	20.0	65.1
Nigeria	82.8	94.7
Pakistan	75.6	72.8
Saudi Arabia	16.8	41.3
Singapore	43.0	72.4
Tanzania	81.9	83.0
Turkey	6.5	67.2

Appendix 3.A
List of Countries Used in Tables 3.1–3.6

List of Countries Used in Tables 3.1–3.2

Albania (2002)

Argentina (1999)

Austria (1999)

Bangladesh (2002)

Belarus (2000)

Belgium (1999)

Bosnia and Herzegovina (2001)

Bulgaria (1999)

Canada (2000)

Chile (2000)

China (2001)

Croatia (1999)

Czech Republic (1999)

Denmark (1999)

Egypt (2000)

Estonia (1999)

Finland (2000)

France (1999)

Germany (1999)

Great Britain (1999)

Greece (1999)

Hungary (1999)

Iceland (1999)

India (2001)

Indonesia (2001)

Iran (2000)

Iraq (2004)

Ireland (1999)

Israel (2001)

Italy (1999)

Japan (2000)

Jordan (2001)

Kyrgyzstan (2003)

Latvia (1999)

Lithuania (1999)

Luxembourg (1999)

Macedonia (2001)

Malta (1999)

Mexico (2000)

Moldova (2002)

Morocco (2001)

Netherlands (1999)

Nigeria (2000)

Pakistan (2001)

Peru (2001)

Philippines (2001)

Poland (1999)

Portugal (1999)

Romania (1999)

Russia (1999)

Saudi Arabia (2003)

Serbia (2001)

Singapore (2002)

Slovakia (1999)

Slovenia (1999)

South Africa (2001)

South Korea (2001)

Spain (2000)

continued

List of Countries Used in Tables 3.1–3.2

Sweden (1999)

Tanzania (2001)

Turkey (2001)

Uganda (2001)

Ukraine (1999)

United States (1999)

Venezuela (2000)

Vietnam (2001)

Zimbabwe (2001)

List of Countries Used in Tables 3.3–3.6

Argentina (2006)

Australia (2005)

Brazil (2006)

Bulgaria (2006)

Burkina Faso (2007)

Chile (2006)

China (2007)

Colombia (2005)

Cyprus (2006)

Egypt (2008)

Ethiopia (2007)

Finland (2005)

France (2006)

Germany (2006)

Ghana (2007)

Great Britain (2006)

India (2006)

Indonesia (2006)

Iran (2005)

Italy (2005)

Japan (2005)

Jordan (2007)

Malaysia (2006)

Mali (2007)

Mexico (2005)

Moldova (2006)

Morocco (2007)

Netherlands (2006)

New Zealand (2004)

Peru (2006)

Poland (2005)

Romania (2005)

Russia (2006)

Rwanda (2007)

Serbia (2006)

Slovenia (2005)

South Africa (2007)

South Korea (2005)

Spain (2007)

Sweden (2006)

Switzerland (2007)

Taiwan (2006)

Thailand (2007)

Trinidad and Tobago (2006)

Turkey (2007)

Ukraine (2006)

United States (2006)

Vietnam (2006)

Zambia (2007)

Appendix 3.B
Model Equations and Summary Statistics for Chapter 3

HIERARCHICAL LEVEL MODELS FOR TABLES 3.2–3.13

Below are the equations for the hierarchical level models presented throughout the chapter. In the interest of space we are only providing the equation for the most saturated models from each table. Simpler models follow the same structure, only with fewer variables.

Table 3.2. Dependent Variable: Sociability Index (0 = no social interactions, 1 = numerous weekly social interactions)

Model 5:

$$Y_{ij} = \beta_{0j} + \beta_{1j}(\text{female})_{ij} + \beta_{2j}(\text{age})_{ij} + \beta_{3j}(\text{education level})_{ij} + \beta_{4j}(\text{Muslim})_{ij} + \beta_{5j}(\text{Christian})_{ij} + \beta_{6j}(\text{importance of God})_{ij} + r_{ij}$$

$$\beta_{0j} = \gamma_{00} + \gamma_{01}(\text{GDP per capita})_{ij} + \gamma_{02}(\text{average age})_{ij} + \gamma_{03}(\text{level of democracy}) + \gamma_{04}(\text{proportion Muslim})_{ij} + \gamma_{05}(\text{proportion Christian})_{ij} + \gamma_{06}(\text{average importance of God})_{ij}$$

$$\beta_{1j} = \gamma_{10} + u_{1j}$$
$$\beta_{2j} = \gamma_{20} + u_{2j}$$
$$\beta_{3j} = \gamma_{30} + u_{3j}$$
$$\beta_{4j} = \gamma_{40} + u_{4j}$$
$$\beta_{5j} = \gamma_{50} + u_{5j}$$
$$\beta_{6j} = \gamma_{60} + u_{6j}$$

Tables 3.4–3.6. Dependent Variables: Membership in Organizations (0 = not a member, 1 = a member)

The models in tables 3.4–3.6 include estimates of eight different dependent variables. The model specification on the right side of the equation, however, was identical for all dependent variables. In some instances, however, u_{kj} has been constrained to equal zero. These instances are noted in the variance components statistics in the relevant tables.

Model 3:

$$\varphi_{ij} = \frac{1}{1 + \exp\{-\eta_{ij}\}}$$

$\eta_{ij} = \beta_{0j} + \beta_{1j}(\text{female})_{ij} + \beta_{2j}(\text{age})_{ij} + \beta_{3j}(\text{education level})_{ij} + \beta_{4j}(\text{Muslim})_{ij} + \beta_{5j}(\text{Christian})_{ij}$

$\beta_{0j} = \gamma_{00} + \gamma_{01}(\text{GDP per capita})_{ij} + \gamma_{02}(\text{average age})_{ij} + \gamma_{03}(\text{level of democracy}) + \gamma_{04}(\text{average memberships})_{ij} + \gamma_{05}(\text{proportion Muslim})_{ij} + \gamma_{06}(\text{proportion Christian})_{ij} + u_{0j}$

$\beta_{1j} = \gamma_{10} + u_{1j}$
$\beta_{2j} = \gamma_{20} + u_{2j}$
$\beta_{3j} = \gamma_{30} + u_{3j}$
$\beta_{4j} = \gamma_{40} + u_{4j}$
$\beta_{5j} = \gamma_{50} + u_{5j}$
$\beta_{6j} = \gamma_{60} + u_{6j}$

Tables 3.8–3.13. Dependent Variables: Tolerance for Controversial and Dishonest Behaviors (1 = never justifiable, 10 = always justifiable)

The models in tables 3.8–3.13 include estimates of five different dependent variables. The model specification on the right side of the equation, however, was identical for all dependent variables.

Model 5:

$Y_{ij} = \beta_{0j} + \beta_{1j}(\text{female})_{ij} + \beta_{2j}(\text{age})_{ij} + \beta_{3j}(\text{education level})_{ij} + \beta_{4j}(\text{Muslim})_{ij} + \beta_{5j}(\text{Christian})_{ij} + \beta_{6j}(\text{importance of God})_{ij} + r_{ij}$

$\beta_{0j} = \gamma_{00} + \gamma_{01}(\text{GDP per capita})_{ij} + \gamma_{02}(\text{average age})_{ij} + \gamma_{03}(\text{level of democracy}) + \gamma_{04}(\text{proportion Muslim})_{ij} + \gamma_{05}(\text{proportion Christian})_{ij} + \gamma_{06}(\text{average importance of God})_{ij}$

$\beta_{1j} = \gamma_{10} + u_{1j}$
$\beta_{2j} = \gamma_{20} + u_{2j}$
$\beta_{3j} = \gamma_{30} + u_{3j}$
$\beta_{4j} = \gamma_{40} + u_{4j}$
$\beta_{5j} = \gamma_{50} + u_{5j}$
$\beta_{6j} = \gamma_{60} + u_{6j}$

SUMMARY STATISTICS

Data for Tables 3.1–3.2

Individual-level variables	Mean (min, max)
Age	41.09 (15, 101)
Education	0.48 (0, 1)

Country-level variables	
GDP per capita (logged)	3.86 (2.68, 4.52)
Freedom House Average (1994–98)	4.99 (1, 7)
Average age	41.56 (30.15, 49.18)
Average importance of God level	7.35 (3.76, 10)
Proportion Muslim	0.20 (0, 0.99)
Proportion Christian	0.53 (0, 0.99)

Data for Tables 3.3–3.6

Individual-level variables	Mean (min, max)
Age	41.08 (15, 98)
Education	0.48 (0, 1)

Country-level variables	
GDP per capita (logged)	3.79 (2.76, 4.47)
Freedom House Average (1994–98)	4.89 (1, 7)
Average age	41.90 (29.79, 52.45)
Average importance of God level	7.56 (3.58, 9.91)
Proportion Muslim	0.19 (0, 0.99)
Proportion Christian	0.53 (0, 0.99)

The summary statistics used in tables 3.7–3.13 are the same as those reported in appendix 2.B.

Appendix 3.C
Alternate Specification of Sociability Index

In addition to the four-item sociability index used in tables 3.1 and 3.2, we constructed a three-item index that excludes time spent with individuals from religious organizations. The following two tables replicate the analysis conducted in tables 3.1 and 3.2 using this alternate measure as the dependent variable.

Table 3.C.1 Mean Scores for Religious Groups on Sociability Index B (0–1)

	Muslims	All Non-Muslims*	Christians	No Denomination
Sociability Index B (average of frequency of time spent with friends, colleagues, and people from sports or recreation group)	0.53 (N = 14,898)	0.52 (N = 57,480)	0.52 (N = 38,363)	0.51 (N = 14,791)

*Includes all individuals who adhere to a religious denomination other than Islam as well as individuals who did not state adherence to a religious tradition.

Table 3.C.2 HLM Analysis of Sociability Index B [0 = no social interactions, 1 = numerous weekly social interactions]

Predictors	Model 1	Model 2	Model 3	Model 4	Model 5
Intercept	0.52***(.01)	0.52***(.01)	0.52***(.01)	0.52***(.01)	0.52***(.01)
Individual-level[a]					
Female			-0.09***(.01)	-0.09***(.01)	-0.09***(.01)
Age			-0.00***(.00)	-0.00***(.00)	-0.00***(.00)
Education level			0.12***(.01)	0.12***(.01)	0.12***(.01)
Muslim	-0.01 (.01)		-0.01 (.01)	-0.01 (.01)	-0.01 (.01)
Christian		-0.01 (.01)			
Importance of God			0.02***(.00)	0.02***(.00)	0.02***(.00)
Country-level[b]					
GDP per capita (log)				0.04 (.03)	0.03 (.03)
Average age				-0.00 (.00)	-0.01 (.00)
Level of democracy				-0.01 (.00)	-0.01 (.00)
Proportion Muslim				0.07 (.05)	0.05 (.06)
Proportion Christian				0.10* (.05)	0.11 (.06)
Average importance of God					-0.01 (.00)

Variance Components[c]

σ^2	0.06	0.06	0.05	0.05	0.05
τ	$u_0 = 0.01$	$u_0 = 0.01$	$u_0 = 0.01$	$u_0 = 0.01$	$u_0 = 0.01$
	$u_M = 0.00$	$u_C = 0.00$	$u_F = 0.00$	$u_F = 0.00$	$u_F = 0.00$
			$u_A = 0.00$	$u_A = 0.00$	$u_A = 0.00$
			$u_E = 0.00$	$u_E = 0.00$	$u_E = 0.00$
			$u_M = 0.00$	$u_M = 0.00$	$u_M = 0.00$
			$u_C = 0.00$	$u_C = 0.00$	$u_C = 0.00$
					$u_I = 0.00$

Entries are restricted maximum likelihood coefficients with robust standard errors, calculated on HLM 6.06.

$N = 69{,}585$ individuals in 64 countries. (Turkey is included in these models; it was excluded in the Sociability Index analyzed in tables 3.1–3.2 because the question about time spent with individuals from religious organizations was not asked.)

[a] All individual-level variables are centered at the group mean; all individual-level error terms were treated as random coefficients and were statistically significant at $p < .001$.

[b] All country-level variables are centered at the grand mean.

[c] The variance components for a null model including only the random Level-2 intercept are: $\sigma^2 = 0.06$; $\tau = 0.01$.

*$p < .05$; **$p < .01$; ***$p < .001$.

Appendix 4
OLS Output for Murder Rates

Regressions of Murder Rates on Hypothesized Predictors

	Model 1	Model 2	Model 3	Model 4	Model 5
(Intercept)	8.036*** (1.098)	6.412 (5.715)	−15.712 (9.536)	−17.429* (8.703)	5.586 (7.651)
Percent Muslim	−0.070*** (0.015)	−0.093*** (0.017)	−0.068*** (0.018)	−0.066*** (0.012)	−0.095*** (0.025)
Income per capita		−0.373*** (0.100)	−0.265** (0.084)	−0.275** (0.096)	−0.367*** (0.083)
Life expectancy		0.083 (0.095)	0.172 (0.131)	0.180† (0.100)	0.094 (0.127)
Ethnic diversity			−1.443 (4.153)		0.908 (3.880)
Income inequality			0.404** (0.136)	0.399** (0.135)	
Level of democracy			−0.179 (0.722)		−0.067 (0.559)
N	151	151	132	132	150
Adjusted R^2	.067	.144	.234	.245	.131

Note: OLS models with robust standard errors in parentheses.

†significant at $p < .10$; *$p < .05$; **$p < .01$; ***$p < .001$.

Appendix 5.A
Comprehensive List of
Major Episodes of Intrastate
Political Violence, 1946–2007

Date	Site	Description	Deaths	Predominant religion(s) of country	Conflict instigated in whole or in part by Islamists?
1945–1947	Iran	Azerbaijani and Kurd rebellions	2,000	Islam	No
1945–1949	Greece	Greek civil war	150,000	Christianity	No
1946	Bolivia	Civil violence	1,000	Christianity	No
1946–1950	China	Chinese civil war	1,000,000	Traditional beliefs	No
1947	China	Repression of Taiwan dissidents	20,000	Traditional beliefs	No
1947	Paraguay	Civil violence (Liberals)	1,000	Christianity	No
1947–1948	Yemen AR	Civil violence (Yahya clan coup attempt)	5,000	Islam	No
1947–1949	India	Kashmir rebellion	4,000	Hinduism	Yes
1948	Colombia	Civil violence (Conservatives)	1,000	Christianity	No
1948	Costa Rica	Civil violence (National Union)	2,000	Christianity	No
1948	South Korea	Civil violence (Army)	1,000	Buddhism	No
1948	India	Civil violence (Hyderabad)	200	Hinduism	No
1948–1956	Malaysia	Repression of Chinese by Malay militia	12,500	Islam	No
1948–	Myanmar (Burma)	Ethnic war (Karen, Shan, and others)	100,000	Buddhism	No
1948–1960	Colombia	"La Violencia" civil war (Liberals)	250,000	Christianity	No
1950	Indonesia	Ethnic violence (Moluccans)	5,000	Islam	No
1950–1951	China	Repression of the landlords	1,500,000	Traditional beliefs	No

1950–1952	Philippines	Civil violence (Huks)	10,000	Christianity	No
1950–1953	North Korea, South Korea	Korean War (civil war)	1,500,000	Buddhism	No
1950–1960	Malaysia	Independence and civil violence	15,000	Islam	No
1951	Thailand	Civil violence	NA	Buddhism	No
1952	Egypt	Civil violence (Nasser coup)	1,000	Islam	No
1952	Bolivia	Civil violence	2,000	Christianity	No
1952–	India	Ethnic war (northeast tribals; Assam separatists)	25,000	Hinduism	No
1953	Indonesia	Civil violence (Darul Islam)	1,000	Islam	Yes
1953–1954	Vietnam	Repression of landlords	15,000	Buddhism	No
1954	Guatemala	Civil violence (coup against Arbenz)	1,000	Christianity	No
1954–1955	Taiwan	Ethnic violence (Native Taiwanese v. KMT)	5,000	Traditional beliefs	No
1955	Costa Rica	Civil violence	1,000	Christianity	No
1955	Taiwan	Civil violence (Taiwanese v. KMT)	5,000	Traditional beliefs	No
1955	Argentina	Civil violence (army rebellion)	3,000	Christianity	No
1956	North Vietnam	Civil violence	NA	Buddhism	No
1956–1957	Haiti	Civil violence	NA	Christianity	No
1956–1960	Yemen AR	Ethnic violence (Yemeni–Adenese clans)	1,000	Islam	No
1956–1967	China	Ethnic war (Tibetans)	100,000	Traditional beliefs	No

continued

Date	Site	Description	Deaths	Predominant religion(s) of country	Conflict instigated in whole or in part by Islamists?
1956–1972	Sudan	Ethnic warfare (Islamic v African)	500,000	Islam	Yes
1957	Oman	Civil violence	NA	Islam	No
1957–1959	Cuba	Civil war (Castro ousts Batista)	5,000	Christianity	No
1957–1961	Indonesia	Civil violence (dissident military)	30,000	Islam	No
1958	Lebanon	Civil violence	2,000	Islam	No
1958	Iraq	Civil violence (coup ousts monarchy)	2,000	Islam	No
1958	Jordan	Civil violence	NA	Islam	No
1958–1975	North Vietnam, South Vietnam	"Vietnam War" (civil war)	2,000,000	Buddhism	No
1959	Iraq	Civil violence (Shammar tribe)	2,000	Islam	No
1959	China	Repression of counter-revolutionaries	50,000	Traditional beliefs	No
1959–1966	Rwanda	PARMEHUTU overthrow of Tutsi monarchy; repression of Tutsis	75,000	Christianity	No
1960–1961	Pakistan	Ethnic violence (Pushtun)	1,000	Islam	No
1960–1965	Zaire	Katanga civil war	100,000	Christianity	No
1960–1973	Laos	Civil war	25,000	Buddhism	No
1961–1993	Iraq	Ethnic warfare (Kurds)	150,000	Islam	No

1962–1963	Algeria	Civil violence (rebel factions)	2,000	Islam	No
1962–1970	Yemen AR	Civil war (following coup)	40,000	Islam	No
1962–1973	Ethiopia	Eritrean separatists	2,000	Islam and Christianity	Yes
1963	Iraq	Civil violence	NA	Islam	No
1963	Iran	Civil violence (land reform)	1,000	Islam	Yes
1963–1968	Cyprus	Civil violence (Makarios crisis)	2,000	Islam and Christianity	No
1963–1993	Indonesia	Ethnic warfare (Papuan–West Irian)	15,000	Islam	No
1964	Guatemala	Civil violence	NA	Christianity	No
1964	Zambia	Civil violence	1,000	Christianity	No
1964	Tanzania	Civil violence	NA	Islam and Christianity	No
1964	Brazil	Civil violence	NA	Christianity	No
1964–1966	Kenya	Shifta; Somali separatism	1,000	Christianity	No
1965	Burundi	Ethnic violence (failed coup; Hutu/Tutsi)	5,000	Christianity	No
1965	Dominican Republic	Civil violence	3,000	Christianity	No
1965	Peru	Civil violence	NA	Christianity	No
1965–1966	Indonesia	Repression of Chinese/Communists	500,000	Islam	Yes
1965–1968	USA	Civil violence (urban Afro-American unrest)	1,000	Christianity	No
1965–1994	Chad	Civil war	75,000	Islam	No

continued

Date	Site	Description	Deaths	Predominant religion(s) of country	Conflict instigated in whole or in part by Islamists?
1965–	Israel	Ethnic war (Arab Palestinians/Palestine Liberation Organization)	20,000	Judaism	No
1966	Nigeria	Repression of Ibo	20,000	Islam and Christianity	No
1966	Uganda	Ethnic violence (Buganda)	2,000	Christianity	No
1966–1970	Nigeria	Ethnic warfare (Biafra separatism)	200,000	Islam and Christianity	No
1966–1975	China	"Cultural Revolution"	500,000	Traditional beliefs	No
1966–1996	Guatemala	Repression of indigenous peoples	150,000	Christianity	No
1967	Zaire	Civil violence	800	Christianity	No
1967–1983	Thailand	Ethnic violence and repression (Malay)	NA	Buddhism	Yes
1968	France	Civil violence (student and labor unrest)	3,000	Christianity	No
1968	Czechoslovakia	"Prague Spring" civil violence	1,000	Christianity	No
1968–1982	India	Repression of Naxalites	2,000	Hinduism	No
1969–1979	Equatorial Guinea	Repression of dissidents	50,000	Christianity	No
1969–1994	UK	Ethnic violence (Northern Ireland/Irish Republican Army)	3,000	Christianity	No
1970	Jordan	Civil violence (Palestinians)	10,000	Islam	No
1970–1975	Oman	Civil violence (Dhofar rebellion)	3,000	Islam	No

continued

1970–1975	Cambodia	Civil war	150,000	Buddhism	No
1970–1982	Italy	Ethnic violence (Sardinians)	2,000	Christianity	No
1971	Sri Lanka	Civil violence (attempted coup)	10,000	Buddhism	No
1971	Bangladesh, Pakistan	Ethnic war (Bengali independence)	1,000,000	Islam	No
1971–1978	Uganda	Ethnic warfare (Idi Amin regime)	250,000	Christianity	No
1972	Burundi	Ethnic violence (Hutus target Tutsis)	2,000	Christianity	No
1972–1973	Burundi	Repression of Hutus	100,000	Christianity	No
1972–1979	Zimbabwe	Ethnic violence (ZANU/ZAPU v Whites)	20,000	Christianity	No
1972–1997	Philippines	Civil warfare (New Peoples Army)	40,000	Christianity	No
1972–	Philippines	Ethnic warfare (Moros)	50,000	Christianity	Yes
1973	Chile	Civil violence (army ouster of Allende)	5,000	Christianity	No
1973–1977	Pakistan	Ethnic warfare (Baluch separatism)	12,000	Islam	No
1974	Cyprus	Civil violence	5,000	Islam and Christianity	No
1974–1976	Chile	Repression of dissidents ("disappeared")	20,000	Christianity	No
1974–1985	Turkey	Civil violence	8,000	Islam	No
1974–1991	Ethiopia	Ethnic warfare (Eritreans and others)	750,000	Islam and Christianity	No
1975	Portugal	Civil violence	NA	Christianity	No
1975–1978	Cambodia	Khmer Rouge repression of dissidents	1,500,000	Buddhism	No
1975–1990	Laos	Civil violence (rebel Lao and Hmong)	10,000	Buddhism	No
1975–1991	Indonesia	Ethnic violence (Aceh)	15,000	Islam	Yes

Date	Site	Description	Deaths	Predominant religion(s) of country	Conflict instigated in whole or in part by Islamists?
1975–1991	Lebanon	Ethnic war (various sects)	100,000	Islam	Yes
1975–1992	Bangladesh	Ethnic war (Chittagong Hills)	25,000	Islam	No
1975–2002	Angola	Civil war (UNITA)	1,000,000	Christianity	No
1975–2005	Angola	Civil violence (Cabinda separatists; FLEC)	3,500	Christianity	No
1975–	Colombia	Civil violence, land reform, and drug trafficking (left: ELN, FARC, ELP, MAO, M-19; right MAS, AUC)	55,000	Christianity	No
1976	South Africa	Ethnic violence	1,000	Christianity	No
1976	Sudan	Islamic Charter Front	1,000	Islam	Yes
1976–1980	Argentina	"The Dirty War" repression of dissidents	20,000	Christianity	No
1976–1992	Indonesia	Colonial war (East Timor)	180,000	Islam	No
1977–1979	Ethiopia	"Ogaden War" ethnic violence (Somalis)	10,000	Islam and Christianity	No
1977–1980	Turkey	Ethnic violence (Armenians)	5,000	Islam	No
1977–1983	Zaire	Repression of dissidents	10,000	Christianity	No
1978	Somalia	Military faction	500	Islam	No
1978–1979	Nicaragua	Civil war (Sandinistas)	40,000	Christianity	No
1978–1993	Iran	Civil war (Islamic state)	50,000	Islam	Yes

continued

1978–2002	Afghanistan	Civil war	1,000,000	Islam	Yes
1979–1980	South Korea	Unrest, riots, and government repression	1,000	Buddhism	No
1979–1985	Iran	Ethnic war (Kurds)	40,000	Islam	No
1979–1992	El Salvador	Civil war (FMLN)	75,000	Christianity	No
1979–1998	Iraq	Ethnic violence (Shias)	25,000	Islam	No
1980	Brazil	Repression of dissidents (death squads)	1,000	Christianity	No
1980	Jamaica	Civil violence (elections)	1,000	Christianity	No
1980–1985	Nigeria	Ethnic violence (Islamic groups)	9,000	Islam and Christianity	Yes
1980–1998	China	Ethnic violence (Uighurs, Kazakhs)	10,000	Traditional beliefs	No
1981	Ghana	Civil violence (Konkomba v Nanumba)	1,000	Christianity	No
1981	Gambia	SRLP rebellion	650	Islam	No
1979–1982	Syria	Repression of dissidents (Muslim Brotherhood)	25,000	Islam	Yes
1981–1986	Uganda	Repression of dissidents	100,000	Christianity	No
1981–1987	Zimbabwe	Ethnic violence (Ndebele)	3,000	Christianity	No
1981–1990	Nicaragua	Civil war (Contras)	30,000	Christianity	No
1981–1992	Mozambique	Civil war (RENAMO)	500,000	Traditional beliefs and Christianity	No
1982–1997	Peru	Civil violence (Sendero Luminoso)	30,000	Christianity	No
1983	India	Civil violence (elections in Assam)	3,000	Hinduism	No

Date	Site	Description	Deaths	Predominant religion(s) of country	Conflict instigated in whole or in part by Islamists?
1983–1984	China	Repression of dissidents	5,000	Traditional beliefs	No
1983–1993	India	Ethnic warfare (Sikhs)	25,000	Hinduism	No
1983–1996	South Africa	Ethnic/civil warfare	20,000	Christianity	No
1983–1998	Pakistan	Ethnic violence (Sindhis; Muhajirs)	5,000	Islam	No
1983–	Sri Lanka	Ethnic war (Tamils)	75,000	Buddhism	No
1983–2002	Sudan	Ethnic war (Islamic v. African)	1,000,000	Islam	Yes
1984	Cameroon	Military faction	750	Traditional beliefs and Christianity	No
1984	Zaire	Ethnic/civil warfare	1,000	Christianity	No
1984–1999	Turkey	Ethnic warfare (Kurds)	40,000	Islam	No
1985	Liberia	Repression of dissidents (failed coup)	5,000	Traditional beliefs	No
1986–1987	Yemen PDR	Civil war	10,000	Islam	No
1986–1993	Nigeria	Ethnic violence (Muslim–Christian)	10,000	Islam and Christianity	Yes
1986–2006	Uganda	Ethnic violence (Lord's Resistance Army: Langi and Acholi)	15,000	Christianity	No
1987	Chile	Civil violence	3,000	Christianity	No

Year	Country	Description	Deaths	Religion	
1987–1990	Sri Lanka	Civil war (Janatha Vimukthi Peramuna–Sinhalese extremists)	25,000	Buddhism	No
1988	Myanmar	Civil violence (student protests)	2,000	Buddhism	No
1988	Burundi	Ethnic violence (Tutsis against Hutus)	10,000	Christianity	No
1988–1997	Azerbaijan	Ethnic war (Nagorno–Karabakh)	15,000	Islam	No
1988–1997	Papua New Guinea	Ethnic warfare (Bougainville)	1,000	Christianity	No
1988–	Somalia	Civil war	100,000	Islam	No
1989	China	Civil violence (Tiananman protests)	2,000	Traditional beliefs	No
1989	Romania	Civil violence	1,000	Christianity	No
1990	China	Repression of dissidents	2,000	Traditional beliefs	No
1990–1991	USSR	Sporadic ethnic/communal violence	5,000	Christianity	No
1990–1994	Rwanda	Ethnic warfare (Tutsis v. Hutu regime)	15,000	Christianity	No
1990–1995	Mali	Ethnic warfare (Tuareg)	1,000	Islam	No
1990–1997	Liberia	Civil war	40,000	Traditional beliefs	No
1990–1997	Niger	Civil war (Azawad and Toubou)	1,000	Islam	No
1990–1997	Cambodia	Civil warfare (Khmer Rouge)	5,000	Buddhism	No
1990–	India	Ethnic war (Kashmiris)	35,000	Hinduism	Yes
1991	Croatia	Civil war (Croatian independence)	10,000	Christianity	No
1991	Burundi	Civil violence	1,000	Christianity	No
1991	Haiti	Civil violence (Aristide presidency)	NA	Christianity	No

continued

Date	Site	Description	Deaths	Predominant religion(s) of country	Conflict instigated in whole or in part by Islamists?
1991–1993	Georgia	Civil war	1,000	Christianity	No
1991–1993	Kenya	Ethnic violence (Kalenjin, Masai, Kikuyu, Luo)	2,000	Christianity	No
1991–1993	Georgia	Ethnic war (Abkhazians–Ossetians)	3,000	Christianity	No
1991–1993	Bhutan	Ethnic violence (Drukpas v. Nepalese)	NA	Buddhism	No
1991–1994	Djibouti	Front for the Restoration of Unity and Democracy (FRUD) rebellion	1,000	Islam	No
1991–1994	Croatia	Ethnic war (Serbs)	40,000	Christianity	No
1991–1997	Moldova	Ethnic violence (Transdniester Russians)	2,000	Christianity	No
1991–2001	Sierra Leone	Civil/ethnic warfare (Revolutionary United Front [RUF]/Mende)	25,000	Islam	No
1991–2004	Algeria	Civil warfare (Islamic militants)	60,000	Islam	Yes
1991–2002	India	Ethnic violence (Hindu v. Muslim)	3,500	Hinduism	No
1992–1995	Bosnia	Ethnic war (Serbs, Croats, Muslims)	200,000	Islam	No
1992–1996	Zaire	Ethnic violence	10,000	Christianity	No
1992–1998	Tajikistan	Civil warfare	25,000	Islam	Yes
1992–1999	Egypt	Civil violence (Islamic militants)	2,000	Islam	Yes

1992–1999	Senegal	Ethnic violence (Casamance)	3,000	Islam	No
1993	Congo-Brazzaville	Ethnic violence	2,000	Christianity	No
1993–2005	Burundi	Ethnic warfare (Tutsis against Hutus)	100,000	Christianity	No
1994	Rwanda	Ethnic violence (Hutus target Tutsis)	500,000	Christianity	No
1994	Ghana	Ethnic violence	1,000	Christianity	No
1994	Yemen	Ethnic warfare (south Yemenis)	3,000	Islam	No
1994–1996	Russia	Civil war (Chechnya secession)	40,000	Christianity	No
1994–1997	Mexico	Ethnic violence (Chiapas)	1,000	Christianity	No
1994–1998	Rwanda	Ethnic warfare (Hutus v. Tutsi regime)	15,000	Christianity	No
1996–1998	Iraq	Ethnic warfare (Kurds)	2,000	Islam	No
1996–2006	Nepal	Civil war (United People's Front [UPF] "People's War")	8,000	Hinduism	No
1996–	Zaire/DRC	Civil war (ouster of Mobutu and aftermath)	1,500,000	Christianity	No
1997–1999	Congo-Brazzaville	Civil warfare	10,000	Christianity	No
1997	Albania	Civil violence (Pyramid schemes)	2,000	Islam	No
1997–2005	Indonesia	Ethnic violence (Aceh; GAM militants)	3,000	Islam	Yes
1997–	Nigeria	Communal violence (Delta province; Ijaw, Itsekeri; and others)	1,500	Islam and Christianity	No
1998	Lesotho	Civil violence (May elections)	1,000	Christianity	No
1998–1999	Yugoslavia	Ethnic war (Kosovar Albanians)	15,000	Christianity	No

continued

Date	Site	Description	Deaths	Predominant religion(s) of country	Conflict instigated in whole or in part by Islamists?
1998	Indonesia	Civil violence (ouster of Suharto)	2,000	Islam	No
1998	Georgia	Ethnic warfare (Abkhazia)	1,000	Christianity	No
1998–1999	Guinea-Bissau	Civil war (coup attempt)	6,000	Traditional beliefs and Islam	No
1998–2003	Solomon Islands	Communal violence (Malaita/ Isatabu islanders)	500	Christianity	No
1999	Indonesia	Ethnic violence (East Timor independence)	3,000	Islam	No
1999–2002	Indonesia	Ethnic violence (Moluccas; Muslim/ Christian)	3,500	Islam	Yes
1999–2000	Ethiopia	Ethnic war (Oromo separatists)	2,000	Islam and Christianity	No
1999–2006	Russia	Ethnic war (Chechen separatists)	30,000	Christianity	No
2000–2001	Guinea	Parrot's Beak clashes	1,000	Islam	No
2000–2003	Liberia	Civil violence (attacks by LURD guerillas)	1,000	Traditional beliefs	No
2000–2005	Côte d'Ivoire	Civil war (north, south, west divisions)	3,000	Traditional beliefs, Islam, and Christianity	No

2001	Indonesia	Communal (Dayaks v. Madurese immigrants)	1,000	Islam	No
2001	Rwanda	Ethnic war (attacks by Hutu guerillas)	2,500	Christianity	No
2001	Central African Republic	Civil violence (attacks by Bozize loyalists; coup)	1,000	Christianity	No
2001–2004	Nigeria	Ethnic violence (Christian–Muslim; Plateau; Kano regions)	55,000	Islam and Christianity	No
2001–	India	Maoist insurgency (People's War Group; Maoist Communist Centre; People's Liberation Guerilla Army)	1,500	Hinduism	No
2001–	Pakistan	Sectarian violence: Sunnis, Shi'ites, and Ahmadis	2,000	Islam	No
2002–2003	Congo-Brazzaville	Civil violence (Ninja militants in Pool region)	500	Christianity	No
2003	Thailand	Anti-Drug Trafficking Campaign	2,500	Buddhism	No
2003–	Saudi Arabia	Islamic militants	700	Islam	Yes
2003–	Sudan	Communal–separatist violence in Darfur	200,000	Islam	No
2004–	Yemen	Followers of al-Huthi in Sada	2,000	Islam	Yes
2004–	Haiti	General unrest surrounding ouster of President Aristide and his Lavalas Family ruling party	2,000	Christianity	No

continued

Date	Site	Description	Deaths	Predominant religion(s) of country	Conflict instigated in whole or in part by Islamists?
2004–	Pakistan	Pashtuns in Federally Administered Tribal Areas, mainly in South Wazirstan and North-West Frontier Province	1,500	Islam	No
2004–	Thailand	Malay–Muslims in southern border region (Narathiwat, Pattani, Songkhla, and Yala provinces)	3,000	Buddhism	Yes
2004–	Turkey	Kurds in southeast	1,000	Islam	No
2005–	Pakistan	Rebellion in Baluchistan	800	Islam	No
2005–	Chad	Anti-Deby regime; United Front for Democratic Change (FUC), Union of Forces for Democracy and Development (UFDD), and others	1,500	Islam	No
2005–	Central African Republic	APRD (northwest) and UFDR (northeast) rebels	1,500	Christianity	No
2006–	Mexico	Federal Army and police offensive against entrenched drug cartels and corrupt police and officials, mainly in the northern region bordering the USA	4,000	Christianity	No

2006–	Chad	Communal fighting between Toroboro ("black" and sedentary farmer) and Janjawid ("Arab")	5,000	Islam	No
2007–	Lebanon	Palestinian/Islamic militants	500	Islam	Yes
2007–	Ethiopia	Somalis and Oromo militants in Ogaden	1,000	Islam and Christianity	No
2007–	Kenya	Communal violence following disputed presidential election	1,000	Christianity	No

Appendix 5.B
OLS Output for Deaths in Major Episodes of Political Violence

Table 5.B.1 Regressions of Deaths in Major Episodes of Political Violence on Hypothesized Predictors

	Model 1	Model 2	Model 3	Model 4	Model 5	Model 6	Model 7
(Intercept)	0.776** (0.236)	-0.339 (0.277)	0.846 (0.595)	0.677 (0.501)	-0.581† (0.313)	-0.494† (0.295)	0.835 (0.525)
Percent Muslim	-0.003 (0.004)	-0.010† (0.006)	-0.012† (0.006)	-0.012† (0.006)	-0.011† (0.006)	-0.011† (0.006)	-0.011† (0.006)
Fertility rate		0.259** (0.099)	0.226* (0.108)	0.180* (0.086)	0.227* (0.091)	0.268* (0.118)	0.185* (0.086)
Ethnic diversity			-0.869 (0.857)			-0.717 (0.835)	
Level of democracy			-0.223* (0.091)	-0.212* (0.083)			-0.228* (0.089)
Late independence			0.227 (0.202)	0.180 (0.183)	0.570* (0.261)	0.624* (0.299)	
N	171	171	171	171	171	171	171
Adjusted R^2	.000	.033	.059	.057	.038	.037	.062

Note: OLS models with robust standard errors in parentheses.

†significant at $p < .10$; *$p < .05$; **$p < .01$; ***$p < .001$.

Table 5.B.2 Regressions of Deaths in Major Episodes of Political Violence on Hypothesized Predictors, Excluding the Major Outliers in the Data

	Model 1	Model 2	Model 3	Model 4	Model 5	Model 6	Model 7
(Intercept)	0.358*** (0.081)	0.029 (0.170)	0.436† (0.225)	0.424† (0.223)	−0.037 (0.164)	−0.036 (0.161)	0.436† (0.254)
Percent Muslim	−0.001 (0.001)	−0.003 (0.002)	−0.003 (0.003)	−0.003 (0.002)	−0.003 (0.002)	−0.003 (0.003)	−0.003 (0.002)
Fertility rate		0.078† (0.046)	0.058 (0.055)	0.053 (0.046)	0.070 (0.047)	0.071 (0.056)	0.053 (0.046)
Ethnic diversity			−0.083 (0.346)			−0.021 (0.356)	
Level of democracy			−0.079** (0.029)	−0.078** (0.029)			−0.079* (0.031)
Late independence			0.019 (0.113)	0.014 (0.111)	0.155 (0.124)	0.156 (0.124)	
N	165	165	165	165	165	164	165
Adjusted R²	.000	.017	.030	.036	.016	.010	.042

Note: OLS models with robust standard errors in parentheses.

†significant at *p* < .10; *p* < .05; **p* < .01; ***p* < .001.

Appendix 5.C
Comprehensive List of High-Casualty Terrorist Bombings (Involving Fifteen or More Deaths), September 11, 1994, to September 10, 2008

Date	Site	Deaths	Description	Predominant religion of country	Target of terrorism	Perpetrated by Islamists?
10/19/1994	Tel Aviv, Israel	23	Suicide bombing on a bus. Responsibility: HAMAS.	Judaism	Civilians	Yes
01/22/1995	Netanya, Israel	22	Suicide bombing at a bus stop. Responsibility: Islamic Jihad.	Judaism	Armed political target	Yes
04/19/1995	Oklahoma City, USA	168	Bombing of the Alfred P. Murrah Federal Building.	Christianity	Unarmed political target	No
11/19/1995	Islamabad, Pakistan	17	Suicide bombing at the Egyptian embassy. Responsibility: Al-Jihad (also known as Egyptian Islamic Jihad, EIJ).	Islam	Unarmed political target	Yes
12/21/1995	Peshawar, Pakistan	45	Explosion of car bomb in a market. Responsibility: Al-Jihad (also known as Egyptian Islamic Jihad, EIJ).	Islam	Civilians	Yes
01/31/1996	Colombo, Sri Lanka	96	Suicide bombing in a bank. Responsibility: Liberation Tigers of Tamil Eelam (LITE).	Buddhism	Civilians	No
02/25/1996	Jerusalem, Israel	23	Suicide bombing on a bus. Responsibility: HAMAS.	Judaism	Civilians	Yes
03/03/1996	Jerusalem, Israel	19	Suicide bombing on a bus. Responsibility: HAMAS.	Judaism	Civilians	Yes
03/04/1996	Tel Aviv, Israel	15	Suicide bombing at a shopping mall, Dizengoff Center.	Judaism	Civilians	Yes
06/25/1996	Dhahran, Saudi Arabia	19	Detonation of a large fuel truck containing explosives outside of a U.S. military housing complex.	Islam	Armed political target	Yes
11/17/1996	Istanbul, Turkey	17	Fire in the Tozbey Hotel. Responsibility: Turkish Islamic Jihad (TIJ).	Islam	Civilians	Yes

Date	Location	Killed	Description	Religion	Target	Unarmed political target
12/17/1996	Lima, Peru	17	Japanese embassy hostage crisis. Responsibility: Túpac Amaru Revolutionary Movement (MRTA).	Christianity	Unarmed political target	No
03/30/1997	Phnom Penh, Cambodia	19	Attack on anti-judiciary demonstrators.	Buddhism	Civilians	No
04/25/1997	Train near Algiers, Algeria (traveling from Algiers to Blida)	22	Destruction of a passenger train by a bomb hidden under railway tracks.	Islam	Civilians	Yes
07/30/1997	Jerusalem, Israel	15	Suicide bombings in an outdoor market. Responsibility: HAMAS.	Judaism	Civilians	Yes
10/15/1997	Colombo, Sri Lanka	18	Truck bombing in Colombo's financial district.	Buddhism	Civilians	No
11/17/1997	Luxor, Egypt	74	Attack on a group of foreign tourists.	Islam	Civilians	Yes
01/11/1998	Sidi Hamed, Algeria	103	Massacre of the town.	Islam	Civilians	Yes
02/14/1998	Wuhan, China	50	Bus bomb.	Traditional beliefs	Civilians	Yes
02/14/1998	Coimbatore, India	40	Car bombs at Bharatiya Janata Party (BJP) election meeting.	Hinduism	Unarmed political target	Yes
02/23/1998	Boufarik, Algeria	18	Train attack.	Islam	Civilians	Yes
03/05/1998	Maradana, Sri Lanka	32	Bomb on a bus. Responsibility: Liberation Tigers of Tamil Eelam.	Buddhism	Civilians	No

continued

Date	Site	Deaths	Description	Predominant religion of country	Target of terrorism	Perpetrated by Islamists?
05/22/1998	El Harrach, Algeria	17	Bombing at the Boumadid market.	Islam	Civilians	Yes
06/07/1998	Khaipur, Pakistan (train from Karachi to Peshawar)	23	Bombing of a passenger train.	Islam	Civilians	No
08/07/1998	Nairobi, Kenya	291	Bombing at the U.S. embassy.	Christianity	Unarmed political target	Yes
08/15/1998	Omagh, UK	29	Car bomb. Responsibility: Real Irish Republican Army (RIRA).	Christianity	Civilians	No
08/25/1998	Masaka, Uganda (buses from Kampala to Rwanda)	30	Bombs on three buses. Responsibility: Allied Democratic Forces/National Army for the Liberation of Uganda (ADF/NALU).	Christianity	Civilians	Yes
08/31/1998	Bab el Oued, Algeria (Algiers)	17	Bombing near a market in the Bab el-Oued district.	Islam	Civilians	Yes
09/05/1998	Makhachkala, Russia (Dagestan)	17	Car bomb.	Christianity	Civilians	No
10/18/1998	Segoria, Colombia (Segovia)	71	Pipeline blast. Responsibility: National Liberation Army (ELN).	Christianity	Civilians	No

Date	Location	Deaths	Description	Religion	Unarmed political target	Yes/No
02/16/1999	Tashkent, Uzbekistan	16	Five synchronized car bombs.	Islam		Yes
03/19/1999	Vladikavkaz, Russia	60	Bomb in a crowded central market.	Christianity	Civilians	No
09/04/1999	Buinsk, Russia (Buinaksk)	32	Bomb exploded in a military housing complex.	Christianity	Armed political target	No
09/09/1999	Moscow, Russia	95	Bombing of an apartment complex.	Christianity	Civilians	No
09/13/1999	Moscow, Russia	121	Bombing of an apartment complex.	Christianity	Civilians	No
09/16/1999	Volgodonsk, Russia	17	Bombing of an apartment complex.	Christianity	Civilians	No
02/25/2000	Ozamiz, Mindanao, Philippines	49	Bombings of two passenger buses aboard a ferry.	Christianity	Civilians	Yes
03/10/2000	Colombo, Sri Lanka	49	Attack on a motorcade on a highway leading to Ceremonial Drive at Sri Lanka's parliament. Responsibility: Liberation Tigers of Tamil Eelam (LTTE).	Buddhism	Armed political target	No
04/12/2000	Mallow Wali, Pakistan	15	Bombing of a Shi'i mosque.	Islam	Civilians	No
05/17/2000	Batticaloa, Sri Lanka	29	Bombing of a Buddhist feast near a temple. Responsibility: Liberation Tigers of Tamil Eelam (LTTE).	Buddhism	Civilians	No
06/07/2000	Ratmalana, Sri Lanka (Colombo)	24	Suicide bomb attack during ceremonies to mark the country's first War Heroes Day. Responsibility: Liberation Tigers of Tamil Eelam (LTTE).	Buddhism	Civilians	No
09/13/2000	Jakarta, Indonesia	15	Bombing of the stock exchange building.	Islam	Civilians	No

continued

Date	Site	Deaths	Description	Predominant religion of country	Target of terrorism	Perpetrated by Islamists?
09/19/2000	Islamabad, Pakistan	19	Bombing of a marketplace.	Islam	Civilians	No
10/03/2000	Muttur, Sri Lanka	26	Suicide bombing at an election rally. Responsibility: Liberation Tigers of Tamil Eelam (LTTE).	Buddhism	Unarmed political target	No
12/09/2000	Alkan-yurt, Russia (Alkhan-yurt)	21	Car bomb explosion in a Chechen village.	Christianity	Civilians	No
12/24/2000	Christian churches, Indonesia	15	Series of coordinated bombings of churches in Jakarta and eight other cities.	Islam	Civilians	Yes
12/30/2000	Manila, Philippines	22	Series of bombings around Metro Manila (Rizal Day Bombings).	Christianity	Civilians	Yes
03/16/2001	Shijianzhuang, Hebei, China (Shijiazhong)	108	Four simultaneous explosions, with one flattening a five-story dormitory building at a cotton mill.	Traditional beliefs	Civilians	No
03/24/2001	Mineralnye vody/ Yesentuky, Russia	24	Three car bombs.	Christianity	Civilians	No
06/01/2001	Tel Aviv, Israel	21	Suicide bombings outside a disco. Responsibility: Islamic Jihad.	Judaism	Civilians	Yes
06/15/2001	Narayanganj, Bangladesh	22	Bombing of the Awami League office.	Islam	Unarmed political target	Yes

Date	Location	Number	Description	Religion	Target	
08/09/2001	Jerusalem, Israel	16	Suicide bombing at Sbarro Pizzeria. Responsibility: Hamas/Islamic Jihad.	Judaism	Civilians	Yes
09/11/2001	New York/Washington DC/Somerset County PA, United States of America	2,982	Several airplane hijackings and crashes, with two crashing into the World Trade Center. Responsibility: Al-Qaeda.	Christianity	Civilians	Yes
10/01/2001	Srinagar, India	40	Attack on the state legislative assembly complex using a car bomb and gunmen. Responsibility: Jaish-e-Muhammad.	Hinduism	Unarmed political target	Yes
10/28/2001	Bahawalpur, Pakistan	15	Massacre of Christian worshipers in church. Responsibility: Lashkar-e-Umar.	Islam	Civilians	Yes
12/2/2001	Haifa, Israel	16	Suicide bombing on a bus. Responsibility: Hamas.	Judaism	Civilians	Yes
03/27/2002	Netanya, Israel	30	Suicide bombing at the Park Hotel on the Passover holiday. Responsibility: Hamas.	Judaism	Civilians	Yes
03/31/2002	Haifa, Israel	16	Suicide bombing in the Matza gas station restaurant. Responsibility: Hamas.	Judaism	Civilians	Yes
04/11/2002	Djerba, Tunisia	17	Attack on a synagogue.	Islam	Civilians	Yes
04/21/2002	Gen. Santos City, Philippines	15	Bombing at a Fitmart Store. Responsibility: Abu Sayyaf.	Christianity	Civilians	Yes

continued

Date	Site	Deaths	Description	Predominant religion of country	Target of terrorism	Perpetrated by Islamists?
05/02/2002 [05/03/2002]	Bojayá, Colombia	119 [60]	Massacre of the town by guerillas. Responsibility: Revolutionary Armed Forces of Colombia (FARC).	Christianity	Civilians	No
05/07/2002	Rishan Letzion, Israel (Rishon Lezion)	17	Bombing at a pool hall. Responsibility: Hamas.	Judaism	Civilians	Yes
05/08/2002	Karachi, Pakistan	17	Bombing of a Pakistani Navy bus.	Islam	Armed political target	Yes
05/09/2002	Kaspiisk, Dagestan, Russia (Kaspiysk)	43	Bombing of a military parade.	Christianity	Armed political target	Yes
06/05/2002	Megiddo, Israel	20	Suicide bus bombing. Responsibility: Islamic Jihad.	Judaism	Civilians	Yes
06/18/2002	Jerusalem, Israel	20	Suicide bus bombing. Responsibility: Hamas.	Judaism	Civilians	Yes
07/05/2002	Larba, Algeria	38	Bombing during a celebration of Algeria's 40th anniversary of independence from France.	Islam	Civilians	Yes
08/07/2002	Bogota, Colombia	21	Attacks against an army base and the presidential palace during an inauguration ceremony. Responsibility: Revolutionary Armed Forces of Colombia (FARC).	Christianity	Armed political target	No
09/05/2002	Kabul, Afghanistan	30	Explosion of two bombs, the second a large car bomb, in front of a shop selling televisions and satellite dishes.	Islam	Civilians	Yes

Date	Location	Deaths	Description	Religion	Target	Suicide
10/10/2002	Grozny, Russia	22	Explosion in a regional police headquarters.	Christianity	Armed political target	No
10/12/2002	Denpasar, Bali, Indonesia	202	Three bombings, two near nightclubs and one outside the United States' consulate office. Responsibility: Jemaah Islamiyah.	Islam	Civilians	Yes
10/21/2002	Pardes Hannah, Israel (Pardes Hanna)	16	Suicide bus bombing. Responsibility: Islamic Jihad.	Judaism	Civilians	Yes
10/23/2002	Moscow, Russia	162	Seizure of crowded Moscow theatre by Chechen rebel fighters.	Christianity	Civilians	No
11/28/2002	Mombasa, Kenya	16	Suicide bombing at the Paradise Hotel.	Christianity	Civilians	Yes
12/07/2002	Mymensingh, Bangladesh	18	Bombings in four movie theatres.	Islam	Civilians	Yes
12/24/2002	Datu Piang, Mindanao, Philippines (Maguindanao)	16	Bombing outside a mayor's home.	Christianity	Unarmed political target	Yes
12/27/2002	Grozny, Chechnya, Russia	80	Bombing of republic's government headquarters by three suicide bombers	Christianity	Unarmed political target	No
01/05/2003	Tel Aviv, Israel	25	Suicide bombing in a pedestrian mall. Responsibility: Al Aqsa Martyrs Brigades.	Judaism	Civilians	No

continued

Date	Site	Deaths	Description	Predominant religion of country	Target of terrorism	Perpetrated by Islamists?
01/31/2003	Rambasa, Afghanistan	18	Bombing of a bridge and bus.	Islam	Armed political target	Yes
02/07/2003	Bogota, Colombia	32	Car bomb at El Nogal Social Club. Responsibility: Revolutionary Armed Forces of Colombia (FARC).	Christianity	Civilians	No
02/14/2003	Neiva, Colombia	17	Bomb targeting the chief of police. Responsibility: Revolutionary Armed Forces of Colombia (FARC).	Christianity	Armed political target	No
03/04/2003	Davao, Mindanao, Philippines	24	Bombing at Davao City International Airport. Responsibility: Abu Sayyaf Group (ASG).	Christianity	Civilians	Yes
03/05/2003	Haifa, Israel	25	Suicide bus bombing.	Judaism	Civilians	Yes
04/02/2003	Davao, Mindanao, Philippines	16	Bombing of a wharf.	Christianity	Civilians	Yes
05/12/2003	Znamenskoye, Chechnya, Russia	59	Truck bombing of local government administration and the Federal Security Service of the Russian Federation directorate complex.	Christianity	Unarmed political target	No
05/12/2003	Riyadh, Saudi Arabia	34	Nearly simultaneous bombings at three compounds housing Westerners.	Islam	Civilians	Yes

Date	Location	Number	Description	Religion	Target	
05/14/2003	Iliskhan Yurt, Chechnya, Russia	20	Female suicide bomb attack during a religious festival.	Christianity	Civilians	No
05/16/2003	Casablanca, Morocco	43	Series of suicide bombings at restaurants, a hotel, and a Jewish community center. Responsibility: Al-Qaeda.	Islam	Civilians	Yes
06/05/2003	Mozdok, N. Ossetia, Russia	18	Female suicide bombing outside of a bus carrying Russian air force pilots.	Christianity	Civilians	No
06/11/2003	Jerusalem, Israel	18	Suicide bus bombing. Responsibility: Hamas.	Judaism	Civilians	Yes
07/04/2003	Quetta, Pakistan	53	Shi'i mosque stormed by armed attackers.	Islam	Civilians	No
07/05/2003	Tushino airfield (outside Moscow), Russia	19	Two female suicide bombings outside of a concert.	Christianity	Civilians	No
08/01/2003	Mozdok, N. Ossetia, Russia	52	Truck bombing beside a military hospital.	Christianity	Armed political target	No
08/19/2003	Jerusalem, Israel	22	Suicide bus bombing. Responsibility: Hamas/Islamic Jihad.	Judaism	Civilians	Yes
08/25/2003	Mumbai, India	52	Two bombings in taxis, one at the Gateway of India and the other at a bazaar.	Hinduism	Civilians	Yes
10/04/2003	Haifa, Israel	22	Suicide bombing in the Maxim Restaurant. Responsibility: Islamic Jihad.	Judaism	Civilians	Yes
11/08/2003	Riyadh, Saudi Arabia	17	Suicide bombings at a Riyadh housing compound. Responsibility: Al-Qaeda.	Islam	Civilians	Yes

continued

Date	Site	Deaths	Description	Predominant religion of country	Target of terrorism	Perpetrated by Islamists?
11/15/2003	Istanbul, Turkey	25	Two truck bomb attacks at synagogues.	Islam	Civilians	Yes
11/20/2003	Istanbul, Turkey	31	Two truck bomb attacks, one at HSBC Bank AS and the other at the British consulate office.	Islam	Civilians	Yes
12/05/2003	Yessentuki, Russia	46	Suicide bombing on a commuter train.	Christianity	Civilians	No
12/25/2003	Rawalpindi, Pakistan	17	Attack of two suicide bombers on the motorcade of President Pervez Musharraf.	Islam	Unarmed political target	Yes
01/04/2004	Parang, Mindano, Philippines	15	Bombing at a basketball game.	Christianity	Unarmed political target	No
02/06/2004	Moscow, Russia	41	Bombing on a train car. Responsibility: Gazoton Murdash.	Christianity	Civilians	No
02/26/2004	Off coast of Manila, Philippines	118	Bombing of a passenger ferry. Responsibility: Abu Sayyaf Group (ASG).	Christianity	Civilians	Yes
03/02/2004	Quetta, Pakistan	47	Bombing and shooting during a Shi'i procession marking the death of Imam Hussein, grandson of the Prophet Mohammed.	Islam	Civilians	No
03/11/2004	Madrid, Spain	191	Series of coordinated bombings against the train system.	Christianity	Civilians	Yes
05/07/2004	Karachi, Pakistan	24	Bombing of a Shi'i mosque.	Islam	Civilians	No

Date	Location	Deaths	Description	Religion	Target	Suicide
05/29/2004	Khobar, Saudi Arabia	22	Attack on two oil industry installations and a foreign worker housing complex. Responsibility: The Jerusalem Squadron.	Islam	Civilians	Yes
05/31/2004	Karachi, Pakistan	21	Bombing of a Shi'i mosque.	Islam	Civilians	No
08/21/2004	Grozny, Chechnya, Russia	58	Simultaneous attack on polling stations and other targets. Responsibility: Chechen combatants.	Christianity	Civilians	No
08/21/2004	Dhaka, Bangladesh	19	Grenade attack at an Awami League rally.	Islam	Unarmed political target	Yes
08/25/2004	Rostov-on-Don/Tula, Russia	90	Two nearly simultaneous airplane crashes.	Christianity	Civilians	No
08/31/2004	Beersheba, Israel	16	Two bus suicide bombings. Responsibility: Hamas.	Judaism	Civilians	Yes
09/01/2004	Beslan, N. Ossetia, Russia	331	Seizure of more than 1,100 schoolchildren and adults as hostages. Responsibility: Chechen combatants.	Christianity	Civilians	No
10/01/2004	Sialkot, Pakistan	30	Suicide bombing at a Shi'i mosque.	Islam	Civilians	No
10/07/2004	Multan, Pakistan	40	Bombings at a gathering to mark the one-year anniversary of the murder of a Sunni leader, the Sipah-e-Sahaba chief.	Islam	Civilians	No
10/07/2004	Taba, Sinai Peninsula, Egypt	34	Attacks on two holiday resorts frequented by Israelis.	Islam	Civilians	Yes
12/12/2004	Gen. Santos City, Philippines	15	Bombing of a supermarket.	Christianity	Civilians	No

continued

Date	Site	Deaths	Description	Predominant religion of country	Target of terrorism	Perpe-trated by Islamists?
02/14/2005	Beirut, Lebanon	23	Bombing near the former Lebanese prime minister's motorcade.	Islam	Unarmed political target	No
03/19/2005	Naseerabad, Pakistan	50	Bombing of a Shi'i shrine.	Islam	Civilians	No
03/20/2005	Fatehpur, Pakistan	43 [30]	Bombing at a Muslim shrine.	Islam	Civilians	No
05/27/2005	Islamabad, Pakistan	20	Suicide bombing at an annual Shi'i congregation at the shrine of Bari Iman.	Islam	Civilians	No
05/28/2005	Tentena, Indonesia	22	Two bombs exploded in a crowded market during peak shopping hours.	Islam	Civilians	No
06/01/2005	Kandahar, Afghanistan	21	Suicide bombing in a mosque during a funeral for a Muslim cleric opposed to the Taliban.	Islam	Civilians	Yes
06/13/2005	Pulwama, India	16	Car bombing outside of a government school and near a Central Reserve Police Force camp.	Hinduism	Armed political target	Yes
07/07/2005	London, UK	56	Coordinated bombings targeting London's transportation system during morning rush hour.	Christianity	Civilians	Yes
07/23/2005	Sharm el-Shiekh, Egypt	88	Series of attacks on Egyptian resort city.	Islam	Civilians	Yes
10/01/2005	Bali, Indonesia	25	Suicide bombings in an area popular with Western tourists.	Islam	Civilians	Yes

Date	Site	Deaths	Description	of country	Target of terrorism	Islamists?
10/29/2005	New Delhi, India	61	Bombings in two markets and a bus. Responsibility: Islamic Revolutionary Front.	Hinduism	Civilians	Yes
11/09/2005	Amman, Jordan	63	Coordinated bombing attacks in three hotels. Responsibility: Al-Qaeda.	Islam	Civilians	Yes
01/16/2006	Spin Boldak, Afghanistan	24	Suicide bombing by a motorcyclist in a crowd. Responsibility: the Taliban.	Islam	Civilians	Yes
02/09/2006	Hangu, Pakistan	27	Suicide bombing during Ashoura, the holiest festival for Shi'i Muslims, which triggered a riot.	Islam	Civilians	No
02/28/2006	Darmagura, Chhattisgarh, India	55	Truck carrying anti-Maoist activists blown up by a landmine.	Hinduism	Civilians	No
03/07/2006	Varanasi, India	21	Bombings at a temple and a railway station.	Hinduism	Civilians	Yes
04/11/2006	Karachi (Nishtar Park), Pakistan	58	Suicide bombing at a celebration of the Prophet Mohammed's birthday.	Islam	Civilians	No
04/24/2006	Dahab, Sinai, Egypt	23	Three bombing attacks on a resort city.	Islam	Civilians	Yes
06/15/2006	Kabithigollewa, Sri Lanka	64	Landmine attack on a commuter bus. Responsibility: Liberation Tigers of Tamil Eelam (LTTE).	Buddhism	Civilians	No
07/11/2006	Mumbai, India	209 [193]	Series of seven bombings on trains on the suburban railway.	Hinduism	Civilians	Yes

continued

Date	Site	Deaths	Description	Predominant religion of country	Target of terrorism	Perpetrated by Islamists?
08/28/2006	Lashkar Gah, Afghanistan	17	Suicide bombing in a bazaar.	Islam	Civilians	Yes
09/08/2006	Malegaon, India	37	Series of bomb blasts in a Muslim cemetery adjacent to a mosque.	Hinduism	Civilians	Yes
09/26/2006	Lashkar Gah, Afghanistan	18	Suicide bombing outside a provincial governor's compound. Responsibility: Taliban.	Islam	Unarmed political target	Yes
10/16/2006	Dambulla, Sri Lanka	94	Suicide bombing of a naval convoy. Responsibility: Liberation Tigers of Tamil Eelam (LTTE).	Buddhism	Armed political target	No
10/18/2006	Galle, Sri Lanka	16	Suicide boats detonated near a navy base. Responsibility: Liberation Tigers of Tamil Eelam (LTTE).	Buddhism	Armed political target	No
11/05/2006	Guwahati, India	15	Two bombings, one in a marketplace and the other near an oil installation.	Hinduism	Civilians	No
11/08/2006	Dargai, Pakistan	42	Suicide bombing at an army base.	Islam	Armed political target	Yes
01/06/2007	Hikkaduwa, Sri Lanka (Ambalangoda Galle Road)	15	Suicide bombing on a bus. Responsibility: Liberation Tigers of Tamil Eelam (LTTE).	Buddhism	Civilians	No
01/27/2007	Peshawar, Pakistan	15	Suicide bombing in the Qissa Khawani Bazaar.	Islam	Civilians	No

02/17/2007	Quetta, Pakistan	16	Suicide bombing in the court of a senior civil judge.	Islam	Unarmed political target	No
02/18/2007	Diwana (train), India (Deewana)	66	Bombings of two train carriages on the Samjhauta Express.	Hinduism	Civilians	Yes
04/02/2007	Ampara, Sri Lanka	16	Bus bombing. Responsibility: Liberation Tigers of Tamil Eelam (LTTE).	Buddhism	Civilians	No
04/11/2007	Algiers, Algeria	33	Two suicide truck bombings near United Nations' offices. Responsibility: Al-Qaeda.	Islam	Unarmed political target	Yes
04/28/2007	Charsada, Pakistan (Charsadda)	28	Suicide bombing while the interior minister, Aftab Sherpao, was addressing a crowd. Responsibility: Taliban.	Islam	Unarmed political target	Yes
05/15/2007	Peshawar, Pakistan	25	Suicide bombing at a hotel/restaurant.	Islam	Civilians	Yes
06/17/2007	Kabul, Afghanistan	35	Police academy bus bombing. Responsibility: Taliban.	Islam	Armed political target	Yes
07/15/2007	Dera Ismail Khan, Pakistan	28	Suicide bombing while candidates took police entrance exams.	Islam	Armed political target	Yes
07/17/2007	Islamabad, Pakistan	18	Suicide bombing at a rally in support of a suspended chief judge.	Islam	Unarmed political target	Yes
07/19/2007	Hub, Pakistan	30	Suicide car bombing that struck a convoy of Chinese workers being escorted by security forces.	Islam	Armed political target	Yes
07/19/2007	Kohat, Pakistan	18	Suicide car bombing that hit a police academy.	Islam	Armed political target	Yes

continued

Date	Site	Deaths	Description	Predominant religion of country	Target of terrorism	Perpetrated by Islamists?
08/25/2007	Hyderabad, India	43	Near-simultaneous explosion of two bombs, one in an amusement park and the other in a restaurant.	Hinduism	Civilians	Yes
09/04/2007	Rawalpindi, Pakistan	25	Suicide bombing attack on a bus carrying government workers followed by bombing in a bazaar.	Islam	Armed political target	Yes
09/06/2007	Batna, Algeria	22	Suicide bombing in a crowd waiting to see the president. Responsibility: Al-Qaeda.	Islam	Unarmed political target	Yes
09/08/2007	Dellys, Algeria	30	Suicide truck bombing at a coast guard barracks. Responsibility: Al-Qaeda.	Islam	Armed political target	Yes
09/10/2007	Gereshk, Afghanistan	29	Suicide bombing in a crowded square just before evening prayers.	Islam	Armed political target	Yes
09/29/2007	Kabul, Afghanistan	31	Suicide bombing on a military bus. Responsibility: Taliban.	Islam	Armed political target	Yes
10/01/2007	Bannu, Pakistan	16	Suicide bombing at a police checkpoint.	Islam	Armed political target	Yes
10/18/2007	Karachi, Pakistan	144	Bombing attack on a motorcade carrying former Prime Minister Benazir Bhutto.	Islam	Unarmed political target	Yes
11/06/2007	Baghlan, Afghanistan	82	Bombing of a sugar factory.	Islam	Unarmed political target	Yes
11/23/2007	Varanasi, Faizabad, and Lucknow, India	15	Six consecutive court bombings. Responsibility: Indian Mujahideen.	Hinduism	Unarmed political target	Yes

Date	Count	Description	Religion	Target	Response
11/24/2007	37	Two suicide bombings targeting the army, one at the Inter-Services Intelligence (ISI) office and the other at an army checkpost.	Islam	Armed political target	Yes
11/28/2007	17	Bomb explosion near the entrance to a department store.	Buddhism	Civilians	No
12/06/2007	16	Roadside explosion targeting a passenger bus.	Buddhism	Civilians	No
12/11/2007	41	Truck bombings near United Nations' offices and an Algerian government building. Responsibility: al-Qaeda.	Islam	Unarmed political target	Yes
12/21/2007	60	Suicide bombing in a mosque targeting the interior minister, Aftab Sherpao.	Islam	Unarmed political target	Yes
12/27/2007	32	Shooting of Benazir Bhutto and bombing of an election rally.	Islam	Unarmed political target	Yes
01/10/2008	25	Suicide bombing targeting a police officer outside the high court.	Islam	Armed political target	Yes
01/16/2008	33	Bombing of a passenger bus.	Buddhism	Civilians	No
01/29/2008	18	Bombing of a school bus.	Buddhism	Civilians	No
02/02/2008	20	Bombing of a bus.	Buddhism	Civilians	No
02/03/2008	16	Bombing in a railway station.	Buddhism	Civilians	No

Locations (first column, left):
11/24/2007 — Rawalpindi, Pakistan
11/28/2007 — Colombo (Nugegoda), Sri Lanka
12/06/2007 — Kabithigollewa, Sri Lanka
12/11/2007 — Algiers, Algeria
12/21/2007 — Charsadda, Pakistan
12/27/2007 — Rawalpindi, Pakistan
01/10/2008 — Lahore, Pakistan
01/16/2008 — Buttala, Sri Lanka
01/29/2008 — Mannar, Sri Lanka
02/02/2008 — Dambulla, Sri Lanka
02/03/2008 — Colombo (Fort station), Sri Lanka

continued

Date	Site	Deaths	Description	Predominant religion of country	Target of terrorism	Perpetrated by Islamists?
02/06/2008	Bossaso, Somalia	20	Two bombings in a building housing mainly Ethiopian migrants. Responsibility: al Shabaab.	Islam	Civilians	Yes
02/09/2008	Charsadda, Pakistan	27	Bombing at a political rally for the Awami National Party.	Islam	Unarmed political target	Yes
02/16/2008	Parachinar, Pakistan	55	Bombing at a political rally for the Pakistan People's Party (PPP).	Islam	Unarmed political target	Yes
02/17/2008	Argandab district (Kandahar), Afghanistan	101	Bombing of a dog fighting competition that targeted a local police chief.	Islam	Unarmed political target	Yes
02/29/2008	Mingora, Pakistan	46	Bombing at the funeral of a police officer.	Islam	Civilians	Yes
03/02/2008	Darra Adam Khel, Pakistan	42	Bombing of a gathering of tribal elders and local officials.	Islam	Unarmed political target	Yes
03/11/2008	Lahore, Pakistan	31	Two car bombings, one at the Federal Investigations Agency (FIA) and another at an advertising agency, which was mistakenly believed to be an undercover office of the Special Investigation Authority (SIA).	Islam	Unarmed political target	Yes
04/06/2008	Weliveriya, Sri Lanka (Weliweriya)	15	Bombing at the opening ceremony of a marathon.	Buddhism	Unarmed political target	No

Date	Location		Description			
04/17/2008	Zaranj, Afghanistan	24	Bombing outside a mosque in a bazaar.	Islam	Armed political target	Yes
04/25/2008	Piliyandala, Sri Lanka	24	Bombing of a bus.	Buddhism	Civilians	No
04/29/2008	Khogiani, Afghanistan	19	Bombing targeting a drug eradication team outside local government headquarters.	Islam	Unarmed political target	Yes
05/02/2008	Saada, Yemen	18	Car bombing outside a mosque.	Islam	Civilians	Yes
05/13/2008	Jaipur, India	80	Nine bombings at various locations in Jaipur, a popular tourist destination. Responsibility: Indian Mujahideen (IM).	Hinduism	Civilians	Yes
05/15/2008	Del Aram, Afghanistan	19	Bombing in a bazaar. Responsibility: Taliban.	Islam	Armed political target	Yes
06/06/2008	Moratuwa, Sri Lanka	21	Bombing of a passenger bus.	Buddhism	Civilians	No
07/06/2008	Islamabad, Pakistan	19	Bombing near the Lal Masjid mosque (Red Mosque) on the one-year anniversary of the same mosque's siege by Pakistani forces.	Islam	Armed political target	Yes
07/07/2008	Kabul, Afghanistan	42	Bombing at the gates of the Indian Embassy.	Islam	Unarmed political target	Yes
07/26/2008	Ahmedabad, India	55	Series of bombings targeting the city bus service and hospitals. Responsibility: Indian Mujahideen (IM).	Hinduism	Civilians	Yes
07/27/2008	Istanbul, Turkey	17	Two bomb explosions in a crowded square.	Islam	Civilians	No
08/02/2008	Mogadishu, Somalia	20	Explosion of a roadside bomb.	Islam	Civilians	Yes

continued

Date	Site	Deaths	Description	Predominant religion of country	Target of terrorism	Perpetrated by Islamists?
08/13/2008	Tripoli, Lebanon	15	Roadside bomb explosion that hit a bus carrying civilians and Lebanese military forces.	Islam	Armed political target	Yes
08/19/2008	Issers, Algeria	48	Bombing in a crowd of paramilitary recruits waiting to take exams outside a police academy.	Islam	Armed political target	Yes
08/19/2008	Dera Ismail Khan, Pakistan	32	Bombing in the compound of a hospital. Responsibility: Tehrik-e-Taleban Pakistan.	Islam	Civilians	No
08/21/2008	Wah, Pakistan	67	Two bombings at the military's Pakistan Ordnance Factories, the center of the country's defense industry. Responsibility: Tehrik-e-Taleban Pakistan.	Islam	Armed political target	Yes
08/24/2008	Gitega province, Burundi	19	Bombing of a wedding reception.	Christianity	Civilians	No

Note: In a handful of cases, my own research turned up dates and numbers of deaths that differed from those provided by Monty Marshall in his "High Casualty Terrorist Bombings" list, which provided the foundation for my own table. In these cases, Marshall's numbers are listed in brackets beneath my own findings in the "Dates" and "Deaths" columns here.

Appendix 6
Model Equations and Summary Statistics for Chapter 6

HIERARCHICAL GENERALIZED LINEAR MODELS FOR TABLES 6.7-6.11

Below are the equations for the hierarchical generalized linear models presented throughout the chapter. In the interest of space we are only providing the equation for the most saturated models from each table. Simpler models follow the same structure, only with fewer variables.

Table 6.7. Dependent Variable: Responses to Statement, "A university education is more important for a boy than a girl"

Model 5:

$$\eta_{mij} = \beta_{0j} + \sum_{q=1}^{Q} \beta_{qj} X_{qj} + \sum_{m=2}^{M-1} D_{mij} \delta_m$$

$$\eta_{mij} = \beta_{0j} + \beta_{1j}(\text{female})_{ij} + \beta_{2j}(\text{age})_{ij} + \beta_{3j}(\text{education level})_{ij} + \beta_{4j}(\text{Muslim})_{ij} + \beta_{5j}(\text{Christian})_{ij}$$
$$+ \beta_{6j}(\text{importance of God})_{ij} + D_{mij} \delta_m$$

$$\beta_{0j} = \gamma_{00} + \gamma_{01}(\text{GDP per capita})_{ij} + \gamma_{02}(\text{average age})_{ij} + \gamma_{03}(\text{average importance of God})_{ij}$$
$$+ \gamma_{04}(\text{proportion Muslim})_{ij} + \gamma_{05}(\text{proportion Christian})_{ij}$$

$$\beta_{1j} = \gamma_{10} + u_{1j}$$
$$\beta_{2j} = \gamma_{20} + u_{2j}$$
$$\beta_{3j} = \gamma_{30} + u_{3j}$$
$$\beta_{4j} = \gamma_{40} + u_{4j}$$
$$\beta_{5j} = \gamma_{50} + u_{5j}$$
$$\beta_{6j} = \gamma_{60} + u_{6j}$$

Table 6.9. Dependent Variable: "When jobs are scarce, men should have more right to a job than women" (1 = agree, 0 = neither agree or disagree/disagree)

Model 5:

$$\varphi_{ij} = \frac{1}{1 + \exp\{-\eta_{ij}\}}$$

$$\eta_{ij} = \beta_{0j} + \beta_{1j}(\text{female})_{ij} + \beta_{2j}(\text{age})_{ij} + \beta_{3j}(\text{education level})_{ij} + \beta_{4j}(\text{Muslim})_{ij} + \beta_{5j}(\text{Christian})_{ij} + \beta_{6j}(\text{importance of God})_{ij}$$

$$\beta_{0j} = \gamma_{00} + \gamma_{01}(\text{GDP per capita})_{ij} + \gamma_{02}(\text{average age})_{ij} + \gamma_{03}(\text{average importance of God})_{ij} + \gamma_{04}(\text{proportion Muslim})_{ij} + \gamma_{05}(\text{proportion Christian})_{ij} + u_{0j}$$

$$\beta_{1j} = \gamma_{10} + u_{1j}$$
$$\beta_{2j} = \gamma_{20} + u_{2j}$$
$$\beta_{3j} = \gamma_{30} + u_{3j}$$
$$\beta_{4j} = \gamma_{40} + u_{4j}$$
$$\beta_{5j} = \gamma_{50} + u_{5j}$$
$$\beta_{6j} = \gamma_{60} + u_{6j}$$

Table 6.11. Dependent Variable: Responses to Statement, "On the whole, men make better political leaders than women do"

Model 5:

$$\eta_{mij} = \beta_{0j} + \sum_{q=1}^{Q} \beta_{qj} X_{qj} + \sum_{m=2}^{M-1} D_{mij} \delta_m$$

$$\eta_{mij} = \beta_{0j} + \beta_{1j}(\text{female})_{ij} + \beta_{2j}(\text{age})_{ij} + \beta_{3j}(\text{education level})_{ij} + \beta_{4j}(\text{Muslim})_{ij} + \beta_{5j}(\text{Christian})_{ij} + \beta_{6j}(\text{importance of God})_{ij} + D_{mij} \delta_m$$

$$\beta_{0j} = \gamma_{00} + \gamma_{01}(\text{GDP per capita})_{ij} + \gamma_{02}(\text{average age})_{ij} + \gamma_{03}(\text{average importance of God})_{ij} + \gamma_{04}(\text{proportion Muslim})_{ij} + \gamma_{05}(\text{proportion Christian})_{ij}$$

$$\beta_{1j} = \gamma_{10} + u_{1j}$$
$$\beta_{2j} = \gamma_{20} + u_{2j}$$
$$\beta_{3j} = \gamma_{30} + u_{3j}$$
$$\beta_{4j} = \gamma_{40} + u_{4j}$$
$$\beta_{5j} = \gamma_{50} + u_{5j}$$
$$\beta_{6j} = \gamma_{60} + u_{6j}$$

SUMMARY STATISTICS

Individual-level variables	Mean (min, max)
Age	40.92 (15, 101)
Education	0.49 (0, 1)
Average importance of God level	7.76 (1,10)
Average importance of God level for pooled Muslim and Christian sample	8.56 (1,10)

Country-level variables	
GDP per capita (logged)	3.81 (2.68, 4.53)
Average age	41.43 (29.79, 52.45)
Average importance of God level	7.54 (3.58, 10)
Proportion Muslim	0.20 (0, 0.99)
Proportion Christian	0.54 (0, 0.99)

Appendix 7.A.1–3
OLS Output for Political Openness, Using Alterative Measures for Political Openness

Table 7.A.1 Dependent variable is Freedom House scores (Political Rights plus Civil Liberties scores), annual average for 2004–2008; 0 is the least democratic and 100 is the most democratic

	Model 1	Model 2	Model 3	Model 4	Model 5	Model 6	Model 7
(Intercept)	70.13*** (2.57)	31.93** (11.21)	32.26* (14.67)	31.79* (14.62)	38.41* (16.08)	31.10** (11.26)	32.18** (10.33)
Percent Muslim	−0.41*** (0.05)	−0.32*** (0.05)	−0.14* (0.06)	−0.20*** (0.04)	−0.31*** (0.05)	−0.22** (0.07)	−0.22*** (0.04)
GDP per capita		1.32*** (0.26)	1.37*** (0.25)	1.35*** (0.24)	1.23*** (0.26)	1.38*** (0.26)	1.46*** (0.25)
Life expectancy		0.41* (0.19)	0.56* (0.26)	0.48* (0.20)	0.38† (0.21)	0.67* (0.26)	0.43* (0.18)
Population size		−0.01 (0.02)	−0.02 (0.02)	−0.02 (0.02)	−0.01 (0.02)		
Ethnic diversity			2.72 (7.04)	5.51 (7.15)	0.28 (7.52)		
Fuels dependence			−0.30*** (0.05)	−0.33*** (0.05)			−0.32*** (0.05)
Late independence			−4.71 (3.23)	−5.57† (3.11)	−5.61 (3.62)		
Arab country			−12.21* (5.21)			−19.17** (6.17)	
Sex literacy ratio			−7.15 (14.30)			−19.65 (14.54)	
N	172	172	168	171	171	169	172
Adjusted R²	.26	.47	.57	.56	.46	.49	.56

Note: OLS regression models with robust standard errors in parentheses.

†significant at $p < .10$; * $p < .05$; ** $p < .01$; *** $p < .001$.

Table 7.A.2 Dependent variable is Economist Intelligence Unit Index of Democracy 2006, recoded 0–100; 0 is the least democratic and 100 is the most democratic

	Model 1	Model 2	Model 3	Model 4	Model 5	Model 6	Model 7
(Intercept)	63.99*** (2.04)	18.43* (8.49)	23.86* (10.55)	27.78** (10.08)	31.45** (11.10)	13.87 (9.03)	18.84* (7.79)
Percent Muslim	−0.33*** (0.03)	−0.26*** (0.04)	−0.10* (0.05)	−0.17*** (0.03)	−0.24*** (0.04)	−0.16** (0.06)	−0.18*** (0.03)
GDP per capita		0.99*** (0.21)	1.03*** (0.19)	0.98*** (0.19)	0.91*** (0.21)	1.05*** (0.21)	1.06*** (0.20)
Life expectancy		0.56*** (0.14)	0.43* (0.18)	0.51*** (0.14)	0.46** (0.15)	0.59** (0.20)	0.58*** (0.13)
Population size		−0.00 (0.02)	−0.00 (0.02)	−0.00 (0.02)	−0.00 (0.02)		
Ethnic diversity			−3.67 (5.26)	−2.88 (5.24)	−6.29 (5.73)		
Fuels dependence			−0.21*** (0.03)	−0.23*** (0.03)			−0.23*** (0.03)
Late independence			−3.92† (2.13)	−4.37* (2.10)	−4.26† (2.41)		
Arab country			−8.21* (4.01)			−14.36** (5.23)	
Sex literacy ratio			9.46 (11.08)			1.53 (11.73)	
N	172	172	168	171	171	169	172
Adjusted R^2	.27	.56	.65	.64	.57	.59	.64

Note: OLS regression models with robust standard errors in parentheses.

†significant at $p < .10$; *$p < .05$; **$p < .01$; ***$p < .001$

Table 7.A.3 Dependent variable is Polity IV Project Polity scores for 2006, recoded 0–100; 0 is the least democratic and 100 is the most democratic

	Model 1	Model 2	Model 3	Model 4	Model 5	Model 6	Model 7
(Intercept)	80.17*** (2.85)	48.28** (14.77)	73.60*** (20.00)	70.53*** (19.84)	77.39*** (21.09)	49.62** (15.52)	49.90*** (13.57)
Percent Muslim	-0.45*** (0.07)	-0.41*** (0.08)	-0.19† (0.10)	-0.24*** (0.07)	-0.37*** (0.08)	-0.29* (0.11)	-0.28*** (0.07)
GDP per capita		0.54 (0.39)	0.51 (0.34)	0.45 (0.33)	0.28 (0.37)	0.67† (0.39)	0.72* (0.36)
Life expectancy		0.43† (0.25)	0.43 (0.36)	0.31 (0.27)	0.21 (0.28)	0.71* (0.35)	0.42† (0.24)
Population size		-0.01 (0.03)	-0.02 (0.02)	-0.02 (0.02)	-0.01 (0.02)		
Ethnic diversity			-5.89 (10.54)	-3.07 (10.66)	-9.35 (11.54)		
Fuels dependence			-0.34*** (0.08)	-0.39*** (0.07)			-0.39*** (0.07)
Late independence			-12.86** (4.70)	-13.61** (4.48)	-14.08** (4.91)		
Arab country			-12.80 (8.69)			-23.58* (10.65)	
Sex literacy ratio			-12.96 (19.78)			-24.69 (20.70)	
N	155	155	152	155	155	152	155
Adjusted R^2	.23	.28	.40	.40	.30	.31	.38

Note: OLS regression models with robust standard errors in parentheses.

†significant at $p < .10$; *$p < .05$; **$p < .01$; ***$p < .001$.

Appendix 7.B
Model Equations and Summary Statistics for Chapter 7

HIERARCHICAL LINEAR MODELS FOR TABLE 7.5

Below are the equations for the hierarchical linear models in table 7.6. In the interest of space we are only providing the equation for the most saturated model. Simpler models follow the same structure, only with fewer variables.

Table 7.5. Dependent Variable: Democracy Support Index (1 = most anti-democracy, 4 = most pro-democracy)

Model 4:

$$Y_{ij} = \beta_{0j} + \beta_{1j}(\text{female})_{ij} + \beta_{2j}(\text{age})_{ij} + \beta_{3j}(\text{education level})_{ij} + \beta_{4j}(\text{Muslim})_{ij} + \beta_{5j}(\text{Christian})_{ij} + r_{ij}$$

$$\beta_{0j} = \gamma_{00} + \gamma_{01}(\text{GDP per capita})_{ij} + \gamma_{02}(\text{average age})_{ij} + \gamma_{03}(\text{level of democracy}) + \gamma_{04}(\text{proportion Muslim})_{ij} + \gamma_{05}(\text{proportion Christian})_{ij}$$

$$\beta_{1j} = \gamma_{10} + u_{1j}$$
$$\beta_{2j} = \gamma_{20} + u_{2j}$$
$$\beta_{3j} = \gamma_{30} + u_{3j}$$
$$\beta_{4j} = \gamma_{40} + u_{4j}$$
$$\beta_{5j} = \gamma_{50} + u_{5j}$$

SUMMARY STATISTICS

Individual-level variables	Mean (min, max)
Age	40.92 (15, 101)
Education	0.49 (0, 1)

Country-level variables	
GDP per capita (logged)	3.81 (2.68, 4.53)
Freedom House Average (1994–1998)	4.92 (1, 7)
Average age	41.43 (29.79, 52.45)
Proportion Muslim	0.20 (0, 0.99)
Proportion Christian	0.54 (0, 0.99)

Appendix 8
Matching Countries as a
Robustness Check

Statistical analysis in which countries constitute the units of analysis is inherently problematic. The population is necessarily finite and is not large enough to yield good statistical properties. Countries are different from each other in many ways that we *know* matter for social outcomes, and are distinct in numerous other ways that *may* matter as well. It is hard to argue that countries are exchangeable or can be thought of as independent observations. For these reasons, the results of regression analyses on country-level variables must be interpreted cautiously.

Some additional statistical problems arise when we try to compare Muslim and non-Muslim countries since they differ on a host of factors *other* than their predominant religious tradition. In particular, the level of socioeconomic development is a challenging confounder when comparing Muslim and non-Muslim countries because non-Muslim countries have a broader range of values than Muslim ones on development indicators. When we "control" for level of development in a regression context, we are in fact comparing wealthy non-Muslim countries to hypothetical wealthy Muslim countries. The results obtained in the regression models are therefore not based on an empirical comparison for all values of our control variables, but rather rest heavily on a linearity assumption—that relationships observed for a low level of economic development also hold for a high level.

To avoid some of these problems, we estimated a series of matching models to examine the difference between being a predominantly Muslim country or not. The matching models, which are non-parametric models resting on fewer assumptions, constitute a robustness check on the cross-national regression analyses presented in this volume. We avoid the linearity assumption by pairing Muslim and non-Muslim countries with similar characteristics and then analyzing their differences on the outcome of interest. Doing so gives us another, potentially more focused, look at the data and provides a check on our findings. For every regression model presented in chapters 4–7, we replicated the analyses using a matching method in which the Muslim countries in the dataset were matched to (or paired with) a non-Muslim country that is as similar as possible on a chosen set of control variables, usually the same control variables that were included in the regression models.

Strictly speaking, in order to analyze the *effect* of being a Muslim country, we should ideally observe two countries that were identical in every way a long time ago, but that subsequently diverged in one respect, which was that one became predominantly Muslim and the other did not. We would then observe how they differed in terms of the dependent variable after time had passed. Since this is historically impossible, we cannot say anything about the *effect* of being a Muslim country, but we can try to make the best possible description of the empirical differences between Muslim and non-Muslim countries in the world today.

In contrast to experimental conditions, in which a clear treatment is randomly applied to one group while a group of exchangeable units experiences a control condition, it is impossible randomly to assign countries to be Muslim and non-Muslim. Likewise, as demonstrated throughout the book, measuring "Muslim" is more precise when done continuously as a percentage of a country's population that adheres to Islam. Matching, however, depends on dichotomization. For the purpose of the matching models a country was determined "Muslim" if more than 55 percent of the population is Muslim, as spelled out at the end of chapter 1. This is the same dichotomization that was used for the descriptive tables presented throughout the book. This crude dichotomization sacrifices the nuance of percentages, yet it was the only option that allowed us to achieve balance on confounding variables.

There are numerous ways of matching countries. For multivariate matching, the best possible matches are found using the genetic matching algorithm GenMatch.[1] GenMatch combines propensity score matching and Mahalanobis distance matching to find the set of matches that minimizes the discrepancy of potential confounding variables between the treatment and control groups. We used GenMatch to establish a set of matched pairs for each country-level dependent variable analyzed in chapters 4–7. The number of matched pairs varied depending on the availability of data. Our smallest number of matched pairs was 25 for the question on murder rates. In other words, we matched 25 predominantly Muslim countries with 25 non-Muslim countries for a set of 25 pairs. The highest number of matched pairs was 44 for the questions on literacy ratio and political openness.

In each case we chose to match based on a parsimonious set of confounding variables most relevant to the outcome at hand. The variables included in different analyses were income per capita, life expectancy, population size, ethnic diversity, fuels dependence, level of democracy, fertility rate, late national independence, healthy life expectancy, and percentage of the population that is infected with HIV. Once Muslim countries were paired with non-Muslim countries through GenMatch, the remaining non-Muslim countries were thrown out of the sample. The matching was done with replacement, which means that some non-Muslim countries were used more than once as a match to a Muslim country if they were the best fit on the chosen control variables. We then estimated the differences between the two groups using the average treatment effect of the treated (ATT). This statistic is found by subtracting the value on the outcome variable for the non-Muslim country in a pair from the value on the outcome variable for the Muslim country in the same pair of countries. This is done for all the country pairs. The ATT is the average of all of these differences.

In most instances, matching greatly improved the balance of the covariates in the model, meaning that the pairs identified by the matching algorithms had highly similar values for the variables we matched on. Thus, we had no reason to believe that the observed differences on the dependent variables were driven by differences in confounding variables. Matching thereby provided a non-parametric way of "controlling" for the variables we see as the main potential confounders. For most of the dependent variables, the findings of the matching estimator corroborated the substantive findings of the regression models. The matching models do not rely upon the parametric assumptions that the OLS and negative binomial models presented in chapters 4–7 do, yet the former yield results that are largely consistent with the latter. The matching exercise therefore serves as a robustness check and increases our confidence in the OLS and negative binomial regressions that we rely upon in much of the empirical analysis presented in chapters 4–7.

A summary of the results is presented in the table below.

COMPARING REGRESSION AND MATCHING RESULTS

Dependent Variable	Regression Coefficient for Percent Muslim[a]	ATT
Corruption perceptions (chapter 4)	0.004 (0.003)	0.28 (0.39)
Control of corruption (chapter 4)	0.07* (0.03)	4.10 (3.20)
Murder rates (chapter 4)	−0.013*** (0.003)	−5.76** (1.96)
Deaths in episodes of large-scale political violence (chapter 5)	−0.01 (0.01)	−0.79 (0.68)
Female-to-male earned income ratio (chapter 6)	−0.13*** (0.03)	−0.10* (0.04)
Female parliamentarians (chapter 6)	−0.08** (0.03)	−7.25* (2.98)

continued

Dependent Variable	Regression Coefficient for Percent Muslim[a]	ATT
Women at ministerial level (chapter 6)	−0.02 (0.02)	−0.98 (1.81)
Female-to-male literacy ratio (chapter 6)	−0.05[†] (0.03)	−2.04 (2.30)
Male-to-female healthy life expectancy gap (chapter 6)	−0.03*** (0.01)	−1.69[†] (0.96)
Gini score (chapter 6)	−0.08*** (0.02)	−3.87* (1.69)
Political openness (chapter 7)	−0.09* (0.04)	−9.40** (3.20)

[a] The coefficients in this column are taken from the most saturated regression model for each dependent variable.

[b] Robust standard errors in parentheses for the regression coefficients. Abadie-Imbens standard errors in parentheses for the ATT estimates.

[†]significant at $p < .10$; * $p < .05$; ** $p < .01$; *** $p < .001$.

Notes

CHAPTER 1

1. Huston Smith is an example. See Huston Smith, *The World Religions: Our Great Wisdom Traditions* (New York: HarperCollins, 1991); Huston Smith, *Islam: A Concise Introduction* (New York: HarperCollins, 2001); and Huston Smith, *The Soul of Christianity: Restoring the Great Tradition* (New York: HarperCollins, 2005).

2. See Amaney Jamal and Nadine Naber, eds., *Race and Arab Americans before and after 9/11: From Invisible Citizens to Visible Subjects* (Syracuse, NY: Syracuse University Press, 2008); Olivier Roy, *Secularism Confronts Islam* (New York: Columbia University Press, 2007); Ali S. Asani, "'So That You May Know One Another': A Muslim American Reflects on Pluralism and Islam," *Annals of the Academy of Political and Social Science* 588 (July 2003), pp. 40–51; Mujeeb R. Khan, "The Islamic and Western Worlds: 'End of History' or the 'Clash of Civilizations'?" in Emran Qureshi and Michael A. Sells, eds., *The New Crusades: Constructing the Muslim Enemy* (New York: Columbia University Press, 2003), pp. 170–201; and Mujeeb R. Khan, "Bosnia-Herzegovina and the Crisis of the Post–Cold War International System," *East European Politics and Societies* 9, 3 (Fall 1995), pp. 459–498.

3. See, for example, Paul Steinhauser, "Poll: Few Americans Have Good View of Muslim World," June 2, 2009, online at <http://www.cnn.com/2009/POLITICS/06/02/us.muslims.poll/index.html> (site consulted June 2009); Sudha Ramachandran, "In India, the Wages of Distrust," *Asia Times*, November 15, 2006, online at <http://www.atimes.com/atimes/South_Asia/HK15Df01.html> (site consulted June 2009); and Organization for Security and Cooperation in Europe, Permanent Council, "OSCE Conference on Anti-Semitism and on Other Forms of Intolerance," Consolidated Summary, Cordoba, Spain, September 23, 2005, online at <http://www.osce.org/documents/cio/2005/06/16402_en.pdf> (site consulted June 2009).

4. Mohammed Arkoun, "Rethinking Islam Today," *Annals of the Academy of Political and Social Science* 588 (July 2003), p. 18.

5. Lara Deeb, *An Enchanted Modern: Gender and Public Piety in Shi'i Lebanon* (Princeton, NJ: Princeton University Press, 2006), pp. 3–4.

6. Amir Taheri, *The Persian Night: Iran under the Khomeinist Revolution* (New York: Encounter, 2009), pp. 46–47.

7. For example, John L. Esposito, *The Future of Islam* (New York: Oxford University Press, 2010); John L. Esposito and Dalia Mogahed, *Who Speaks for Islam? What a Billion Muslims Really Think* (New York: Gallop Press, 2008); and John L. Esposito, *Unholy War: Terror in the Name of Islam* (New York: Oxford University Press, 2003).

8. For example, Karen Armstrong, *Islam: A Short History* (New York: Random House, 2002); Karen Armstrong, *Muhammad: A Biography of the Prophet* (New York: HarperCollins, 1992); and Bruce B. Lawrence, *Shattering the Myth: Islam beyond Violence* (Princeton, NJ: Princeton University Press, 1998).

9. For example, Daniel Pipes, *Militant Islam Reaches America* (New York: Norton, 2003); *Miniatures: Views of Islamic and Middle Eastern Politics* (Piscataway, NJ: Transaction, 2003); and Daniel Pipes, *In the Path of God: Islam and Political Power* (Piscataway, NJ: Transaction, 1983).

10. Samuel P. Huntington, *The Clash of Civilizations and the Remaking of World Order* (New York: Simon and Schuster, 1998). See also Christopher Caldwell, *Reflections on the Revolution in Europe: Immigration, Islam, and the West* (New York: Doubleday, 2009).

11. Esposito and Mogahed, *Who Speaks for Islam?*

12. Huntington, *Clash of Civilizations and the Remaking of World Order.*

13. See Oliver Roy, *The Politics of Chaos in the Middle East* (New York: Columbia University Press, 2008), pp. 73–120.

14. Peter J. Katzenstein and Robert O. Keohane, eds., *Anti-Americanisms in World Politics* (Ithaca, NY: Cornell University Press, 2007).

15. John Gerring, *Social Science Methodology: A Criterial Framework* (New York: Cambridge University Press, 2001), p. 124.

16. Milton Viorst, "Puritanism and Stagnation," in Khaled Abou El Fadl, ed., *The Place of Tolerance in Islam* (Boston: Beacon, 2002), p. 27.

17. Akbar S. Ahmed, *Islam under Siege* (Cambridge, UK: Polity, 2003), p. 144. See also Fazlur Rahman, *Islam and Modernity: Transformation of an Intellectual Tradition* (Chicago: University of Chicago Press, 1982); Bassam Tibi, *Islam between Culture and Politics* (New York: Palgrave, 2001); and Tariq Ramadan, *Islam, the West and Challenges of Modernity* (Leicester, UK: The Islamic Foundation, 2001).

18. Association of Religion Data Archives, online at <http://www.thearda.com> (site consulted September 2008).

CHAPTER 2

This chapter was coauthored with Danielle Lussier.

1. Ernest Gellner, "Marxism and Islam: Failure and Success," in Azzam Tamimi, ed., *Power-Sharing Islam?* (London: Liberty for Muslim World Publications, 1993), p. 36.

2. "Flags, Veils, and Sharia," *The Economist*, July 19–25, 2008, p. 36.

3. "Major Religions of the World Ranked by Number of Adherents," online at <http://www.Adherents.com> (site consulted June 2008). See also Saeed M. Mohtsham, "Vision and Visionary Leadership: An Islamic Perspective," *International Review of Business Research Papers* 3, 2 (June 2007), pp. 248–277, online at <http://www.bizresearchpapers.com/Mohtsham.pdf> (site consulted June 2008).

4. Jytte Klausen, *The Islamic Challenge: Politics and Religion in Western Europe* (New York: Oxford University Press, 2005), pp. 139–142.

5. The WVS data may be accessed online at <http://www.worldvaluessurvey.org>. All analyses in this book that use the WVS data rely upon the raw data files downloaded from the website. The World Values Survey Integrated Questionnaire and the fourth-wave data were downloaded in July 2008 and the fifth-wave data in January 2009. The WVS is not the only source of data that covers a broad swath of the world. The Barometer surveys and the Pew Global Attitudes project surveys also do so, but they are not as extensive as the WVS and they do not offer as much information in the public domain. They also are less useable for other reasons as well. The Barometer surveys (such as the Eurobarometer, the Latinobarometer, the Afrobarometer, and the Asian Barometer) furnish valuable information. Yet the Barometer surveys are decentralized; the survey effort is carried out by different organizations in different regions, and somewhat different questions are asked from region to region. These circumstances sometimes make

comparing data drawn from different regions difficult. Furthermore, the data are not gathered and managed at any central office, and accessing them for all regions is problematic. For scholars working on one particular region the Barometer surveys may be especially valuable, but for those who wish to take a global view using a unified data set they are more problematic. The Barometer surveys also mostly query people about their political views; they are more political than sociological and do not focus on religiosity and other nonpolitical personal matters. For the purposes of this book, the WVS provides much better and more accessible data than the Barometer surveys. For some of the Barometer surveys, see "The Eurobarometer Survey Series," online at <http://www.gesis.org/en/data_service/eurobarometer> (site consulted October 2008); "The Afrobarometer," online at <http://www.afrobarometer.org> (site consulted October 2008); "Latinobarómetro," online at <http://www.latinobarometro.org> (site consulted October 2008); and "The Asian Barometer" online at <http://www.asianbarometer.org> (site consulted July 2009). The Pew Global Attitudes Project reports provide some interesting insights, but they are much less globally comprehensive. Furthermore, Pew does not make publicly available the individual-level data used to prepare its reports, which renders impossible doing the type of analyses we conduct here using the WVS data. The Pew reports and data may be accessed online at <http://www.pewglobal.org> (site consulted November 2008).

6. For example, while most of the WVS is based on face-to-face interviews, in Japan the survey is administered through a postal questionnaire.

7. Katherine Meyer, Helen Rizzo, and Yousef Ali, "Changed Political Attitudes in the Middle East: The Case of Kuwait," *International Sociology* 22, 3 (May 2007), pp. 289–324.

8. Michael Coppedge, "Thickening Thin Concepts: Issues in Large-N Data Generation," in Geraldo Munck, ed., *Regimes and Democracy in Latin America: Theories and Methods* (New York: Oxford University Press, 2007), p. 122.

9. These cases were included in the early release data available on the World Values Survey website <http://www.worldvaluessurvey.org> as of February 1, 2009.

10. Although Algeria was included in the fourth wave of the WVS, the question about religious denomination was not asked. We were unable to include Algeria in this analysis since we could not accurately measure religious denomination.

11. The two questions are F024 and F025 in the WVS Integrated Questionnaire.

12. For more details on the creation of these groups, see appendix 2.A.

13. This large proportion of nondenominationalists in Pakistan appears incongruous with other sources, which estimate that the population of Pakistan is almost universally Muslim. Indeed, all respondents in the WVS from Pakistan who listed a religious denomination said they were Muslim. It is possible that the large proportion of respondents without a denomination is an error in the survey, but we have no way of verifying this.

14. World Values Survey question F035 provides a good example. The question asks: "Generally speaking, do you think that churches in your country are giving adequate answers to the moral problems and needs of the individual?" The question centers on personal opinion about a religious matter. But it does not necessarily elicit answers that reflect respondents' own religiosity, since it asks whether people think that *churches in their country* are performing a potentially important function well. Answers depend on what religious organizations are doing from country to country, whether they are meeting people's needs, and what people expect from their country's religious organizations. Thus, while the question deals with personal views on a religious matter, it does not necessarily yield answers that give us good data on respondents' own religious commitment.

15. For example, World Values Survey question F066 asks, "How often do you pray to God outside of religious services?" The question is a potentially excellent source of information on personal religiosity. But data are still a bit sparse, and the question was not asked in the most recent fifth wave.

16. World Values Survey, question F063 on the Integrated Questionnaire: "How important is God in your life?" (possible answers range from 10, meaning "very important," to 1, meaning "not at all important"; respondents are asked to score their answer on the 1–10 scale).

17. World Values Survey, question F034 on the Integrated Questionnaire: "Independently of whether you go to church or not, would you say you are: 1) a religious person; 2) not a religious person; or 3) a convinced atheist."

18. World Values Survey, question F028: "Apart from weddings, funerals, and christenings, about how often do you attend religious services these days?" (possible answers in the fourth-wave surveys are "more than once a week"; "once a week"; "once a month"; "only on special holy days/Christmas/Easter days"; "other specific holy days"; "once a year"; "less often"; and "never/practically never"; in the fifth-wave surveys the options are "more than once a week"; "once a week"; "once a month"; "only on special holy days"; "once a year"; "less often"; and "never/practically never." For the purposes of analysis, we have combined the two responses from the surveys "only on special holy days/ Christmas/Easter days" and "other specific holy days" to align with the question wording in the fifth-wave surveys.

19. The fourth-wave sample included sixty-six countries.

20. Question X047 on the World Values Survey Integrated Questionnaire.

21. There are other good methodological reasons for excluding the income variable. First, the question on income was not asked in Argentina and Jordan, thereby forcing us to exclude two important cases from the study. Second, data on income are missing in all country cases, for a total of over 7,500 missing cases in the full data set. In contrast to most other variables, we have good reason to believe that data on income are not missing at random: Survey researchers have documented that it is generally individuals in higher income brackets who choose not to report income data to public opinion polls. Including income as a variable risks excluding important respondents from our sample and biasing the results. Lastly, the data on income and education level are highly correlated. We ran several preliminary models using the income variable and found that education was generally the only variable in the model affected by the inclusion or exclusion of individual-level income. We believe that the education variable adequately captures socioeconomic status for the purposes of our study and that nothing is lost by excluding the measure of relative income.

22. In that year, incomes ranged from those of the fortunate inhabitants of Luxembourg, who averaged $33,505 per person, to those of the hard-pressed citizens of Sierra Leone, who averaged $458.

23. Average age was calculated by aggregating the data for respondents in each country in the WVS. In initial runs we also included a variable for the average educational attainment of the country's population. This was not found to show a relationship to religiosity and was trimmed from the final models. The variables for average age and average educational attainment were included in initial tests not only for substantive interest but to ensure precise calculation estimates. Because our data have a hierarchical structure, we must consider the possibility that an individual's attitudes and behaviors can be influenced not only by individual circumstances but also by the aggregate experiences of the society in which he or she resides. Thus, it is possible to consider these aggregate statistics as "controls" for isolating the statistical relationship of individual-level characteristics.

24. Average age among WVS respondents ranges from a low of 30 in Zambia to a high of 53 in Switzerland. It is important to bear in mind that these numbers are higher than those that include the entire population. Since the WVS respondents are all adults, children are excluded from our average age statistic. In contrast, if we examine cross-national statistics for the average age of the entire population of countries for the year 2000, we find a low of 14 in Uganda and a high of 41 in Japan.

25. Source: Freedom House, "Freedom in the World," online at <http://www.freedomhouse.org> (site consulted December 2008). Following common practice, we use the "freedom ratings," which are averages of countries' "political rights" and "civil liberties" scores. Scores run from 1 (most free) to 7 (least free). For more intuitive presentation, we flip the scores such that 7 stands for most free and 1 for least free. In preliminary analyses we tested separate measures of "political rights" and "civil liberties" scores and found no substantive difference in the results between these measures and the combined "freedom ratings."

26. For more on HLM, see Stephen W. Raudenbush and Anthony S. Bryk, *Hierarchical Linear Models: Applications and Data Analysis Methods* (Thousand Oaks, CA: Sage, 2002); Tom A. Snijders and Roel J. Bosker, *Multilevel Analysis: An Introduction to Basic and Advanced Multilevel Modeling* (London: Sage, 1999); and Andrew Gelman and Jennifer Hill, *Data Analysis Using Regression and Multilevel/Hierarchical Models* (Cambridge: Cambridge University Press, 2007).

27. As with any multiple regression models, the coefficients and standard errors of HLM and HGLM models may change depending on the inclusion or exclusion of specific variables. In testing hypotheses about whether Muslims are distinctive, a relevant question for HLM analysis is whether to include a Christian dummy variable at the individual level and a percent Christian variable at the country level. Does the exclusion of relevant controls for Christianity—the denomination that is claimed by the largest number of survey respondents—constitute an omitted variable bias? We ran all of the models presented in this book excluding the Christian self-identification and percent Christian variables to assess which model specification was a more honest representation of the data and hypothesis test. We determined that controlling for Christian at the individual and country levels was the most accurate way to present global, individual-level data analysis. If we exclude the dummy variable for self-identified Christians from the model, Christians become the largest group in the non-Muslim base category and the coefficient for "Muslim" changes. Since in many instances Christians and Muslims appear to behave quite similarly, the size of a "Muslim" effect is suppressed when we do not control for self-identification as a Christian. By controlling for Christian, we are able to compare Muslims and Christians as distinct from nondenominationalists, yet we are also able to compare them to each other. Controlling for percent Christian at the country level is a bit more problematic. Since our number of countries ranges from 49 to 83 in the models, including percent Christian may introduce some multicollinearity in the models. Yet, in order to be consistent, we have included percent Christian at the country level. On the whole, in almost all of the analyses we conducted excluding controls for being a Christian and percent Christian in national populations, the results were nearly identical in terms of statistical significance and direction of effect to those presented in this volume. In the handful of instances in which the results differ, we present the information in footnotes to the respective models.

28. Average age of the population and the average score on the importance-of-God scale are measured by taking the average for all of the respondents in the WVS for each country. The proportion of Muslims and Christians is based on the proportion of respondents in each country in the WVS that self-identify as Muslims and Christians. The proportion Muslim

correlates at 0.98 with data on Muslim populations published by the Association of Religion Data Archives, online at <http://www.thearda.com> (site consulted September 2008).

29. This finding was robust across multiple model specifications, including models that tested the proportions of Muslims and proportions of Christians separately.

30. For more on binary outcome models, see Raudenbush and Bryk, *Hierarchical Linear Models*, pp. 294–309.

31. Predicted probabilities are calculated by taking the beta coefficients from the model (or, if the model is hierarchical, the gamma coefficients) and solving the model equation by inserting specific values of interest on the independent variables. Predicted probabilities aid our understanding of the relationship between particular independent variables and the outcome of interest by allowing us to consider probable independent variable values and the different scores they provide on the dependent variable. By using predicted probabilities to examine values of the independent variables of interest, we develop a clearer interpretation of the relationship between two variables than what can be obtained by looking only at the beta or gamma coefficients. For more on predicted probabilities, see J. Scott Long, *Regression Models for Categorical and Limited Dependent Variables* (Thousand Oaks, CA: Sage, 1997), pp. 63–68.

32. Although the wording of this question offered several response categories, "more than once a week"; "once a week"; "once a month"; "only on special holy days"; "once a year"; "less often"; and "never/practically never," we found that treating the dependent variable as an ordered response model that could be analyzed with ordered logit was not particularly illuminating. An ordered response model assumes that the difference between categories "once a week" and "once a month" is the same as the difference between categories "less often" and "once a year" with regard to differences in the independent variable. We did not find this assumption convincing on a theoretical level and therefore decided that the most appropriate way to analyze religious practice was to consider weekly attendees against those who attend less frequently.

33. As'ad AbuKhalil, "Against the Taboos of Islam," in Charles E. Butterworth and I. William Zartman, eds., *Between the State and Islam* (Washington, DC: Woodrow Wilson Center Press, 2001), p. 115.

34. Elaine Howard Ecklund, "Religion and Spirituality among University Scientists," *Social Science Research Council Forum*, February 5, 2007. Online at <http://religion.ssrc.org/reforum/Ecklund.pdf> (site consulted July 2008).

35. Mark Tessler, "Do Islamic Orientations Influence Attitudes toward Democracy in the Arab World? Evidence from Egypt, Jordan, Morocco, and Algeria," *International Journal of Comparative Sociology* 43, 3–5 (October 2002), pp. 229–249.

36. Mark Tessler, "Islam and Democracy in the Middle East: The Impact of Religious Orientations on Attitudes toward Democracy in Four Arab Countries," *Comparative Politics* 34 (April 2002), pp. 337–354; online version at <http://polisci.lsa.umich.edu/documents/tesslerCPArticle.pdf> (cited passage in online version, pp. 4–5).

37. Bernard Lewis, "Islam and Liberal Democracy: A Historical Overview," *Journal of Democracy* 7, 2 (April 1996), p. 61.

38. Mohammad Amjad, "Shi'ism and Revolution in Iran," *Journal of Church and State* 31, 1 (1989), p. 35.

39. Samuel P. Huntington, *The Clash of Civilizations and the Remaking of World Order* (New York: Simon and Schuster, 1998), p. 70.

40. Jamal al-Suwaidi, "Arab and Western Conceptions of Democracy," in David Garnham and Mark Tessler, eds., *Democracy, War, and Peace in the Middle East* (Bloomington: Indiana University Press, 1995), p. 87.

41. Lahouari Addi, "Islamist Utopia and Democracy," *Annals of the American Academy of Political and Social Science* 524 (November 1992), p. 122.

42. Mounira M. Charrad, *States and Women's Rights: The Making of Postcolonial Tunisia, Algeria, and Morocco* (Berkeley: University of California Press, 2001), p. 29. See also Binnaz Toprak, *Islam and Political Development in Turkey* (Leiden: E. J. Brill, 1981), pp. 20–34.

43. World Values Survey, question F103: "How much do you agree or disagree with the following statement: Religious leaders should not influence how people vote in elections?" (possible answers are "agree strongly"; "agree"; "neither agree nor disagree"; "disagree"; and "strongly disagree").

44. World Values Survey, question F105: "How much do you agree or disagree with the following statement: Religious leaders should not influence government?" (possible answers are "agree strongly"; "agree"; "neither agree nor disagree"; "disagree"; and "strongly disagree").

45. Question F105, which measures agreement with the statement that "religious leaders should not influence government," was not asked in China, Colombia, France, Iraq, Israel, Netherlands, Nigeria, Pakistan, Russia, Saudi Arabia, Singapore, Switzerland, Egypt, and Britain. The absence of data for a number of countries with large Muslim populations reduces the number of Muslims in our sample by almost half, thus making us less confident in the results of the models for this question. The substantive findings of this analysis were essentially the same as what we present here for question F103, which asks whether "religious leaders should not influence how people vote in elections," except that the proportion of Christians in a country's population was also statistically significant and positive.

46. This model was also estimated using the "do you consider yourself a religious person" question as the control for religiosity, yielding substantively similar results.

47. It is difficult, though, to link this finding in a satisfactory way to any real-world examples, since several of our country-level variables are highly correlated. For example, if we compare the predicted probabilities of two hypothetical Muslim men with average age, education level, and religiosity, one living in France, where the levelcs of income and democracy are above the global average, but the levels of religiosity and proportion Muslim are below the global average, and the other living in Egypt, where the levels of income and democracy are below the global average while the levels of religiosity and the proportion Muslim are above the global average, we find that the Muslim man in Egypt has a predicted probability of agreement of .61, while that of the Muslim man in France is .77.

48. World Values Survey, question F104: "How much do you agree or disagree with the following statement: It would be better for [this country] if more people with strong religious beliefs held public office" (possible answers are "agree strongly"; "agree"; "neither agree nor disagree"; "disagree"; and "strongly disagree").

49. World Values Survey, question F102: "How much do you agree or disagree with the following statement: Politicians who do not believe in God are unfit for public office" (possible answers are "agree strongly"; "agree"; "neither agree nor disagree"; "disagree" and "strongly disagree").

50. al-Suwaidi, "Arab and Western Conceptions of Democracy," p. 87.

51. Huntington, *Clash of Civilizations and the Remaking of World Order*, p. 70.

52. Marshall G. S. Hodgson, *The Venture of Islam: Conscience and History in a World Civilization*, vol. 2, *The Expansion of Islam in the Middle Periods* (Chicago: University of Chicago Press, 1974), p. 48.

53. In addition to the volume cited in the previous note, see Marshall G. S. Hodgson, *The Venture of Islam: Conscience and History in a World Civilization*, vol. 1, *The Classical Age of Islam* (Chicago: University of Chicago Press, 1974); and Marshall G. S. Hodgson, *The Venture of Islam: Conscience and History in a World Civilization*, vol. 3, *The Gunpowder Empire and Modern Times* (Chicago: University of Chicago Press, 1974).

54. Jonathan P. Berkey, *The Formation of Islam: Religion and Society in the Near East, 600–1800* (New York: Cambridge University Press, 2003), pp. 123, 125, and 184; also pp. 203–215. See also Şerif Mardin, "An Islamic Political Formula in Transformation: Islam, Identity, and Nationalism in the History of the Volga Tatars," in Charles E. Butterworth and I. William Zartman, eds., *Between the State and Islam* (Washington, DC: Woodrow Wilson Center Press, 2001), pp. 62–63; Ira M. Lapidus, "The Golden Age: The Political Concepts of Islam," *Annals of the Academy of Political and Social Science* 524 (November 1992), pp. 13–25; and Baber Johansen, *Contingency in a Sacred Law: Legal and Ethical Norms in the Muslim Fiqh* (Leiden: Brill, 1998).

55. Fazlur Rahman, *Islam and Modernity: Transformation of an Intellectual Tradition* (Chicago: University of Chicago Press, 1982), pp. 79–80.

56. Hodgson, *Venture of Islam*, vol. 1, p. 241.

57. Bernard Haykel, *Revival and Reform in Islam: The Legacy of Muhammad al-Shawkānī* (Cambridge: Cambridge University Press, 2003), p. 6.

58. Ibrahim A. Karawan, "Monarchs, Mullahs, and Marshals: Islamic Regimes?" *Annals of the American Academy of Political and Social Science* 524 (November 1992), p. 103.

59. Ibid., p. 119.

60. As'ad AbuKhalil, *The Battle for Saudi Arabia: Royalty, Fundamentalism, and Global Power* (New York: Seven Stories Press, 2004); John R. Bradley, *Saudi Arabia Exposed: Inside a Kingdom in Crisis* (New York: Palgrave Macmillan, 2005); Ali Gheissari and Vali Nasr, *Democracy in Iran: History and the Quest for Liberty* (New York: Oxford University Press, 2009); Ali M. Ansari, *Iran under Ahmadinejad: The Politics of Confrontation* (London: Routledge, 2008); and Abbas Milani, "Iran in Ferment: Cracks in the Regime," *Journal of Democracy* 20, 4 (October 2009), pp. 11–15.

61. Muhammad 'Abduh, *The Theology of Unity* (Kuala Lumpur: Islamic Book Trust, 2004); and M. Rashīd Rida, *The Muhammadan Revelation* (Alexandria, VA: Al-Saadawi Publications, 1996). See also Hodgson, *Venture of Islam*, vol. 1, p. 206; Berkey, *Formation of Islam*, p. 6; AbuKhalil, "Against the Taboos of Islam," pp. 110–111; L. Carl Brown, *Religion and State: The Muslim Approach to Politics* (New York: Columbia University Press, 2000), pp. 31–42; and Nikki R. Keddie, *Modern Iran: Roots and Results of Revolution* (New Haven, CT: Yale University Press, 2006), pp. 1–21.

62. Hodgson, *Venture of Islam*, vol. 2, p. 53.

63T. Without the controls for Christian self-identification and percent Christian, neither Muslim self-identification nor percent Muslim is statistically significant. This does not change the substantive conclusions. While the models presented here show that Muslims are less likely to agree with this statement, the finding when Christian controls are excluded shows that there is no difference between Muslims and non-Muslims.

64T. Without the controls for Christian self-identification and percent Christian, percent Muslim is no longer statistically significant.

65T. Without the controls for Christian self-identification and percent Christian, percent Muslim remains statistically significant when we control for individual- and country-level religiosity.

CHAPTER 3

This chapter was coauthored with Danielle Lussier.

1. Robert D. Putnam, *Bowling Alone: The Collapse and Revival of American Community* (New York: Simon and Schuster, 2001), p. 19.

2. For an overview of the use of social capital in contemporary literature, see Alejandro Portes, "Social Capital: Its Origins and Applications in Modern Sociology," *Annual Review of Sociology* 24 (August 1998), pp. 1–24.

3. Putnam, *Bowling Alone*; Robert D. Putnam, *Making Democracy Work: Civic Traditions in Modern Italy* (Princeton, NJ: Princeton University Press, 1993); and Alexis de Tocqueville, *Democracy in America* (New York: Mentor, 1956).

4. Ariel C. Armony, *The Dubious Link: Civic Engagement and Democratization* (Stanford, CA: Stanford University Press, 2004); Sheri Berman, "Civil Society and the Collapse of the Weimar Republic," *World Politics* 49, 3 (April 1997), pp. 401–429; Simone Chambers and Jeffrey Kopstein, "Bad Civil Society," *Political Theory* 29, 6 (December 2001), pp. 838–866; and Omar G. Encarnación, *The Myth of Civil Society: Social Capital and Democratic Consolidation in Spain and Brazil* (New York: Palgrave Macmillan, 2003).

5. Émile Durkheim, *Suicide* (New York: Free Press, 1951); Émile Durkheim, *The Elementary Forms of Religious Life* (New York: Free Press, 1995); and William James, *The Varieties of Religious Experience* (New York: The Library of America, 2009).

6. For example, Amaney A. Jamal, *Barriers to Democracy: The Other Side of Social Capital in Palestine and the Arab World* (Princeton, NJ: Princeton University Press, 2007); Jane Harrigan and Hamed El-Said, *Economic Liberalisation, Social Capital and Islamic Welfare Provision* (Basingstoke, Hampshire: Palgrave Macmillan, 2008); Eva Bellin, "Civil Society: Effective Tool of Analysis for Middle East Politics?" *PS: Political Science and Politics* 27, 3 (September 1994), pp. 509–510; Ziad Abdel Samad, "Civil Society in the Arab Region: Its Necessary Role and the Obstacles to Fulfillment," *International Journal of Not-for-Profit Law* 9, 2 (April 2007), online at <http://www.icnl.org/knowledge/ijnl/vol9iss2/special_1.htm> (site consulted July 2008); Fatima Mernissi, *ONG rurales du Haut Atlas: Les Aït Débrouille* (Casablanca: Editions le Fennec, 1997); E. Fuat Keyman and Ahmet Içduygu, "Globalization, Civil Society, and Citizenship in Turkey: Actors, Boundaries, and Discourses," *Citizenship Studies* 7, 2 (July 2003), pp. 219–34; Arif T. Payaslyoglu and Ahmet Içduygu, "Awareness of and Support for Human Rights among Turkish University Students," *Human Rights Quarterly* 21, 2 (May 1999), pp. 513–34; Şerif Mardin, "Power, Civil Society, and Culture in the Ottoman Empire," *Comparative Studies in Society and History* 11, 3 (June 1969), pp. 258–81; Şerif Mardin, *Religion and Social Change in Modern Turkey: The Case of Bediüzzaman Said Nursi* (Albany: State University of New York Press, 1989); and Peter Brigaitis, "Religious Engagement and Social Capital in the Islamic Context," M.A. thesis, University of North Texas, May 2005, online at <http://digital.library.unt.edu/permalink/meta-dc- 4788:1> (site consulted July 2008).

7. World Values Survey, Integrated Questionnaire number A058: "How often do you [spend] time with friends?" (possible answers are "weekly"; "once or twice a month"; "only a few times a year"; and "not at all").

8. World Values Survey, Integrated Questionnaire number A059: "How often do you spend time socially with colleagues from your work or your profession?" (possible answers are "weekly"; "once or twice a month"; "only a few times a year"; and "not at all").

9. World Values Survey, Integrated Questionnaire number A060: "How often you do spend time with people at your mosque, church, or synagogue?" (possible answers are "weekly"; "once or twice a month"; "only a few times a year"; and "not at all").

10. World Values Survey, Integrated Questionnaire number A061: "How often you do spend time socially with people at sports clubs or voluntary or service organizations?" (possible answers are "weekly"; "once or twice a month"; "only a few times a year"; and "not at all").

11. For a list of countries included in this analysis, see appendix 3.A.

12. Note that in contrast to a traditional regression analysis, the independent variables here are not measured in their original scale but are centered around their group means.

13. We also calculated an alternate three-item sociability index that excludes time spent with people from religious organizations. The results from these models can be seen in appendix 3.C.

14. Question numbers V24–V33 in the World Values Survey 2005 Codebook.

15. For a full list of countries included in this analysis, see appendix 3.A. It is important to bear in mind that individual survey respondents, not countries, are our units of analysis here. Individual Muslim respondents come not only from these eight countries but from numerous others as well. Among the 67,955 individual respondents for whom we have data on organizational memberships, 14,719 (22 percent) identify as Muslim.

16. In addition to these eight organizations, respondents were also asked about belonging to a "consumer organization." The numbers who were members were too small to warrant reliable analysis, so this category was excluded from further study. Respondents were also asked if they belong an "other" organization. We found, however, that the coding of the data for this question was inconsistent both within and across country cases, making analysis of these data impossible.

17. Foreign language questionnaires available at <http://www.worldvaluessurvey.org>.

18. Daniel Pipes, *Militant Islam Reaches America* (New York: Norton, 2003); Robert Spencer, *The Truth about Muhammad: Founder of the World's Most Intolerant Religion* (Washington, DC: Regnery, 2006); and Robert Spencer, ed., *The Myth of Islamic Tolerance: How Islamic Law Treats Non-Muslims* (Amherst, NY: Prometheus, 2005).

19. John L. Esposito, *What Everyone Needs to Know about Islam* (New York: Oxford University Press, 2002); Karen Armstrong, *Islam: A Short History* (New York: Modern Library, 2002); Karen Armstrong, *Holy War: The Crusades and Their Impact on Today's World* (New York: Anchor, 2001); and Abid Ullah Jan, "The Limits of Tolerance," in Khaled Abou El Fadl, ed., *The Place of Tolerance in Islam* (Boston: Beacon, 2002), pp. 42–50.

20. Khaled Abou El Fadl, "The Place of Tolerance in Islam," in Khaled Abou El Fadl, ed., *The Place of Tolerance in Islam* (Boston: Beacon, 2002), pp. 3–23; Sohail H. Hashmi, "A Conservative Legacy," in Khaled Abou El Fadl, ed., *The Place of Tolerance in Islam* (Boston: Beacon, 2002), pp. 31–36; Khaled Abou El Fadl, *The Great Theft: Wrestling Islam from the Extremists* (San Francisco: HarperOne, 2005); and As'ad AbuKhalil, *The Battle for Saudi Arabia: Royalty, Fundamentalism, and Global Power* (New York: Seven Stories Press, 2004).

21. World Values Survey, Integrated Questionnaire number F118: "Please tell me for each of the following statements whether you think it can always be justified, never be justified, or something in between: homosexuality" (1 = "never justifiable"; 10 = "always justifiable").

22. World Values Survey, Integrated Questionnaire number F120: "Please tell me for each of the following statements whether you think it can always be justified, never be justified, or something in between: abortion" (1 = "never justifiable"; 10 = "always justifiable").

23. World Values Survey, Integrated Questionnaire number F121: "Please tell me for each of the following statements whether you think it can always be justified, never be justified, or something in between: divorce" (1 = "never justifiable"; 10 = "always justifiable").

24. World Values Survey, Integrated Questionnaire number F117: "Please tell me for each of the following statements whether you think it can always be justified, never be

justified, or something in between: someone accepting a bribe in the course of their duties" (1 = "never justifiable"; 10 = "always justifiable").

25. World Values Survey, Integrated Questionnaire number F114: "Please tell me for each of the following statements whether you think it can always be justified, never be justified, or something in between: claiming government benefits to which you are not entitled" (1 = "never justifiable"; 10 = "always justifiable").

26. World Values Survey, Integrated Questionnaire number F116: "Please tell me for each of the following statements whether you think it can always be justified, never be justified, or something in between: cheating on taxes if you have a chance" (1 = "never justifiable"; 10 = "always justifiable").

27. For citations, I rely upon *The Koran*, trans. N. J. Dawood (London: Penguin, 1997).

28. For the relevant passages in the Qur'an, see 52:24, 56:17, 76:19. For contemporary discussions, see Al-Fatiah Foundation, "Homosexuality and Same-Sex Acts in Islam," online at <http://web.archive.org/web/20030622050907/http://www.al-fatiha.org/pamphlet.html> (site consulted July 2008); TheReligionofPeace.com, "What Does the Religion of Peace Teach about Homosexuality?" online at <http://www.thereligionofpeace.com/Quran/026-homosexuality.htm> (site consulted July 2008); and Scott Siraj al-Haqq Kugle, "Sexuality, Diversity, and Ethics in the Agenda of Progressive Muslims," in Omid Safi, ed., *Progressive Muslims: On Justice, Gender, and Pluralism* (Oxford: Oneworld, 2003), pp. 190–234.

29. For biblical references here and elsewhere, I rely upon the New International Version (NIV) (Grand Rapids, MI: Zondervan, 1984).

30. Daniel A. Heminiak, *What the Bible Really Says about Homosexuality* (Tajique, NM: Alamo Square Press, 2000); and Michael Vasey, *Strangers and Friends: New Exploration of Homosexuality and the Bible* (London: Hodder & Stoughton, 1997).

31. For example, Tariq Ali, "Theological Distractions," in Khaled Abou El Fadl, ed., *The Place of Tolerance in Islam* (Boston: Beacon, 2002), pp. 37–41.

32. Akbar S. Ahmed, *Islam under Siege: Living Dangerously in a Post-Honor World* (Oxford: Polity Press, 2003), p. 105.

33. The Qur'an 16:58–59; 60:12.

34. For example, Ps. 139:13.

35. The Qur'an 2:229–233; 65:1–6.

36. Matt. 5:31–32 and 19:3–9.

37T. In preliminary models we also included a measure for individual-level and country-level religiosity. Not surprisingly, both were found to be statistically significant and positive. When religiosity is included, the size of the coefficients for both Muslim and Christian self-identification is reduced, and the female variable is no longer statistically significant. The size of the coefficient for the proportion Christian was also reduced.

38T$_1$. In the analysis that treated "active membership" as the dependent variable, self-identification as a Muslim was statistically significant and negative, while self-identification as a Christian was not statistically significant across model specifications.

38T$_2$. In the analysis that treated "active membership" as the dependent variable, Christian self-identification, Christian proportion, and Muslim proportion were all statistically significant and negative across model specifications.

39T$_1$. In the analysis treating "active membership" as the dependent variable, self-identification as a Christian was not statistically significant.

39T$_2$. In the analysis treating "active membership" as the dependent variable, Christian proportion was statistically significant and negative.

39T$_3$. In the analysis treating "active membership" as the dependent variable, self-identification as Muslim was statistically significant and negative. Self-identification as a Christian and the Christian proportion were not statistically significant.

CHAPTER 4

1. There are exceptions, but they do not focus on Islam. Daniel Treisman, for example, includes in his inquiry on the causes of corruption a variable for the percentage of the population that is made up of Protestants. Treisman finds a link between Protestantism and lower levels of corruption. See Daniel Treisman, "The Causes of Corruption: A Cross-National Study," *Journal of Public Economics* 76, 3 (June 2000), pp. 399–457. See also Omer Gokcekus, "Is It Protestant Tradition or Current Protestant Population That Affects Corruption?" *Economic Letters* 99, 1 (April 2008), pp. 59–62.

2. Jonathan P. Berkey, *The Formation of Islam: Religion and Society in the Near East, 600–1800* (New York: Cambridge University Press, 2003), pp. 39–82; Marshall G. S. Hodgson, *The Venture of Islam*, vol. 1, *The Classical Age of Islam* (Chicago: University of Chicago Press, 1974), pp. 229–230; Timothy J. Piro, "Liberal Professionals in the Contemporary Arab World," in Charles E. Butterworth and I. William Zartman, eds., *Between the State and Islam* (Washington, DC: Woodrow Wilson Center Press, 2001), pp. 200–204; and Akbar S. Ahmed, *Islam under Siege: Living Dangerously in a Post-Honor World* (Oxford: Polity, 2003), pp. 141–143.

3. Edward C. Banfield, *The Moral Basis of a Backward Society* (New York: Free Press, 1967).

4. Abdullahi Ahmed An-Na'im, *Islam and the Secular State: Negotiating the Future of Shari'a* (Cambridge, MA: Harvard University Press, 2008), p. 69.

5. Transparency International, "The Corruption Perceptions Index," online at <http://www.transparency.org/policy_research/surveys_indices/cpi> (site consulted April 2008).

6. Daniel Kaufmann, Aart Kraay, and Massimo Mastruzzi, "Governance Matters, 2008: Worldwide Governance Indicators, 1996–2007," online at <http://info.worldbank.org/governance/wgi/mc_countries.asp> (site consulted August 2008).

7. Figures are for 2007 and are drawn from the *CIA World Factbook 2008* (New York: Skyhorse, 2007).

8. In a Welch two-sample t-test, $t = -3.8$ with 104.5 degrees of freedom. This yields a p-value = 0.0002, which means that the means of the two groups are statistically significantly different from each other at conventional levels of significance.

9. A boxplot is a plot that shows the distribution of the data for a group. Often several boxplots are placed next to each other to compare the values for different population groups. Each plot is a summary of the percentiles of the data. The box shows the range of values for the middle 50 percent of the data. The line in the middle of the box shows the median value of the data. The bottom line of the graph shows the 25th percentile of the data, and the lowest point is the smallest value that the data takes on for this group. Similarly, the top line of the graph marks the 75th percentile of the data, and the top point shows that highest value that the data takes on for this group.

10. For overviews of the literature as well as valuable analyses, see John Gerring and Strom C. Thacker, "Political Institutions and Corruption: The Role of Unitarism and Parliamentarism," *British Journal of Political Science* 34, 2 (April 2004), pp. 295–330; and Treisman, "Causes of Corruption."

11. Data for GNI are for GNI per capita at purchasing power parity in the year 2000 and are from The World Bank, *World Development Report 2002: Building Institutions for Markets* (New York: Oxford University Press, 2002), pp. 232–235, 240. Data for life expectancy in the year 2000 are from the United Nations Development Programme, *Human*

Development Report 2002 (New York: Oxford University Press, 2002), pp. 149–152; except for Timor Leste, which are for 2003 and are drawn from the 2005 version of the same publication; and for Afghanistan, Bosnia, Myanmar, the Palestinian Territories, Taiwan, and Yugoslavia, which are for 1999 and are from *CIA World Factbook 2000* (Washington, DC: Brassay's, 2000). Ethnic diversity is measured using the ethnic fractionalization index created by Alberto Alesina and colleagues. Source: Alberto Alesina, Arnaud Devleeschauwer, William Easterly, Sergio Kurlat, and Romain Wacziarg, "Fractionalization," *Journal of Economic Growth* 8, 2 (June 2003), pp. 155–94. A legacy of Soviet-type rule is measured as a dichotomous variable for whether a country has a history of Soviet-type communism. The twenty-eight countries in the data set of the former USSR, Eastern Europe, and Mongolia make up this group. Economic dependence on hydrocarbons is measured as the percentage of merchandise exports accounted for by oil and gas in the year 2000 (or the closest year for which data are available). Source: World Development Bank, *World Development Indicators 2002* (Washington, DC: The World Bank, 2002); and International Monetary Fund, "Statistical Appendices from reports for 2000, 2001, and 2002," online at <http://imf.org/external/country/index.htm> (site consulted May 2003). A legacy of British colonial heritage is measured as a dichotomous variable indicating whether or not the country is a former colony of Great Britain. Unitarism of state structure (or the structure of government) is measured using an indicator created by John Gerring and Strom Thacker to control for that variable. The measure ranges from 1 to 5, with higher scores representing more unitarism and lower scores more decentralization. Source: Gerring and Thacker, "Political Institutions and Corruption," p. 329. Level of democracy is assessed using the "freedom ratings" published on an annual basis for all countries of the world by Freedom House. The scores range from 1 (most open polity) to 7 (least open polity). I invert the scores to provide for more intuitive presentation. Here I use the average ratings for 2002–2004. Source: Freedom House, *Freedom in the World*, online at <http://freedomhouse.org> (site consulted July 2008).

12. Association of Religion Data Archives, online at <http://www.thearda.com> (site consulted September 2008).

13. As a robustness check, we also ran the models presented in table 4.3 and all other cross-national regression models presented in the book using a subset of the data. In the alternative analyses, we eliminated all observations in which gross national income (GNI) at purchasing power parity (PPP) for the year 2000 exceeded the highest GNI at PPP for a Muslim country. The cut-off was $25,320, the figure for predominantly Muslim Brunei. The operation therefore excluded from the analysis the world's thirteen wealthiest countries, all of them predominantly non-Muslim. The excluded countries are Luxembourg, the United States, Switzerland, Norway, Iceland, Belgium, Canada, Denmark, Japan, Austria, the Netherlands, Ireland, and Australia. The result was a data set that composed 44 Muslim countries and 115 non-Muslim countries. We found no substantive differences in the models estimated on this truncated data set. This check gives us confidence that the broader range of income present in non-Muslim countries, and in particular the presence among non-Muslim societies of a substantial number of countries that are wealthier than even the richest Muslim country, is not biasing the results of our regression models.

14. In a Welch two-sample t-test, $t = -3.9$ with 120.5 degrees of freedom. This yields a p-value = 0.0002, which means that the means of the two groups are statistically significantly different from each other at conventional levels of significance.

15. One should not attribute too much substantive significance to the negative sign for the percent Muslim coefficient in models 1, 2, and 4. The controls for level of democracy and

fuels dependence are not included in any of these models. Both of these variables are highly and negatively correlated with percent Muslim. In the absence of controls for level of democracy and fuels dependence, it is likely that the negative sign for percent Muslim is picking up these other factors that are not accounted for in the models.

16. Bertrand Russell, *Power* (London: Routledge, 1992), p. 182.

17. Sandra S. Evans and Joseph E. Scott, "The Seriousness of Crime Cross-Culturally," *Criminology* 22, 1 (February 1984), pp. 39–59.

18. Ineke Haen Marshall and Carolyn Rebecca Block, "Maximizing the Availability of Cross-National Data on Homicide," *Homicide Studies* 8, 3 (August 2004), pp. 267–310.

19. United Nations Development Programme (UNDP), *Human Development Report 2007/2008* (New York: Palgrave Macmillan, 2007), pp. 322–325. Data are taken from this source where available. The UNDP reports data for an available year between 2000 and 2004. Data for Brazil, Pakistan, Bangladesh, Uzbekistan, Niger, Senegal, and Mali are from Interpol. They were taken from data for a year between 1995 and 2000 that Interpol posted on its online site at <http://www.interpol.int> and that I consulted in January 2002. Interpol subsequently took the data out of the public domain and began providing them exclusively to police organizations. Data for Central African Republic, Congo-Brazzaville, Gabon, Guinea, Guinea-Bissau, Iraq, Kenya, and Malawi are drawn from Jerome L. Neapolitan, "Homicides in Developing Nations: Results of Research Using a Large and Representative Sample," *International Journal of Offender Therapy and Comparative Criminology* 41, 4 (1997), pp. 369–370. Neapolitan's data, which he draws from Interpol, are for an available year between 1988 and 1994. What may appear to be a low number for Iraq, given the violence that besets that country, is explicable given that the statistic for Iraq is drawn from a year predating the invasion by the United States and several of its allies in 2003.

20. In a Welch two-sample *t*-test, $t = -4.8176$ with 134.6 degrees of freedom. This means that the means for the two groups are highly statistically significantly different.

21. Louise I. Shelley, *Crime and Modernization: The Impact of Industrialization and Urbanization on Crime* (Carbondale: Southern Illinois University Press, 1981); William R. Avison and Pamela A. Loring, "Population Diversity and Cross-National Homicide: The Effects of Inequality and Heterogeneity," *Criminology* 24, 4 (November 1986), pp. 733–749; Neapolitan, "Homicides in Developing Nations."

22. For measures of ethnic fractionalization, Alesina et al., "Fractionalization," 2003. For level of democracy, the average "freedom ratings" (inverted scale) for 2001, from Freedom House, *Freedom in the World*, online at <http://freedomhouse.org> (site consulted July 2008). Socioeconomic inequality is measured using the Gini Index. Data are drawn from United Nations Development Programme (UNDP), *Human Development Report 2007/2008*, pp. 281–284. The UNDP reports data from the most recent available study of inequality for each country, which generally were conducted between 1995 and 2004. Data are taken from this source where available. Data for Cyprus, Iceland, Malta, and Serbia/Yugoslavia are from the Central Intelligence Agency, *CIA World Factbook*, online at <https://www.cia.gov/library/publications/the-world-factbook/index.html> (site consulted January 2008).

23. For example, Wesley G. Skogan, "Social Change and the Future of Violent Crime," in Ted Robert Gurr, ed., *Violence in America*, vol. 1, *The History of Crime* (Newbury Park, CA: Sage, 1989), pp. 235–250.

24. Marshall and Block, "Maximizing the Availability of Cross-National Data on Homicide," p. 301. Marshall and Block not only use cross-national data on homicide; they also enrich and organize the available data and point to ways in which shortcomings in the available data may be overcome. But their sample of countries is limited largely to the

advanced industrialized countries of Western Europe and North America and the post-communist region of the former USSR and East Europe.

25. Poisson models, binomial models, and negative binomial models are the most commonly used models for studying count data. These models generally, and in this case, give a much better model fit than the OLS models, since the normality assumption underlying an OLS model usually is violated when using count data. Poisson models make an assumption that the mean and the variance in the distribution is the same, while negative binomial models are often recommended for over-dispersed data. Over-dispersion in the data can arise when the occurrence of one event increases the probability of further events, as is the case in data on murders. See Joseph M. Hilbe, *Negative Binomial Regression* (Cambridge: Cambridge University Press, 2008).

26. Neapolitan, "Homicides in Developing Nations."

27. W. Byron Groves, Graeme Newman, and Charles Corrado, "Islam, Modernization, and Crime: A Test of the Religious Ecology Thesis," *Journal of Criminal Justice* 15, 6 (1987), pp. 495–503.

28. Émile Durkheim, *Suicide* (New York: Free Press, 1951).

29. Freda Adler, *States Not Obsessed with Crime* (Littleton, CO: Fred B. Rothman and Co., 1983).

30. Olena Antonaccio and Charles R. Tittle, "A Cross-National Test of Bonger's Theory of Criminality and Economic Conditions," *Criminology* 45, 4 (November 2007), pp. 925–958; and De Li, "Economic Development, Social Control, and Murder Rates: A Cross-National Approach," *Cross-Cultural Research* 29, 4 (November 1995), pp. 361–382.

31. Neapolitan, "Homicides in Developing Nations," pp. 368–369.

32. Adel A. Helal and Charisse T. M. Coston, "Low Crime Rates in Bahrain: Muslim Social Control Testing the Theory of Synnomie," in Charles B. Fields and Richter H. Moore, eds., *Comparative Criminal Justice: Traditional and Nontraditional Systems of Law and Control* (Long Grove, IL: Waveland, 1995), pp. 30–47.

33. Sam S. Souryal, "The Religionization of Society: The Continuing Application of Sharia Law in Saudi Arabia," *Journal for the Scientific Study of Religion* 26, 4 (December 1987), pp. 429–449.

34. Rudolph Peters, "The Islamization of Criminal Law: A Comparative Analysis," *Die Welt des Islams* 34 (1994), p. 269.

35. Souryal, "Religionization of Society," p. 448. See also Marcus Felson, "Linking Criminal Choices, Routine Activities, Informal Control, and Criminal Outcomes," in Derek B. Cornish, ed., *The Reasoning Criminal: Rational Choice Perspectives on Offending* (New York: Springer, 1986), pp. 119–128.

36. Peters, "Islamization of Criminal Law," pp. 266–267.

37. Seyed Hossein Serajzadeh, "Islam and Crime: The Moral Community of Muslims," *Journal of Arabic and Muslim Studies* 4 (2001–2002), p. 125.

38. Robert D. Putnam, *Bowling Alone: The Collapse and Revival of American Community* (New York: Simon and Schuster, 2000), p. 294.

CHAPTER 5

1. Charles Louis de Secondat (Montesquieu), *The Spirit of the Laws*, ed. Anne M. Cohler, Basia Carolyn Miller, and Harold Samuel Stone (Cambridge: Cambridge University Press, 1995), pp. 461–462.

2. For example, Serge Trifkovic, *The Sword of the Prophet* (Boston: Regina Orthodox Press, 2002); and Gregory M. Davis, *Religion of Peace? Islam's War against the World* (Los Angeles: World Ahead Publishing, 2006).

3. Samuel P. Huntington, *The Clash of Civilizations and the Remaking of World Order* (New York: Simon and Schuster, 1998), pp. 256–258.

4. Michael Bonner, *Jihad in History: Doctrines and Practice* (Princeton, NJ: Princeton University Press, 2008); David Cook, *Understanding Jihad* (Berkeley: University of California Press, 2005); Richard Bonney, *Jihad from Qu'ran to Bin Laden* (New York: Palgrave Macmillan, 2004); and John Kelsay, *Arguing the Just War in Islam* (Cambridge, MA: Harvard University Press, 2007).

5. For example, Rachid Al-Ghannouchi, "Secularism in the Arab Maghreb," in Azzam Tamimi and John L. Esposito, eds., *Islam and Secularism in the Middle East* (New York: New York University Press, 2000), pp. 114–115; Ronald Lukens-Bull, *A Peaceful Jihad: Negotiating Identity and Modernity in Muslim Java* (New York: Palgrave Macmillan, 2005), pp. 119–126; and Bruce B. Lawrence, *Shattering the Myth: Islam beyond Violence* (Princeton, NJ: Princeton University Press, 2000), pp. 157–185.

6. Monty G. Marshall, "Major Episodes of Political Violence 1946–2008," online at <http://systemicpeace.org/warlist.htm> (site consulted October 2008).

7. The Palestinian Territories are not included in this total or in this section, since they are not treated as a national entity in Marshall's data set. Hence, the total of 171 rather than 172 countries.

8. I use 1990 as the year for population in the divisor, since it is the earliest year for which we have good data on the population of all of what were or became the world's countries as of the present time. Use of an alternative year (such as 1945, 1975, or 2000) for population yields no substantive difference in the findings.

9. In a Welch two-sample t-test of the difference of means between the Muslim and non-Muslim countries, $t = -0.2456$ with 116.3 degrees of freedom. This gives a p-value of 0.8, suggesting that the means for the groups of countries are not statistically significantly different.

10. For example, Mitchell's *International Historical Statistics* contains a rich body of data, but for national income, figures are given only in local currencies, which makes cross-national standardization (at least for the time until the 1970s or so) impossible. The only other good indicator of socioeconomic development for which this source provides data is on infant mortality. Here it furnishes useful data stretching back to the nineteenth century, but for Africa prior to the 1980s provides data for only four countries. B. R. Mitchell, *International Historical Statistics,* 2nd revised ed. (3 vols.) (New York: Stockton Press, 1993). Such shortages are found in other sources as well.

11. United Nations Development Programme, *Human Development Report 2007–2008* (New York: Palgrave Macmillan, 2007), pp. 243–246. Numbers are unavailable in that source for Afghanistan, Iraq, Liberia, North Korea, Somalia, Taiwan, and Yugoslavia. For those countries, data for fertility rates are for 1989 and are drawn from *CIA World Factbook 1989* (Washington, DC: Central Intelligence Agency, 1989).

12. The Polity project provides scores, which range from –10 (most autocratic) to +10 (most democratic), for years all the way back to the early nineteenth century. It codes countries', and some territories and principalities', level of democracy, to 1825. These data are hardly problem-free. Retrospectively coding how democratic Ethiopia, Greece, and Guatemala—not to mention Baden, the Orange Free State, and the Papal States—were in 1860 may be an attempt to do the impossible, though the effort is indeed heroic and appreciated by scholars who rely on the data. As an alternative to the Freedom House ratings for 1975, I used Polity scores for 1946 for all countries for which numbers are available, which is most countries that were independent at that time. For all others, I used the Polity score for the first year of national independence. For many African countries,

which were generally the last to gain independence, that time is usually 1960 or there-abouts. The Polity data are less plentiful than the Freedom House data, however, and using them requires the loss of a substantial number of cases. I therefore present the results of the analyses using Freedom House ratings here. Using the Polity scores did not appreciably change the results.

13. Use of data for the year 1975 is advisable, since those numbers, like the data used for fertility rates, represent conditions at roughly the midpoint in the interval of time we are considering. The year is also one of the first for which Freedom House data are available. Data are missing for some countries for 1975, however. For them, data for the closest available year are used. Data for Belize are for 1981; for Djibouti, 1977; for Namibia, 1974; for Palestinian Territories, 1977; for the Solomon Islands, 1978. Data for Germany is for the Federal Republic in 1975; for Yemen, an average of scores for North and South Yemen in 1975.

14. Daniel Kaufmann, Aart Kraay, and Massimo Mastruzzi, "Governance Matters, 2008: Worldwide Governance Indicators, 1996–2007," online at <http://info.worldbank.org/governance/wgi/mc_countries.asp> (site consulted August 2008); and Monty G. Marshall and Benjamin R. Cole, "Global Report on Conflict, Governance, and State Fragility, 2008," *Foreign Policy Bulletin* (Winter 2008), online at <http://www.systemicpeace.org/Global%20Report%202008.pdf> (site consulted September 2008).

15. See Abdelwahab El-Affendi, *Who Needs an Islamic State?* 2nd ed. (London: Malaysia Think Tank, 2008); William Hale and Ergun Özbudun, *Islamism, Democracy, and Liberalism in Turkey: The Case of the AKP* (New York: Routledge, 2010); Carrie Rosefsky Wickham, *Mobilizing Islam: Religion, Activism, and Political Change in Egypt* (New York: Columbia University Press, 2002); Edward W. Walker, "Islam, Islamism and Political Order in Central Asia," *Journal of International Affairs* 56, 2 (Spring 2003), pp. 1–21; Oliver Roy, *The Failure of Political Islam* (London: I. B. Tauris, 1999); and Jillian Schwedler, *Faith in Moderation: Islamist Parties in Jordan and Yemen* (Cambridge: Cambridge University Press, 2006).

16. Monica Duffy Toft, "Getting Religion? The Puzzling Case of Islam and Civil War," *International Security* 31, 4 (Spring 2007), pp. 97–131.

17. I am especially indebted to Katherine E. Michel for assistance in assembling and coding the data used in this chapter.

18. For example, Zachary Abuza, *Militant Islam in Southeast Asia: Crucible of Terror* (Boulder, CO: Lynne Rienner, 2003); Daniel Benjamin and Steven Simon, *The Age of Sacred Terror* (New York: Random House, 2002); Gérard Chaliand and Arnaud Blin, eds., *The History of Terrorism: From Antiquity to al-Qaeda* (Berkeley: University of California Press, 2007); Malise Ruthven, *A Fury for God: The Islamist Attack on America* (London: Granta, 2004); Caroline Cox and John Marks, *The West, Islam and Islamism* (London: Civitas, 2006); Jalil Roshandel and Sharon Chadha, *Jihad and International Security* (New York: Palgrave Macmillan, 2006); Antonio Giustozzi, *Koran, Kalashnikov, and Laptop: The Neo-Taliban Insurgency in Afghanistan* (New York: Columbia University Press, 2007); Rohan Gunaratna, *Inside Al-Qaeda: Global Network of Terror* (New York: Penguin, 2003); Bruce Hoffman, *Inside Terrorism* (New York: Columbia University Press, 2006); Amir Taheri, *Holy Terror: Inside the World of Islamic Terrorism* (Bethesda, MD: Alder and Adler, 1987); Brynjar Lia, *Architect of Global Jihad: The Life of al-Qaeda Strategist Abu Mus'ab Al-Suri* (New York: Columbia University Press, 2008); Mia Bloom, *Dying to Kill: The Allure of Suicide Terror* (New York: Columbia University Press, 2007); Robert A. Pape, *Dying to Win: The Strategic Logic of Suicide Terrorism* (New York: Random House, 2006); Marc Sageman, *Leaderless Jihad: Terror Networks in the Twenty-First*

Century (Philadelphia: University of Pennsylvania Press, 2008); and Harun Yahya, *Islam Denounces Terrorism* (Elmhurst, NY: Tahrike Tarsile Qur'an, 2002).

19. Mahmood Mamdani, "Good Muslim, Bad Muslim: A Political Perspective on Culture and Terrorism," *American Anthropologist* 104, 3 (September 2002), pp. 769–770.

20. Monty G. Marshall, "High Casualty Terrorist Bombings, 9/11/94–9/10/08," online at <http://www.systemicpeace.org/inscr/HCTBSep08.pdf> (site consulted September 2008).

21. A bit of explication is in order on how we determined responsibility for each attack. If a group claimed responsibility, we verify that at least two printed sources reported that claim. In the table that constitutes appendix 5.C, only in these cases where a group claimed responsibility and multiple press sources reported it do we name a responsible party under the "description" column. Where an Islamist group claimed responsibility and where multiple press sources reported the claim, we code the incident as having been "perpetrated by Islamists" (shown in the rightmost column of the table). In some cases, no one claimed responsibility. In these instances we identify no specific group in the "description" column of the table. In order to assess whether Islamists were responsible in these cases, we searched newspapers, reports, and investigations. Where every possible group mentioned as a potential perpetrator was Islamist in orientation, we assume the attack was perpetrated by Islamists. We code it as such and classify it as such in the rightmost column of the table. Where one of more of the groups under suspicion for the attack was not Islamist, we coded the attack as not perpetrated by Islamists and note it as such in the rightmost column of the table.

22. For a variety of well-informed views, see Gail W. Lapidus, "Contested Sovereignty: The Tragedy of Chechnya," *International Security* 23, 1 (Summer 1998), pp. 5–49; Anatol Lieven, *Chechnya: Tombstone of Russian Power* (New Haven, CT: Yale University Press, 1999); James Hughes, *Chechnya: From Nationalism to Jihad* (Philadelphia: University of Pennsylvania Press, 2008); and Gordon M. Hahn, *Russia's Islamic Threat* (New Haven, CT: Yale University Press, 2007).

23. Richard Wike and Nilanthi Samaranayake, "Where Terrorism Finds Support in the Muslim World," *Pew Research Center Publications*, May 23, 2006, online at <http://pewresearch.org/pubs/26/where-terrorism-finds-support-in-the-muslim-world> (site consulted January 2009); Terror Free Tomorrow, online at <http://terrorfreetomorrow.org> (site consulted December 2008); Simon Haddad and Hilal Khashan, "Islam and Terrorism: Lebanese Muslim Views on September 11," *Journal of Conflict Resolution* 46, 6 (2002), pp. 812–828; and C. Christine Fair and Bryan Shepherd, "Who Supports Terrorism? Evidence from Fourteen Muslim Countries," *Studies in Conflict and Terrorism* 29 (2002), pp. 51–74.

24. Quoted in Robert W. Hefner, "Global Violence and Indonesian Politics," *American Anthropologist* 104, 3 (September 2002), p. 754.

25. "A Major Change of Public Opinion in the Muslim World: Results from a New Poll of Indonesians," survey conducted in 2003 by Terror Free Tomorrow, online at <http://terrorfreetomorrow.org> (site consulted December 2008). See also Thomas Reuter, "Winning Hearts and Minds? Religion and Politics in Post-Suharto Indonesia," in Thomas Reuter, ed., *The Return of Constitutional Democracy in Indonesia* (Victoria, Australia: Monash Asia Institute, 2010), pp. 81–83.

26. Robert Spencer, *Islam Unveiled: Disturbing Questions about the World's Fastest-Growing Religion* (San Francisco: Encounter, 2002), pp. 34–35. See also Bruce Bawer, *Surrender: Appeasing Islam, Sacrificing Freedom* (New York: Doubleday, 2009).

27. Mark A. Gabriel, *Islam and Terrorism* (Lake Mary, FL: Strang, 2002). For similar views, see Andrew G. Bostom, ed., *The Legacy of Jihad: Islamic Holy War and the Fate of Non-Muslims*

(Amherst, NY: Prometheus, 2005); and Laurent Murawiec, *Pandora's Boxes: The Mind of Jihad* (Washington, DC: The Hudson Institute, 2007).

28. Khaled Abou El Fadl, "The Place of Tolerance in Islam," in Khaled Abou El Fadl, ed., *The Place of Tolerance in Islam* (Boston: Beacon, 2002), pp. 8, 19.

29. Ibid., p. 19.

30. Ibid., p. 17.

31. Ibid., p. 23.

32. Efraim Karsh, *Islamic Imperialism: A History* (New Haven, CT: Yale University Press, 2007). See also Paul Marshall, Roberta Green, and Lela Gilbert, *Islam at the Crossroads: Understanding Its Beliefs, History, and Conflicts* (Grand Rapids, MI: Baker Books, 2002).

33. Karen Armstrong, *Holy War: The Crusades and Their Impact on Today's World* (New York: Doubleday, 1991), p. xiii.

34. See Tariq Ali, *The Clash of Fundamentalisms: Crusades, Jihads, and Modernity* (London: Verso, 2003); and Alan Heston, "Crusades and Jihads: A Long-Run Economic Perspective," *Annals of the Academy of Political and Social Sciences* 588 (July 2003), pp. 112–135.

35. Mark Juergensmeyer, *Terror in the Mind of God: The Global Rise of Religious Violence* (Berkeley: University of California Press, 2003), ch. 10; Satoshi Kanazawa, "The Evolutionary Psychological Imagination: Why You Can't Get a Date on a Saturday Night and Why Most Suicide Bombers Are Muslim," *Journal of Social, Evolutionary, and Cultural Psychology* 1, 2 (2007), pp. 7–17; Carol R. Ember and Melvin Ember, eds., *The Encyclopedia of Sex and Gender: Men and Women in the World's Cultures* (New York: Springer, 2004); and Nicholas D. Kristof, "Divorced before Puberty," *New York Times*, March 4, 2010.

36. "Fight Poverty and Terrorism," *Development Outreach*, Fall 2001, online at <http://www1.worldbank.org/devoutreach/fall01/special.asp>[3] (site consulted October 2008).

37. Marc Sageman, *Understanding Terror Networks* (Philadelphia: University of Pennsylvania Press, 2004).

38. Barry Rubin, *The Tragedy of the Middle East* (New York: Cambridge University Press, 2002), p. 189.

39. Dore Gold, *Hatred's Kingdom: How Saudi Arabia Supports the New Global Terrorism* (Washington, DC: Regnery, 2003).

40. Pape, *Dying to Win*.

41. Pape, *Dying to Win*, pp. 199–216; and Sageman, *Understanding Terror Networks*, pp. 73–77.

42. The Social Security Administration, "Popular Baby Names," online at <http://www.ssa.gov/OACT/babynames> (site consulted October 2008).

43. Abou El Fadl, "The Place of Tolerance in Islam," pp. 7–8.

44. Sageman, *Understanding Terror Networks*, pp. 78–80. See also Martha Crenshaw, "The Causes of Terrorism," *Comparative Politics* 13, 4 (July 1981), pp. 379–99.

CHAPTER 6

1. Leila Ahmed, *Women and Gender in Islam: Historical Roots of a Modern Debate* (New Haven, CT: Yale University Press, 1993); Jan Goodwin, *Price of Honor: Muslim Women Lift the Veil of Silence on the Islamic World* (New York: Plume, 1994); Fatima Mernissi, *The Veil and the Male Elite: A Feminist Interpretation of Women's Rights in Islam* (New York: Basic, 1987); Pauline Jones Luong, ed., *The Transformation of Central Asia: States and Societies from Soviet Rule to Independence* (Ithaca, NY: Cornell University Press, 2004); Mounira M. Charrad, *States and Women's Rights: The Making of Postcolonial Tunisia, Algeria, and Morocco* (Berkeley: University of California Press, 2001); Mahnaz Afkhami, *Faith and Freedom: Women's Human Rights in the Muslim World* (Syracuse, NY:

Syracuse University Press, 1995); Valentine M. Moghadam, ed., *From Patriarchy to Empowerment: Women's Participation, Movements, and Rights in the Middle East, North Africa, and South Asia* (Syracuse, NY: Syracuse University Press, 2007); Ellen R. Sheeley, *Reclaiming Honor in Jordan: A National Public Opinion Survey on "Honor" Killings* (San Francisco: Ellen R. Sheeley, 2007); Parvin Paidar, *Women and the Political Process in Twentieth Century Iran* (Cambridge: Cambridge University Press, 1995); Hisham Sharabi, *Neopatriarchy: A Theory of Distorted Change in Arab Society* (Oxford: Oxford University Press, 1992); Abdellah Hammoudi, *Master and Disciple: The Cultural Foundations of Moroccan Authoritarianism* (Chicago: University of Chicago Press, 1997); Akbar Ganji, *The Road to Democracy in Iran* (Cambridge, MA: MIT Press, 2008); and Ziba Mir-Hosseini, *Islam and Gender: The Religious Debate in Contemporary Iran* (Princeton, NJ: Princeton University Press, 1999).

2. Leila Ahmed, *A Border Passage: From Cairo to America—A Woman's Journey* (New York: Penguin, 1999); Jean Sasson, *Princess: The True Story of Life behind the Veil in Saudi Arabia* (Atlanta: Windsor-Brooke, 2001); Parvin Darabi and Romin P. Thompson, *Rage against the Veil: The Courageous Life and Death of an Islamic Dissident* (Amherst, NY: Prometheus, 1999); Zarah Ghahramani, *My Life as a Traitor: An Iranian Memoir* (New York: Farrar, Straus and Giroux, 2008); Carmen bin Laden, *Inside the Kingdom: My Life in Saudi Arabia* (New York: Time Warner, 2004); Asra Nomani, *Standing Alone: An American Woman's Struggle for the Soul of Islam* (San Francisco: HarperOne, 2006); Marina Nemat, *Prisoner of Tehran: One Woman's Story of Survival inside an Iranian Prison* (New York: Free Press, 2008).

3. One of the few studies that has done so is Robert Inglehart and Pippa Norris, *Rising Tide: Gender Equality and Cultural Change around the World* (New York: Cambridge University Press, 2003). Inglehart and Norris's book, while laudable in its rigorous use of empirical evidence, nonetheless tends to steer around religion and the issues of structural inequality addressed in the current chapter.

4. Lila Abu-Lughod, *Veiled Sentiments: Honor and Poetry in a Bedouin Society* (Berkeley: University of California Press, 2000); Lila Abu-Lughod, "Do Muslim Women Really Need Saving? Anthropological Reflections on Cultural Relativism and Its Others," *American Anthropologist* 104, 3 (September 2002), pp. 783–790; Nilüfer Göle, *The Forbidden Modern: Civilization and Veiling* (Ann Arbor: University of Michigan Press, 1997); Fadwa El Guindi, *Veil: Modesty, Privacy and Resistance* (Oxford, UK: Berg, 2003); and Balaghi Shiva and Fatma Muge Gocek, eds., *Reconstructing Gender in the Middle East* (New York: Columbia University Press, 1995).

5. United Nations Development Programme (UNDP), *Human Development Report 2007/2008* (New York: Palgrave Macmillan, 2007), pp. 330–333. Data are for the most recent year available between 1996 and 2005.

6. Interparliamentary Union, "Women in National Parliaments," online at <http://www.ipu.org> (site consulted December 2008). Data are for November 2008. In bicameral legislatures, data are for the lower house.

7. United Nations Development Programme (UNDP), *Human Development Report 2007/2008* (New York: Palgrave Macmillan, 2007), pp. 343–346. Data are for deputy prime ministers and ministers, and include prime ministers who hold ministerial portfolios and vice presidents and heads of ministerial-level departments or agencies who exercise a ministerial function.

8. Welch two-sample *t*-tests of the difference in means show that the mean values for Muslim and non-Muslim countries for all the three variables listed in table 6.1 are statistically significantly different at the 0.001 level. For ratio of female-to-male earned

income, $t = -5.14$ with 55.4 degrees of freedom. For women in parliament, $t = -5.18$ with 94.1 degrees of freedom. For women at the ministerial level, $t = -5.61$ with 137.0 degrees of freedom.

9. Data for GDP per capita at purchasing power parity in 1998 and for life expectancy in 1998 are from the United Nations Development Programme, *Human Development Report 2000* (New York: Oxford University Press, 2000), pp. 157–160; except for Afghanistan, Liberia, North Korea, the Palestinian Territories, Somalia, Taiwan, and Yugoslavia, which are for 1999 and are from *CIA World Factbook 2000* (Washington, DC: Brassay's, 2000); and for Timor Leste, which are for 2003 and are drawn from the 2003 version of the *CIA World Factbook*. Level of democracy is a five-year average, covering 1994–1998, of the Freedom House "freedom ratings." The scores range from 1 (most open polity) to 7 (least open polity). I invert the scores to provide for more intuitive presentation. Source: Freedom House, *Freedom in the World*, online at <http://freedomhouse.org> (site consulted July 2008). Economic dependence on fuels is measured as the percentage of merchandise exports accounted for by oil and gas in the year 2000 (or the closest year for which data are available). Source: World Development Bank, *World Development Indicators 2002* (Washington, DC: World Bank, 2002); and International Monetary Fund, "Statistical Appendices from Reports for 2000, 2001, and 2002," online at <http://imf.org/external/country/index.htm> (site consulted May 2003).

10. Michael L. Ross, "Oil, Islam, and Women," *American Political Science Review* 1, 102(February 2008), pp. 107–123.

11. World Values Survey, Integrated Questionnaire number D060: "A university education is more important for a boy than for a girl" (possible answers are "agree strongly"; "agree"; "disagree"; and "strongly disagree").

12. World Values Survey, Integrated Questionnaire number C001: "When jobs are scarce, men should have more right to a job than women" (possible answers are "agree" and "disagree").

13. World Values Survey, Integrated Questionnaire number D059: "On the whole, men make better political leaders than women do" (possible answers are "agree strongly"; "agree"; "disagree"; and "strongly disagree").

14. In preliminary analyses we also included marital status as an individual-level control. It was not statistically significant and did not appear to influence other variables in the models.

15. Interestingly, we find that while self-identification as a Christian had no effect on agreement with the statement, the percentage of the population that is Christian has a statistically significant and negative effect. The larger a country's Christian population, the more likely an individual is to disagree or strongly disagree that university education is more important for a boy than a girl.

16. In preliminary analyses a control for marital status was included. This variable was found to be statistically significant and positive. When it is included, the size of the Muslim and Christian coefficients decreased slightly, but otherwise the marital status variable had minimal impact on the other variables included in the model.

17. In contrast to the question on university education, self-identification as a Christian is statistically significant and positive in models 3 and 4. Additionally, while individual-level religiosity was not statistically significant in table 6.7, we see that it is statistically significant and positive in model 5 of table 6.9. Individuals who are more religious are slightly more likely to agree that men have more of a right to a job than women.

18. Table 6.10 displays predicted probabilities for individuals of average age and education, who have a score on the importance-of-God scale equal to the average for the pooled

sample of Muslims and Christians (8.56) living in countries with average GDP per capita and with populations of average age and religiosity, varying only the percentage of the population that is Muslim and Christian. The values in table 6.10 come from model 5 of table 6.9. The predicted probabilities for model 4 are approximately 0.03 higher than those estimated according to model 5.

19. Preliminary models included a control for marital status. This variable was not statistically significant.

20. In preliminary models we also tested the level of democracy (measured by a five-year average of Freedom House scores) as a possible predictor variable. It was not statistically significant.

21. Table 6.12 includes predicted probabilities for Muslim and Christian men and women of average age and education with a scores on the importance-of-God scale equal to the average for the pooled sample of Muslims and Christians (8.56), living in countries with average GDP per capita, average population age, and average levels of religiosity. We varied the size of the Muslim and Christian populations, according to both models 4 and 5 of table 6.11.

22. Research on women's support for fundamentalist Islam by Lisa Blaydes and Drew Linzer that employs several of the same WVS questions used here points to a similar finding. The authors find that men are considerably more likely than women to ascribe to fundamentalist beliefs. The authors also show that the effect of education was consistent for both men and women; individuals with more education are more likely to hold liberal attitudes regarding religion and the role of women in society. See Lisa Blaydes and Drew A. Linzer, "The Political Economy of Women's Support for Fundamentalist Islam," *World Politics* 60, 4 (July 2008), pp. 576–609.

23. United Nations Development Programme (UNDP), *Human Development Report 2007/2008* (New York: Palgrave Macmillan, 2007), pp. 334–337.

24. A Welch two-sample *t*-test of the difference in means in the female-to-male literacy ratio for Muslim and non-Muslim countries yields a *t* of –3.66 with 62.1 degrees of freedom and a *p*-value smaller than 0.001. This means that the means are highly statistically significantly different from each other.

25. United Nations Development Programme (UNDP), *Human Development Report 2007/2008* (New York: Palgrave Macmillan, 2007), pp. 229–232.

26. World Health Organization, "Healthy Life Expectancy (HALE) at Birth (Years)," online at <http://www.who.int/whosis/indicators/compendium/2008/1hat/en/index.html> (site consulted December 2008). Data are drawn from World Health Organization, "Data and Statistics," online at <http://www.who.int/research/en> (site consulted June 2006).

27. A Welch two-sample *t*-test of the difference in means in the sex difference in healthy life expectancy for Muslim and non-Muslim countries yields a *t* of –5.01 with 83.6 degrees of freedom and a *p*-value smaller than 0.001. This means that the means are highly statistically significantly different from each other.

28. United Nations Development Programme (UNDP), *Human Development Report 2001* (New York: Oxford University Press, 2001), pp. 162–165. Estimates are of the portion of the population aged 15–49 that is infected with HIV, including those living with AIDS.

29. Anne E. Preston, *Leaving Science: Occupational Exit from Scientific Careers* (New York: Russell Sage Foundation, 2004); and Lisa Belkin, "The Opt-Out Revolution," *New York Times Magazine*, October 26, 2003, pp. 42–47, 58, 85–86.

30. *Al'Bukhari's Sahih: The Correct Traditions of Al'Bukhari* (Beirut: Dar Al-Kotob Al-ilmi-yah, 2003), vol. 1, bk. 6, no. 304.

31. Ibn Warraq, *Why I Am Not a Muslim* (Amherst, NY: Prometheus, 2003). See also Anwar Hekmat, *Women and the Koran: The Status of Women in Islam* (Amherst, NY: Prometheus, 1997); and Ali Dashti, *Twenty-Three Years: A Study of the Prophetic Career of Mohammad* (Costa Mesa, CA: Mazda Publishers, 1994).

32. Ayaan Hirsi Ali, *Infidel* (New York: Free Press, 2008).

33. Amina Wadud, *Qur'an and Woman: Rereading the Sacred Text from a Woman's Perspective* (New York: Oxford University Press, 1999), pp. ix–x.

34. For example, Barbara Freyer Stowasser, *Women in the Qur'an, Traditions, and Interpretation* (New York: Oxford University Press, 1994); Asghar Ali Engineer, *The Rights of Women in Islam* (Elgin, IL: New Dawn Press, 2004); Syafiq Hasyim, *Understanding Women in Islam: An Indonesian Perspective* (Jakarta: Solstice, 2006); Nimat Hafez Barazangi, *Women's Identity and the Qur'an: A New Reading* (Gainesville: University Press of Florida, 2004); Mohammad Ali Syed, *The Position of Women in Islam: A Progressive View* (Albany: State University of New York Press, 2004); Niaz A. Shah, *Women, the Koran and International Human Rights Law: The Experience of Pakistan* (Boston: Martinus Nijhoff, 2006); and Fazlur Rahman, *Islam* (Chicago: University of Chicago Press, 1979). For an especially rigorous jurisprudential analysis, see Khaled Abou El Fadl, *Speaking in God's Name: Islamic Law, Authority and Women* (Oxford: Oneworld, 2001).

35. Asma Barlas, *"Believing Women" in Islam: Unreading Patriarchal Interpretations of the Qur'an* (Austin: University of Texas Press, 2002), p. 9. See also Ahmed E. Souaiaia, *Contesting Justice: Women, Islam, Law, and Society* (Albany: State University of New York Press, 2008); and Judith E. Tucker, *Women, Family, and Gender in Islamic Law* (Cambridge: Cambridge University Press, 2008).

36. Barlas, *"Believing Women" in Islam*, pp. 188–189; Wadud, *Qur'an and Woman*, pp. 74–78.

37. Barlas, *"Believing Women" in Islam*, p. 189.

38. For example, *Al'Bukhari's Sahih*, vol. 1, bk. 1, no. 3.

39. For example, ibid., vol. 1, bk. 4, nos. 227 and 228; and vol. 1, bk. 5, no. 282.

40. For example, ibid., vol. 1, bk. 10, no. 837; and vol. 1, bk. 11, no. 900.

41. Al-Bukhari in *A Treasury of Hadith and Sunnah: 551 Hadith*, compiled by Mazhar U. Kazi (Claymont, DE: Alminar, 2000), nos. 541 and 542, p. 131.

42. Al-Tirmidhi in ibid., no. 197, p. 64.

43. Abu Da'ud in ibid., no. 534, p. 130.

44. Ziba Mir-Hosseini, "The Construction of Gender in Islamic Legal Thought and Strategies for Reform," *Hawwa* 1, 1 (2003), p. 3.

45. Abdulaziz Sachedina, "The Ideal and the Real in Islamic Law," in R. S. Khare, ed., *Perspectives on Islamic Law, Justice, and Society* (New York: Rowman and Littlefield, 1999), p. 29.

46. Nikki R. Keddie, *Women in the Middle East: Past and Present* (Princeton, NJ: Princeton University Press, 2007), p. 14.

47. See Marshall G. S. Hodgson, *The Venture of Islam: Conscience and History in a World Civilization*, vol. 1, *The Classical Age of Islam* (Chicago: University of Chicago Press, 1974), pp. 172–183, 223–230; and Marshall G. S. Hodgson, *The Venture of Islam: Conscience and History in a World Civilization*, vol. 2, *The Expansion of Islam in the Middle Periods* (Chicago: University of Chicago Press, 1974), pp. 140–146.

48. United Nations Development Programme, *The Arab Human Development Report 2005* (New York: UNDP Regional Bureau for Arab States, 2005), pp. 167–169. See also Halim Barakat, *The Arab World: Society, Culture, and State* (Berkeley: University of California Press, 1993); and Sharabi, *Neopatriarchy*.

49. Michele Penner Angrist, "Women in Parliament in the Arab and Muslim World" (unpublished ms., 2007). See also Kathleen Collins, *Clan Politics and Regime Transition in Central Asia* (New York: Cambridge University Press, 2009).

50. Michael L. Ross, "Oil, Islam, and Women," *American Political Science Review* 102, 1 (February 2008), pp. 107–123.

51. See also Mounira M. Charrad, "Kinship, Islam, or Oil: Culprits of Gender Inequality?" *Politics and Gender* 5, 4 (December 2009), pp. 546–553; Pippa Norris, "Petroleum Patriarchy? A Response to Ross," *Politics and Gender* 5, 4 (December 2009), pp. 553–560; Alice Kang, "Studying Oil, Islam, and Women as if Political Institutions Mattered," *Politics and Gender* 5, 4 (December 2009), pp. 560–568; Teri L. Caraway, "Comparative Political Economy, Gender, and Labor Markets," *Politics and Gender* 5, 4 (December 2009), pp. 568–575; and Michael L. Ross, "Does Oil Hurt Women? A Reply to Caraway, Charrad, Kang, and Norris," *Politics and Gender* 5, 4 (December 2009), pp. 575–582.

52. For example, Michael Bonner, Mine Ener, and Amy Singer, eds., *Poverty and Charity in Middle Eastern Contexts* (Albany: State University of New York Press, 2003); Janine A. Clark, *Islam, Charity, and Activism: Middle Class Networks and Social Welfare in Egypt, Jordan, and Yemen* (Bloomington: Indiana University Press, 2003); Louise Marlow, *Hierarchy and Egalitarianism in Islamic Thought* (Cambridge: Cambridge University Press, 1997); Mohammad Hashim Kamali, *Freedom, Equality, and Justice in Islam* (Cambridge, UK: Islamic Texts Society, 2002); Charles Tripp, *Islam and the Moral Economy: The Challenge of Capitalism* (Cambridge: Cambridge University, 2006); Michael Cook, *Commanding Right and Forbidding Wrong in Islamic Thought* (Cambridge: Cambridge University Press, 2000); Mine Ener, *Egypt's Poor and the Politics of Benevolence, 1800–1952* (Princeton, NJ: Princeton University Press, 2003); and Yaacov Lev, *Charity, Endowments, and Charitable Institutions in Medieval Islam* (Gainesville: University Press of Florida, 2005).

53. Kenneth Scheve and David Stasavage, "Religion and Preferences for Social Insurance," *Quarterly Journal of Political Science* 1, 3 (2006), pp. 255–286; Kenneth Scheve and David Stasavage, "The Political Economy of Religion and Social Insurance in the United States, 1910–1939," *Studies in American Political Development* 20, 2 (Fall 2006), pp. 132–159; Luigi Guiso, Paola Sapienza, and Luigi Zingales, "People's Opium? Religion and Economic Attitudes," *Journal of Monetary Economics* 50, 1 (January 2003), pp. 225–282; Luigi Giuso, Paola Sapienza, and Liugi Zingales, "Does Culture Affect Economic Outcomes?" *Journal of Economic Perspectives* 20, 2 (Spring 2006), pp. 23–48; John D. Huber and Piero Stanig, "Church–State Separation and Redistribution," typescript, Columbia University, May 5, 2009; and Rajeev Dehejia, Thomas DeLeire, and Erzo F. P. Luttmer, "Insuring Consumption and Happiness through Religious Organizations," *Journal of Public Economics* 91, 1–2 (February 2007), pp. 259–279.

54. *Human Development Report 2007/2008*, 2007, pp. 281–284.

55. A Welch two-sample *t*-test of the difference in means in the Gini scores for Muslim and non-Muslim countries yields a *t* of −1.98 with 66.3 degrees of freedom and a *p*-value smaller than 0.1. This means that the means are statistically significantly different at the 0.1 level.

56. Amy Singer, *Charity in Islamic Societies* (Cambridge: Cambridge University Press, 2008), p. 30.

57. See also Colin Turner, "Wealth as an Immortality Symbol in the Qur'an: A Reconsideration of the *māl/amwāl* Verses," *Journal of Qur'anic Studies* 8, 2 (2006), pp. 58–83.

58. Jonathan Benthall and Jérôme Bellion-Jourdan, *The Charitable Crescent: Politics of Aid in the Muslim World* (London: I. B. Tauris, 2003), p. 19.

59. See ibid., pp. 37–44.

60. See Vali Nasr, *Forces of Fortune: The Rise of the New Muslim Middle Class and What It Will Mean for Our World* (New York: Free Press, 2009).

61. Max Weber, *The Protestant Ethic and the Spirit of Capitalism* (Padstow, UK: Routledge, 2002).

62. For example, Brian D. McLaren, *Everything Must Change: Jesus, Global Crises, and a Revolution of Hope* (Nashville: Thomas Nelson, 2007); and Jim Wallis, *God's Politics: Why the Right Gets It Wrong and the Left Doesn't Get It* (San Francisco: HarperCollins, 2005).

63. Kenneth L. Woodward, "A $1 Million Habit," *Newsweek*, September 15, 1980, p. 35.

64. For example, Paul Zane Pilzer, *God Wants You to Be Rich: How and Why Everyone Can Enjoy Material and Spiritual Wealth in Our Abundant World* (New York: Simon and Schuster, 2007); Scot Anderson, *God Wants You Rich* (Shippensburg, PA: Destiny Image, 2009); C. Thomas Anderson: *Becoming a Millionaire God's Way: Getting Money to You, Not from You* (Mesa, AZ: Winword, 2004); and Toye Ademola, *Seven Secrets of Bible-Made Millionaires* (Peabody, MA: Selah, 2007).

65. Author's interview with Hamid Basyaib, March 27, 2007, Surabaya, Indonesia.

66. Author's interview with Ali Maschan Musa, March 20, 2007, Surabaya, Indonesia.

67. Author's interview with Salahuddin Wahid, April 10, 2007, Jombang, East Java, Indonesia.

68. Author's interview with Abdurrahman Wahid, April 18, 2007, Jakarta, Indonesia.

69. Author's interview with Muhammad Adnan, June 7, 2007, Semarang, Central Java, Indonesia.

70. Walter Rodgers, "Stop Picking on Jimmy Carter," *Christian Science Monitor*, January 5, 2009.

71. *Human Development Report 2007/2008*, pp. 238–240.

72T. Without the controls for Christian self-identification and percent Christian, percent Muslim is statistically significant and positive. This further reinforces the substantive finding including the Christian controls: Muslims are less supportive of equality between the sexes in education access.

73T. Without the controls for Christian self-identification and percent Christian, percent Muslim is statistically significant and positive when controlling for religiosity. This finding confirms the substantive result when including the Christian controls: Muslims are less supportive of equality between the sexes.

CHAPTER 7

1. Khaled Abou El Fadl, *The Great Theft: Wrestling Islam from the Extremists* (San Francisco: HarperOne, 2005), p. 180.

2. Sayyid Qutb, *Milestones* (Indianapolis, IN: American Trust Publications, 1990); Albert Hourani, *Arabic Thought in the Liberal Age, 1798–1939* (Cambridge: Cambridge University Press, 1983); Nikki R. Keddie, ed., *An Islamic Response to Imperialism: Political and Religious Writings of Sayyid Jamal ad-Din al-Afghani* (Berkeley: University of California Press, 1983); Bassam Tibi, *The Challenge of Fundamentalism: Political Islam and the New World Disorder* (Berkeley: University of California Press, 2002); Anthony Shadid, *Legacy of the Prophet: Despots, Democrats, and the New Politics of Islam* (Boulder, CO: Westview, 2001); and Charles Kurzman, ed., *Liberal Islam: A Sourcebook* (New York: Oxford University Press, 1998).

3. Ernest Gellner, *Conditions of Liberty: Civil Society and Its Rivals* (London: Penguin, 1996); Bernard Lewis, *Islam and the West* (New York: Oxford University Press, 1994);

Amir Taheri, *The Persian Night: Iran under the Khomeinist Revolution* (New York: Encounter, 2009); Fareed Zakaria, "Islam, Democracy, and Constitutional Liberalism," *Political Science Quarterly* 119, 1 (March 2004), pp. 1–20; Mehran Kamrava, *Democracy in the Balance: Culture and Society in the Middle East* (Chappaqua, NY: Seven Bridges Press, 1998); Daniel Pipes, *In the Path of God: Islam and Political Power* (New York: Basic, 1983); Elie Kedourie, *Democracy and Arab Political Culture* (London: Frank Cass, 1994); and V. S. Naipaul, *Among the Believers: An Islamic Journey* (New York: Random House, 1982).

4. Khaled Abou El Fadl, "Islam and the Challenge of Democratic Commitment," *Fordham International Law Journal* 27, 1 (December 2003), pp. 4–71; E. Fuat Keyman, ed., *Remaking Turkey: Globalization, Alternative Modernities, and Democracies* (Lanham, MD: Lexington, 2008); John L. Esposito and John O. Voll, *Islam and Democracy* (New York: Oxford University Press, 1996); Bruce K. Rutherford, *Egypt after Mubarak: Liberalism, Islam, and Democracy in the Arab World* (Princeton, NJ: Princeton University Press, 2008); John L. Esposito and James P. Piscatori, "Democratization and Islam," *Middle East Journal* 45, 3 (Summer 1991), pp. 427–440; Sohail H. Hashmi, ed., *Islamic Political Ethics: Civil Society, Pluralism, and Conflict* (Princeton, NJ: Princeton University Press, 2002); Asef Bayat, *Making Islam Democratic: Social Movements and the Post-Islamist Turn* (Stanford, CA: Stanford University Press, 2007); Jillian Schwedler, *Faith in Moderation: Islamist Parties in Jordan and Yemen* (Cambridge: Cambridge University Press, 2006); Vickie Langohr, "Of Islamists and Ballot Boxes: Rethinking the Relationship between Islamists and Electoral Politics," *International Journal of Middle East Studies* 33, 4 (November 2001), pp. 591–610; Ergun Özbudun, "Democratization Reforms in Turkey, 1993–2004," *Turkish Studies* 8, 2 (June 2007), pp. 179–96; Ihsan Dagi, "Turkey's AKP in Power," *Journal of Democracy* 19, 3 (July 2008), pp. 25–30; Laith Kubba, "Institutions Make the Difference," *Journal of Democracy* 19, 3 (July 2008), pp. 37–42; Bora Kanra, "Democracy, Islam, and Dialogue: The Case of Turkey," *Government and Opposition* 40, 4 (Autumn 2005), pp. 515–39; Tamara Cofman Wittes, *Freedom's Unsteady March: America's Role in Building Arab Democracy* (Washington, DC: Brookings, 2008); Abdolkarim Soroush, *Reason, Freedom, and Democracy in Islam* (New York: Oxford University Press, 2002); Benazir Bhutto, *Reconciliation: Islam, Democracy, and the West* (New York: HarperCollins, 2008); Noah Feldman, *The Fall and Rise of the Islamic State* (Princeton, NJ: Princeton University Press, 2008); Larbi Sadiki, "Popular Uprisings and Arab Democratization," *International Journal of Middle East Studies* 32, 1 (February 2000), pp. 71–95; Abdullahi Ahmed An-Na'im, *Toward and Islamic Reformation: Civil Liberties, Human Rights, and International Law* (Syracuse, NY: Syracuse University Press, 1996); Eva Bellin, "The Robustness of Authoritarianism in the Middle East: Exceptionalism in Comparative Perspective," *Comparative Politics* 36, 2 (January 2004), pp. 139–157; Robert W. Hefner, *Civil Islam: Muslims and Democracy in Indonesia* (Princeton, NJ: Princeton University Press, 2000); Douglas Ramage, *Politics in Indonesia: Democracy, Islam, and the Politics of Tolerance* (New York: Routledge, 1995); Matthew J. Nelson, *In the Shadow of Shari'ah: Islam, Islamic Law, and Democracy in Pakistan* (New York: Columbia University Press, 2009); Abdulaziz Sachedina, *The Islamic Roots of Democratic Pluralism* (New York: Oxford University Press, 2001); Mohammed Ayoob, *The Many Faces of Political Islam: Religion and Politics in the Muslim World* (Ann Arbor: University of Michigan Press, 2008); Azzam S. Tamimi, *Rachid Ghannouchi: A Democrat within Islamism* (New York: Oxford University Press, 2001); Joel Benin and Joe Stork, eds., *Political Islam* (Berkeley: University of California Press, 1997); Sayed Khatab and Gary D. Bouma, *Democracy in*

Islam (New York: Routledge, 2007); Jennifer Noyon, *Islam, Politics, and Pluralism: Theory and Practice in Turkey, Jordan, Tunisia, and Algeria* (London: Royal Institute of International Affairs, 2003); Robert Pringle, *Democratization in Mali: Putting History to Work* (Washington, DC: United States Institute of Peace, 2006); Caroline Cox and John Marks, *The West, Islam, and Islamism* (London: Civitas, 2006); Abdou Filali-Ansary, "Muslims and Democracy," *Journal of Democracy* 10, 3 (July 1999), pp. 18–32; Shireen T. Hunter and Huma Malik, *Modernization, Democracy, and Islam* (Westport, CT: Praeger, 2005); John P. Entelis, "The Democratic Imperative vs. the Authoritarian Impulse: The Maghreb State between Transition and Terrorism," *Middle East Journal* 59, 4 (October 2005), pp. 537–558; Binnaz Toprak, "Islam and Democracy in Turkey," *Turkish Studies* 6, 2 (June 2005), pp. 167–186; and Sheldon Gellar, *Democracy in Senegal: Tocquevillian Analytics in Africa* (New York: Palgrave Macmillan, 2005).

5. Michael Bratton, "Briefing: Islam, Democracy and Public Opinion in Africa," *African Affairs* 102, 408 (July 2003), pp. 493–501; Michael Bratton, Robert Mattes, and E. Gyimah-Boadi, *Public Opinion, Democracy, and Market Reform in Africa* (New York: Cambridge University Press, 2005); and Steven Ryan Hofmann, "Islam and Democracy: Micro-Level Indicators of Compatibility," *Comparative Political Studies* 37, 6 (August 2004), pp. 652–676.

6. Manus I. Midlarsky, "Democracy and Islam: Implications for Civilizational Conflict and the Democratic Peace," *International Studies Quarterly* 42, 3 (September 1998), pp. 485–511; M. Steven Fish, "Islam and Authoritarianism," *World Politics* 55, 1 (October 2002), pp. 4–37; and Daniela Donno and Bruce Russet, "Islam, Authoritarianism, and Female Empowerment: What Are the Linkages?" *World Politics* 56, 4 (July 2004), pp. 582–607.

7. Juan J. Linz, *The Breakdown of Democratic Regimes: Crisis, Breakdown, and Reequilibration* (Baltimore: Johns Hopkins University Press, 1978), p. 5.

8. Robert A. Dahl, *Polyarchy* (New Haven, CT: Yale University Press, 1971); Norberto Bobbio, *The Future of Democracy* (Minneapolis: University of Minnesota Press, 1987); and Ian Shapiro, *Democracy's Place* (Ithaca, NY: Cornell University Press, 1996).

9. Freedom House, *Freedom in the World*, online at <http://freedomhouse.org> (site consulted March 2009).

10. The Economist Intelligence Unit, "The Economist Intelligence Unit's Index of Democracy, 2006," online at <http://www.economist.com/media/pdf/Democracy_Index_2007_v3.pdf> (site consulted October 2008); The Polity IV Project, "Political Regime Characteristics and Transitions," online at <http://www.systemicpeace.org/polity/polity4.htm> (site consulted July 2008).

11. Daniel Kaufmann, Aart Kraay, and Massimo Mastruzzi, "Governance Matters VI: Aggregate and Individual Governance Indicators 1996–2006," World Bank Policy Research Working Paper 4280, July 2007, accessible online at <http://papers.ssrn.com/sol3/papers.cfm?abstract_id=999979#> (site consulted July 2008).

12. See M. Steven Fish, *Democracy Derailed in Russia: The Failure of Open Politics* (New York: Cambridge University Press, 2005), pp. 20–23.

13. A Welch two-sample t-test of the difference in the means in the Voice and Accountability scores for Muslim and non-Muslim countries yields a t of -8.01 with 139.2 degrees of freedom and a p-value smaller than 0.001. This means that the means are highly statistically significantly different from each other.

14. For information on measurement and sources of data, see chapter 4, note 11.

15. Valerie Bunce, "Comparative Democratization: Big and Bounded Generalizations," *Comparative Political Studies* 33, 6 (August 2000), pp. 703–734.

16. Alvin Rabushka and Kenneth A. Shepsle, *Politics in Plural Societies* (Columbus, OH:

Merrill, 1972); Adrian Karatnycky, "The 2001 Freedom House Survey," *Journal of Democracy* 13, 1 (January 2002), pp. 99–112; and Donald L. Horowitz, "Democracy in Divided Societies," *Journal of Democracy* 4, 4 (October 1993), pp. 18–38.

17. Michael Ross, "Does Oil Hinder Democracy?" *World Politics* 53, 3 (April 2001), pp. 325–361. For an alternative view on the effects of oil, see Pauline Jones Luong and Erika Weinthal, "Rethinking the Resource Curse: Ownership Structure, Institutional Capacity, and Domestic Constraints," *Annual Review of Political Science* 9 (2006), pp. 241–263.

18. Donno and Russet, "Islam, Authoritarianism, and Female Empowerment"; and Alfred C. Stepan and Graeme B. Robertson, "An 'Arab' More Than a 'Muslim' Gap," *Journal of Democracy* 14, 3 (July 2003), pp. 30–44.

19. M. Steven Fish and Jason Wittenberg, "Failed Democratization," in Christian W. Haerpfer, Patrick Bernhagen, Ronald F. Inglehart, and Christian Welzel, eds., *Democratization* (New York: Oxford University Press, 2009), pp. 249–265; M. Steven Fish, "Why Has Democracy Fared Well in Post-communist Space? The Primacy of Basic Sex Equality," in Hilary Appel, ed., *Evaluating the Success and Failure of Post-Communist Reform* (Claremont, CA: Keck Center for International and Strategic Studies, 2005), pp. 115–134; and Fish, "Islam and Authoritarianism."

20. Aristotle, *The Politics*, trans. Ernest Barker (Oxford: Oxford University Press, 1952); Charles Louis de Secondat (Montesquieu), *The Spirit of the Laws*, ed. Anne M. Cohler, Basia Carolyn Miller, and Harold Samuel Stone (Cambridge: Cambridge University Press, 1995); Robert A. Dahl and Edward R. Tufte, *Size and Democracy* (Stanford, CA: Stanford University Press, 1973); and Carsten Anckar, "Size, Islandness, and Democracy: A Global Comparison," *International Political Science Review* 29, 4 (September 2008), pp. 433–459.

21. Fish, *Democracy Derailed in Russia*, pp. 127–134.

22. United States Department of State, *Country Reports on Terrorism 2007: Indonesia*, April 30, 2008, online at <http://www.unhcr.org/refworld/docid/48196ca22.html> (site consulted April 2009); United States Department of State, *Country Reports on Terrorism 2007: Pakistan*, April 30, 2008, online at <http://www.unhcr.org/refworld/docid/48196cc628.html> (site consulted April 2009).

23. Abdellah Hammoudi, *Master and Disciple: The Cultural Foundations of Moroccan Authoritarianism* (Chicago: University of Chicago Press, 1997); David S. Landes, *The Wealth and Poverty of Nations: Why Some Are So Rich and Others Are So Poor* (New York: Norton, 1999); Hisham Sharabi, *Neopatriarchy: A Theory of Distorted Change in Arab Society* (New York: Oxford University Press, 1988); Yesim Arat, "Feminists, Islamists, and Political Change in Turkey," *Political Psychology* 19, 1 (March 1998), pp. 117–132; Fadia Faqir, "Engendering Democracy in Islam in the Arab World," *Third World Quarterly* 18, 1 (March 1997), pp. 165–174; and Fatima Mernissi, *Beyond the Veil: Male–Female Dynamics in A Modern Muslim Society* (Bloomington: Indiana University Press, 1987).

24. Rose McDermott and Jonathan A. Cowden, "The Effects of Uncertainty and Sex in a Crisis Simulation Game," *International Interactions* 27, 4 (2002), pp. 353–380.

25. Felicia Pratto, L. M. Stallworth, and Jim Sidanius, "The Gender Gap: Differences in Political Attitudes and Social Dominance Orientation," *British Journal of Social Psychology* 36, 1 (March 1997), pp. 49–68; Janet Flammang, *Women's Political Voice* (Philadelphia: Temple University Press, 1997).

26. Fish, "Islam and Authoritarianism."

27. Guillermo O'Donnell, "Human Development, Human Rights, and Democracy," in Guillermo O'Donnell, Jorge Vargas Cullell, and Osvaldo M. Iazzetta, eds., *The Quality of*

Democracy: Theory and Applications (Notre Dame, IN: Notre Dame University Press, 2004), pp. 9–92.

28. Seymour Martin Lipset, *Political Man: The Social Bases of Politics* (Baltimore: Johns Hopkins University Press, 1981); and Daron Acemoglu and James A. Robinson, *Economic Origins of Dictatorship and Democracy* (New York: Cambridge University Press, 2006).

29. Alexis de Tocqueville, *Democracy in America* (New York: Mentor, 1956); Robert D. Putnam, *Making Democracy Work: Civic Traditions in Modern Italy* (Princeton, NJ: Princeton University Press, 1993); and Robert D. Putnam, *Bowling Alone: The Collapse and Revival of American Community* (New York: Simon and Schuster, 2001).

30. For a differentiated, ambitious effort to grasp the possible influence of adherence to Islam and Muslim religiosity in particular on attitudes toward democracy, see Kathleen Collins and Erica Owen, "Religion and Political Preferences in Transition: Islam and Democratic Support in Azerbaijan and Kyrgyzstan," paper prepared for the annual meeting of the American Association for the Advancement of Slavic Studies, November 2009, Boston, MA.

31. Anthony Shadid, *Legacy of the Prophet: Despots, Democrats, and the New Politics of Islam* (Boulder, CO: Westview, 2001), pp. 64–65.

32. Author's interview with Yoyok Tindyo Prasetyo, July 5, 2007, Yogyakarta, Indonesia.

33. Amaney A. Jamal and Mark Tessler, "Attitudes in the Arab World," *Journal of Democracy* 19, 1 (January 2008), pp. 97–110; Mark Tessler and Eleanor Gao, "Gauging Arab Support for Democracy," *Journal of Democracy* 16, 3 (July 2005), pp. 83–97; and Richard Rose, "How Muslims View Democracy: Evidence from Central Asia," *Journal of Democracy* 13, 4 (October 2002), pp. 102–111.

34. Question numbers E114–E117 in the WVS Integrated Questionnaire.

35. This indexing of responses from the WVS was first used by Russell J. Dalton and Nhu-Ngoc T. Ong in "Authority Orientations and Democratic Attitudes: A Test of the 'Asian Values' Hypothesis," *Japanese Journal of Political Science* 6, 2 (August 2005), pp. 1–21.

36. In creating this variable, we only included respondents for whom we had complete responses to all four questions. Consequently, 20 percent of the overall sample could not be used in this analysis. In the raw data file available from <http://www.worldvalues-survey.org>, "don't know" responses are recoded to missing data. Thus, there is no way to distinguish individuals who did not answer the question from those who answered "don't know." Nevertheless, the World Values Survey online data analysis tool, also available at <http://www.worldvalues.survey.org>, provides some general information about the rates of "don't know" responses. According to information available on this site as of March 29, 2010, across the entire sample, fewer than 10 percent of respondents answered "don't know" to one of the four questions. High rates of "don't know" responses were evident in China and India. As a result, less than 50 percent of the China sample and less than 60 percent of the India sample is used in this analysis. With the exception of these two cases, in which there were high rates of "don't know" responses, we believe that most of the other missing data is missing at random. Our findings should not be biased from these missing data.

37. Preliminary models also included a control for religiosity at both the individual and country level. It had no effect on the index and was dropped from final models.

38. Donno and Russet, "Islam, Authoritarianism, and Female Empowerment"; Stepan and Robertson, "An 'Arab' More Than a 'Muslim' Gap"; and Hammoudi, *Master and Disciple*.

39. In a Welch two-sample *t*-test of the level of political openness in non-Arab Muslim countries and non-Muslim countries, $t = -5.508$, $df = 44.543$, p-value = 1.715e-06. In a Welch

two-sample *t*-test between level of political openness in Arab and non-Arab Muslim countries, $t = 1.3522$, $df = 39.56$, p-value = 0.184.

CHAPTER 8

1. "Nearly One in Four People Worldwide is Muslim, Report Says," online at <http://edition.cnn.com/2009/WORLD/asiapcf/10/07/muslim.world.population> (site consulted October 2009).

2. M. Steven Fish, "Islam and Authoritarianism," *World Politics* 55, 1 (October 2002), pp. 4–37.

3. Émile Durkheim, *Suicide* (New York: Free Press, 1951); and Émile Durkheim, *The Elementary Forms of Religious Life* (New York: Free Press, 1995).

4. Robert Huckfeldt, "Citizenship in Democratic Politics: Density Dependence and the Micro–Macro Divide," in Mark Irving Lichbach and Alan S. Zuckerman, eds., *Comparative Politics: Rationality, Culture, and Structure*, 2nd ed. (New York: Cambridge University Press, 2009), pp. 291–313.

5. Jason Brownlee, "Political Crisis and Restabilization: Iraq, Libya, Syria, and Tunisia," in Marsha Pripstein Posusney and Michele Penner Angrist, eds., *Authoritarianism in the Middle East: Regimes and Resistance* (Boulder, CO: Lynne Rienner, 2005), pp. 43–62; and Steven Levitsky and Lucan A. Way, "International Linkage and Democratization," in Larry Diamond and Marc F. Plattner, eds., *Democracy: A Reader* (Baltimore: Johns Hopkins University Press, 2009), pp. 289–303.

6. Christian Lowe and Tarek Amara, "Ben Ali Secures Another Term," Reuters report published online at <http://www.iol.co.za/index.php?set_id=1&click_id=85&art_id=nw20091026222937849C507360> (site consulted November 2009).

7. "Are Rankings Unfair to U.S. Higher Ed?" Associated Press report, November 3, 2009, published online at <http://www.msnbc.msn.com/id/33606263> (site consulted November 2009).

8. For information on a robustness check carried out on the findings generated by cross-national statistical analyses, see appendix 8.

APPENDIX 8

1. Jasjeet S. Sekhon, "Multivariate and Propensity Score Matching Software with Automated Balance Optimization: The Matching Package for R," *Journal of Statistical Software* (forthcoming). Online at http://sekhon.berkeley.edu/matching (site consulted October 2009); and Jasjeet S. Sekhon, "Opiates for the Matches: Matching Methods for Causal Inference," *Annual Review of Political Science* 12, 2009, pp. 487–508. For more on matching methods, see Donald B. Rubin, *Matched Sampling for Causal Effects* (Cambridge: Cambridge University Press, 2006); and Paul R. Rosenbaum, *Observational Studies* (New York: Springer-Verlag, 2002).

Index

"This book is a profound achievement. Reading it has been an eye-opening experience to the point that I feel that I will never be able to approach my own work and scholarship in the same way. As far as I am concerned, this book will be mandatory reading for all of my students. This book deserves to be widely read and debated by every student of Islam, by every reader who believes that he or she knows what Islam and Muslims are about, and even by every person who might have the most casual interest in the contemporary Muslim realm."

—KHALED ABOU EL FADL, UCLA SCHOOL OF LAW

"This book constitutes a major milestone, moving beyond stereotypes and anecdotal evidence and identifying the ways in which Muslim-majority societies actually are distinctive from other types of societies, using a huge base of empirical cross-national evidence. Many of the findings are surprising. "

—RONALD INGLEHART, UNIVERSITY OF MICHIGAN

"There's no book to my knowledge that does what Fish accomplishes here. This book should have been written at least five years ago!"

—AMANEY A. JAMAL, PRINCETON UNIVERSITY

"*Are Muslims Distinctive?* is a refreshingly brash book. Skilled in empirical analysis, Steven Fish has avoided the temptation to define questions narrowly. Both scholarly and non-scholarly audiences will find the book by turns comforting and unsettling."

—NATHAN J. BROWN, GEORGE WASHINGTON UNIVERSITY

Are Muslims Distinctive? represents the first major social-scientific effort to assess how Muslims and non-Muslims differ—and do not differ—in the contemporary world. Using rigorous methods and data drawn from around the globe, M. Steven Fish reveals that in some areas Muslims and non-Muslims differ less than is commonly imagined. Muslims are not inclined to favor the fusion of religious and political authority or especially prone to mass political violence. Yet there are differences: Gender inequality is more severe among Muslims, Muslims are unusually averse to homosexuality and other controversial behaviors, and democracy is rare in the Muslim world. Other areas of divergence bear the marks of a Muslim advantage: Homicide rates and class-based inequities are less severe among Muslims than non-Muslims. Fish's findings have vital implications for human welfare, interfaith understanding, and international relations.

M. STEVEN FISH is Professor of Political Science at the University of California–Berkeley.

Cover design: Anne Fink
Cover image: Young Afghans share a laugh in the hallway of a house.
(Photo by Tyler Hicks/Getty Images)

ISBN 978-0-19-976921-6

OXFORD
UNIVERSITY PRESS

www.oup.com